Withdrawn

BRENT WEEKS

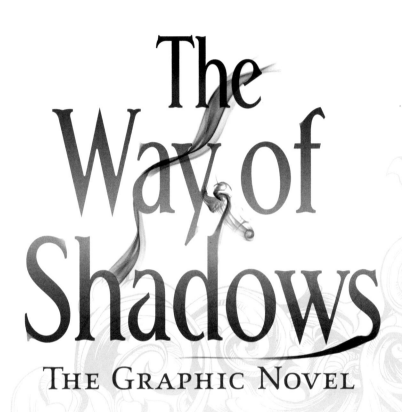

The Way of Shadows

THE GRAPHIC NOVEL

IVAN BRANDON
ANDY MACDONALD

Yen
Press

NEW YORK

FOREWORD

I'm terrified and proud. In many ways, what you're about to read has been a labor of more than a decade. When I started dreaming about The Night Angel Trilogy, I didn't dream of words. I dreamt of action, of fights to dazzle the mind's eye: Bruce Lee's kinetic genius and baffling strength, and *Crouching Tiger, Hidden Dragon*'s grace and speed. Later, after the first draft of *The Way of Shadows*, I spent half a year adapting it into a screenplay, learning the visual language of film.

That screenplay wasn't great, but what it taught me was. I went back and rewrote *The Way of Shadows* with what I'd learned. Beyond that, I learned about visual adaptation—what a picture can say, and what it can't. A picture's worth a thousand words, but its vocabulary is limited. A picture's no sesquipedalian.

Immediately after *The Way of Shadows* was published in 2008, Yen Press Publishing Director Kurt Hassler brought up the idea of a graphic novel adaptation. And here comes the terror. I didn't grow up reading thousands of comics. Oh, sure, I'd read some, but ladies in body paint weren't welcome in the Weeks household. "It's not body paint, it's Spandex, Mom! So she can move more freely!" When you find yourself arguing for the practicality of Emma Frost's "armor," you know you're going to lose.

So I dove into educating myself about the storytelling tools and conventions of the medium. I read works of genius I won't even compare mine to, and I read dreck. As I'd learned years before, an adaptation needs to be faithful to the spirit of the original: it's an adaptation, not a translation. I read adaptations of science fiction and fantasy novels that didn't understand that a four-hundred-word monologue can work fine in a one-hundred-fifty-thousand-word novel, but stretch those four hundred words over twelve panels of a talking head? (I don't know much, but you aren't supposed to do THAT, are you?) But...hold on, the legendary *Locke & Key* has a couple places where the pages of talking heads are necessary and add to the tension and depth of character. (Oh, great. The rules have exceptions? Of course they do.)

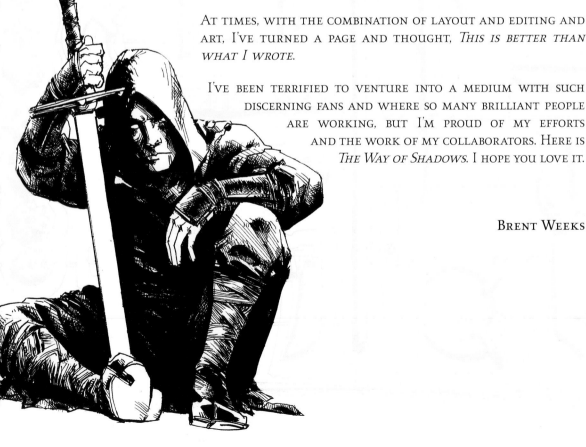

THE BEAUTY OF A COLLABORATIVE WORK OF ART IS THAT WHEN EVERYONE IS PULLING TOGETHER, YOU CAN GET SOMETHING GREATER THAN ANY OF US COULD PRODUCE ALONE. DESPITE MY EFFORTS, THERE'S NO WAY I COULD HAVE PUSHED THIS BOOK TO THIS LEVEL WITHOUT THE WRITING AND ADAPTATION WORK OF IVAN BRANDON. HE DID THE HEAVY LIFTING. ADAPTING A TRILOGY IS PARTICULARLY DAUNTING BECAUSE ANY SUBPLOT CUT HAS REPERCUSSIONS IN LATER BOOKS. MY ASSISTANT, ELISA, WAS INVALUABLE IN KEEPING TIME LINES AND PLOTLINES AND FORESHADOWING STRAIGHT WHILE MY BRAIN WAS STEEPED IN WRITING *LIGHTBRINGER*. ("NO, THAT DOESN'T HAPPEN ANYMORE IN THIS VERSION; YOU DECIDED THAT IF WE CUT X IN THIS SCRIPT, THEN IN A POSSIBLE FUTURE GRAPHIC NOVEL OF *BEYOND THE SHADOWS* THAT Y COULD DO Z IN HER PLACE." OH, RIGHT, RIGHT.)

OF COURSE, WHAT IS A GRAPHIC NOVEL WITHOUT ITS ART? MY DEEPEST THANKS AND RESPECT TO ANDY MACDONALD, WHO I THINK HAS DONE SOME OF HIS BEST WORK EVER HERE. IN THE SUBTLY CURLED LIP OR IN THE MAJESTY OF A CASTLE, ANDY CAPTURES AND COMMUNICATES IN AN INSTANT WHAT MINUTES OF READING COULD ONLY APPROXIMATE.

AT TIMES, WITH THE COMBINATION OF LAYOUT AND EDITING AND ART, I'VE TURNED A PAGE AND THOUGHT, *THIS IS BETTER THAN WHAT I WROTE.*

I'VE BEEN TERRIFIED TO VENTURE INTO A MEDIUM WITH SUCH DISCERNING FANS AND WHERE SO MANY BRILLIANT PEOPLE ARE WORKING, BUT I'M PROUD OF MY EFFORTS AND THE WORK OF MY COLLABORATORS. HERE IS *THE WAY OF SHADOWS*. I HOPE YOU LOVE IT.

BRENT WEEKS

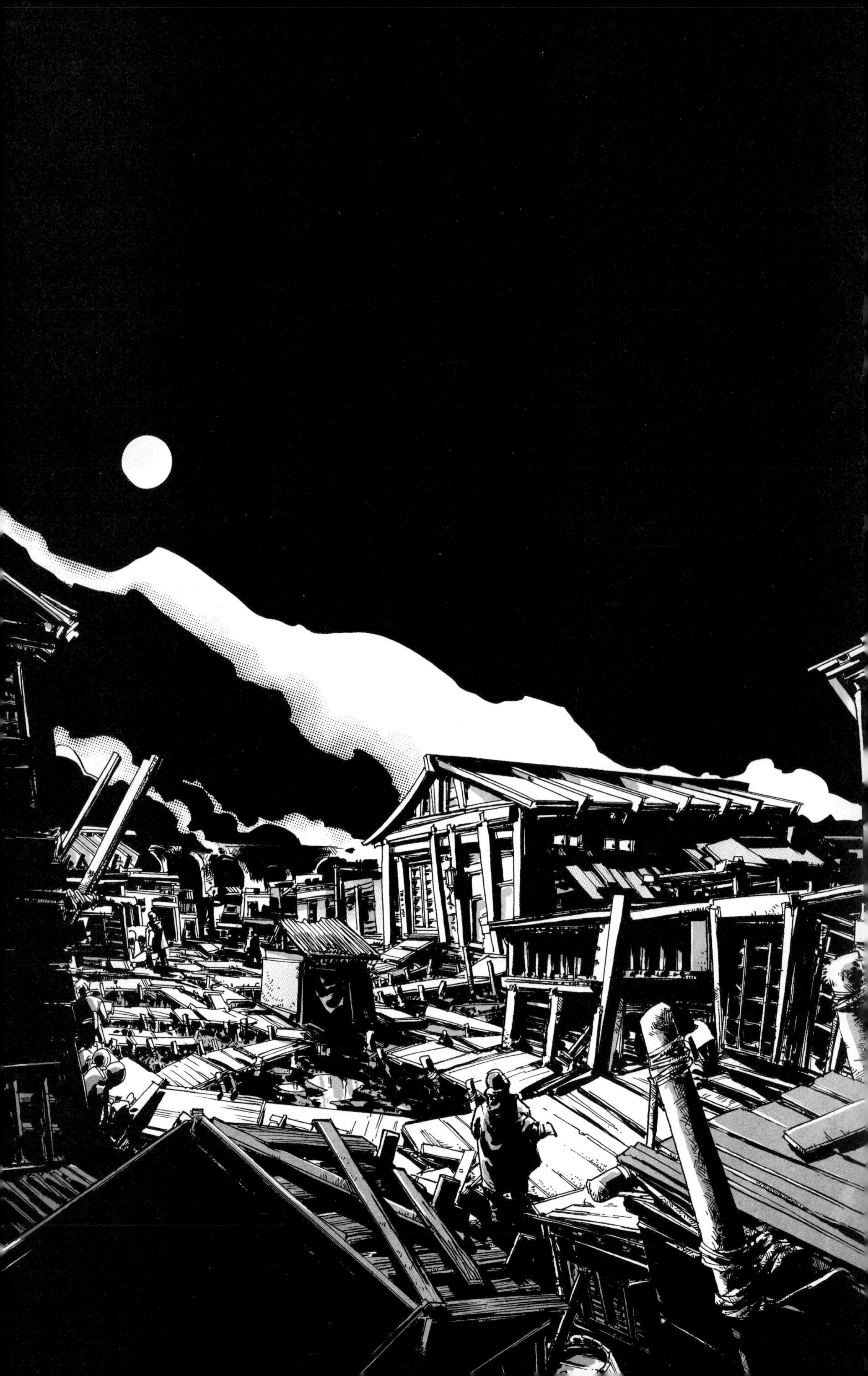

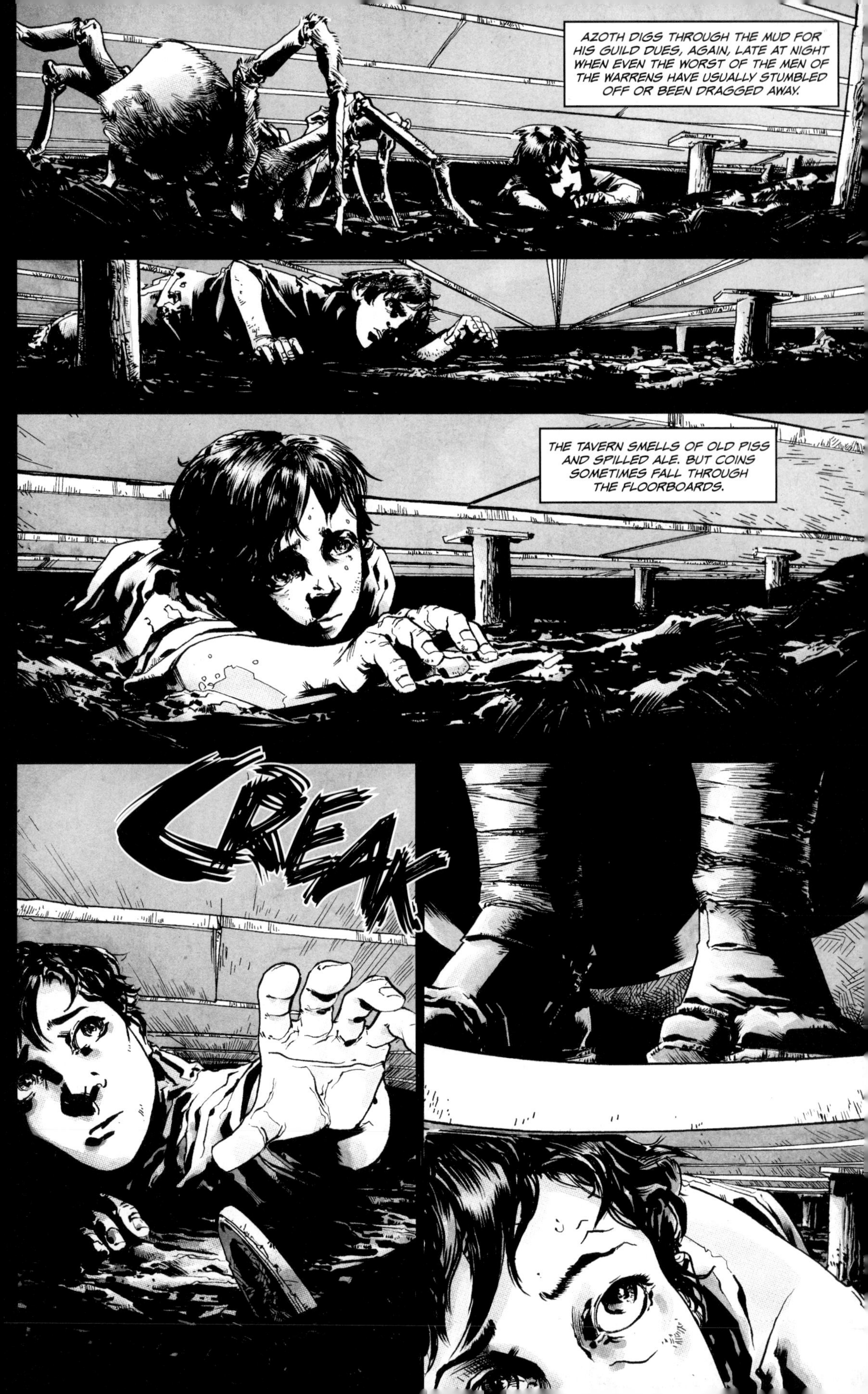
AZOTH DIGS THROUGH THE MUD FOR HIS GUILD DUES, AGAIN, LATE AT NIGHT WHEN EVEN THE WORST OF THE MEN OF THE WARRENS HAVE USUALLY STUMBLED OFF OR BEEN DRAGGED AWAY.
THE TAVERN SMELLS OF OLD PISS AND SPILLED ALE. BUT COINS SOMETIMES FALL THROUGH THE FLOORBOARDS.
CREAK

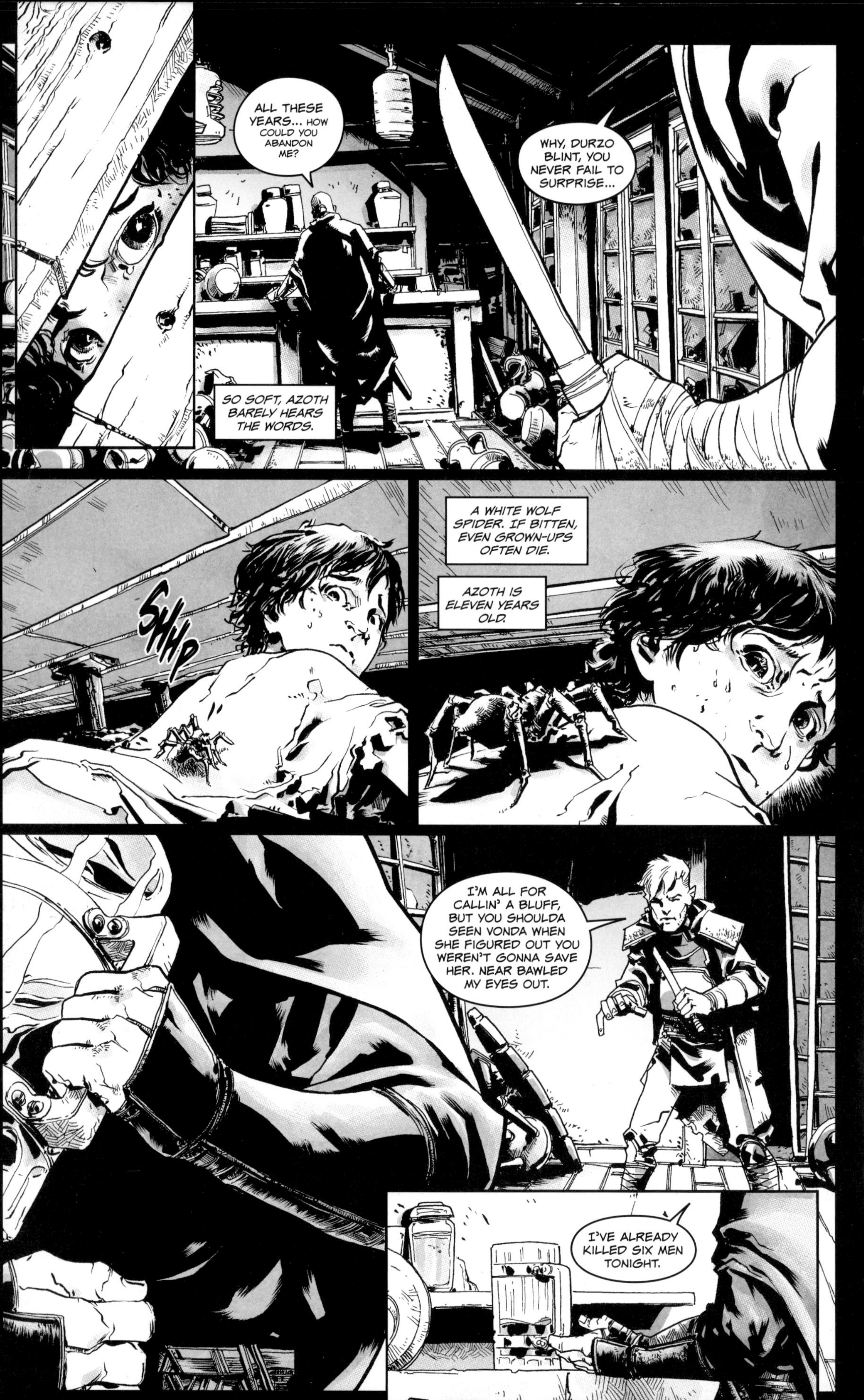
ALL THESE YEARS... HOW COULD YOU ABANDON ME?
SO SOFT, AZOTH BARELY HEARS THE WORDS.
WHY, DURZO BLINT, YOU NEVER FAIL TO SURPRISE...
SHHP
A WHITE WOLF SPIDER. IF BITTEN, EVEN GROWN-UPS OFTEN DIE.
AZOTH IS ELEVEN YEARS OLD.
I'M ALL FOR CALLIN' A BLUFF, BUT YOU SHOULDA SEEN VONDA WHEN SHE FIGURED OUT YOU WEREN'T GONNA SAVE HER. NEAR BAWLED MY EYES OUT.
I'VE ALREADY KILLED SIX MEN TONIGHT.

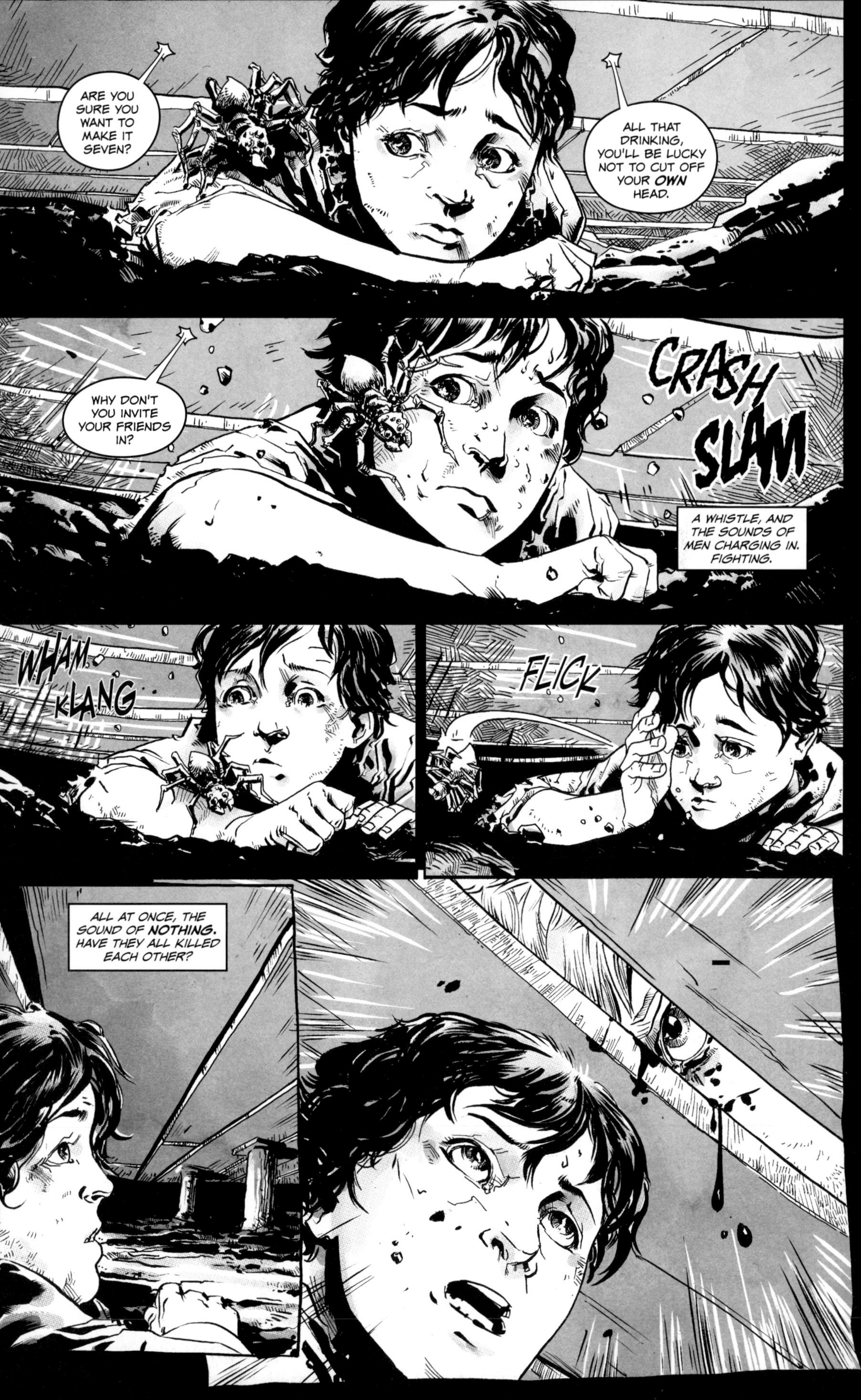

ARE YOU SURE YOU WANT TO MAKE IT SEVEN?
ALL THAT DRINKING, YOU'LL BE LUCKY NOT TO CUT OFF YOUR OWN HEAD.
WHY DON'T YOU INVITE YOUR FRIENDS IN?
CRASH
SLAM
A WHISTLE, AND THE SOUNDS OF MEN CHARGING IN. FIGHTING.
WHAM
KLANG
FLICK
ALL AT ONCE, THE SOUND OF NOTHING. HAVE THEY ALL KILLED EACH OTHER?

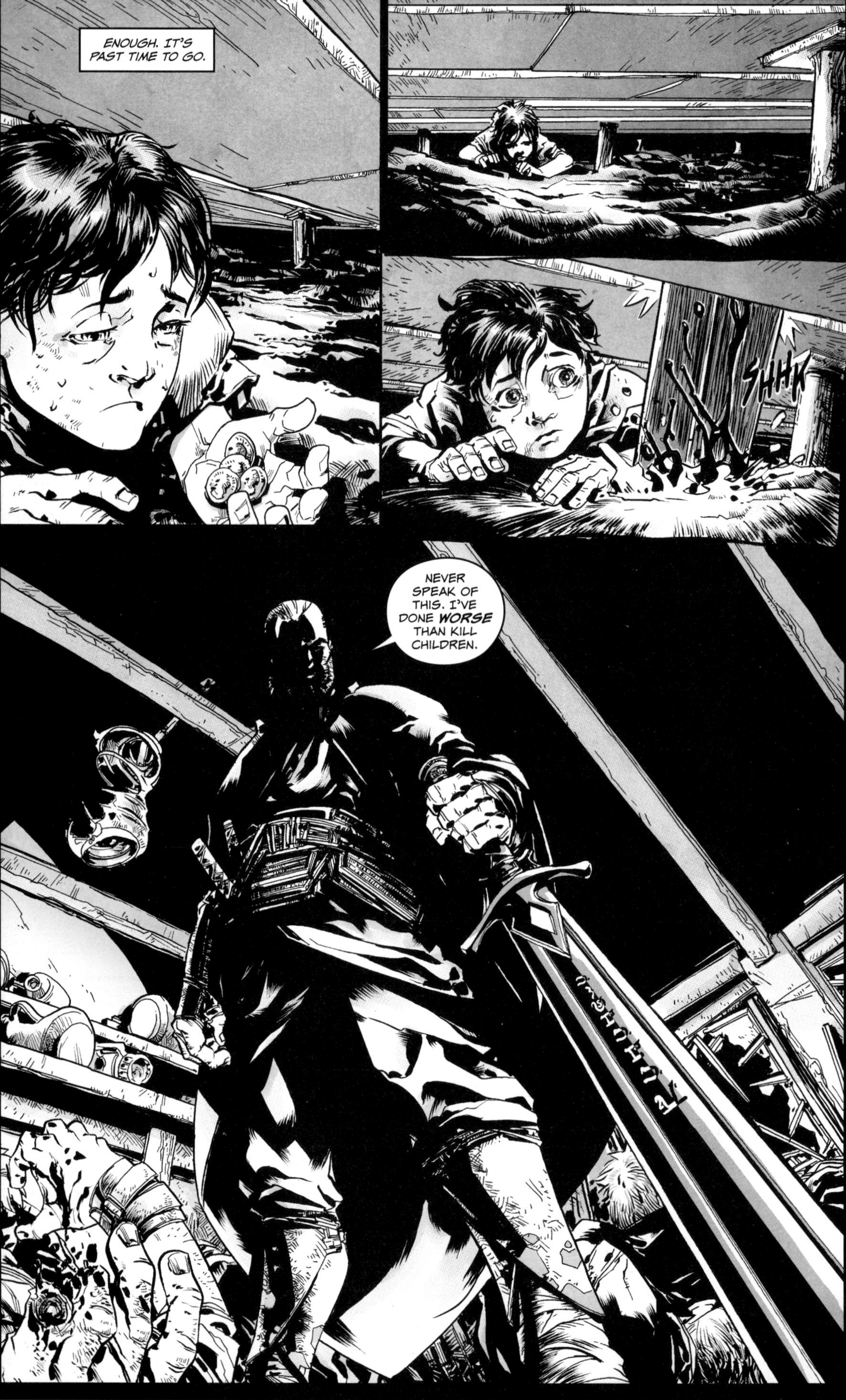
ENOUGH. IT'S PAST TIME TO GO.
SHHK
NEVER SPEAK OF THIS. I'VE DONE ***WORSE*** THAN KILL CHILDREN.

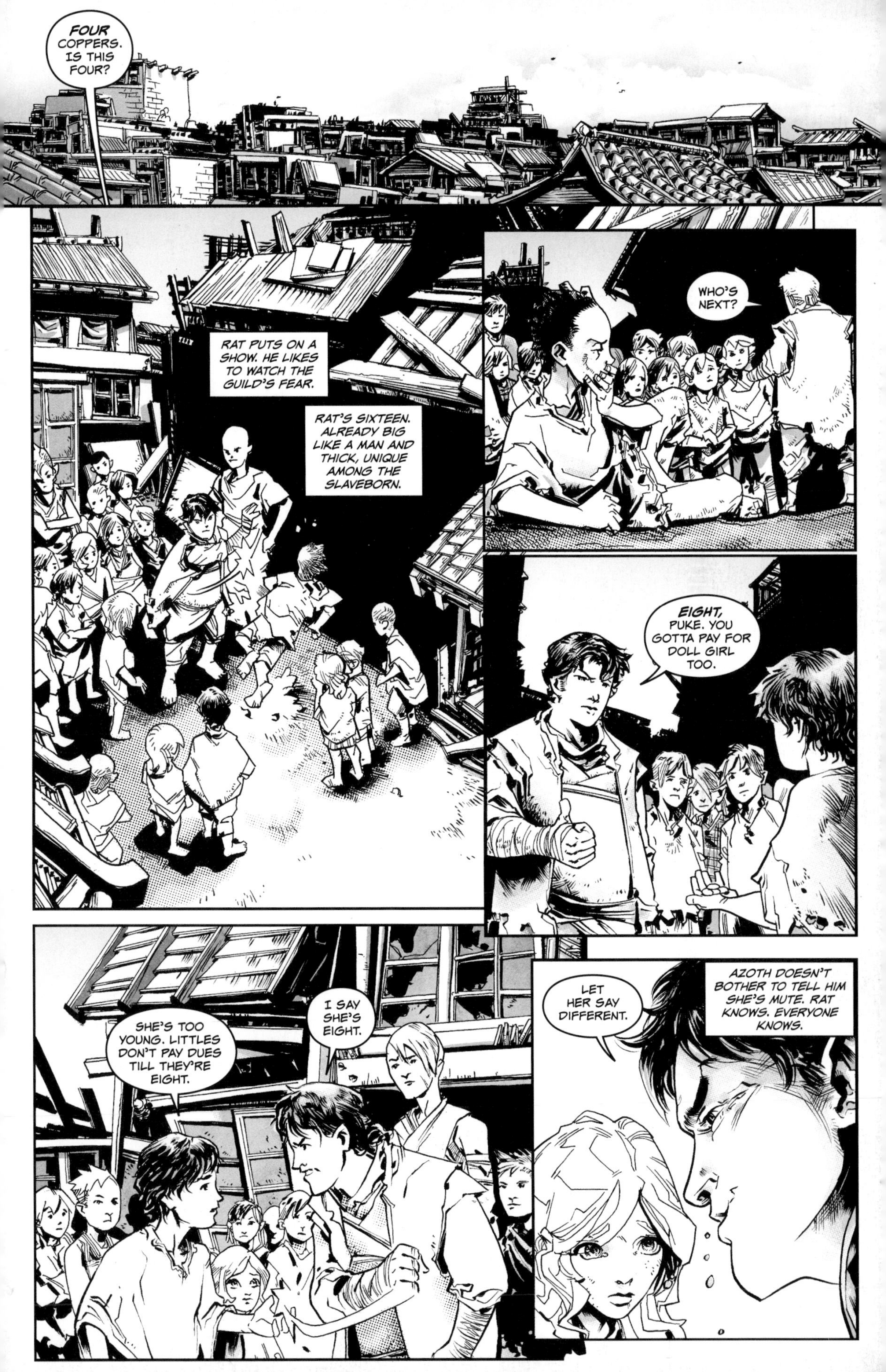

FOUR COPPERS. IS THIS FOUR?
RAT PUTS ON A SHOW. HE LIKES TO WATCH THE GUILD'S FEAR.
RAT'S SIXTEEN. ALREADY BIG LIKE A MAN AND THICK, UNIQUE AMONG THE SLAVEBORN.
WHO'S NEXT?
EIGHT, PUKE. YOU GOTTA PAY FOR DOLL GIRL TOO.
SHE'S TOO YOUNG. LITTLES DON'T PAY DUES TILL THEY'RE EIGHT.
I SAY SHE'S EIGHT.
LET HER SAY DIFFERENT.
AZOTH DOESN'T BOTHER TO TELL HIM SHE'S MUTE. RAT KNOWS. EVERYONE KNOWS.

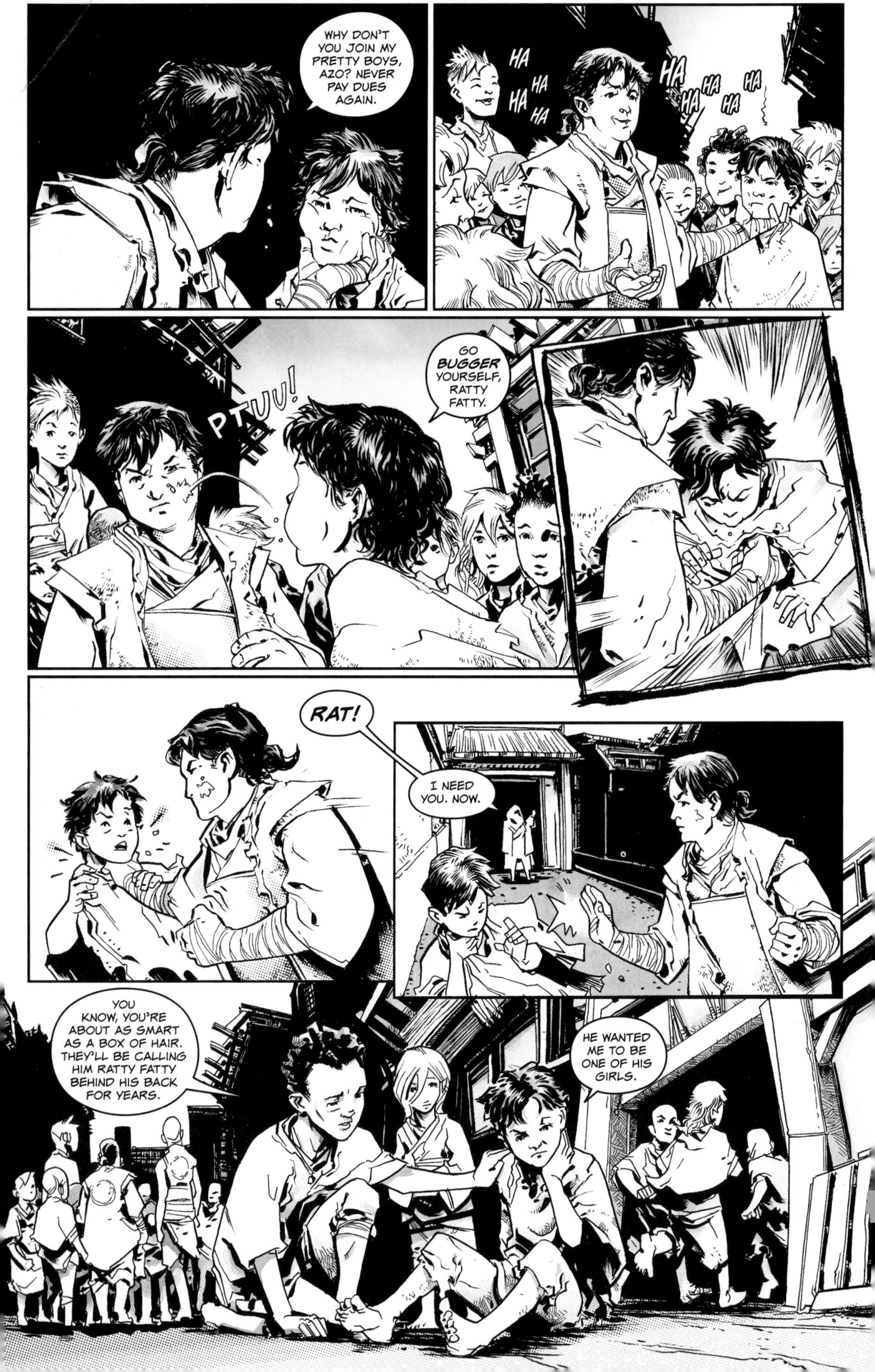
WHY DON'T YOU JOIN MY PRETTY BOYS, AZO? NEVER PAY DUES AGAIN.
HA HA HA HA
HA HA HA HA HA
GO BUGGER YOURSELF, RATTY FATTY.
PTUU!
RAT!
I NEED YOU. NOW.
YOU KNOW, YOU'RE ABOUT AS SMART AS A BOX OF HAIR. THEY'LL BE CALLING HIM RATTY FATTY BEHIND HIS BACK FOR YEARS.
HE WANTED ME TO BE ONE OF HIS GIRLS.

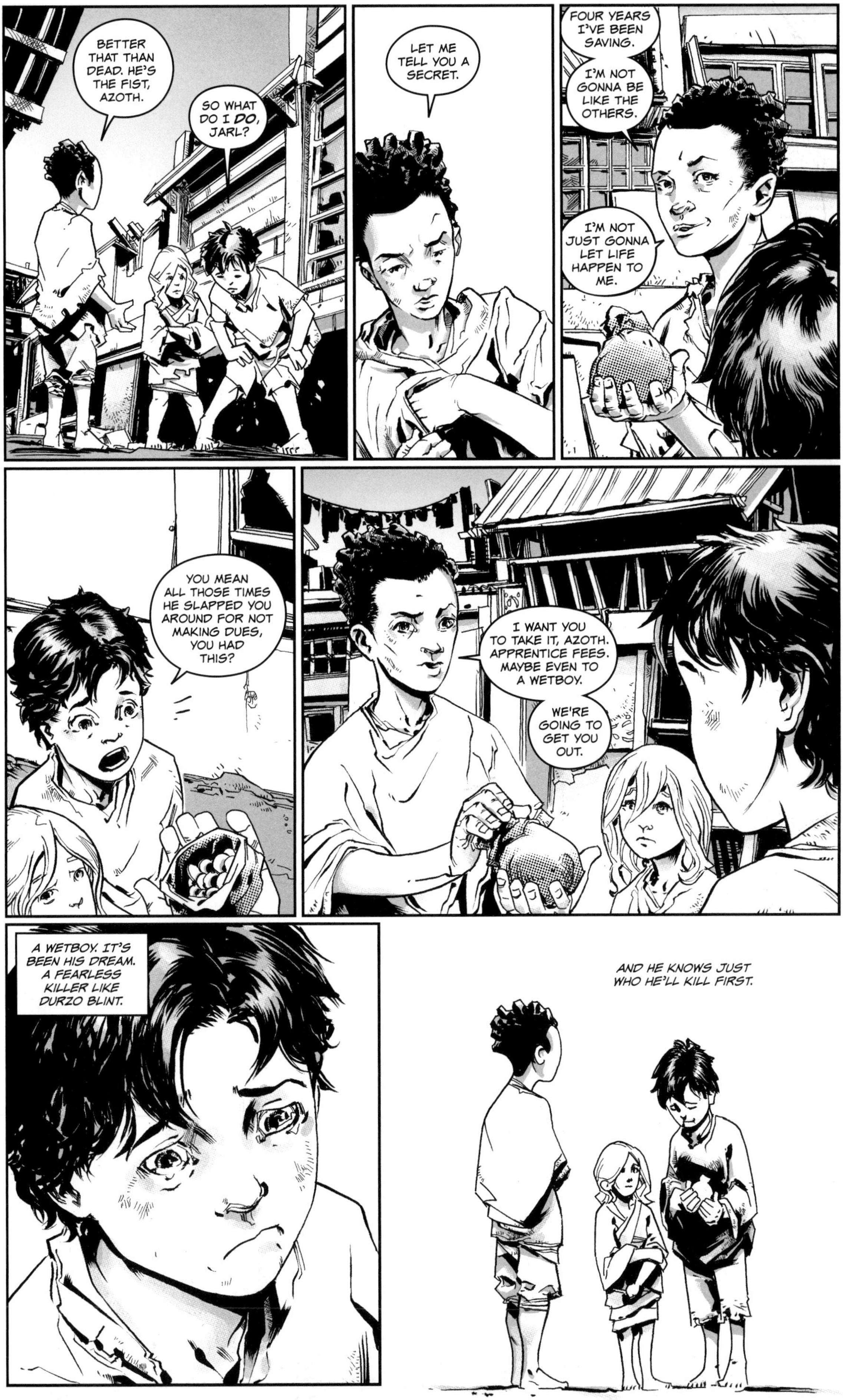
BETTER THAT THAN DEAD. HE'S THE FIST, AZOTH.
SO WHAT DO I DO, JARL?
LET ME TELL YOU A SECRET.
FOUR YEARS I'VE BEEN SAVING.
I'M NOT GONNA BE LIKE THE OTHERS.
I'M NOT JUST GONNA LET LIFE HAPPEN TO ME.
YOU MEAN ALL THOSE TIMES HE SLAPPED YOU AROUND FOR NOT MAKING DUES, YOU HAD THIS?
I WANT YOU TO TAKE IT, AZOTH. APPRENTICE FEES. MAYBE EVEN TO A WETBOY.
WE'RE GOING TO GET YOU OUT.
A WETBOY. IT'S BEEN HIS DREAM. A FEARLESS KILLER LIKE DURZO BLINT.
AND HE KNOWS JUST WHO HE'LL KILL FIRST.

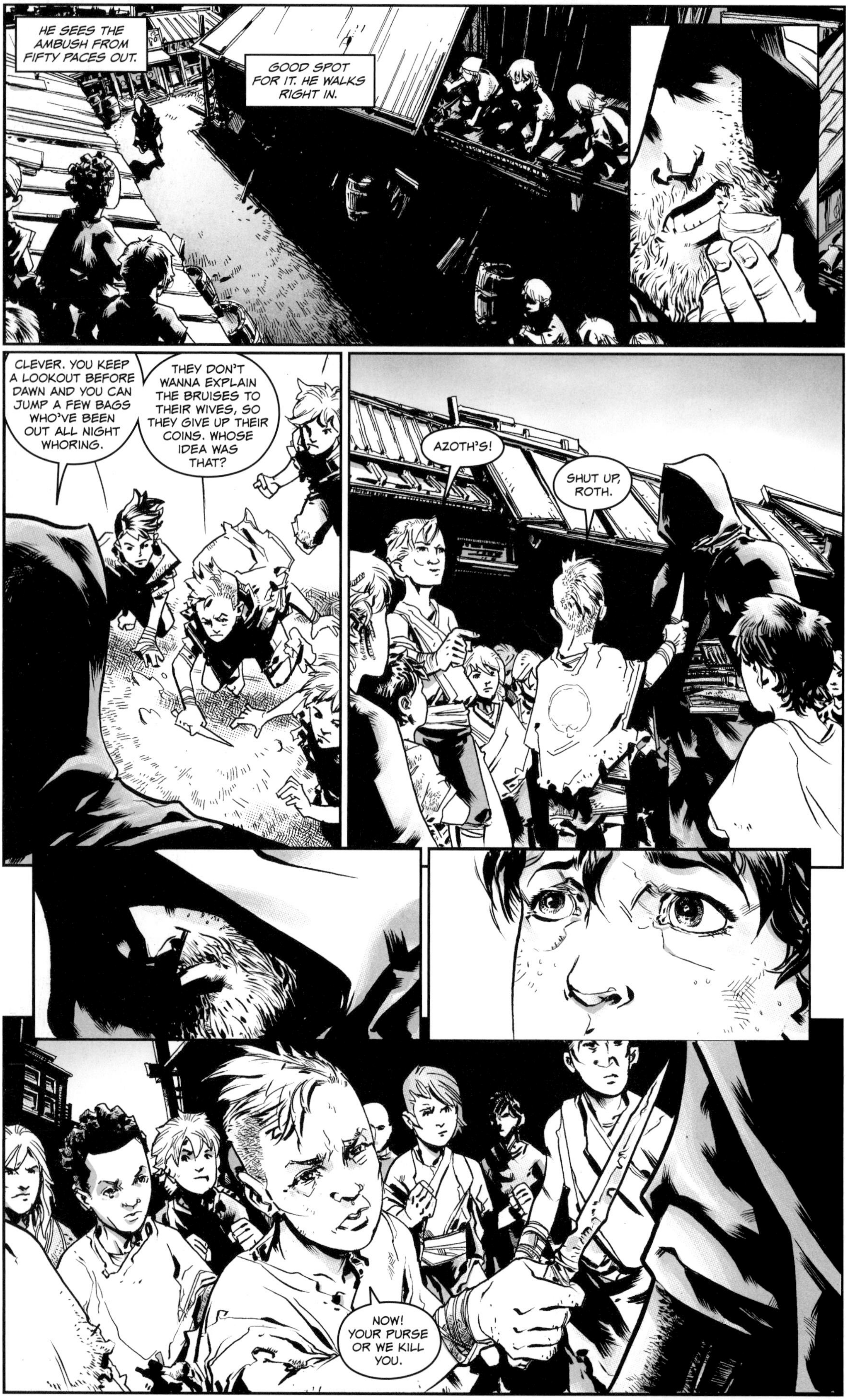
HE SEES THE AMBUSH FROM FIFTY PACES OUT.
GOOD SPOT FOR IT. HE WALKS RIGHT IN.
CLEVER. YOU KEEP A LOOKOUT BEFORE DAWN AND YOU CAN JUMP A FEW BAGS WHO'VE BEEN OUT ALL NIGHT WHORING.
THEY DON'T WANNA EXPLAIN THE BRUISES TO THEIR WIVES, SO THEY GIVE UP THEIR COINS. WHOSE IDEA WAS THAT?
AZOTH'S!
SHUT UP, ROTH.
NOW! YOUR PURSE OR WE KILL YOU.

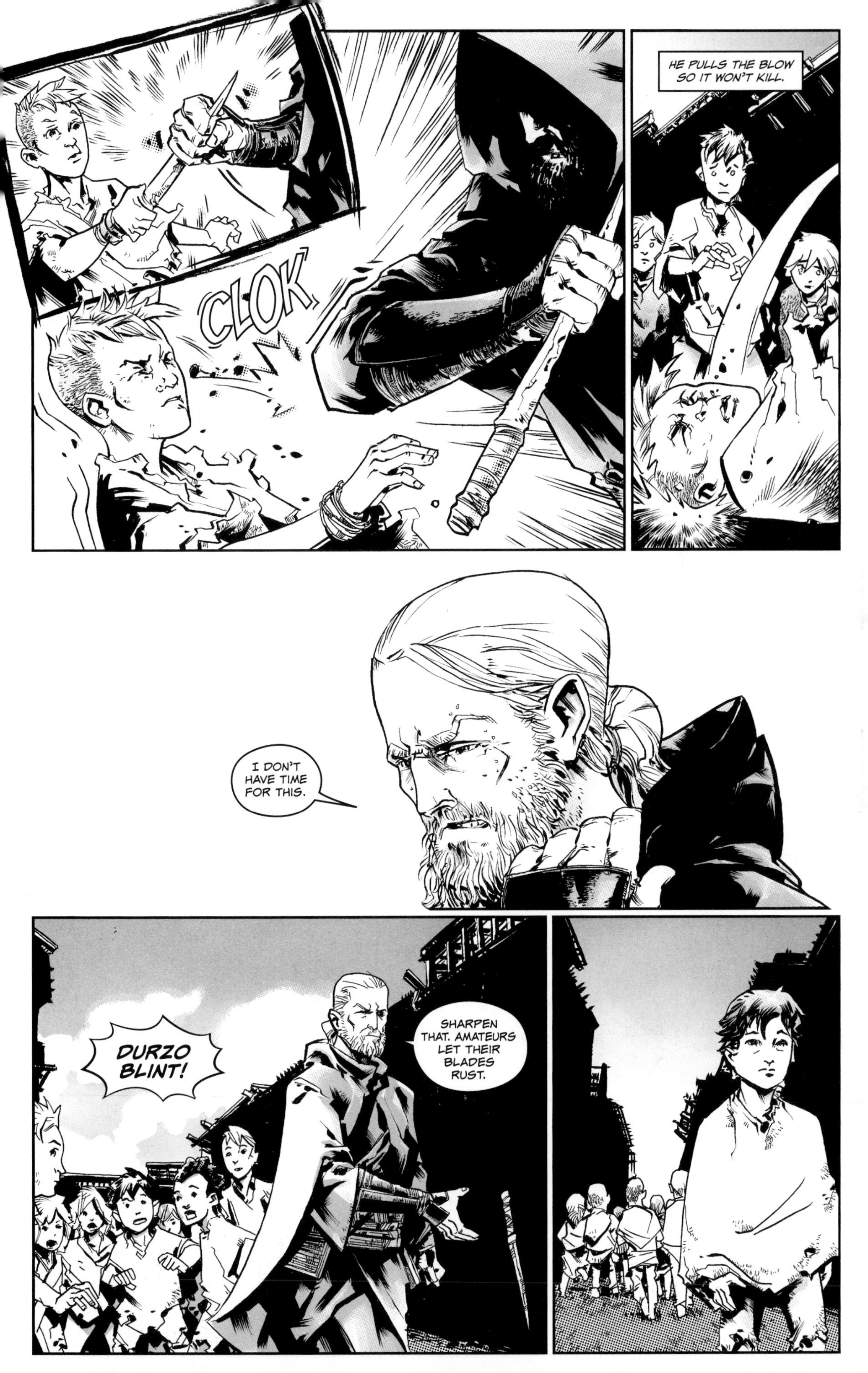
CLOK
HE PULLS THE BLOW SO IT WON'T KILL.
I DON'T HAVE TIME FOR THIS.
DURZO BLINT!
SHARPEN THAT. AMATEURS LET THEIR BLADES RUST.

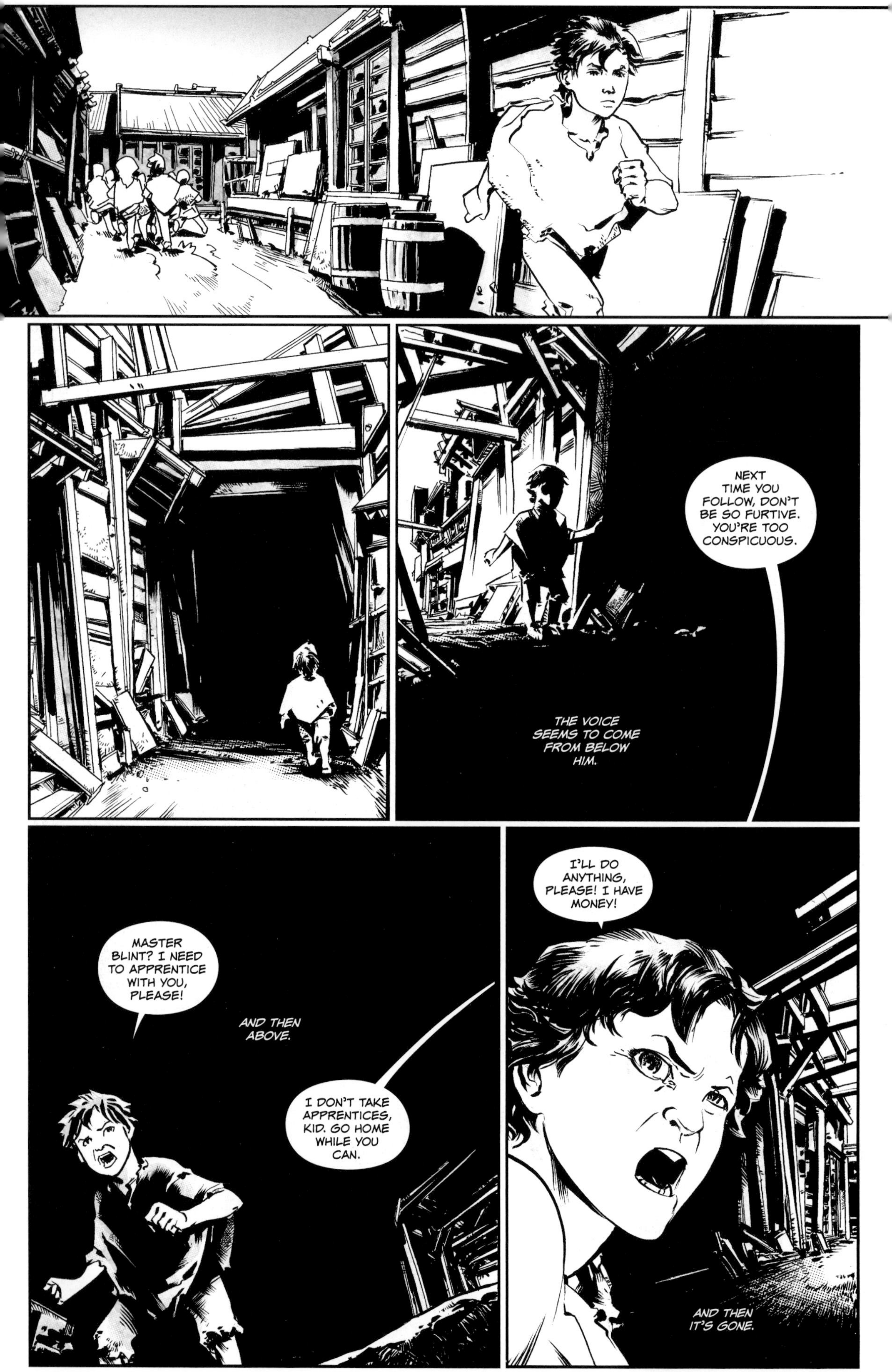
NEXT TIME YOU FOLLOW, DON'T BE SO FURTIVE. YOU'RE TOO CONSPICUOUS.
THE VOICE SEEMS TO COME FROM BELOW HIM.
MASTER BLINT? I NEED TO APPRENTICE WITH YOU, PLEASE!
AND THEN ABOVE.
I DON'T TAKE APPRENTICES, KID. GO HOME WHILE YOU CAN.
I'LL DO ANYTHING, PLEASE! I HAVE MONEY!
AND THEN IT'S GONE.

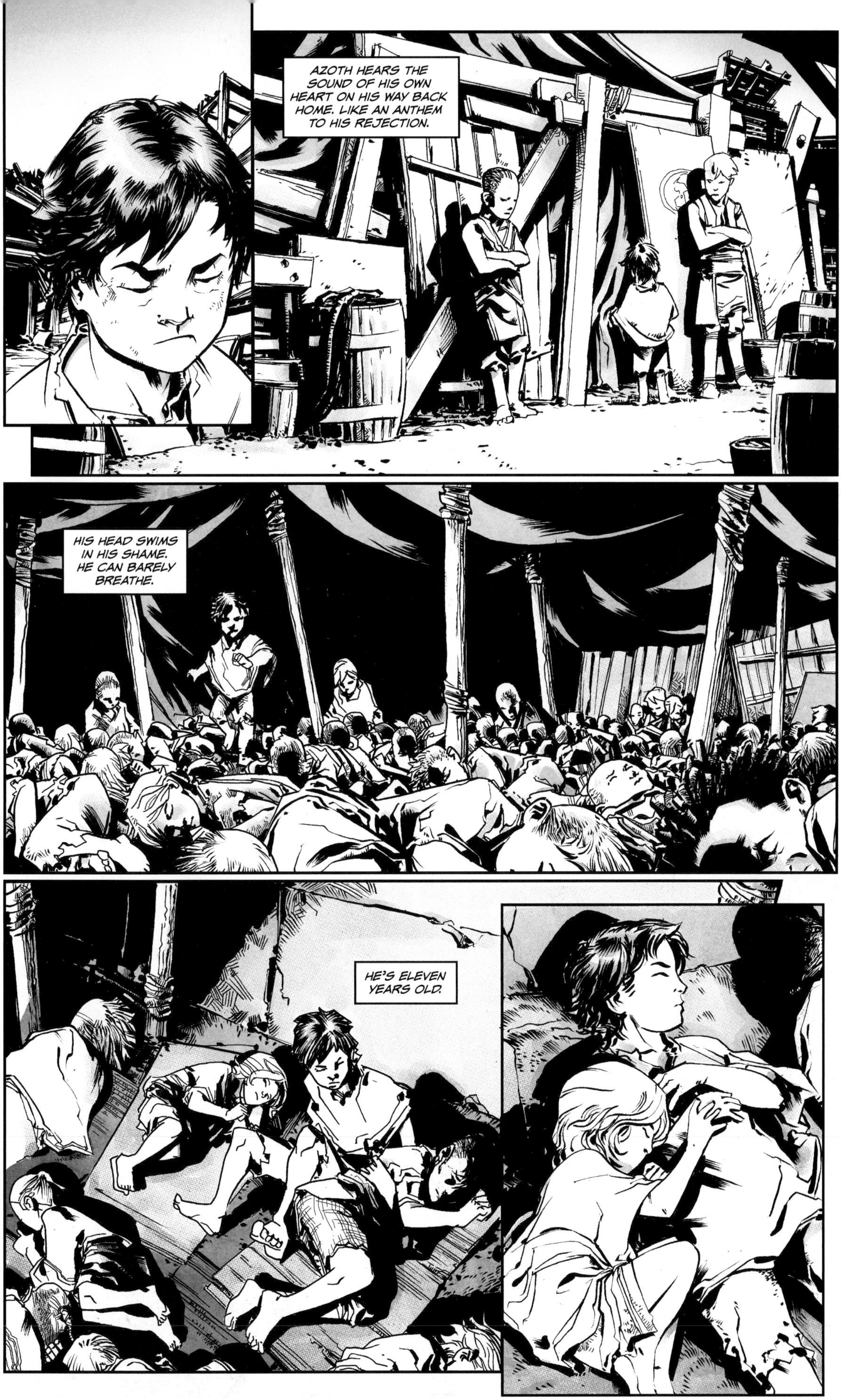
AZOTH HEARS THE SOUND OF HIS OWN HEART ON HIS WAY BACK HOME. LIKE AN ANTHEM TO HIS REJECTION.
HIS HEAD SWIMS IN HIS SHAME. HE CAN BARELY BREATHE.
HE'S ELEVEN YEARS OLD.

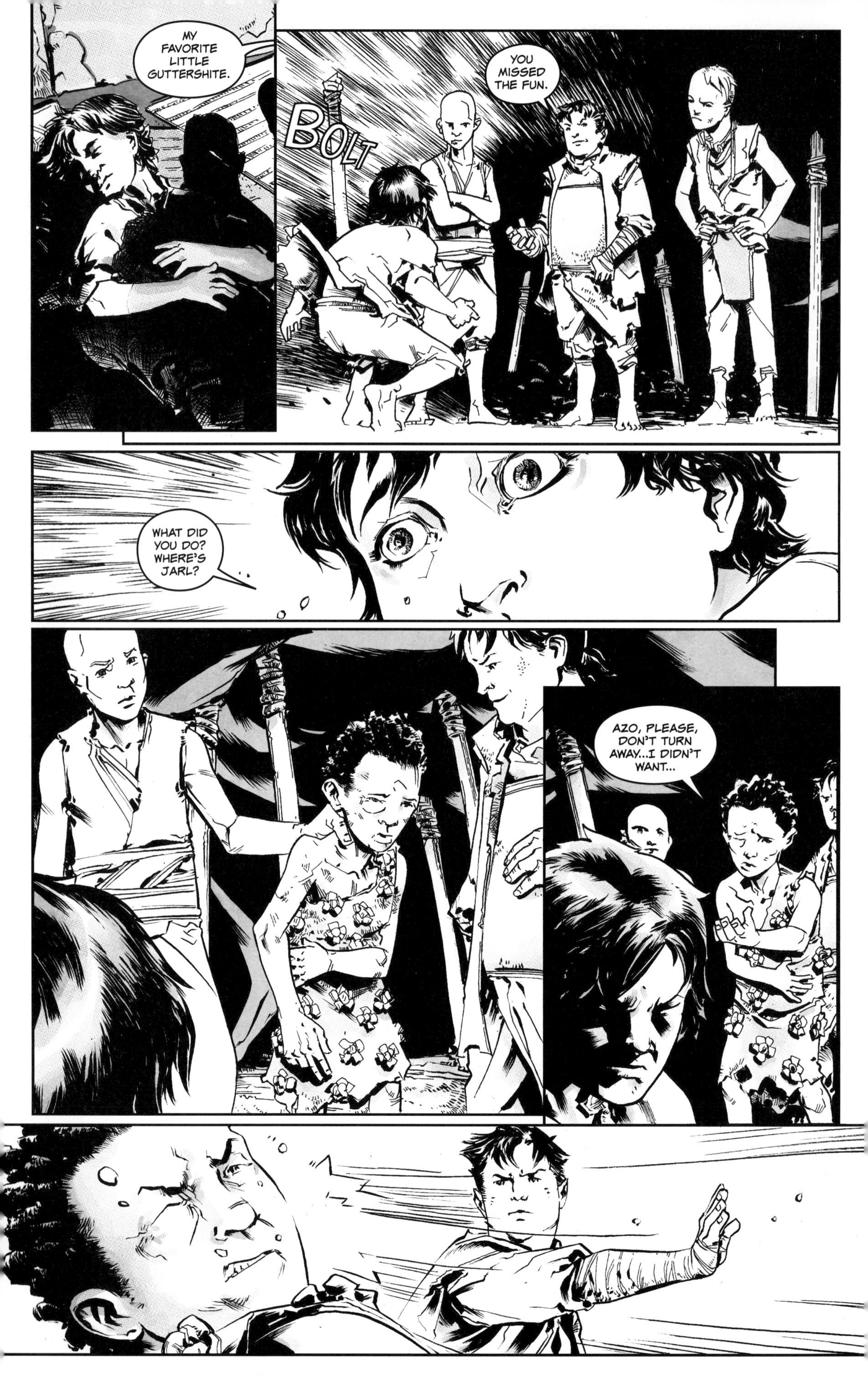
MY FAVORITE LITTLE GUTTERSHITE.
BOLT
YOU MISSED THE FUN.
WHAT DID YOU DO? WHERE'S JARL?
AZO, PLEASE, DON'T TURN AWAY...I DIDN'T WANT...

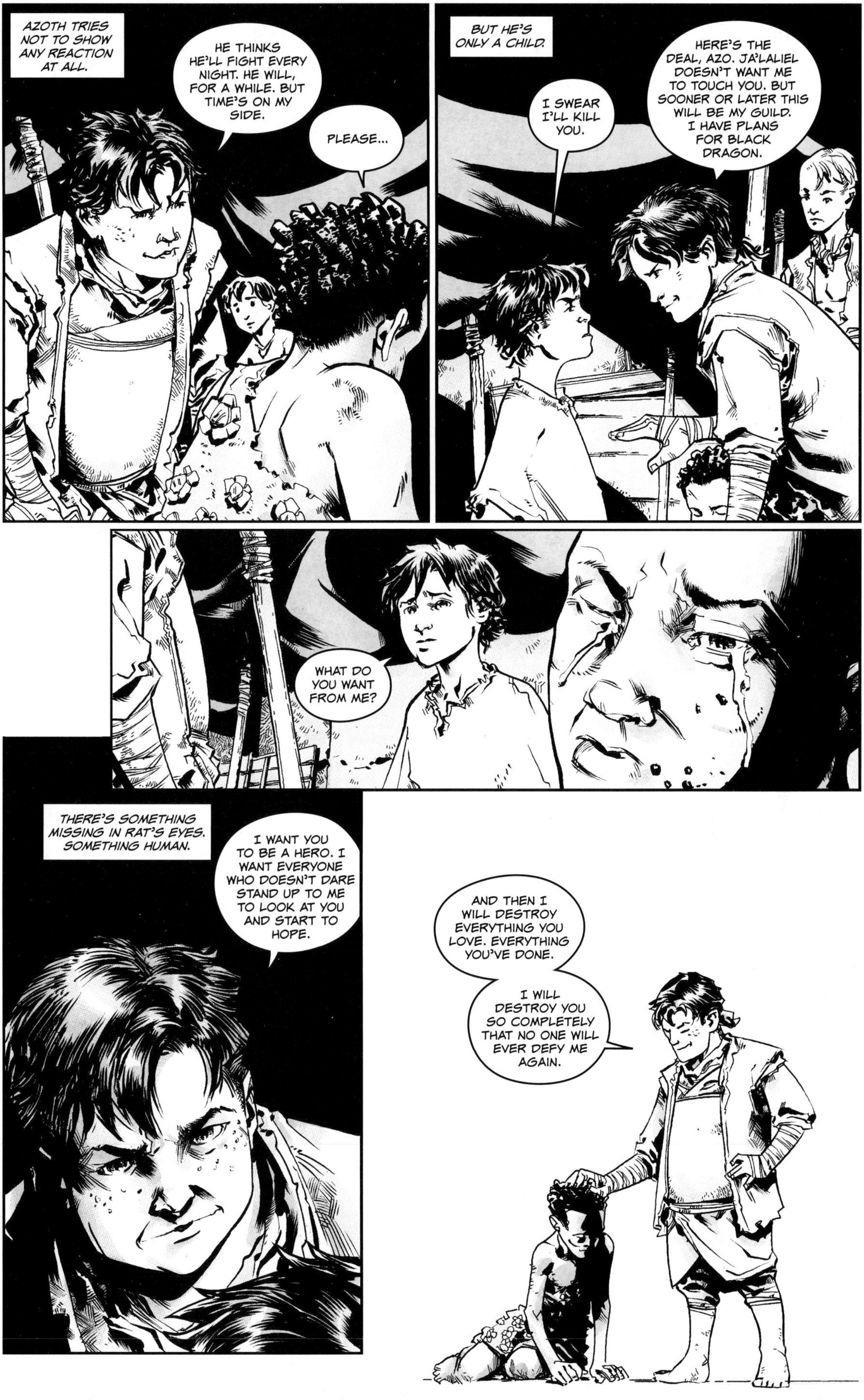
AZOTH TRIES NOT TO SHOW ANY REACTION AT ALL.
HE THINKS HE'LL FIGHT EVERY NIGHT. HE WILL, FOR A WHILE. BUT TIME'S ON MY SIDE.
PLEASE...
BUT HE'S ONLY A CHILD.
I SWEAR I'LL KILL YOU.
HERE'S THE DEAL, AZO. JA'LALIEL DOESN'T WANT ME TO TOUCH YOU. BUT SOONER OR LATER THIS WILL BE MY GUILD. I HAVE PLANS FOR BLACK DRAGON.
WHAT DO YOU WANT FROM ME?
THERE'S SOMETHING MISSING IN RAT'S EYES. SOMETHING HUMAN.
I WANT YOU TO BE A HERO. I WANT EVERYONE WHO DOESN'T DARE STAND UP TO ME TO LOOK AT YOU AND START TO HOPE.
AND THEN I WILL DESTROY EVERYTHING YOU LOVE. EVERYTHING YOU'VE DONE.
I WILL DESTROY YOU SO COMPLETELY THAT NO ONE WILL EVER DEFY ME AGAIN.

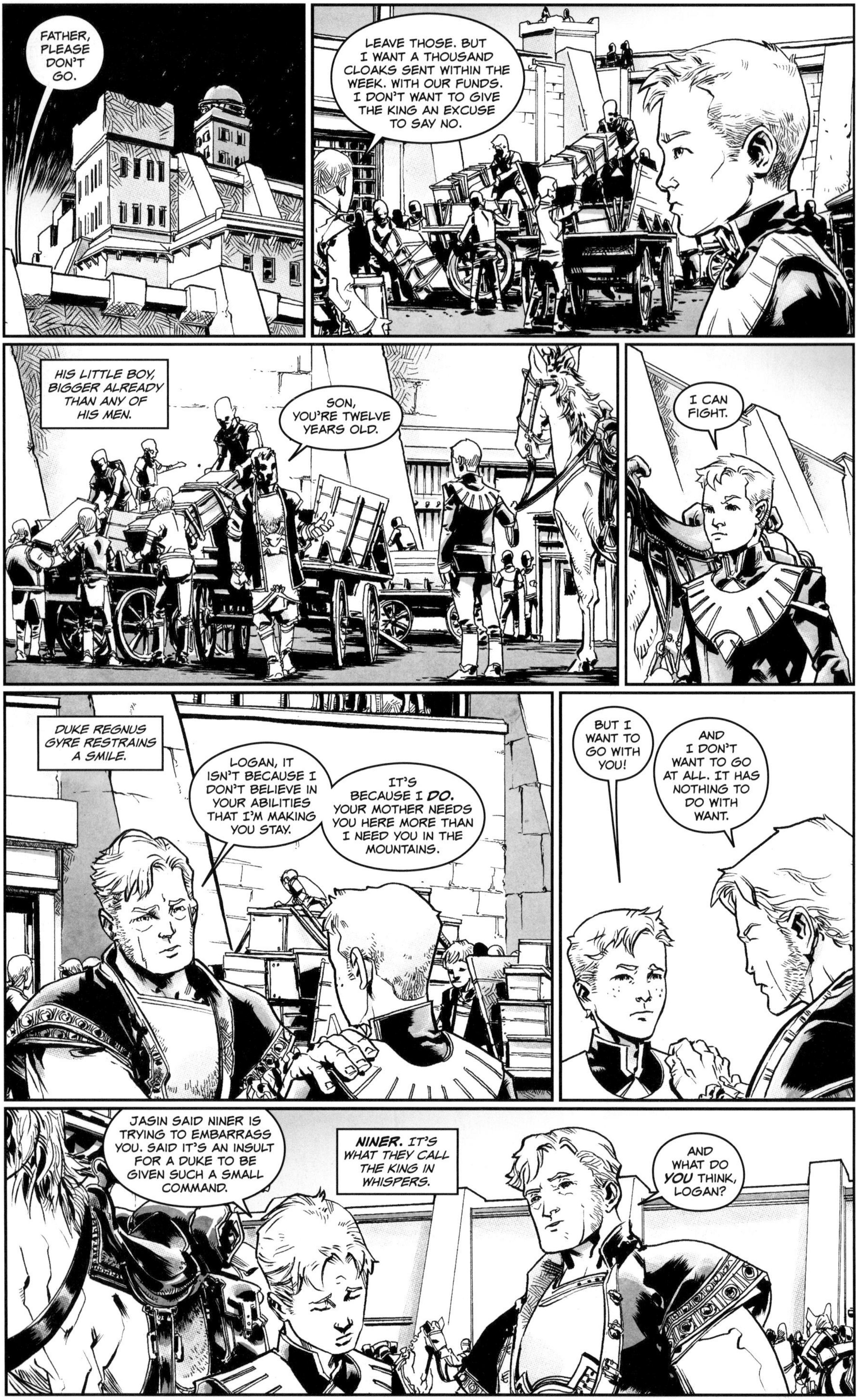
FATHER, PLEASE DON'T GO.
LEAVE THOSE. BUT I WANT A THOUSAND CLOAKS SENT WITHIN THE WEEK. WITH OUR FUNDS. I DON'T WANT TO GIVE THE KING AN EXCUSE TO SAY NO.
HIS LITTLE BOY, BIGGER ALREADY THAN ANY OF HIS MEN.
SON, YOU'RE TWELVE YEARS OLD.
I CAN FIGHT.
DUKE REGNUS GYRE RESTRAINS A SMILE.
LOGAN, IT ISN'T BECAUSE I DON'T BELIEVE IN YOUR ABILITIES THAT I'M MAKING YOU STAY.
IT'S BECAUSE I DO. YOUR MOTHER NEEDS YOU HERE MORE THAN I NEED YOU IN THE MOUNTAINS.
BUT I WANT TO GO WITH YOU!
AND I DON'T WANT TO GO AT ALL. IT HAS NOTHING TO DO WITH WANT.
JASIN SAID NINER IS TRYING TO EMBARRASS YOU. SAID IT'S AN INSULT FOR A DUKE TO BE GIVEN SUCH A SMALL COMMAND.
NINER. IT'S WHAT THEY CALL THE KING IN WHISPERS.
AND WHAT DO YOU THINK, LOGAN?

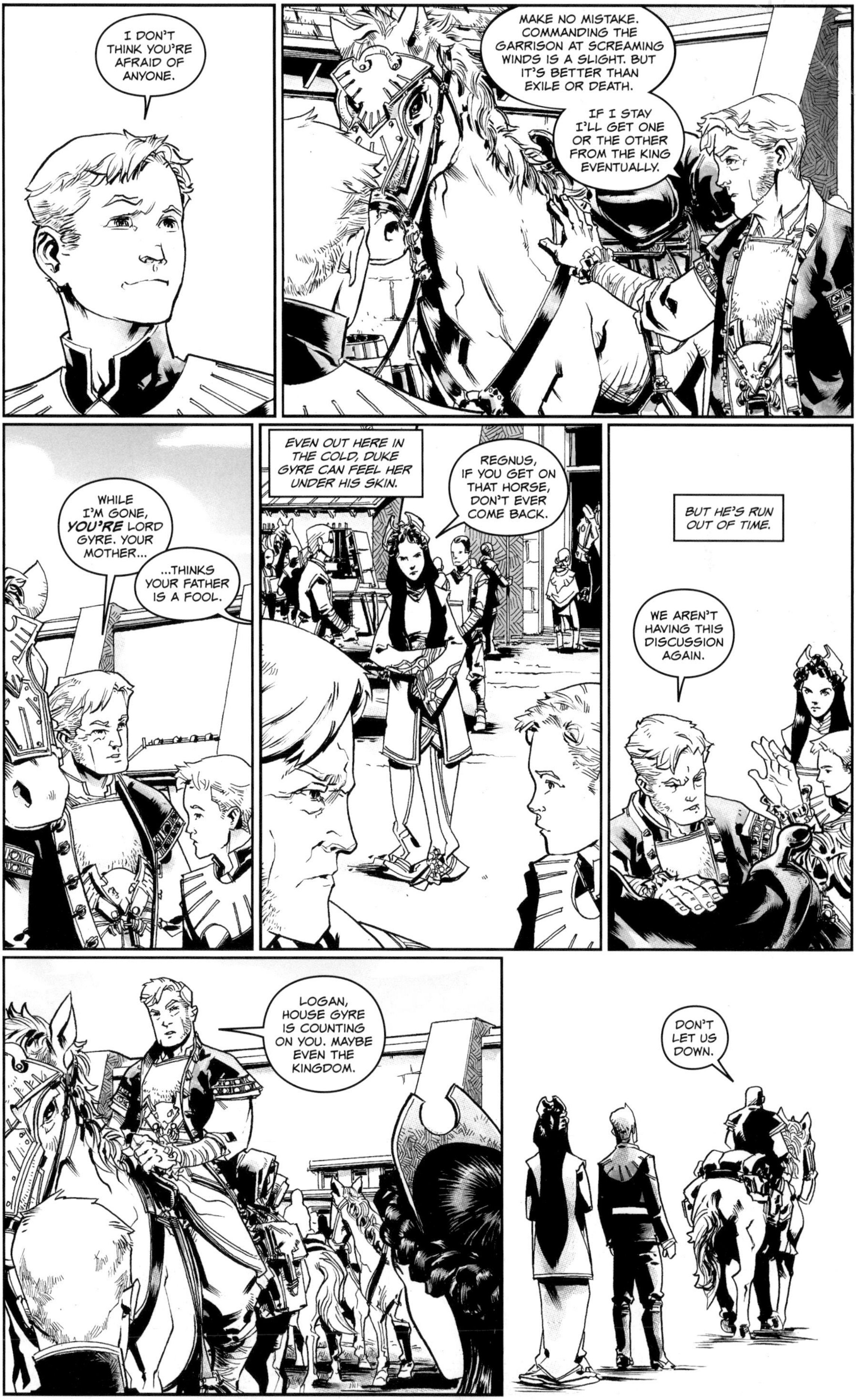
I DON'T THINK YOU'RE AFRAID OF ANYONE.
MAKE NO MISTAKE. COMMANDING THE GARRISON AT SCREAMING WINDS IS A SLIGHT. BUT IT'S BETTER THAN EXILE OR DEATH.
IF I STAY I'LL GET ONE OR THE OTHER FROM THE KING EVENTUALLY.
WHILE I'M GONE, YOU'RE LORD GYRE. YOUR MOTHER...
...THINKS YOUR FATHER IS A FOOL.
EVEN OUT HERE IN THE COLD, DUKE GYRE CAN FEEL HER UNDER HIS SKIN.
REGNUS, IF YOU GET ON THAT HORSE, DON'T EVER COME BACK.
BUT HE'S RUN OUT OF TIME.
WE AREN'T HAVING THIS DISCUSSION AGAIN.
LOGAN, HOUSE GYRE IS COUNTING ON YOU. MAYBE EVEN THE KINGDOM.
DON'T LET US DOWN.

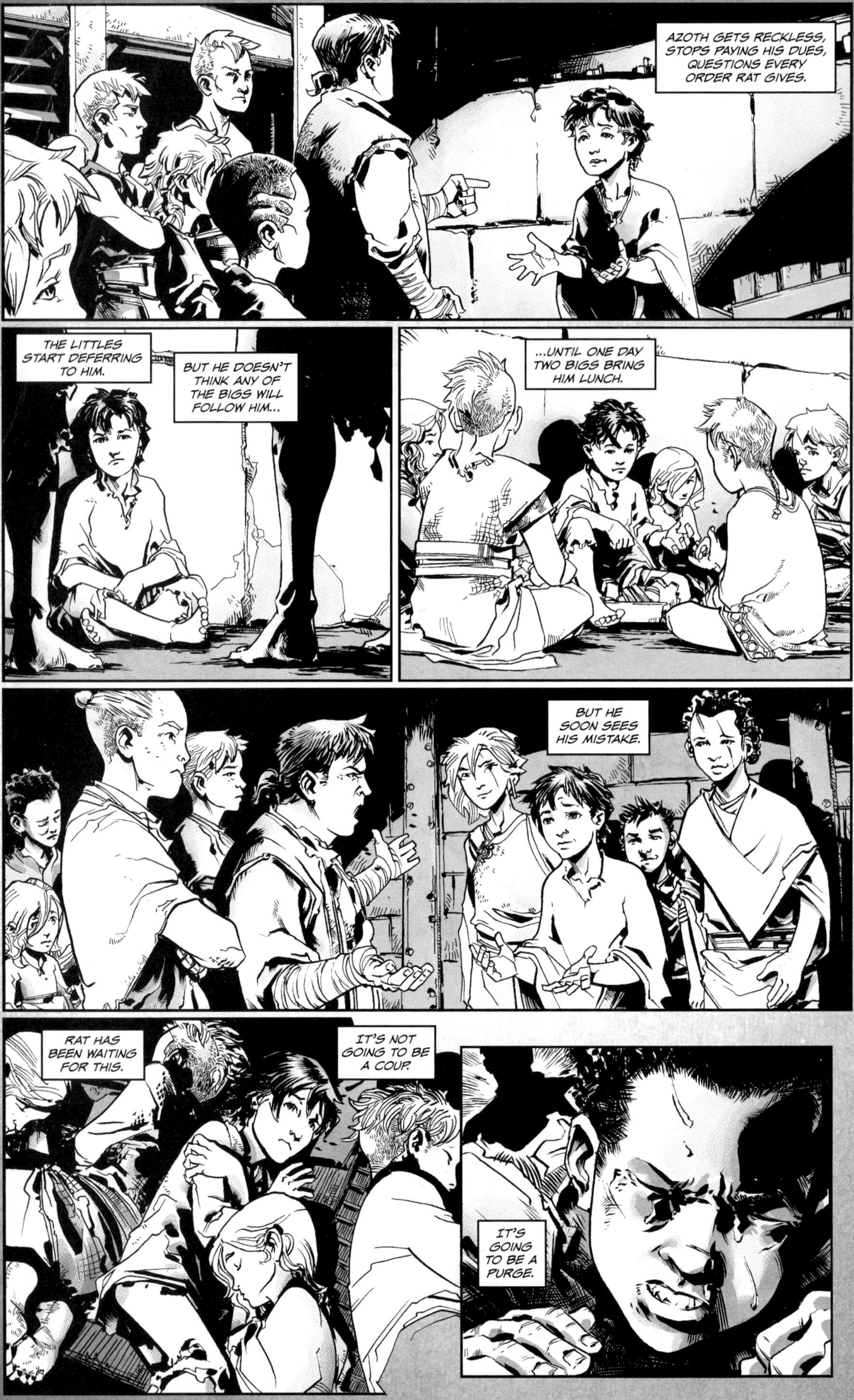
AZOTH GETS RECKLESS, STOPS PAYING HIS DUES, QUESTIONS EVERY ORDER RAT GIVES.
THE LITTLES START DEFERRING TO HIM.
BUT HE DOESN'T THINK ANY OF THE BIGS WILL FOLLOW HIM...
...UNTIL ONE DAY TWO BIGS BRING HIM LUNCH.
BUT HE SOON SEES HIS MISTAKE.
RAT HAS BEEN WAITING FOR THIS.
IT'S NOT GOING TO BE A COUP.
IT'S GOING TO BE A PURGE.

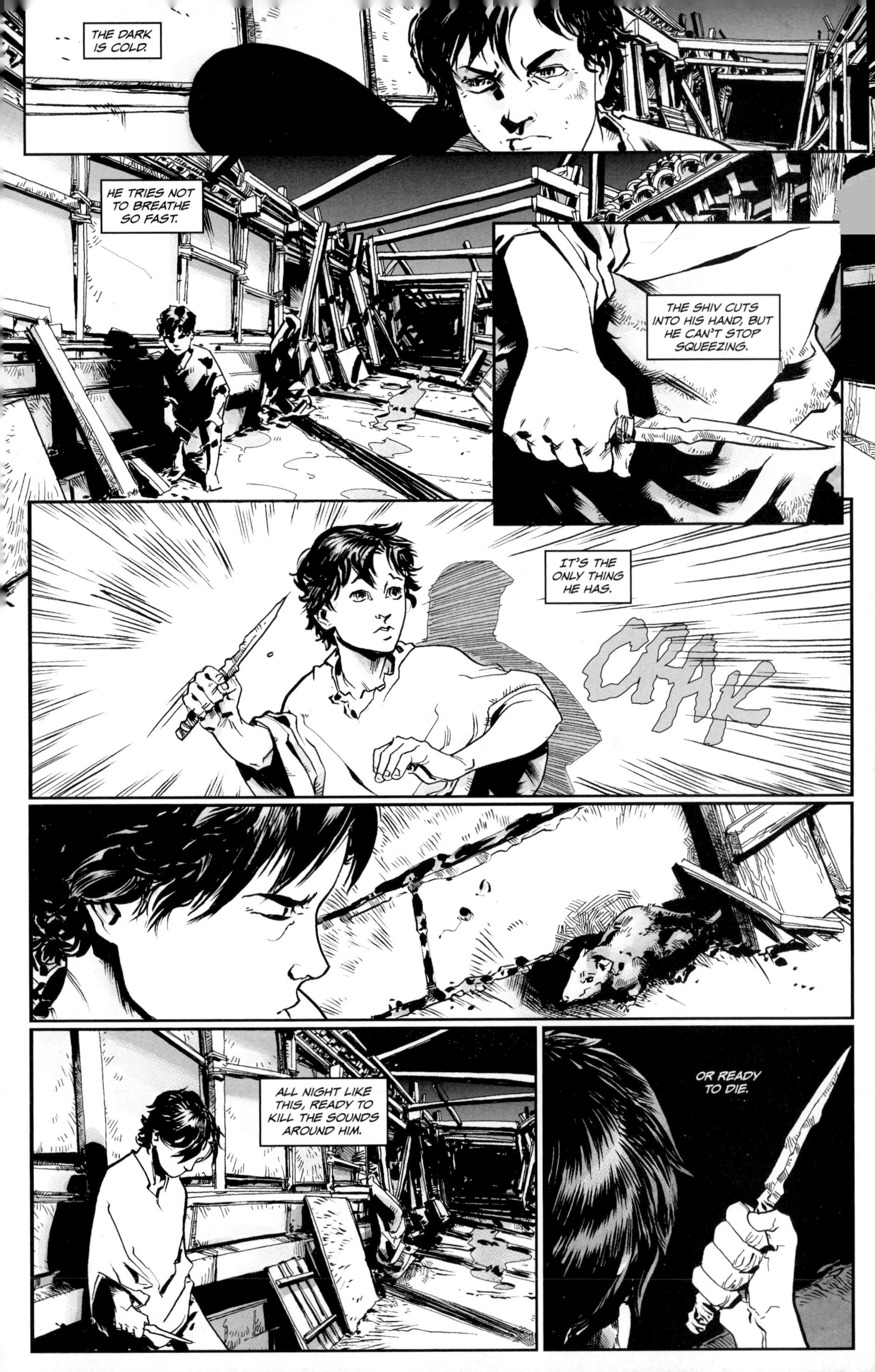
THE DARK IS COLD.
HE TRIES NOT TO BREATHE SO FAST.
THE SHIV CUTS INTO HIS HAND, BUT HE CAN'T STOP SQUEEZING.
IT'S THE ONLY THING HE HAS.
CRAK
ALL NIGHT LIKE THIS, READY TO KILL THE SOUNDS AROUND HIM.
OR READY TO DIE.

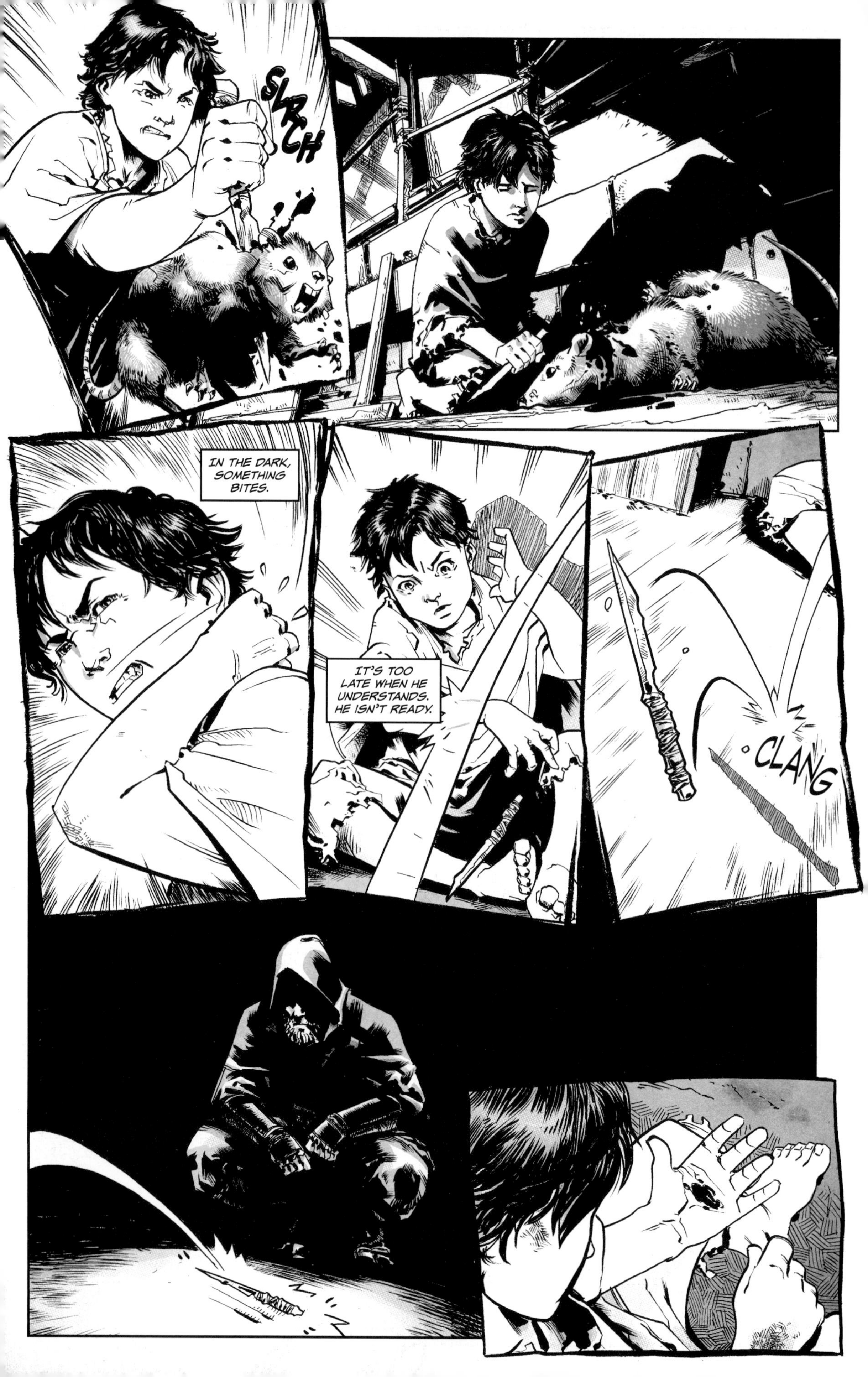
SLRCH
IN THE DARK, SOMETHING BITES.
IT'S TOO LATE WHEN HE UNDERSTANDS. HE ISN'T READY.
CLANG

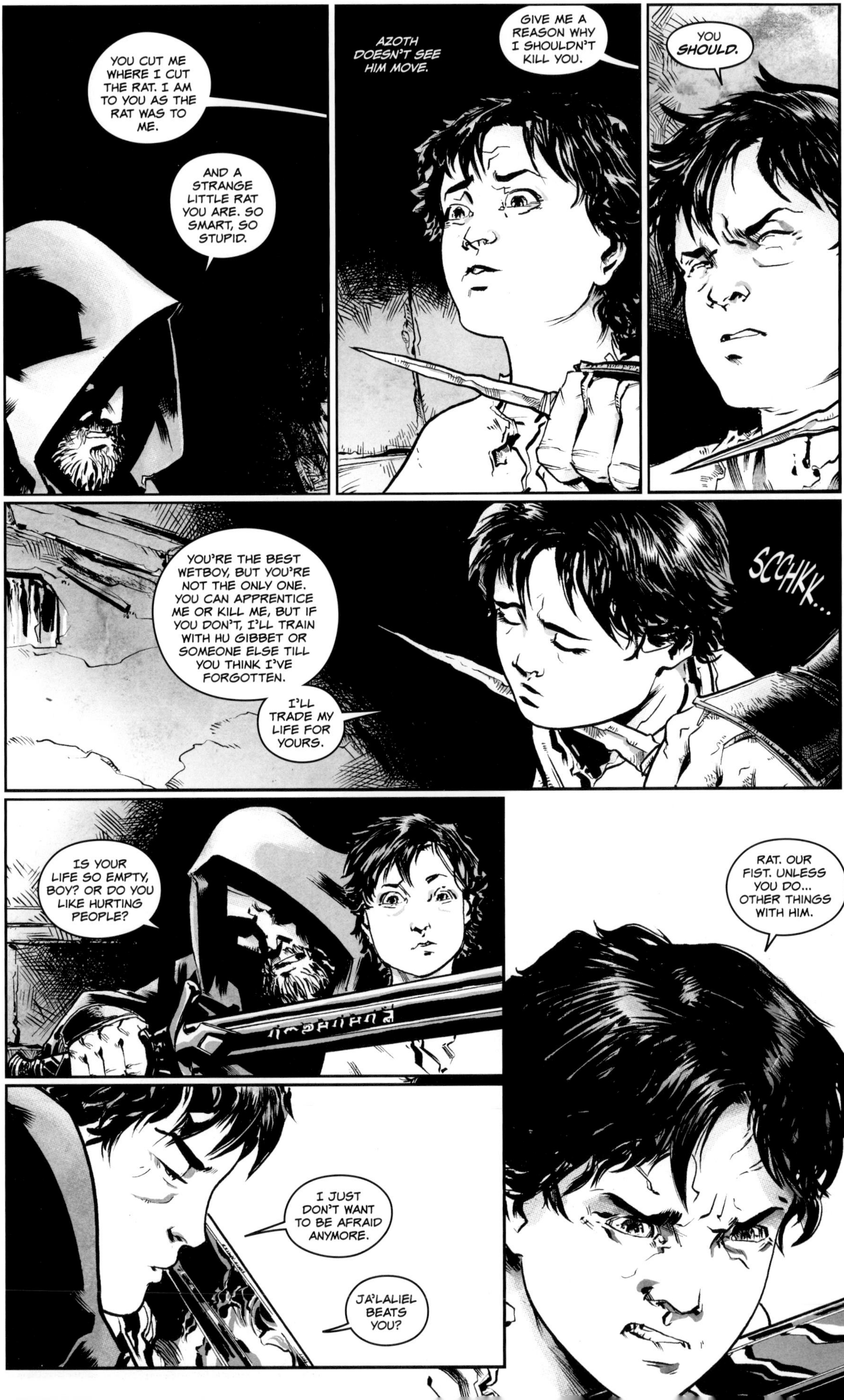
YOU CUT ME WHERE I CUT THE RAT. I AM TO YOU AS THE RAT WAS TO ME.
AND A STRANGE LITTLE RAT YOU ARE. SO SMART, SO STUPID.
AZOTH DOESN'T SEE HIM MOVE.
GIVE ME A REASON WHY I SHOULDN'T KILL YOU.
YOU SHOULD.
YOU'RE THE BEST WETBOY, BUT YOU'RE NOT THE ONLY ONE. YOU CAN APPRENTICE ME OR KILL ME, BUT IF YOU DON'T, I'LL TRAIN WITH HU GIBBET OR SOMEONE ELSE TILL YOU THINK I'VE FORGOTTEN.
I'LL TRADE MY LIFE FOR YOURS.
SCCHKK...
IS YOUR LIFE SO EMPTY, BOY? OR DO YOU LIKE HURTING PEOPLE?
I JUST DON'T WANT TO BE AFRAID ANYMORE.
JA'LALIEL BEATS YOU?
RAT. OUR FIST. UNLESS YOU DO... OTHER THINGS WITH HIM.

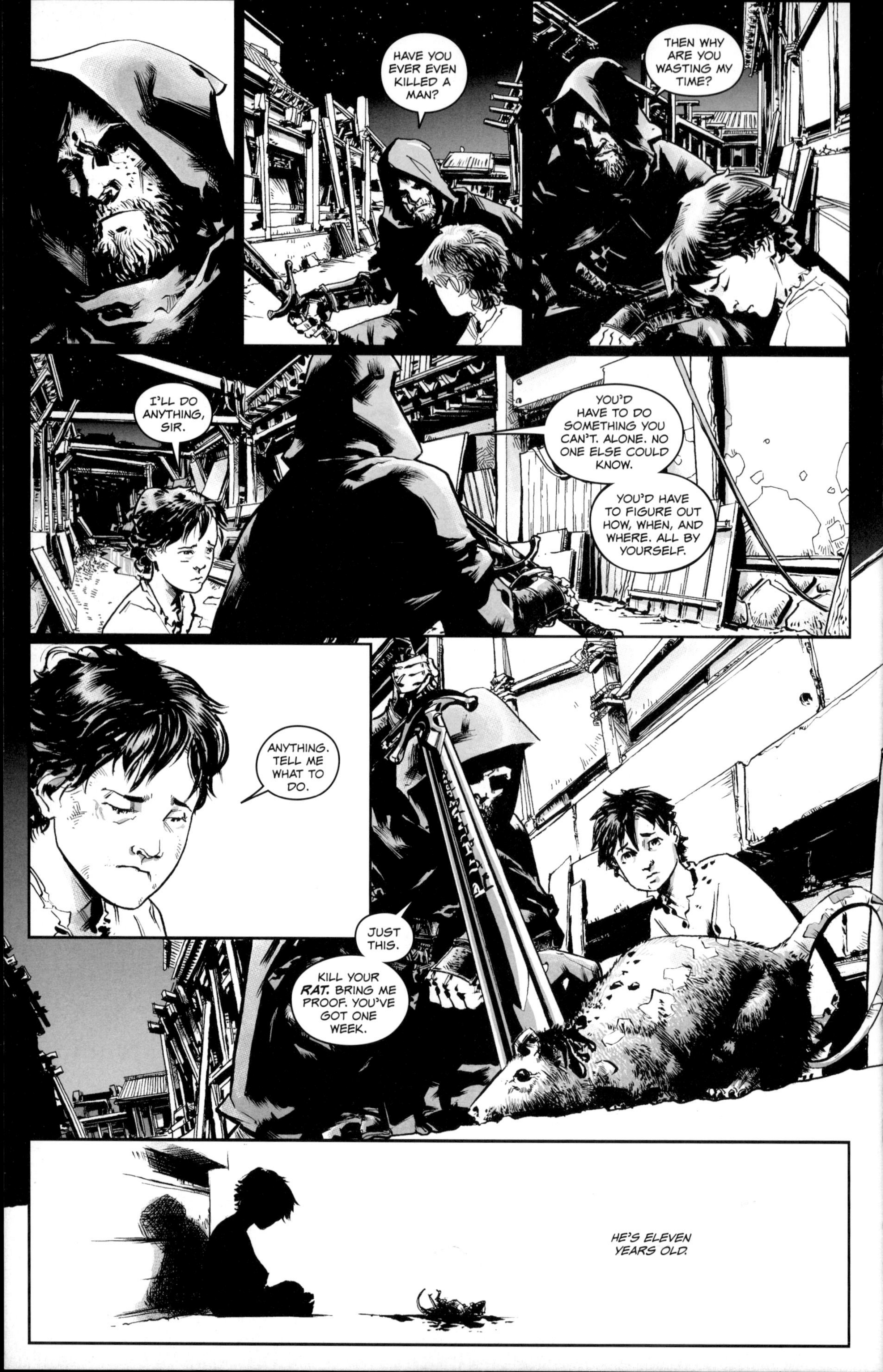
HAVE YOU EVER EVEN KILLED A MAN?
THEN WHY ARE YOU WASTING MY TIME?
I'LL DO ANYTHING, SIR.
YOU'D HAVE TO DO SOMETHING YOU CAN'T. ALONE. NO ONE ELSE COULD KNOW.
YOU'D HAVE TO FIGURE OUT HOW, WHEN, AND WHERE. ALL BY YOURSELF.
ANYTHING. TELL ME WHAT TO DO.
JUST THIS.
KILL YOUR RAT. BRING ME PROOF. YOU'VE GOT ONE WEEK.
HE'S ELEVEN YEARS OLD.

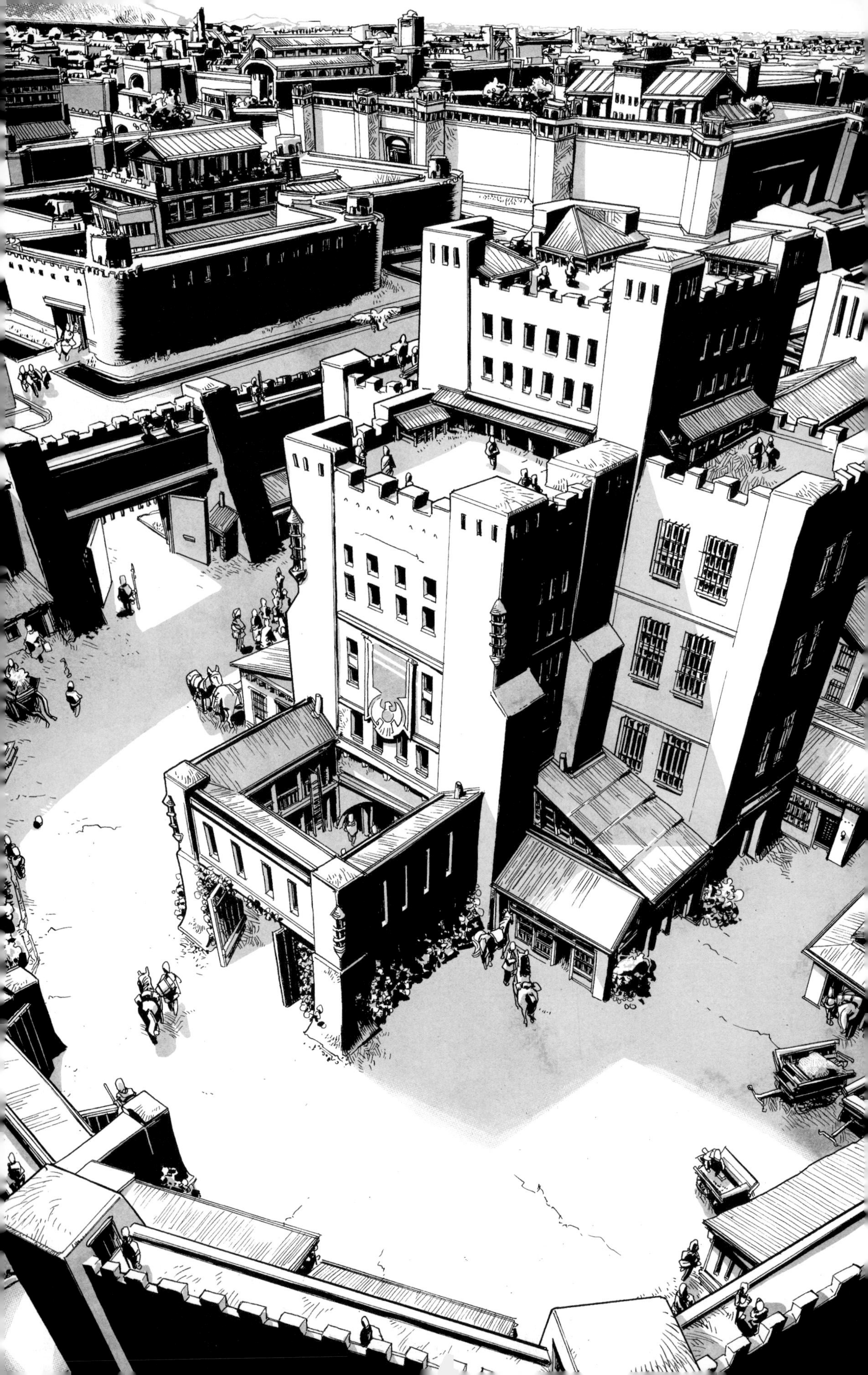

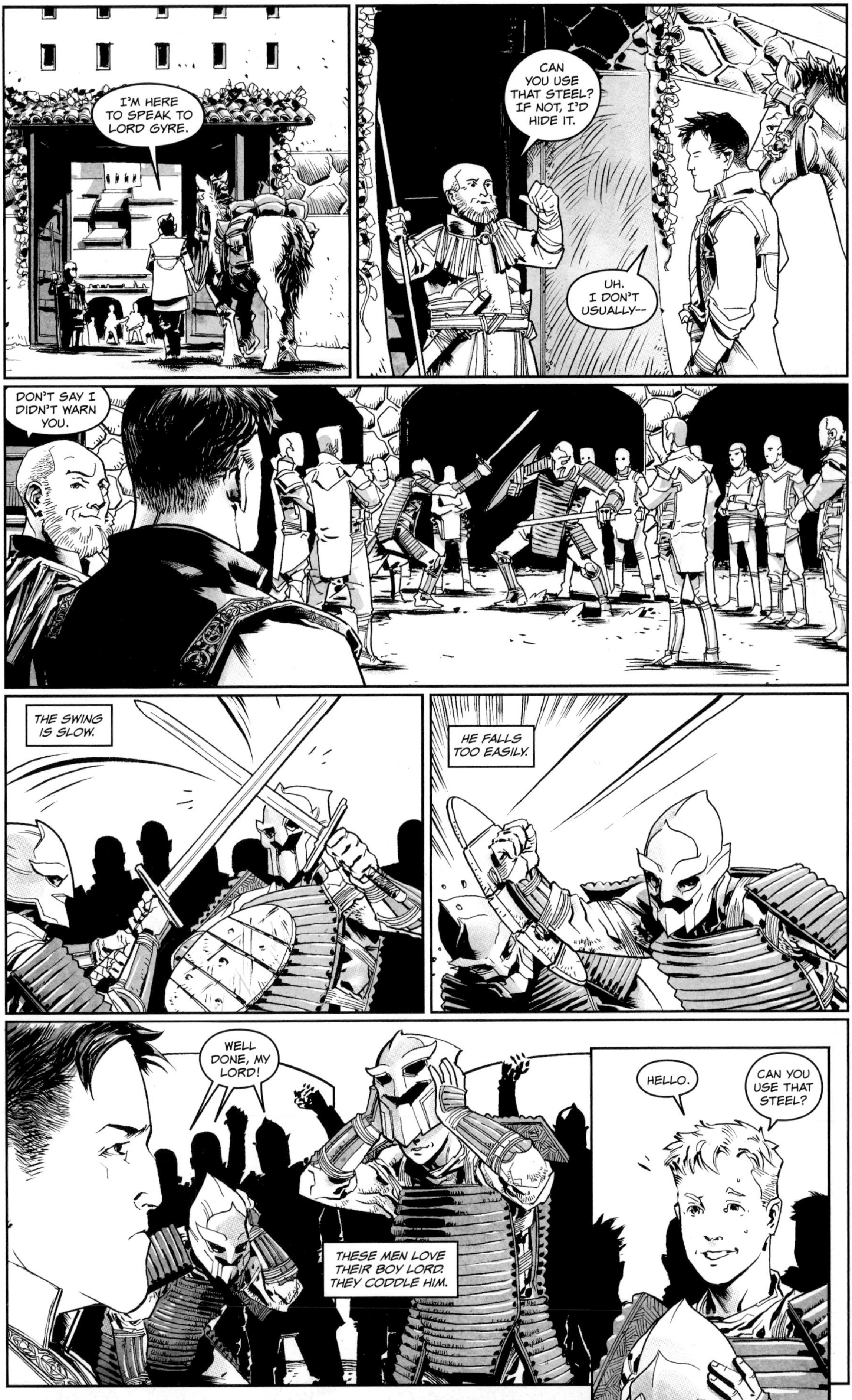
I'M HERE TO SPEAK TO LORD GYRE.
CAN YOU USE THAT STEEL? IF NOT, I'D HIDE IT.
UH. I DON'T USUALLY--
DON'T SAY I DIDN'T WARN YOU.
THE SWING IS SLOW.
HE FALLS TOO EASILY.
WELL DONE, MY LORD!
THESE MEN LOVE THEIR BOY LORD. THEY CODDLE HIM.
HELLO.
CAN YOU USE THAT STEEL?

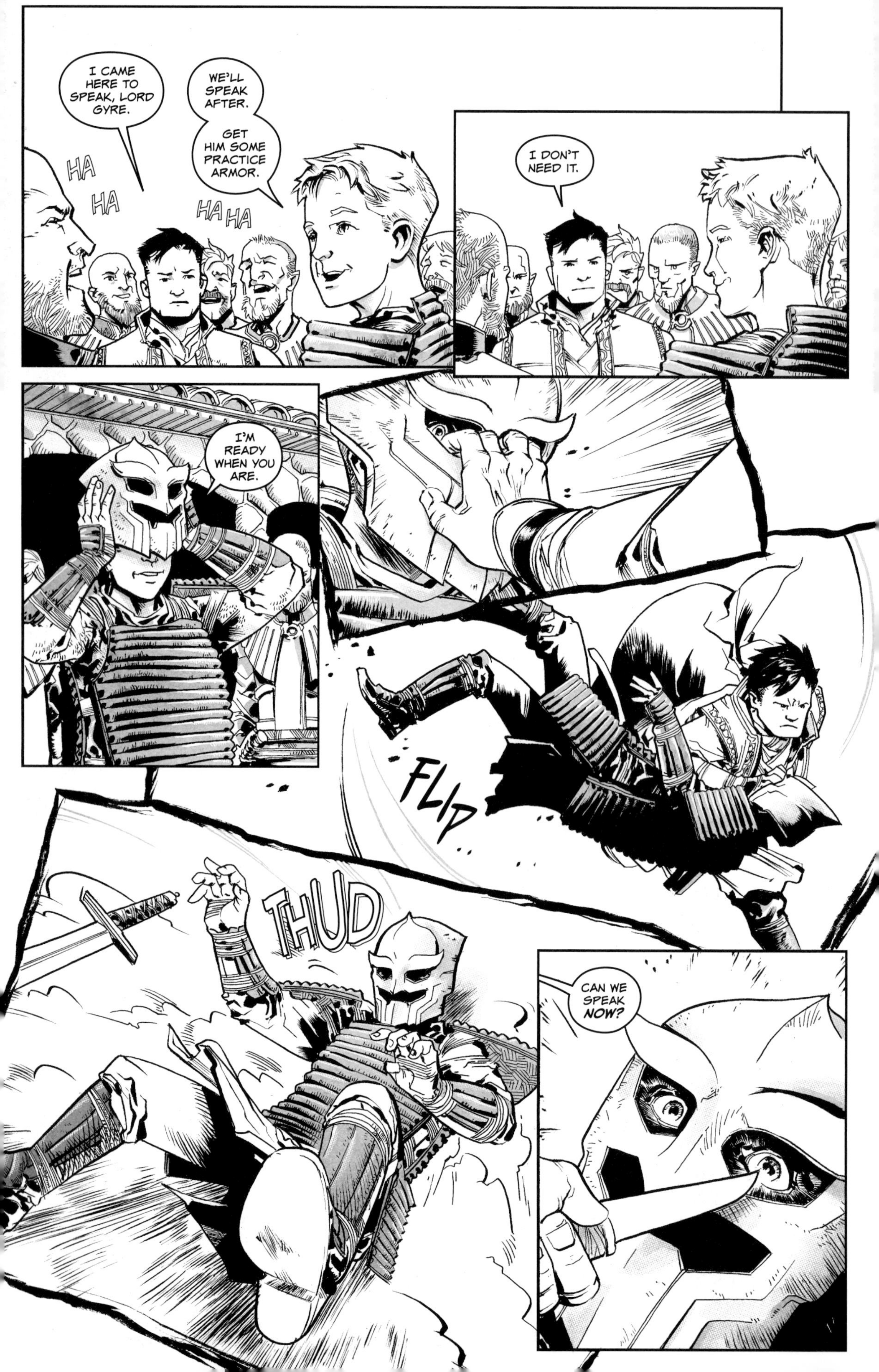
I CAME HERE TO SPEAK, LORD GYRE.
WE'LL SPEAK AFTER.
GET HIM SOME PRACTICE ARMOR.
HA HA
HA HA
I DON'T NEED IT.
I'M READY WHEN YOU ARE.
FLIP
THUD
CAN WE SPEAK NOW?

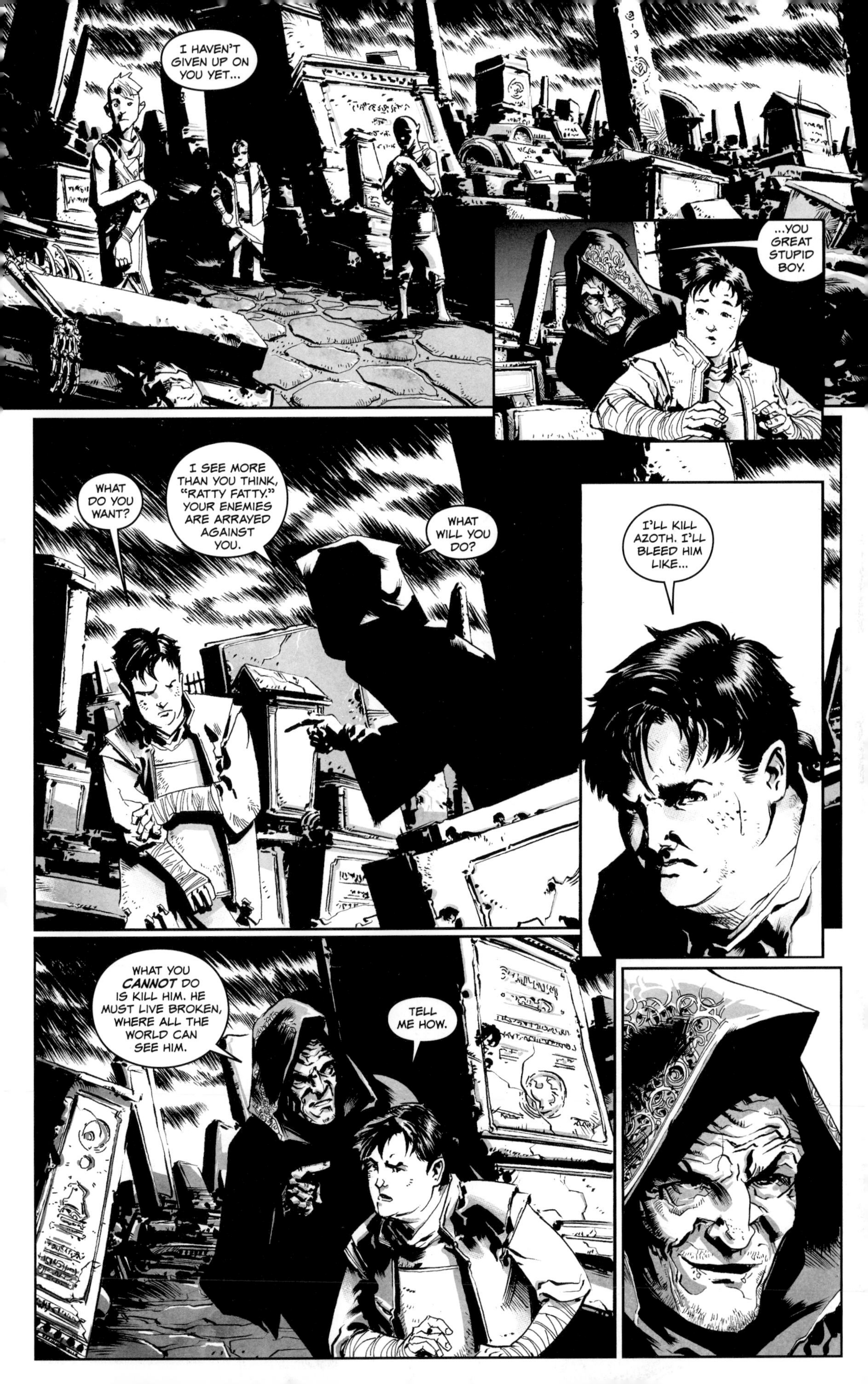
I HAVEN'T GIVEN UP ON YOU YET...
...YOU GREAT STUPID BOY.
WHAT DO YOU WANT?
I SEE MORE THAN YOU THINK, "RATTY FATTY." YOUR ENEMIES ARE ARRAYED AGAINST YOU.
WHAT WILL YOU DO?
I'LL KILL AZOTH. I'LL BLEED HIM LIKE...
WHAT YOU *CANNOT* DO IS KILL HIM. HE MUST LIVE BROKEN, WHERE ALL THE WORLD CAN SEE HIM.
TELL ME HOW.

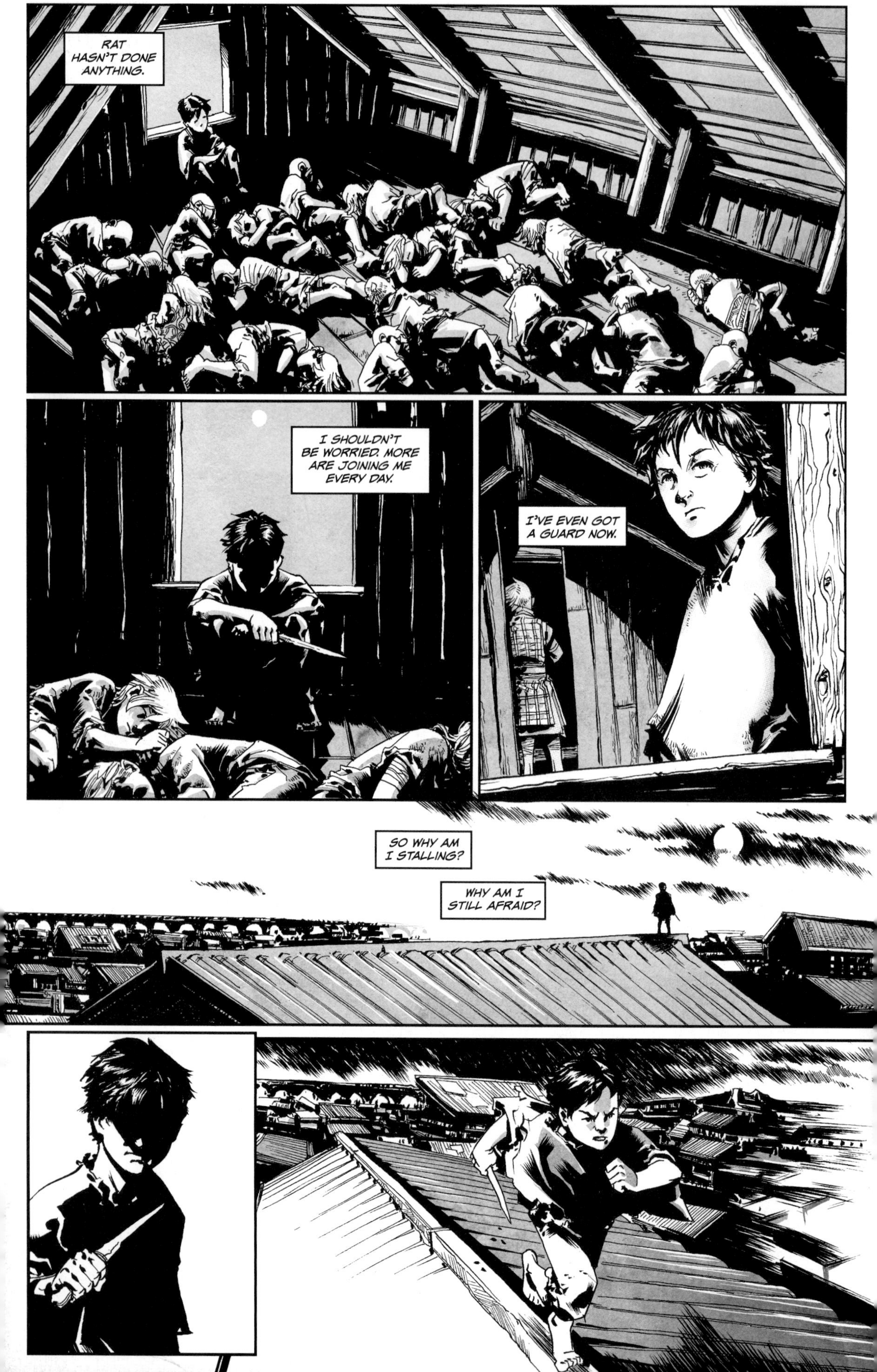
RAT HASN'T DONE ANYTHING.
I SHOULDN'T BE WORRIED. MORE ARE JOINING ME EVERY DAY.
I'VE EVEN GOT A GUARD NOW.
SO WHY AM I STALLING?
WHY AM I STILL AFRAID?

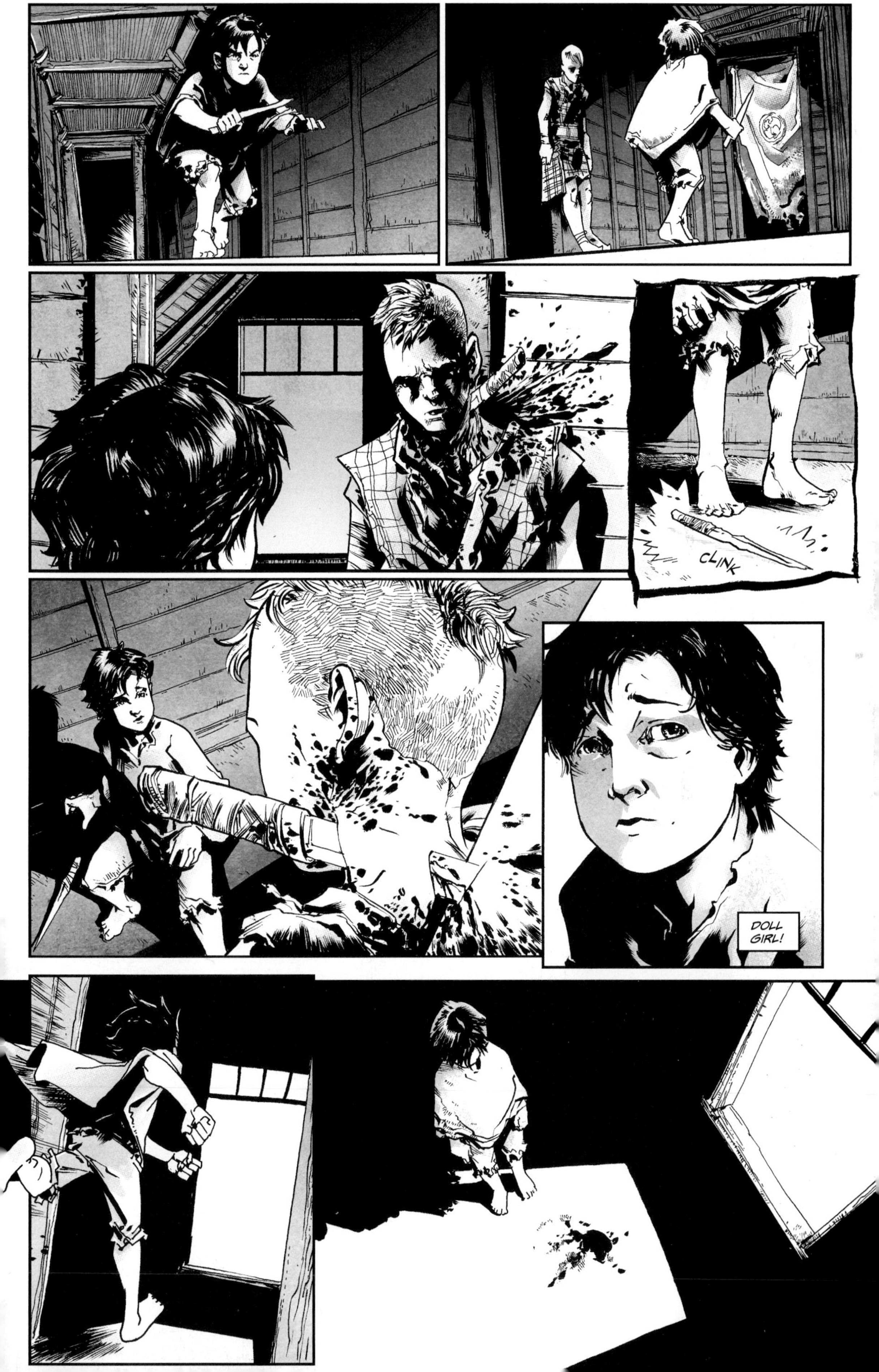
CLINK
DOLL GIRL!

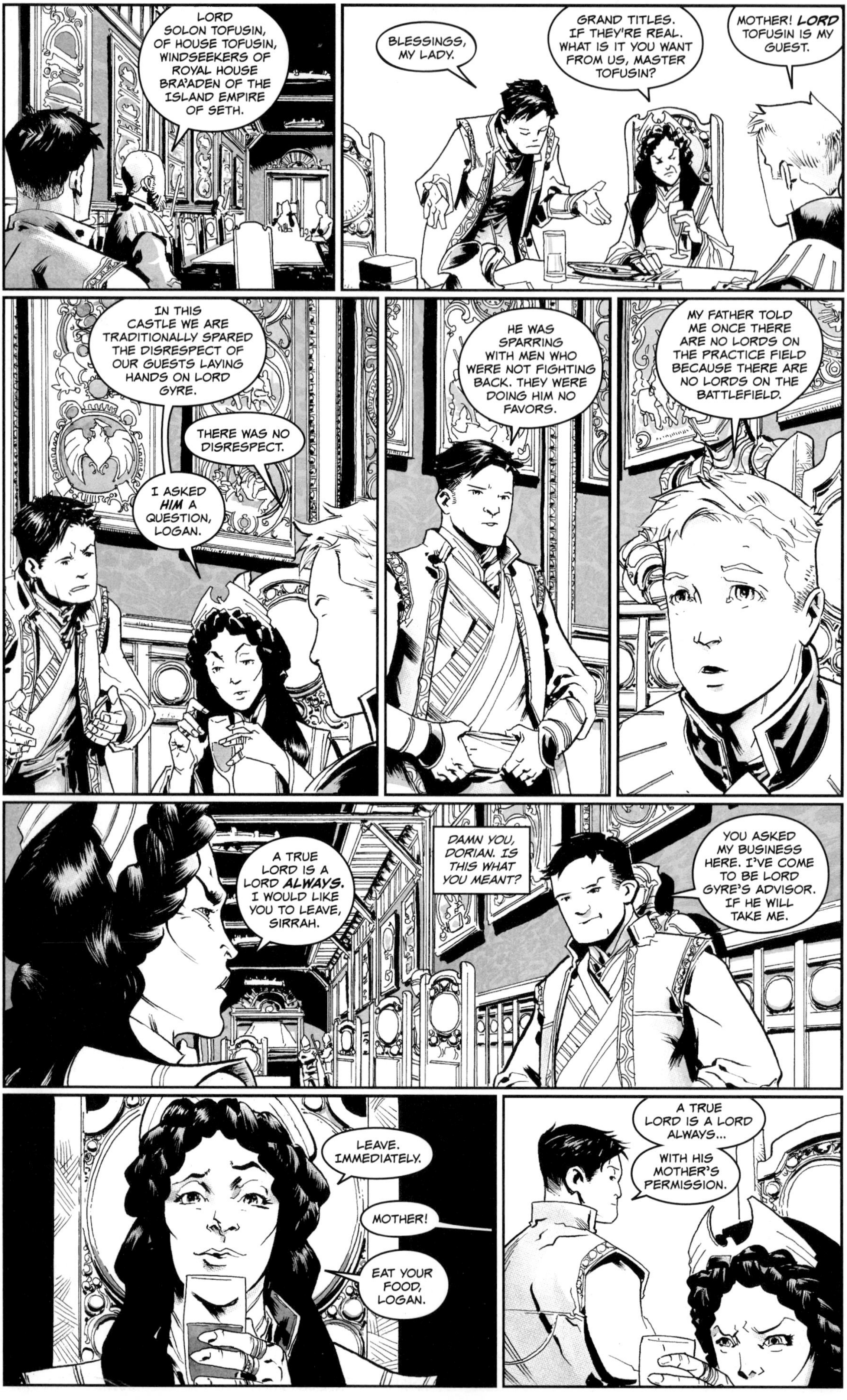
LORD SOLON TOFUSIN, OF HOUSE TOFUSIN, WINDSEEKERS OF ROYAL HOUSE BRA'ADEN OF THE ISLAND EMPIRE OF SETH.
BLESSINGS, MY LADY.
GRAND TITLES. IF THEY'RE REAL. WHAT IS IT YOU WANT FROM US, MASTER TOFUSIN?
MOTHER! LORD TOFUSIN IS MY GUEST.
IN THIS CASTLE WE ARE TRADITIONALLY SPARED THE DISRESPECT OF OUR GUESTS LAYING HANDS ON LORD GYRE.
THERE WAS NO DISRESPECT.
I ASKED HIM A QUESTION, LOGAN.
HE WAS SPARRING WITH MEN WHO WERE NOT FIGHTING BACK. THEY WERE DOING HIM NO FAVORS.
MY FATHER TOLD ME ONCE THERE ARE NO LORDS ON THE PRACTICE FIELD BECAUSE THERE ARE NO LORDS ON THE BATTLEFIELD.
A TRUE LORD IS A LORD ALWAYS. I WOULD LIKE YOU TO LEAVE, SIRRAH.
DAMN YOU, DORIAN. IS THIS WHAT YOU MEANT?
YOU ASKED MY BUSINESS HERE. I'VE COME TO BE LORD GYRE'S ADVISOR. IF HE WILL TAKE ME.
LEAVE. IMMEDIATELY.
MOTHER!
EAT YOUR FOOD, LOGAN.
A TRUE LORD IS A LORD ALWAYS...
WITH HIS MOTHER'S PERMISSION.

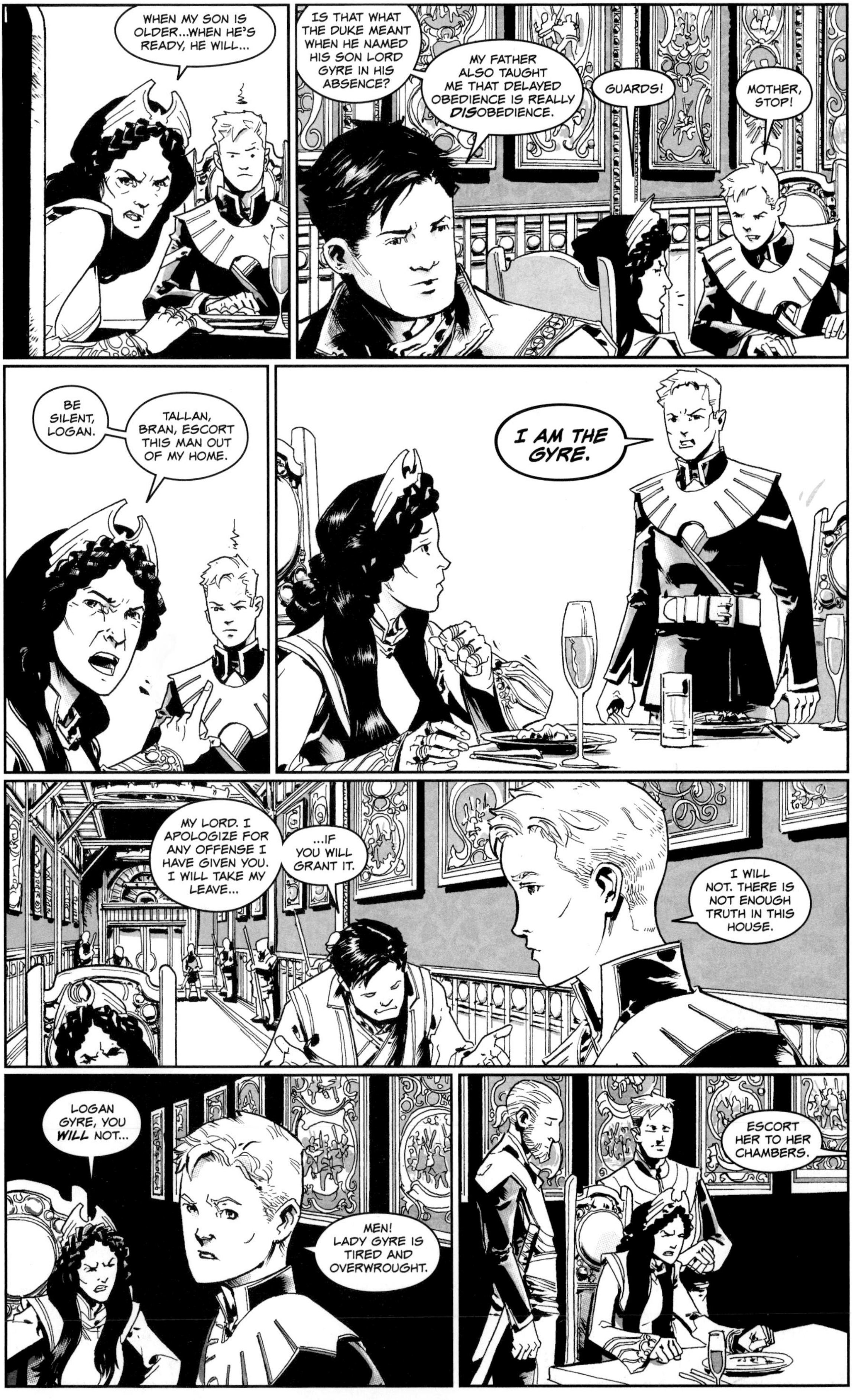
WHEN MY SON IS OLDER...WHEN HE'S READY, HE WILL...
IS THAT WHAT THE DUKE MEANT WHEN HE NAMED HIS SON LORD GYRE IN HIS ABSENCE?
MY FATHER ALSO TAUGHT ME THAT DELAYED OBEDIENCE IS REALLY DISOBEDIENCE.
GUARDS!
MOTHER, STOP!
BE SILENT, LOGAN.
TALLAN, BRAN, ESCORT THIS MAN OUT OF MY HOME.
I AM THE GYRE.
MY LORD. I APOLOGIZE FOR ANY OFFENSE I HAVE GIVEN YOU. I WILL TAKE MY LEAVE...
...IF YOU WILL GRANT IT.
I WILL NOT. THERE IS NOT ENOUGH TRUTH IN THIS HOUSE.
LOGAN GYRE, YOU WILL NOT...
MEN! LADY GYRE IS TIRED AND OVERWROUGHT.
ESCORT HER TO HER CHAMBERS.

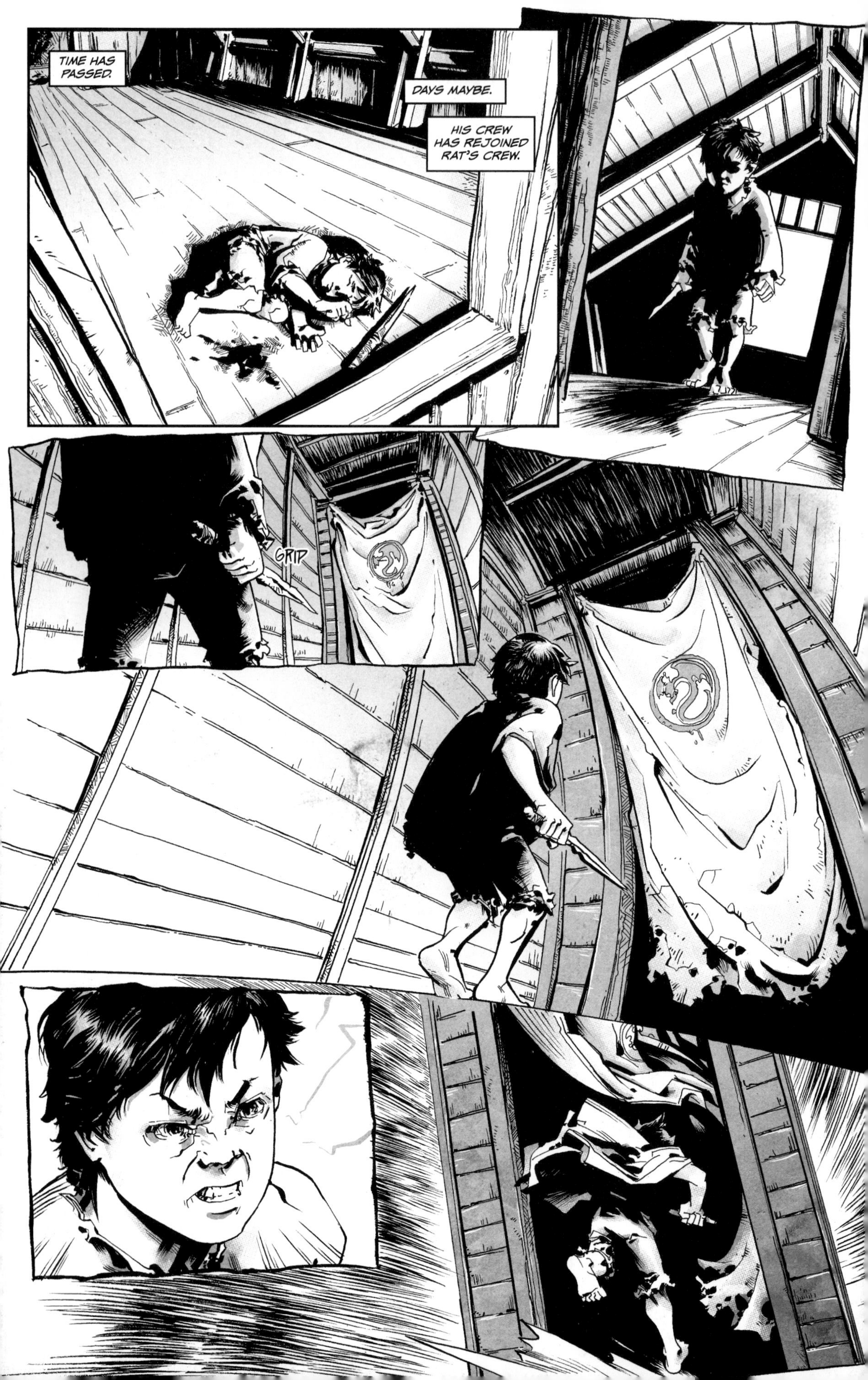
TIME HAS PASSED.
DAYS MAYBE.
HIS CREW HAS REJOINED RAT'S CREW.
GRIP

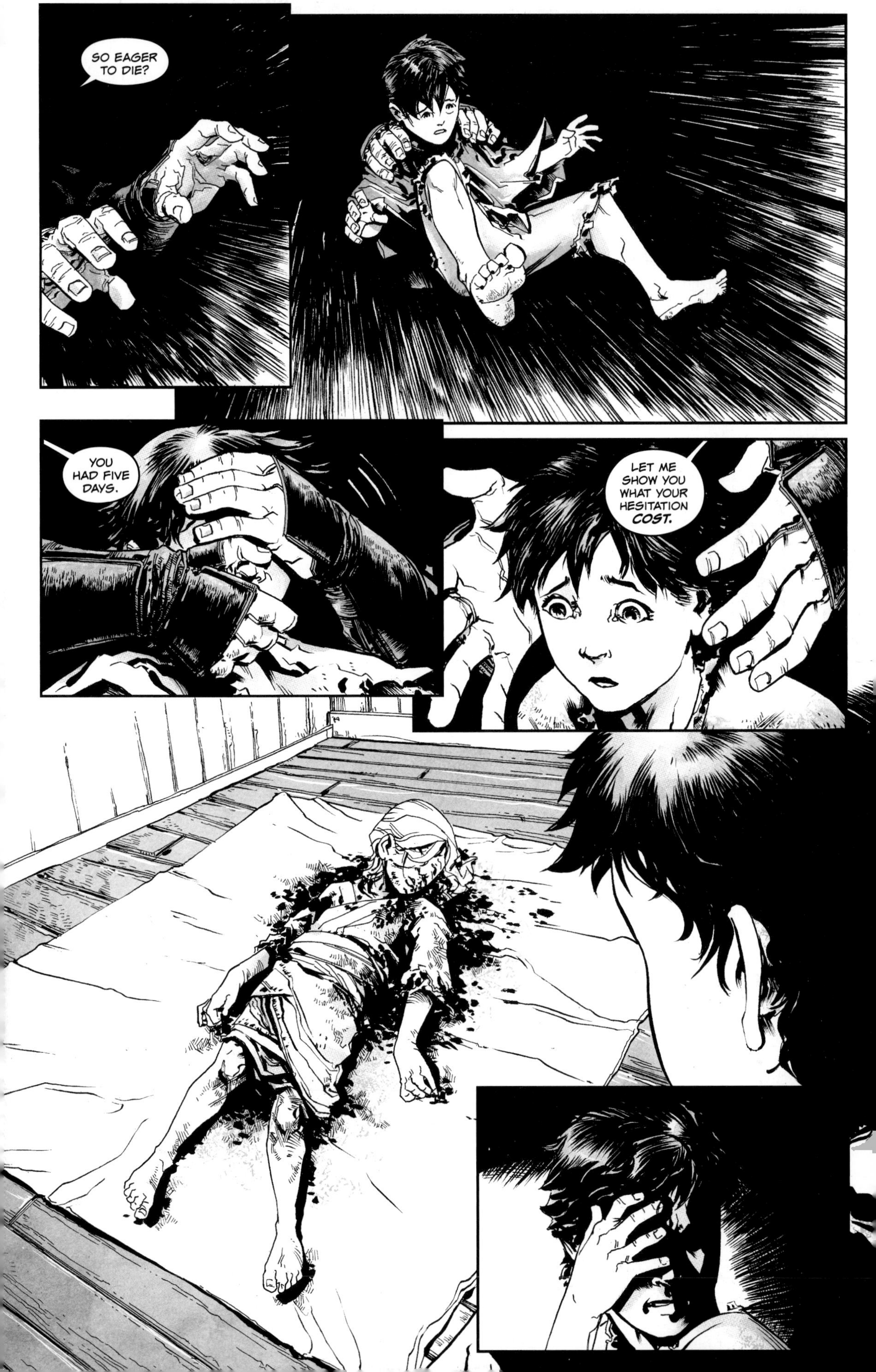
SO EAGER TO DIE?
YOU HAD FIVE DAYS.
LET ME SHOW YOU WHAT YOUR HESITATION COST.

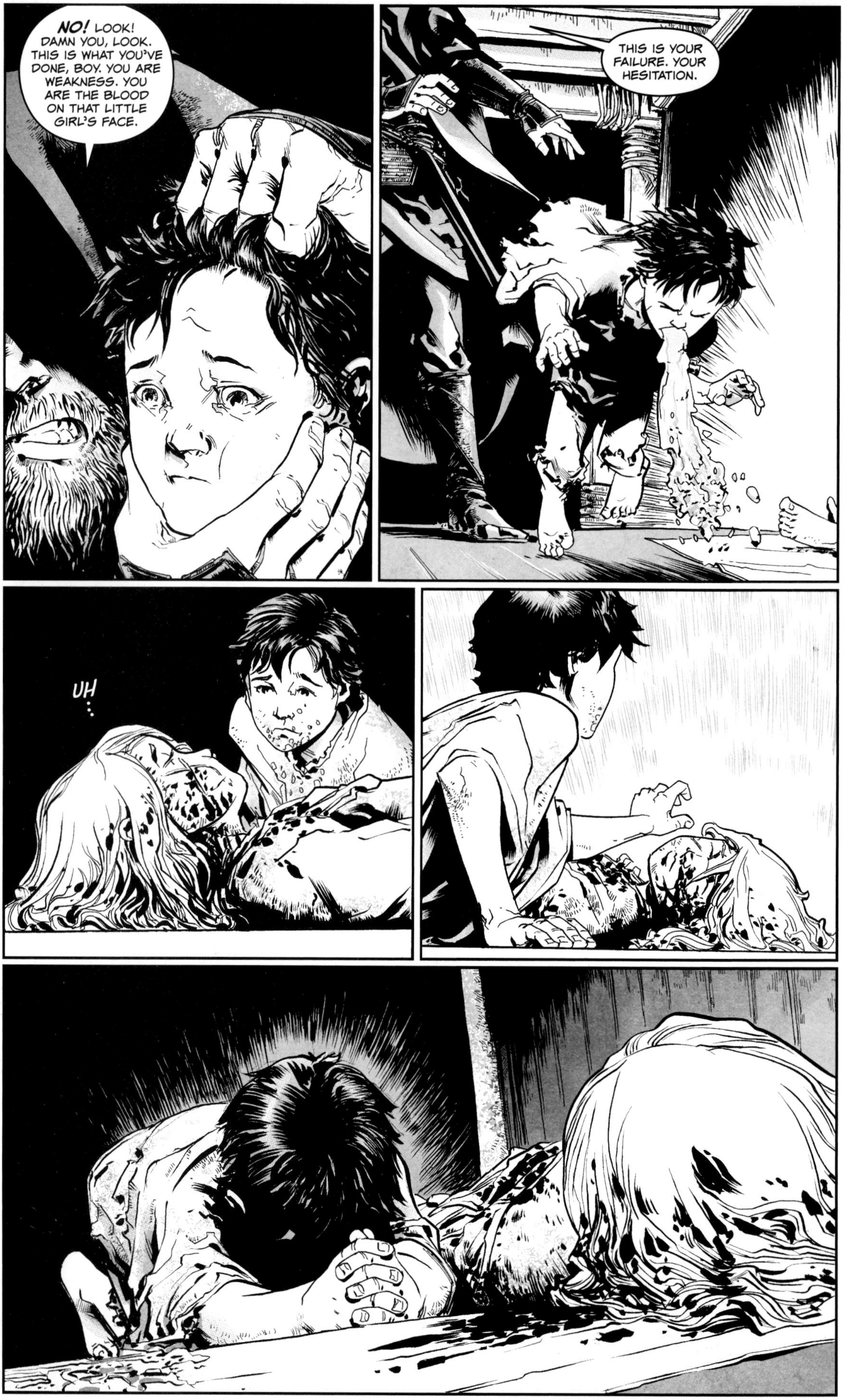
NO! LOOK! DAMN YOU, LOOK. THIS IS WHAT YOU'VE DONE, BOY. YOU ARE WEAKNESS. YOU ARE THE BLOOD ON THAT LITTLE GIRL'S FACE.
THIS IS YOUR FAILURE. YOUR HESITATION.
UH...

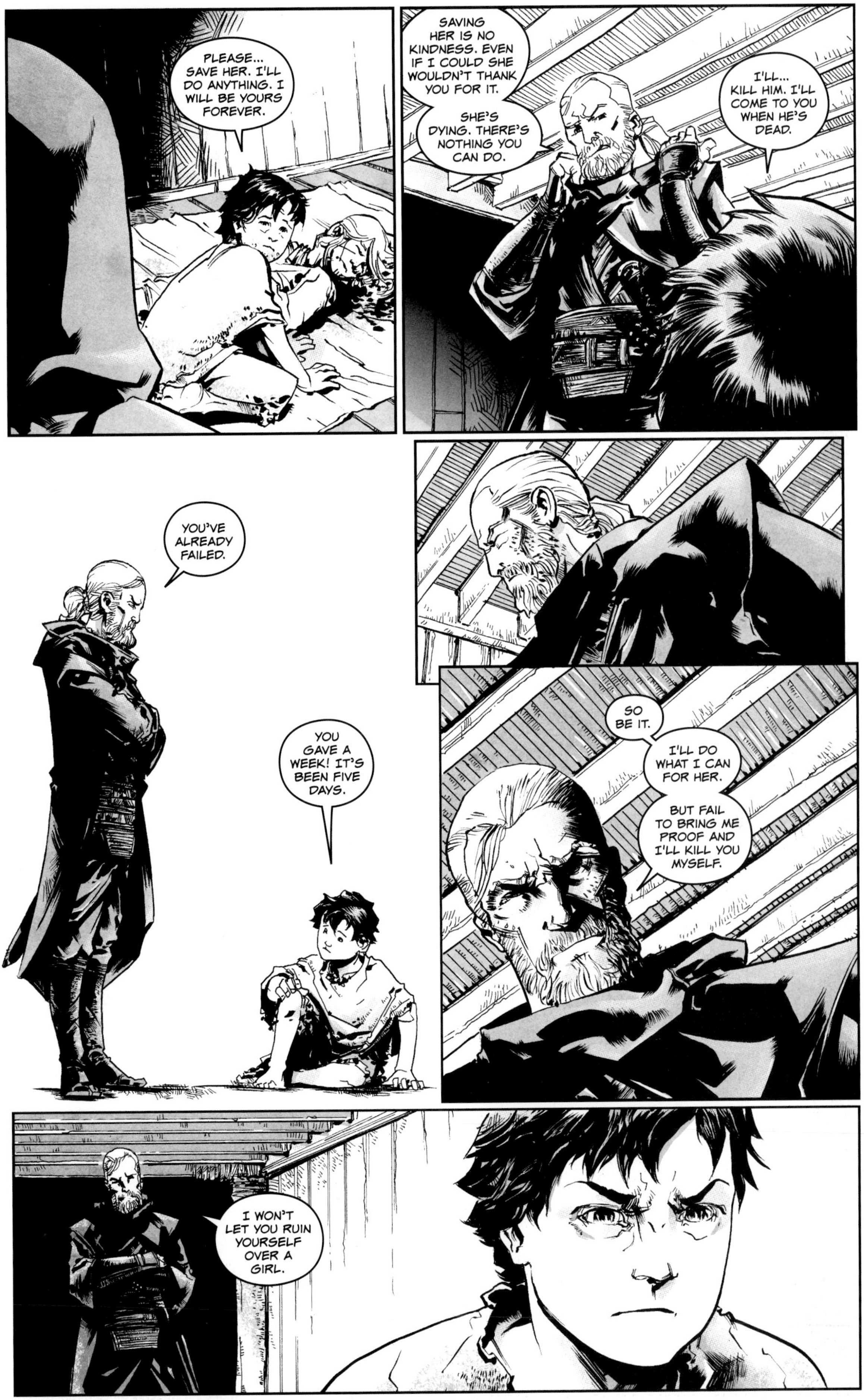
PLEASE... SAVE HER. I'LL DO ANYTHING. I WILL BE YOURS FOREVER.
SAVING HER IS NO KINDNESS. EVEN IF I COULD SHE WOULDN'T THANK YOU FOR IT.
SHE'S DYING. THERE'S NOTHING YOU CAN DO.
I'LL... KILL HIM. I'LL COME TO YOU WHEN HE'S DEAD.
YOU'VE ALREADY FAILED.
YOU GAVE A WEEK! IT'S BEEN FIVE DAYS.
SO BE IT.
I'LL DO WHAT I CAN FOR HER.
BUT FAIL TO BRING ME PROOF AND I'LL KILL YOU MYSELF.
I WON'T LET YOU RUIN YOURSELF OVER A GIRL.

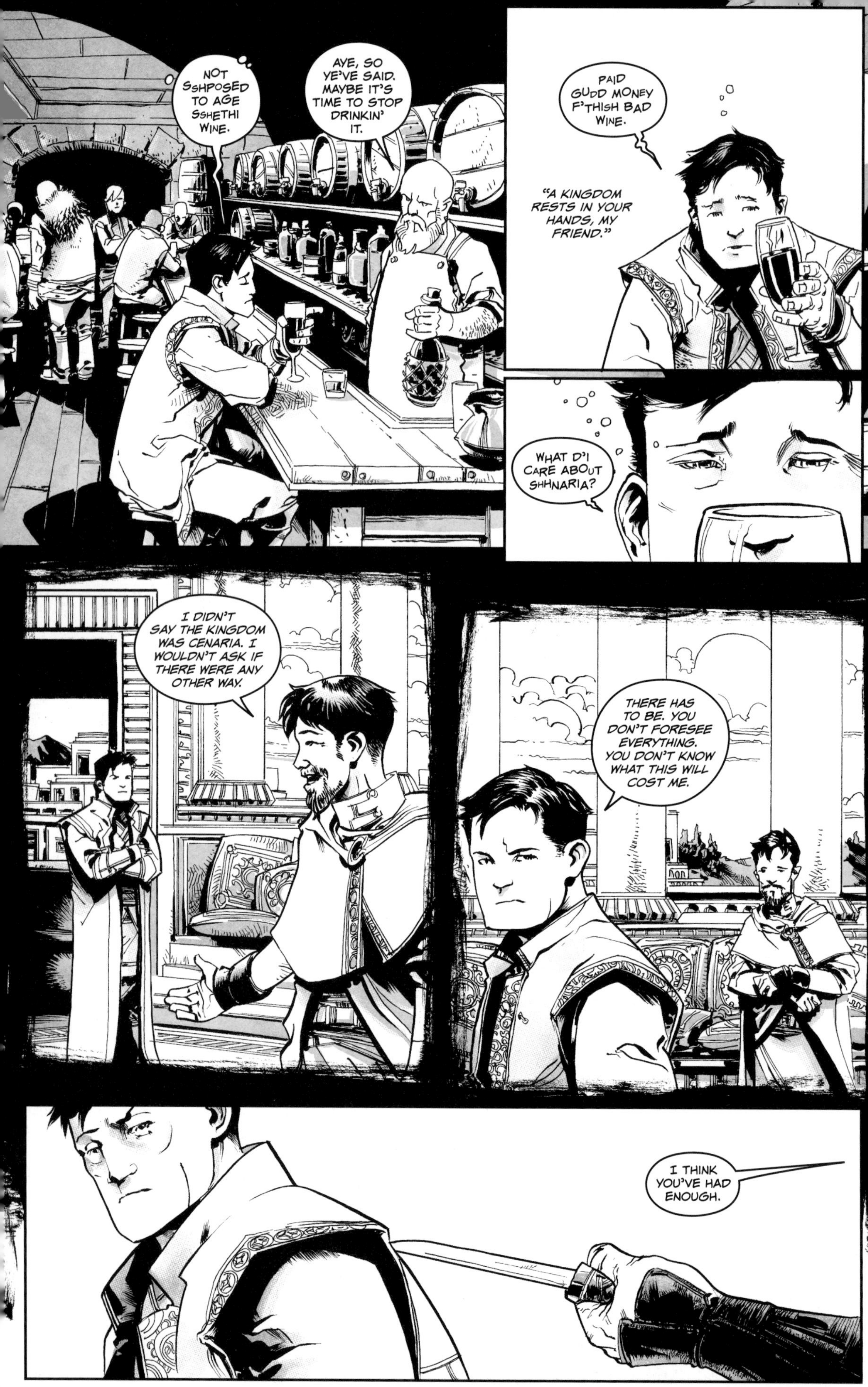
NOT SSHPOSED TO AGE SSHETHI WINE.
AYE, SO YE'VE SAID. MAYBE IT'S TIME TO STOP DRINKIN' IT.
PAID GUDD MONEY F'THISH BAD WINE.
"A KINGDOM RESTS IN YOUR HANDS, MY FRIEND."
WHAT D'I CARE ABOUT SHHNARIA?
I DIDN'T SAY THE KINGDOM WAS CENARIA. I WOULDN'T ASK IF THERE WERE ANY OTHER WAY.
THERE HAS TO BE. YOU DON'T FORESEE EVERYTHING. YOU DON'T KNOW WHAT THIS WILL COST ME.
I THINK YOU'VE HAD ENOUGH.

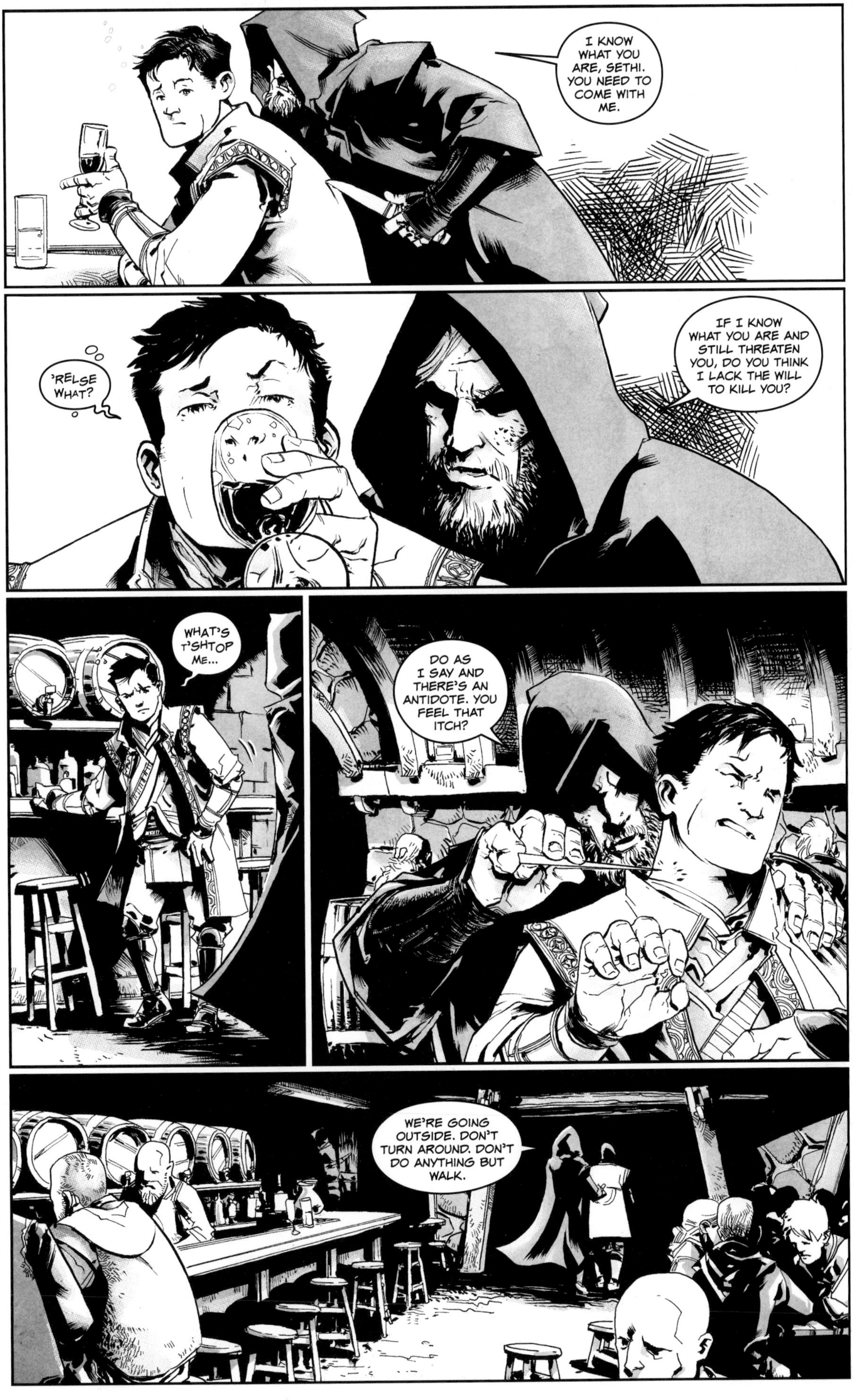
I KNOW WHAT YOU ARE, SETHI. YOU NEED TO COME WITH ME.
'RELSE WHAT?
IF I KNOW WHAT YOU ARE AND STILL THREATEN YOU, DO YOU THINK I LACK THE WILL TO KILL YOU?
WHAT'S T'SHTOP ME...
DO AS I SAY AND THERE'S AN ANTIDOTE. YOU FEEL THAT ITCH?
WE'RE GOING OUTSIDE. DON'T TURN AROUND. DON'T DO ANYTHING BUT WALK.

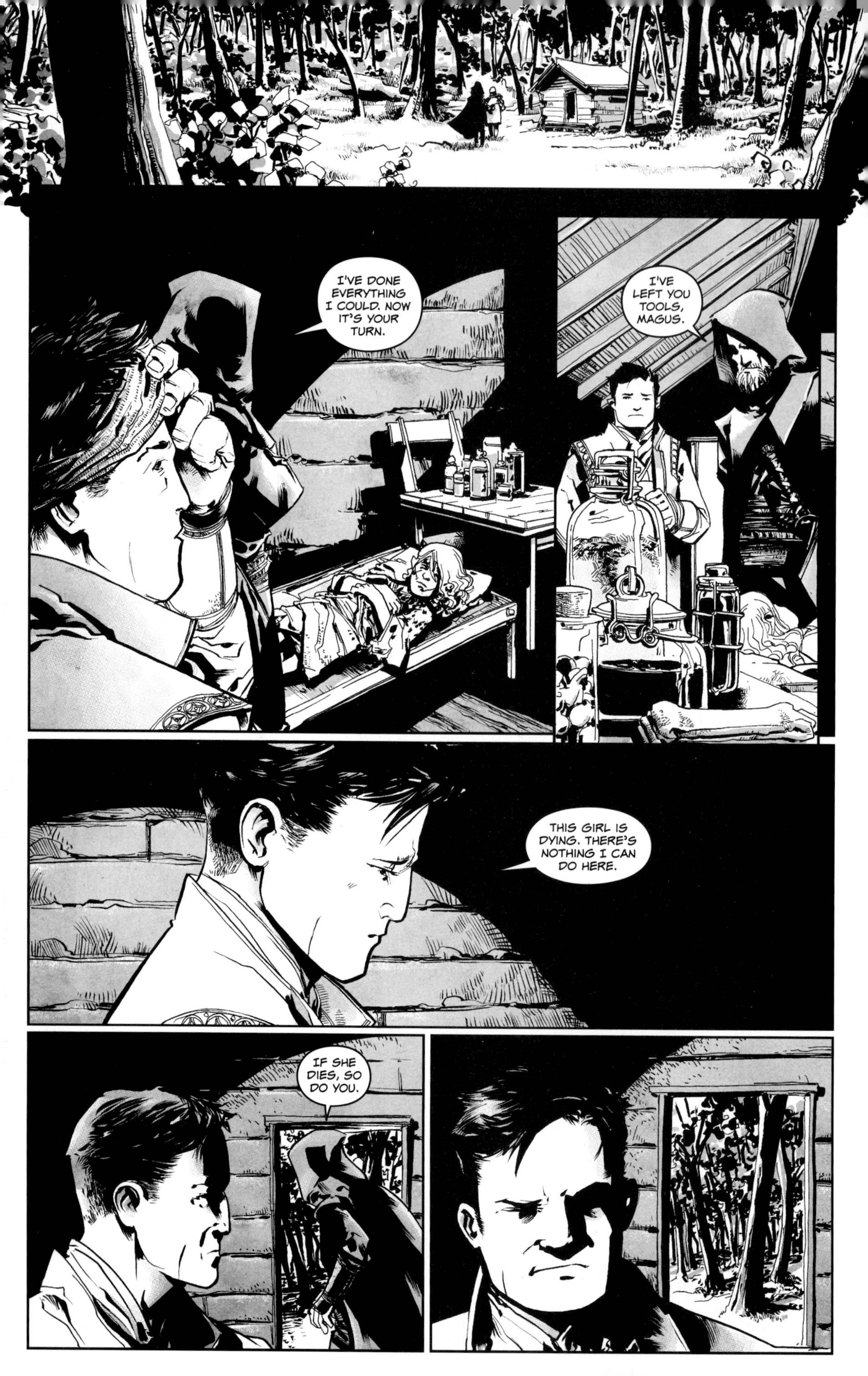
I'VE DONE EVERYTHING I COULD. NOW IT'S YOUR TURN.
I'VE LEFT YOU TOOLS, MAGUS.
THIS GIRL IS DYING. THERE'S NOTHING I CAN DO HERE.
IF SHE DIES, SO DO YOU.

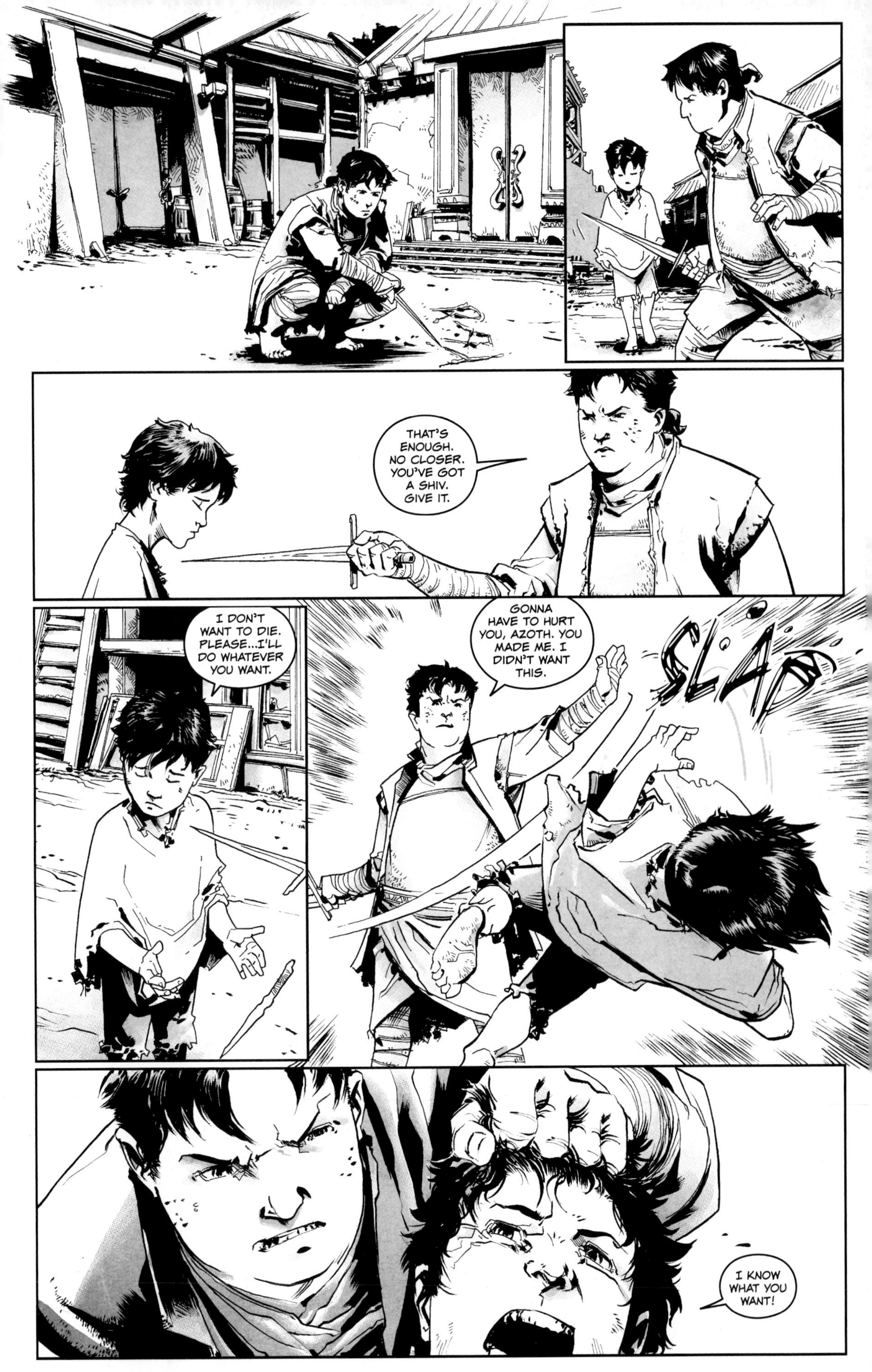
THAT'S ENOUGH. NO CLOSER. YOU'VE GOT A SHIV. GIVE IT.
I DON'T WANT TO DIE. PLEASE...I'LL DO WHATEVER YOU WANT.
GONNA HAVE TO HURT YOU, AZOTH. YOU MADE ME. I DIDN'T WANT THIS.
SLAP
I KNOW WHAT YOU WANT!

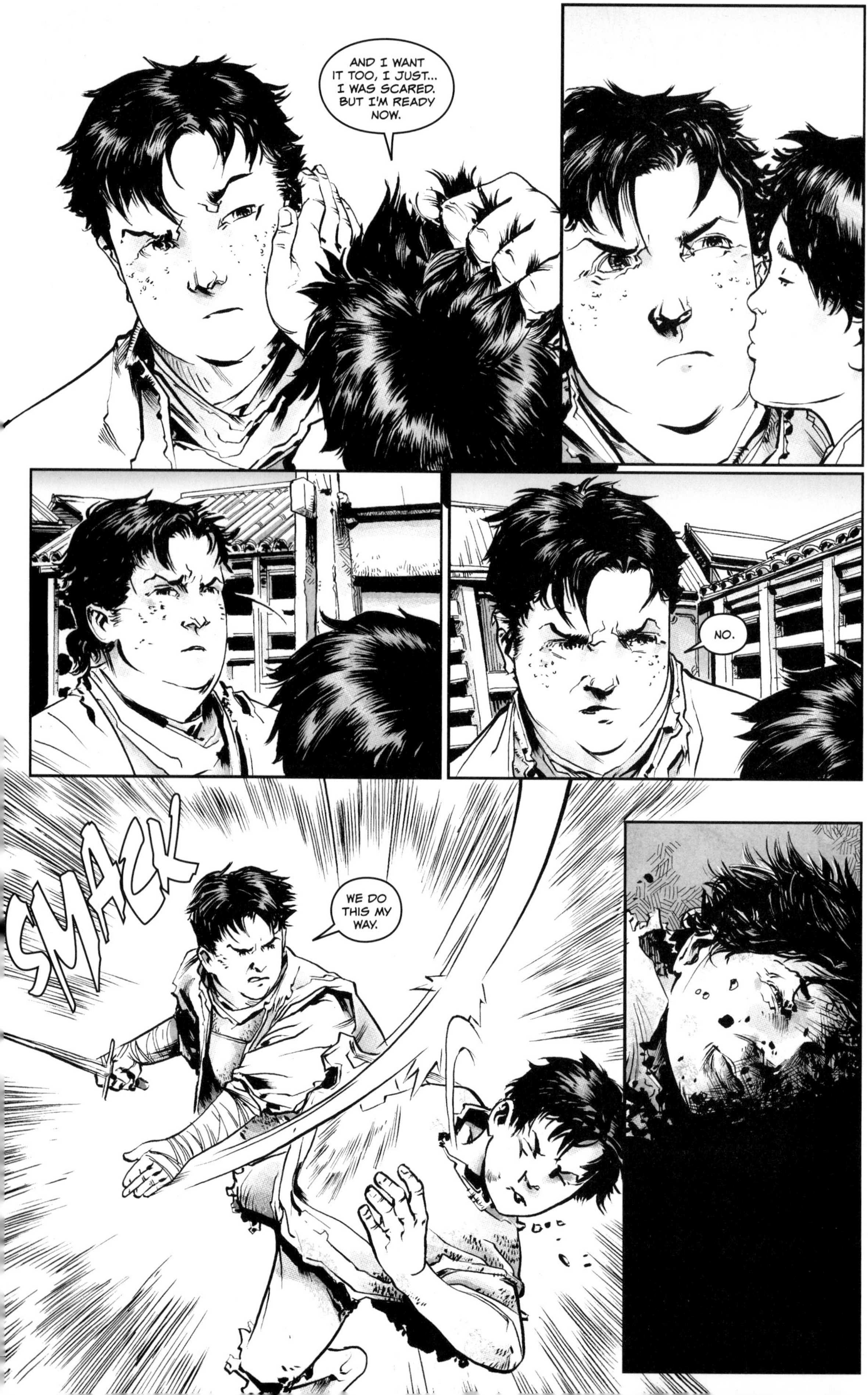
AND I WANT IT TOO, I JUST... I WAS SCARED. BUT I'M READY NOW.
NO.
SMACK
WE DO THIS MY WAY.

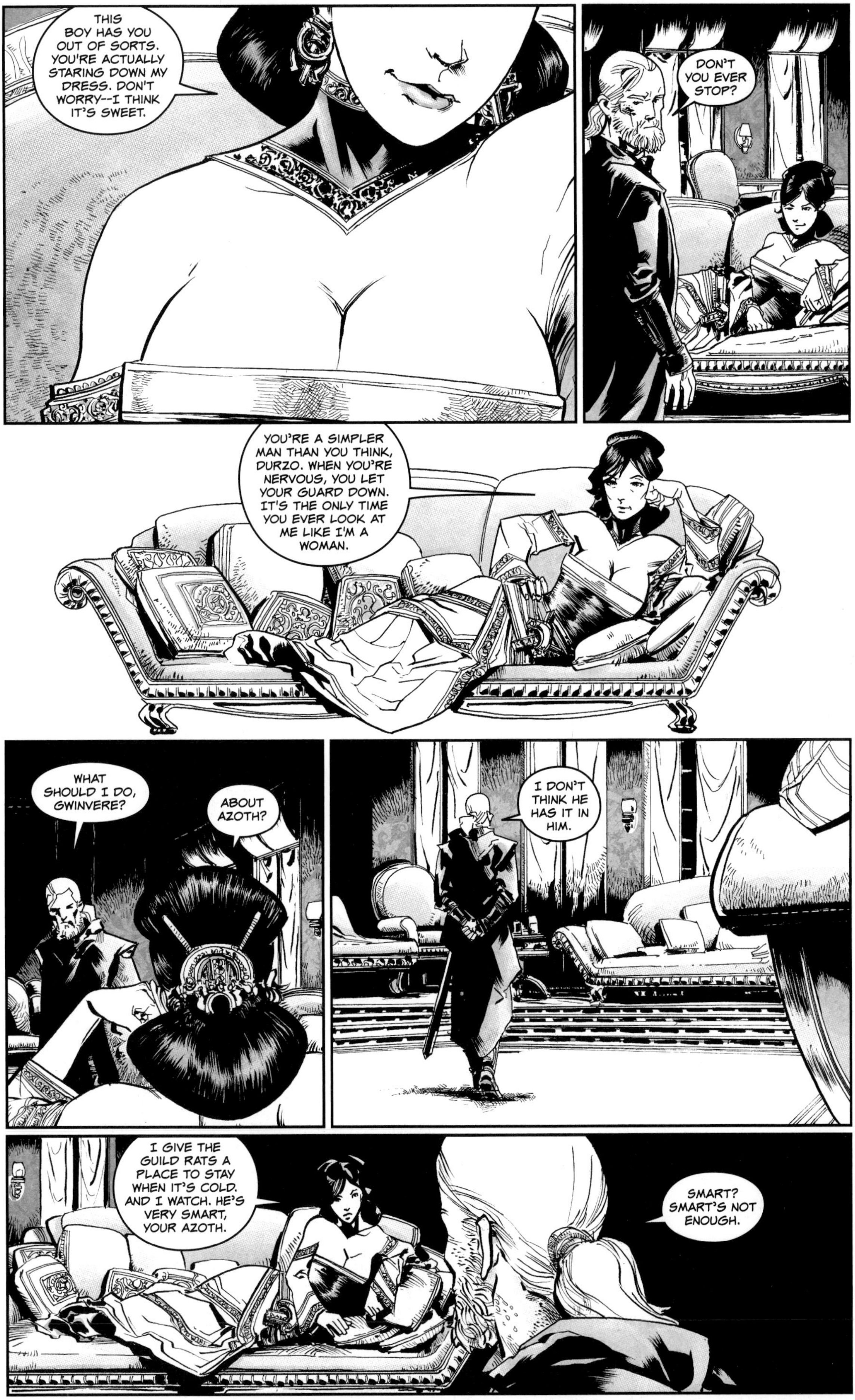
THIS BOY HAS YOU OUT OF SORTS. YOU'RE ACTUALLY STARING DOWN MY DRESS. DON'T WORRY--I THINK IT'S SWEET.
DON'T YOU EVER STOP?
YOU'RE A SIMPLER MAN THAN YOU THINK, DURZO. WHEN YOU'RE NERVOUS, YOU LET YOUR GUARD DOWN. IT'S THE ONLY TIME YOU EVER LOOK AT ME LIKE I'M A WOMAN.
WHAT SHOULD I DO, GWINVERE?
ABOUT AZOTH?
I DON'T THINK HE HAS IT IN HIM.
I GIVE THE GUILD RATS A PLACE TO STAY WHEN IT'S COLD. AND I WATCH. HE'S VERY SMART, YOUR AZOTH.
SMART? SMART'S NOT ENOUGH.

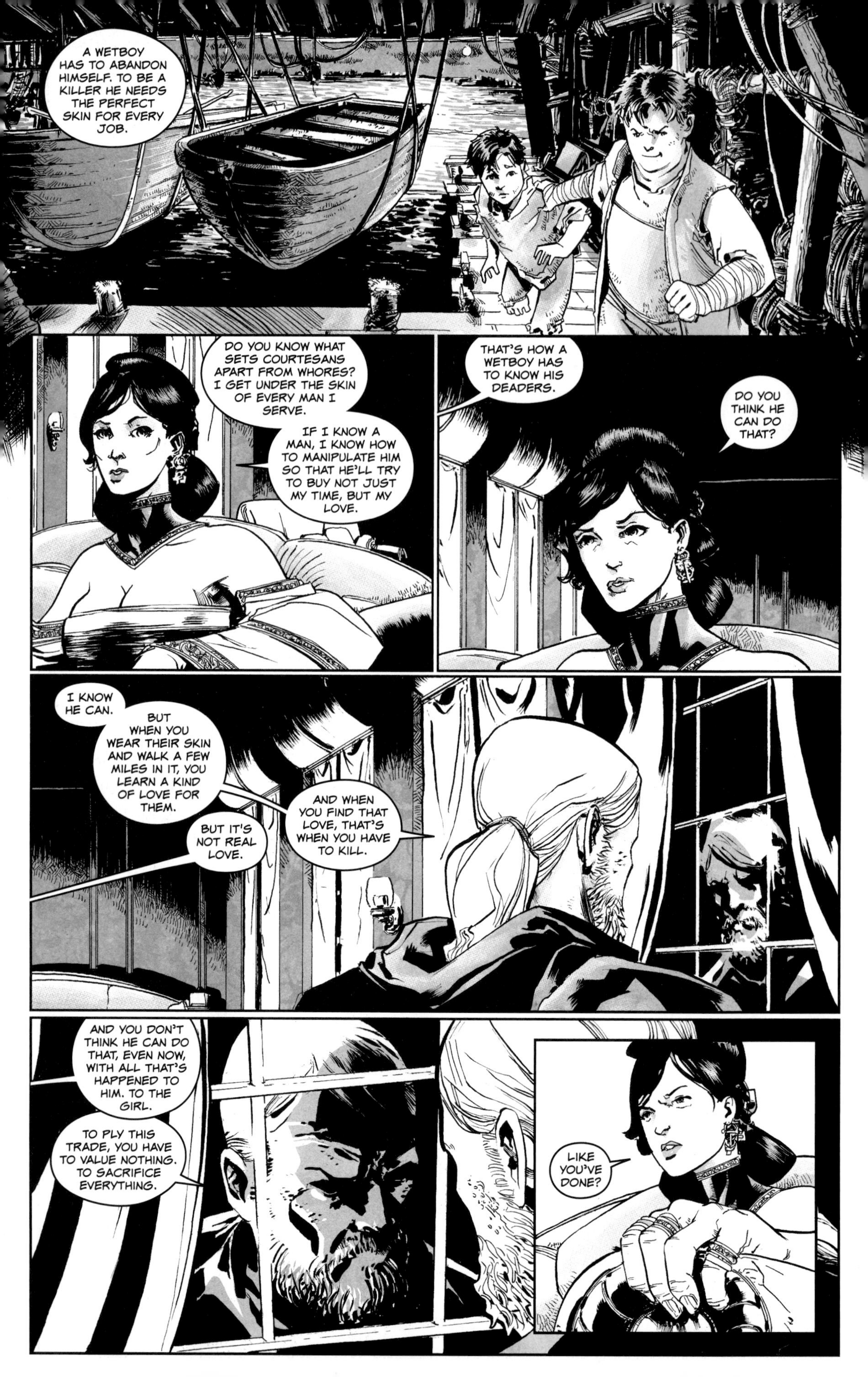
A WETBOY HAS TO ABANDON HIMSELF. TO BE A KILLER HE NEEDS THE PERFECT SKIN FOR EVERY JOB.
DO YOU KNOW WHAT SETS COURTESANS APART FROM WHORES? I GET UNDER THE SKIN OF EVERY MAN I SERVE.
IF I KNOW A MAN, I KNOW HOW TO MANIPULATE HIM SO THAT HE'LL TRY TO BUY NOT JUST MY TIME, BUT MY LOVE.
THAT'S HOW A WETBOY HAS TO KNOW HIS DEADERS.
DO YOU THINK HE CAN DO THAT?
I KNOW HE CAN.
BUT WHEN YOU WEAR THEIR SKIN AND WALK A FEW MILES IN IT, YOU LEARN A KIND OF LOVE FOR THEM.
BUT IT'S NOT REAL LOVE.
AND WHEN YOU FIND THAT LOVE, THAT'S WHEN YOU HAVE TO KILL.
AND YOU DON'T THINK HE CAN DO THAT, EVEN NOW, WITH ALL THAT'S HAPPENED TO HIM. TO THE GIRL.
TO PLY THIS TRADE, YOU HAVE TO VALUE NOTHING. TO SACRIFICE EVERYTHING.
LIKE YOU'VE DONE?

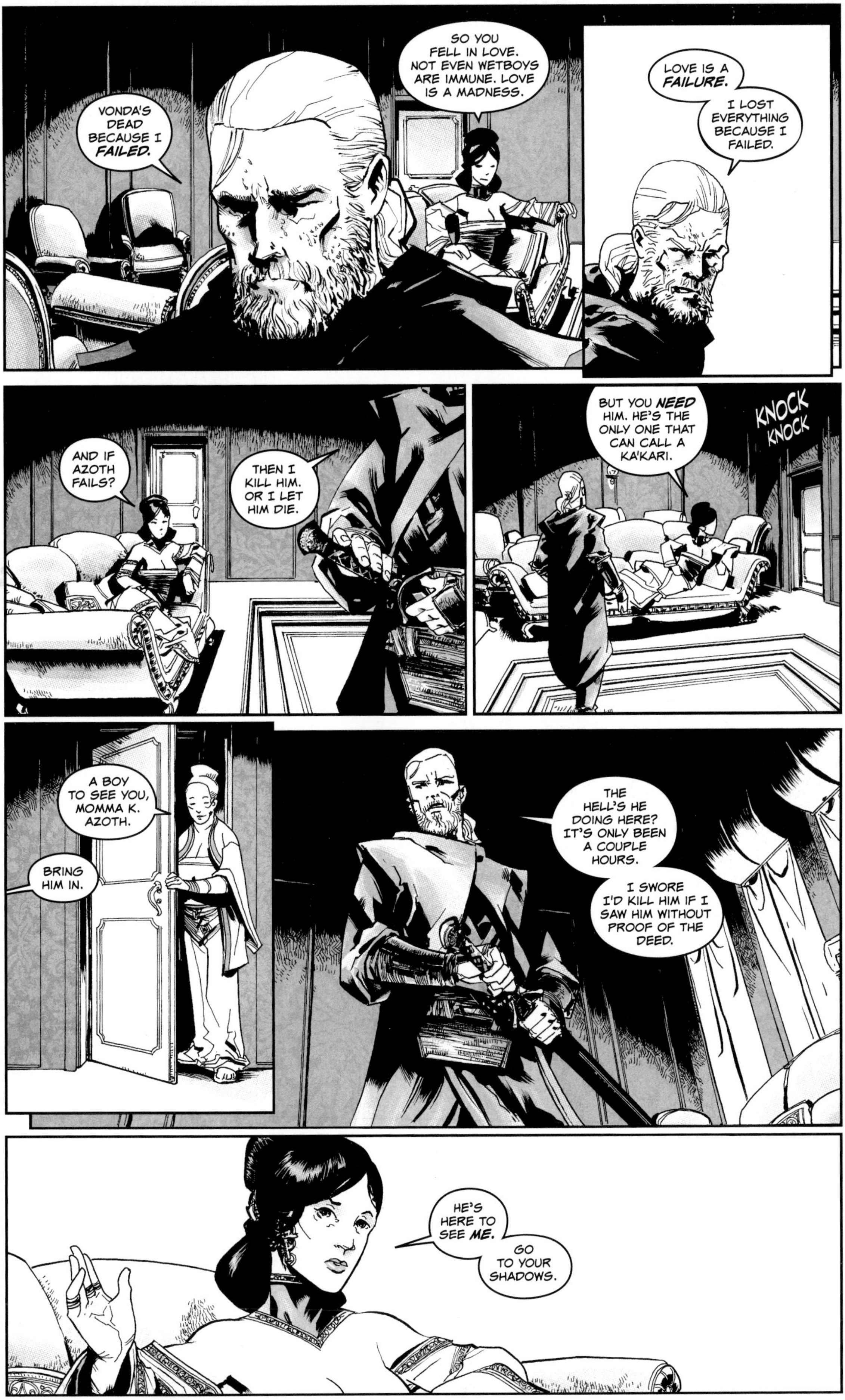
VONDA'S DEAD BECAUSE I FAILED.
SO YOU FELL IN LOVE. NOT EVEN WETBOYS ARE IMMUNE. LOVE IS A MADNESS.
LOVE IS A FAILURE.
I LOST EVERYTHING BECAUSE I FAILED.
AND IF AZOTH FAILS?
THEN I KILL HIM. OR I LET HIM DIE.
BUT YOU NEED HIM. HE'S THE ONLY ONE THAT CAN CALL A KA'KARI.
KNOCK KNOCK
A BOY TO SEE YOU, MOMMA K. AZOTH.
BRING HIM IN.
THE HELL'S HE DOING HERE? IT'S ONLY BEEN A COUPLE HOURS.
I SWORE I'D KILL HIM IF I SAW HIM WITHOUT PROOF OF THE DEED.
HE'S HERE TO SEE ME.
GO TO YOUR SHADOWS.

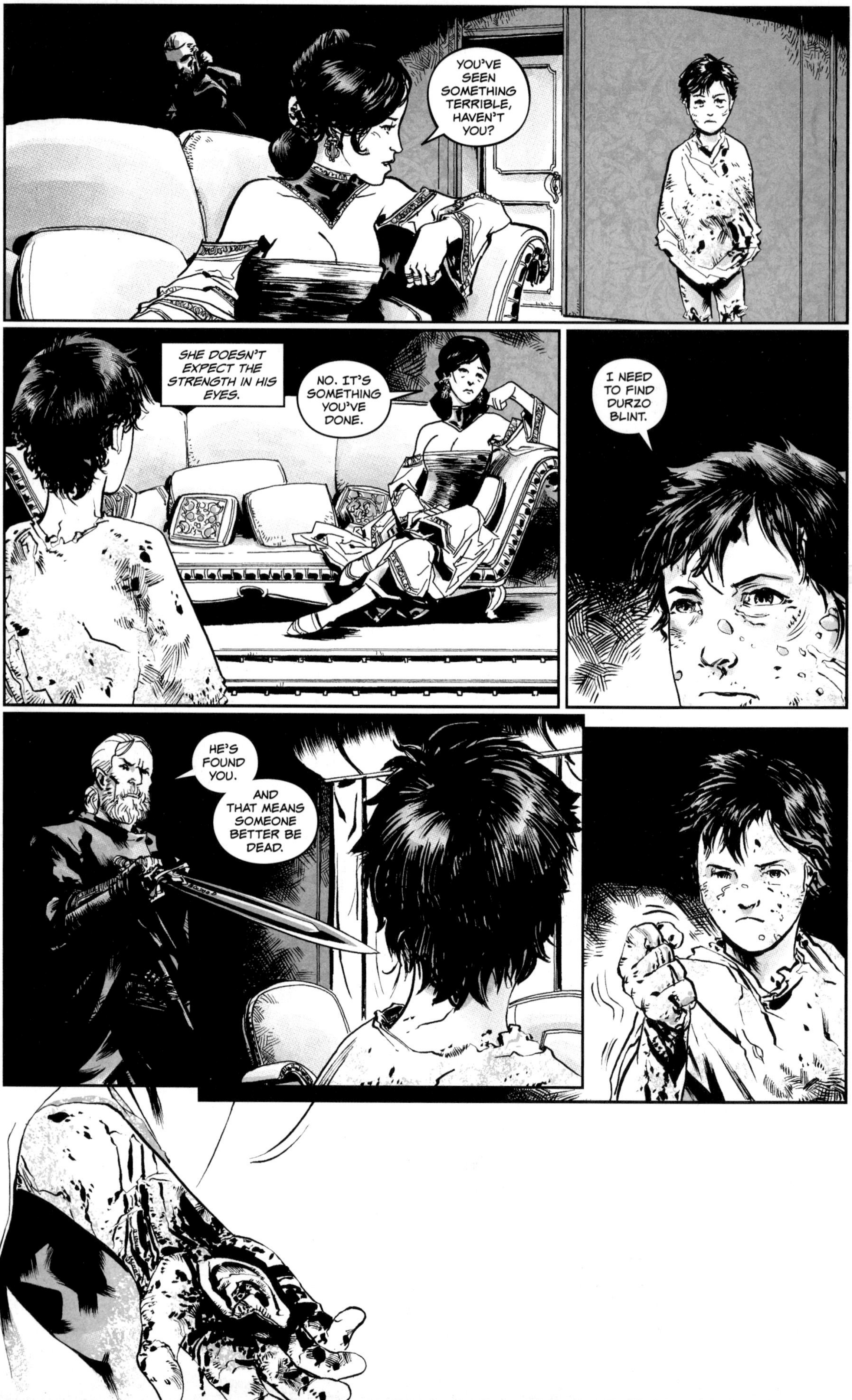
YOU'VE SEEN SOMETHING TERRIBLE, HAVEN'T YOU?
SHE DOESN'T EXPECT THE STRENGTH IN HIS EYES.
NO. IT'S SOMETHING YOU'VE DONE.
I NEED TO FIND DURZO BLINT.
HE'S FOUND YOU.
AND THAT MEANS SOMEONE BETTER BE DEAD.

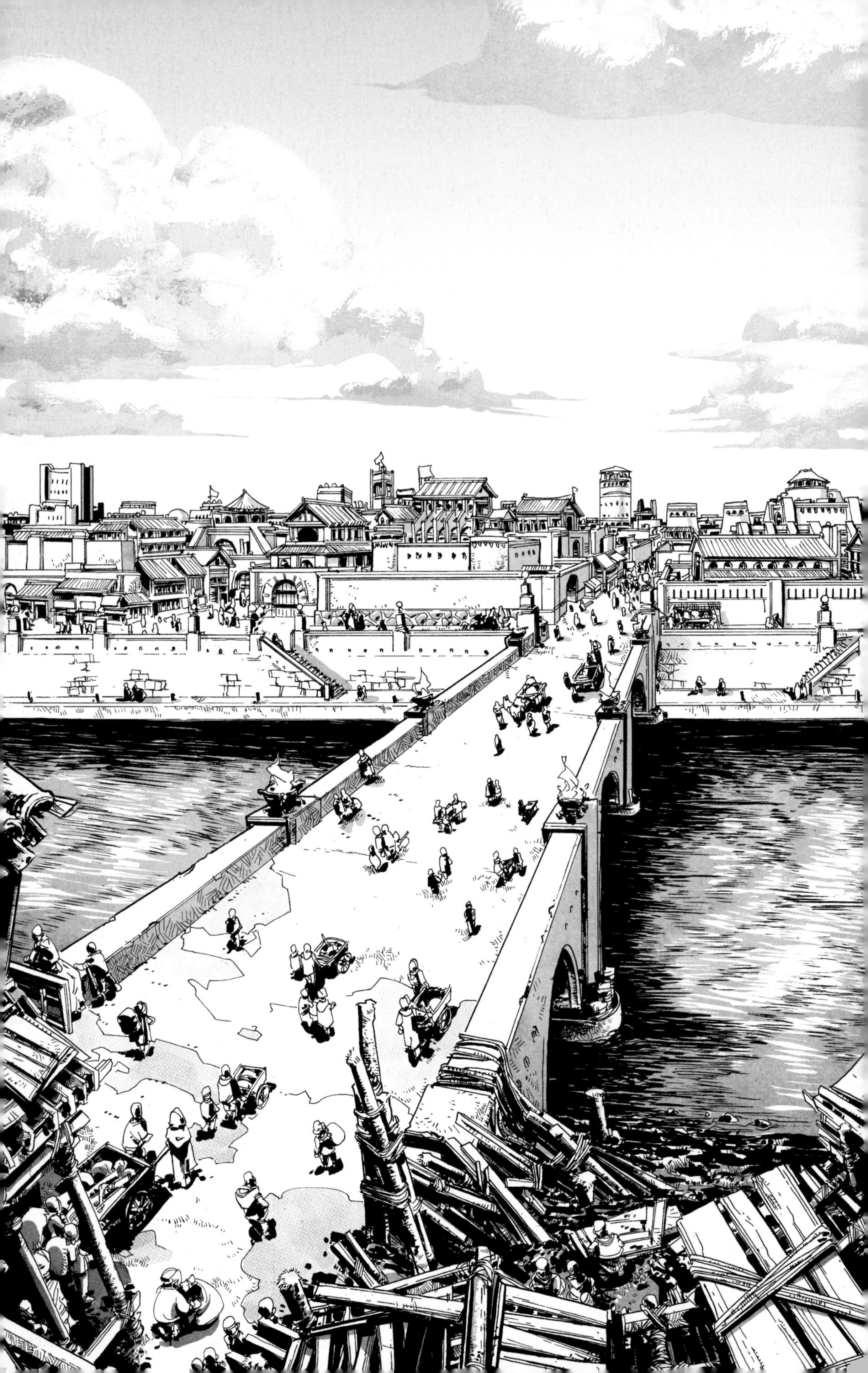

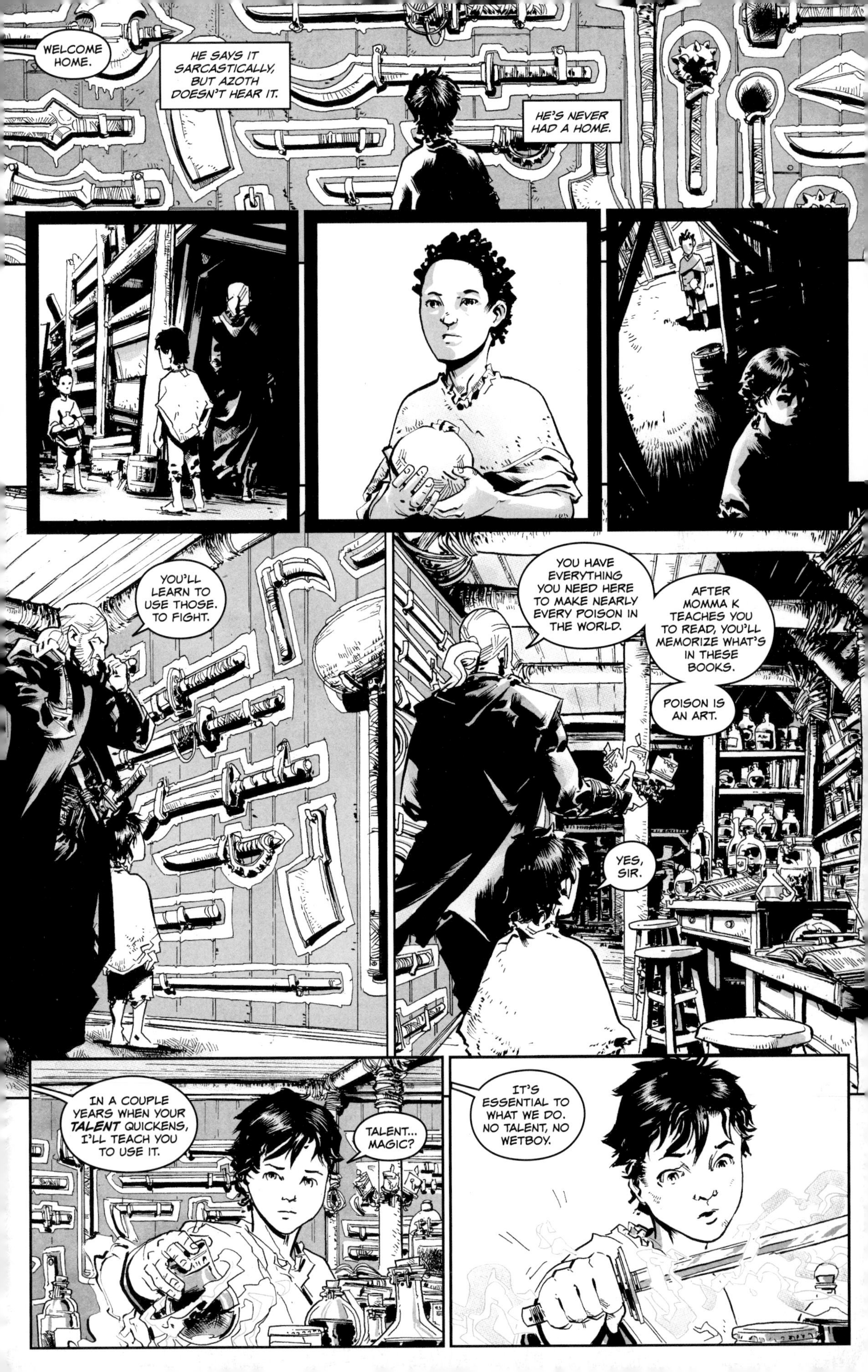
WELCOME HOME.
HE SAYS IT SARCASTICALLY, BUT AZOTH DOESN'T HEAR IT.
HE'S NEVER HAD A HOME.
YOU'LL LEARN TO USE THOSE. TO FIGHT.
YOU HAVE EVERYTHING YOU NEED HERE TO MAKE NEARLY EVERY POISON IN THE WORLD.
AFTER MOMMA K TEACHES YOU TO READ, YOU'LL MEMORIZE WHAT'S IN THESE BOOKS.
POISON IS AN ART.
YES, SIR.
IN A COUPLE YEARS WHEN YOUR TALENT QUICKENS, I'LL TEACH YOU TO USE IT.
TALENT... MAGIC?
IT'S ESSENTIAL TO WHAT WE DO. NO TALENT, NO WETBOY.

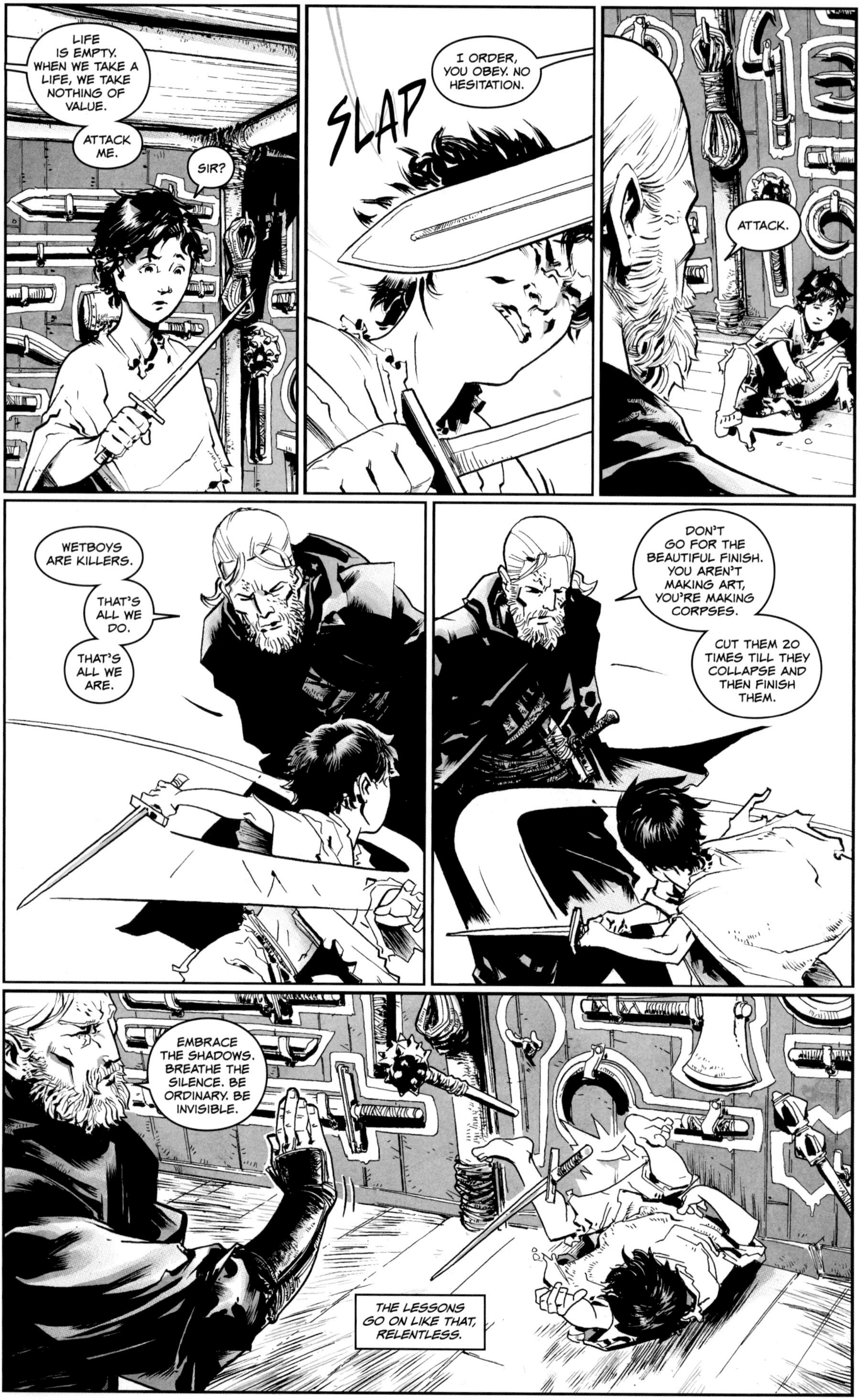
LIFE IS EMPTY. WHEN WE TAKE A LIFE, WE TAKE NOTHING OF VALUE.
ATTACK ME.
SIR?
SLAP
I ORDER, YOU OBEY. NO HESITATION.
ATTACK.
WETBOYS ARE KILLERS.
THAT'S ALL WE DO.
THAT'S ALL WE ARE.
DON'T GO FOR THE BEAUTIFUL FINISH. YOU AREN'T MAKING ART, YOU'RE MAKING CORPSES.
CUT THEM 20 TIMES TILL THEY COLLAPSE AND THEN FINISH THEM.
EMBRACE THE SHADOWS. BREATHE THE SILENCE. BE ORDINARY. BE INVISIBLE.
THE LESSONS GO ON LIKE THAT, RELENTLESS.

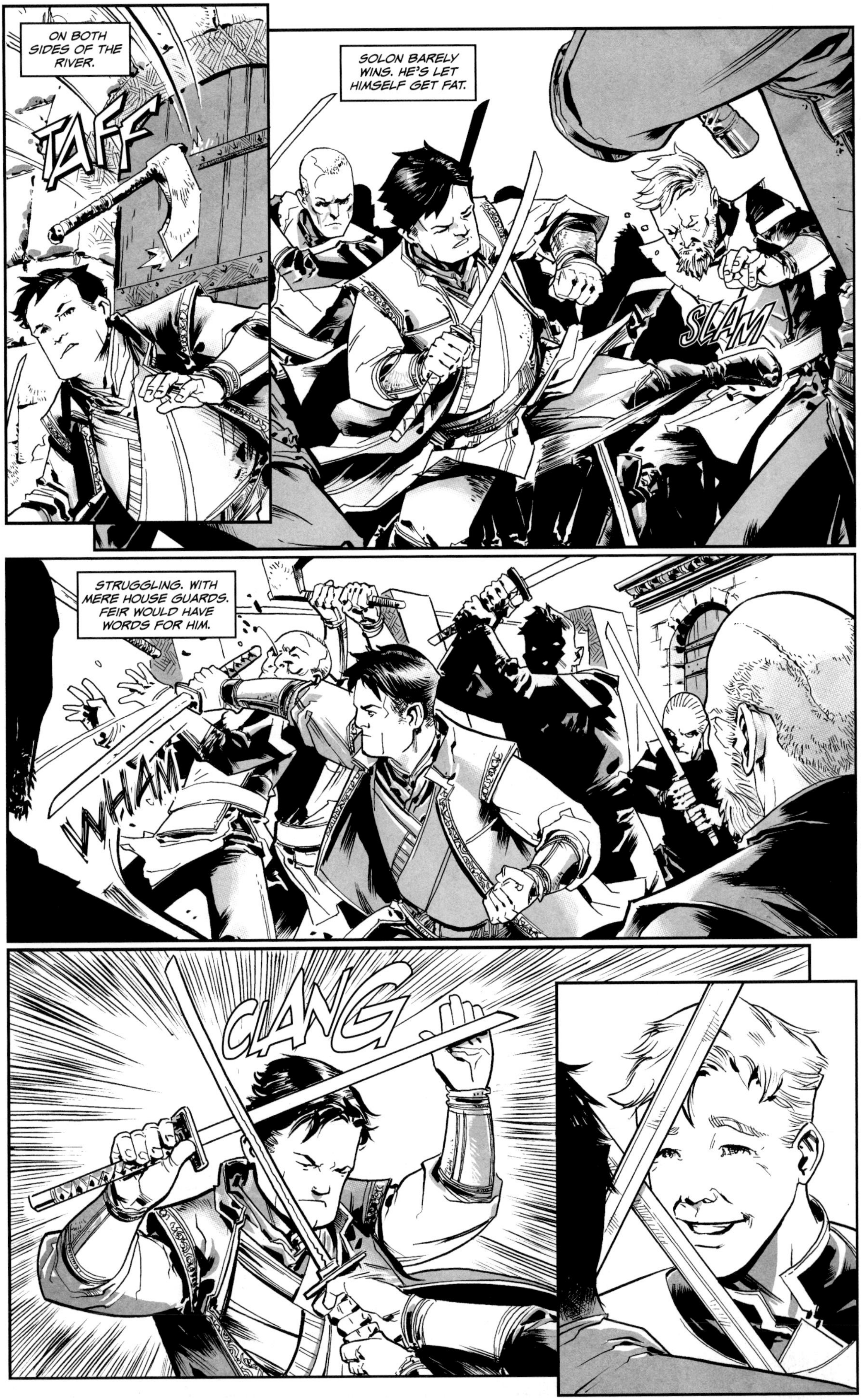
ON BOTH SIDES OF THE RIVER.
TAFF
SOLON BARELY WINS. HE'S LET HIMSELF GET FAT.
SLAM
STRUGGLING. WITH MERE HOUSE GUARDS. FEIR WOULD HAVE WORDS FOR HIM.
WHAM
CLANG

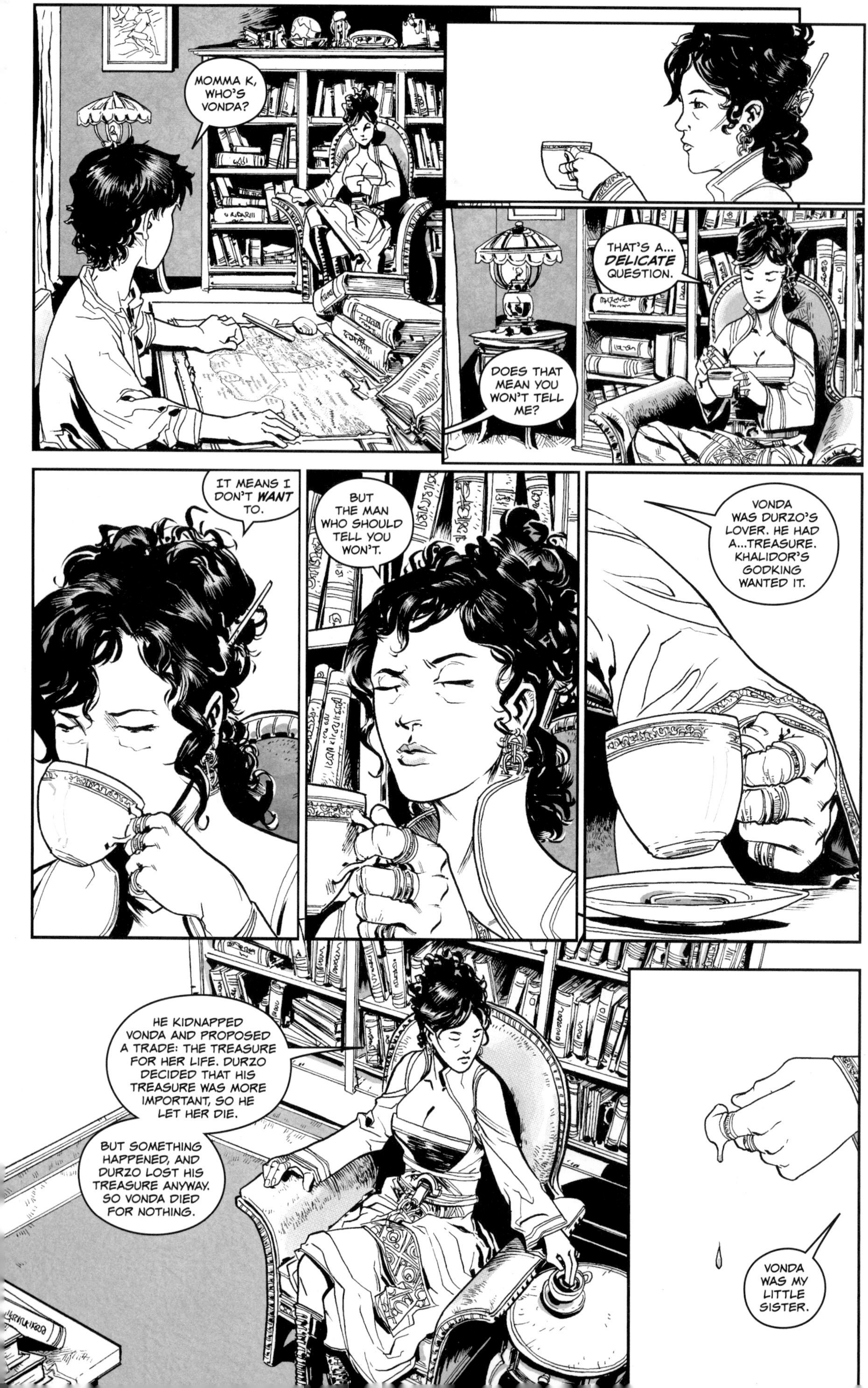
MOMMA K, WHO'S VONDA?
THAT'S A... DELICATE QUESTION.
DOES THAT MEAN YOU WON'T TELL ME?
IT MEANS I DON'T WANT TO.
BUT THE MAN WHO SHOULD TELL YOU WON'T.
VONDA WAS DURZO'S LOVER. HE HAD A...TREASURE. KHALIDOR'S GODKING WANTED IT.
HE KIDNAPPED VONDA AND PROPOSED A TRADE: THE TREASURE FOR HER LIFE. DURZO DECIDED THAT HIS TREASURE WAS MORE IMPORTANT, SO HE LET HER DIE.
BUT SOMETHING HAPPENED, AND DURZO LOST HIS TREASURE ANYWAY. SO VONDA DIED FOR NOTHING.
VONDA WAS MY LITTLE SISTER.

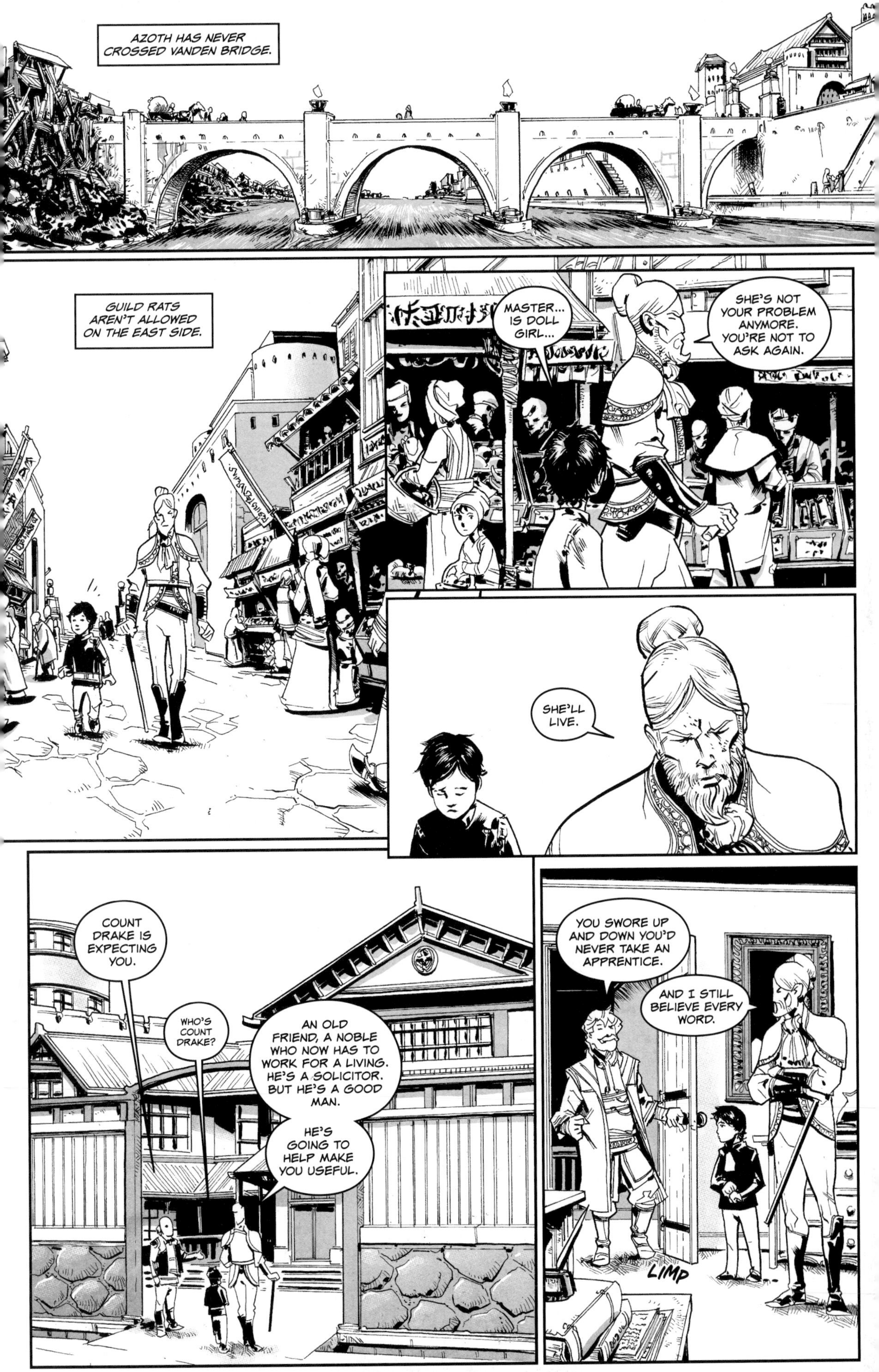

AZOTH HAS NEVER CROSSED VANDEN BRIDGE.
GUILD RATS AREN'T ALLOWED ON THE EAST SIDE.
MASTER... IS DOLL GIRL...
SHE'S NOT YOUR PROBLEM ANYMORE. YOU'RE NOT TO ASK AGAIN.
SHE'LL LIVE.
COUNT DRAKE IS EXPECTING YOU.
WHO'S COUNT DRAKE?
AN OLD FRIEND, A NOBLE WHO NOW HAS TO WORK FOR A LIVING. HE'S A SOLICITOR. BUT HE'S A GOOD MAN.
HE'S GOING TO HELP MAKE YOU USEFUL.
YOU SWORE UP AND DOWN YOU'D NEVER TAKE AN APPRENTICE.
AND I STILL BELIEVE EVERY WORD.
LIMP

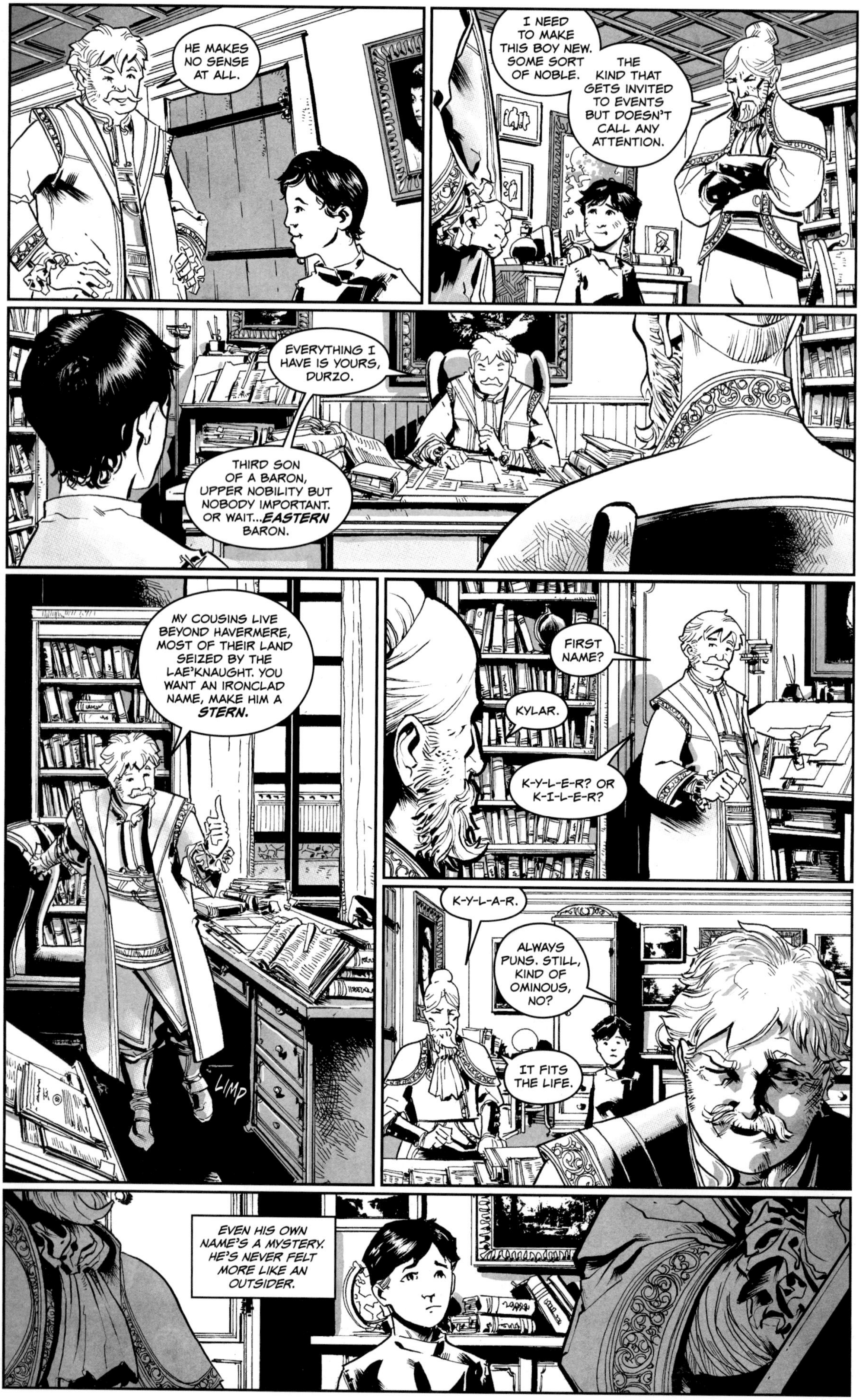
HE MAKES NO SENSE AT ALL.
I NEED TO MAKE THIS BOY NEW. SOME SORT OF NOBLE.
THE KIND THAT GETS INVITED TO EVENTS BUT DOESN'T CALL ANY ATTENTION.
EVERYTHING I HAVE IS YOURS, DURZO.
THIRD SON OF A BARON, UPPER NOBILITY BUT NOBODY IMPORTANT. OR WAIT...EASTERN BARON.
MY COUSINS LIVE BEYOND HAVERMERE, MOST OF THEIR LAND SEIZED BY THE LAE'KNAUGHT. YOU WANT AN IRONCLAD NAME, MAKE HIM A STERN.
LIMP
FIRST NAME?
KYLAR.
K-Y-L-E-R? OR K-I-L-E-R?
K-Y-L-A-R.
ALWAYS PUNS. STILL, KIND OF OMINOUS, NO?
IT FITS THE LIFE.
EVEN HIS OWN NAME'S A MYSTERY. HE'S NEVER FELT MORE LIKE AN OUTSIDER.

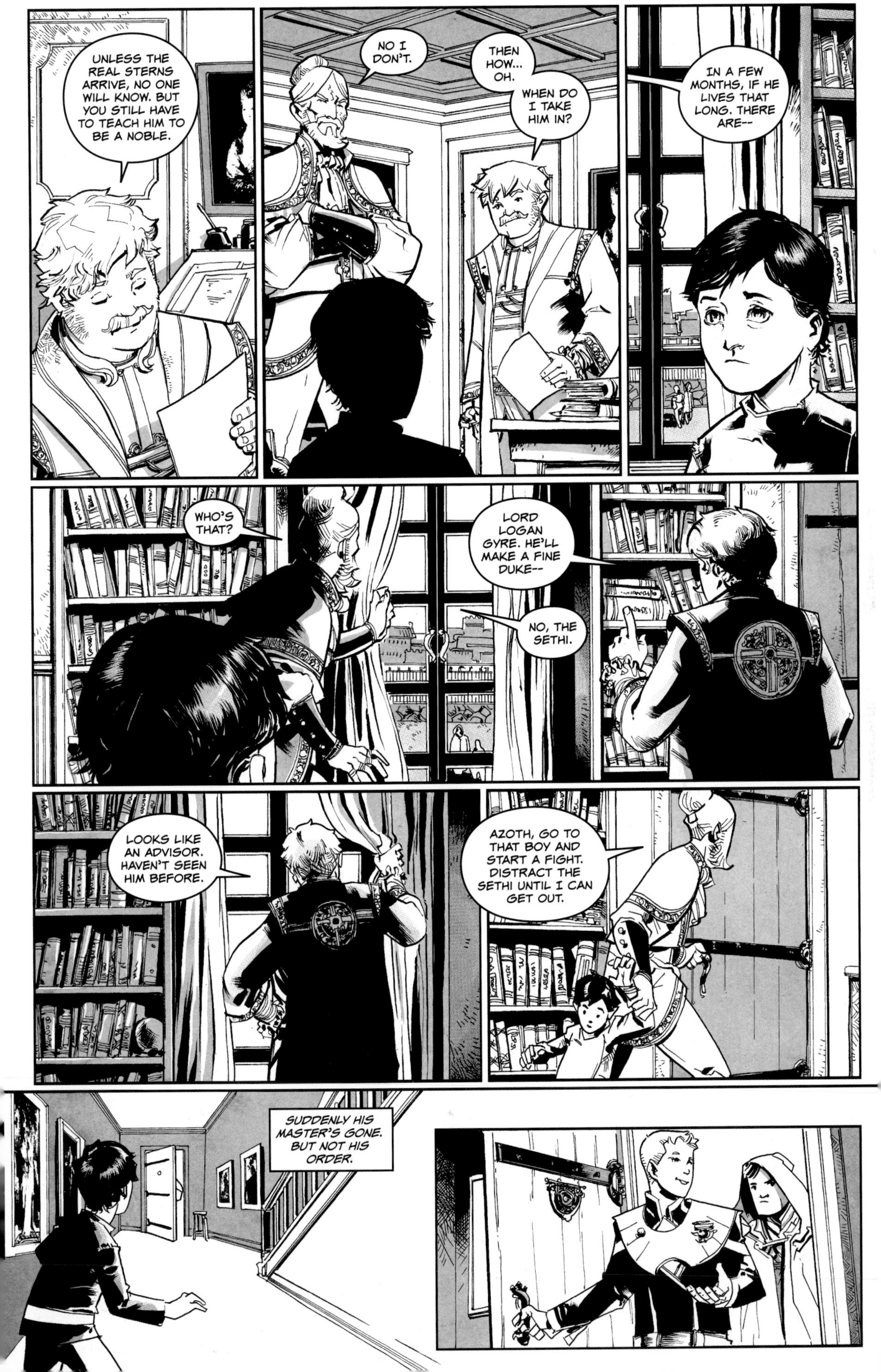
UNLESS THE REAL STERNS ARRIVE, NO ONE WILL KNOW. BUT YOU STILL HAVE TO TEACH HIM TO BE A NOBLE.
NO I DON'T.
THEN HOW... OH.
WHEN DO I TAKE HIM IN?
IN A FEW MONTHS, IF HE LIVES THAT LONG. THERE ARE--
WHO'S THAT?
LORD LOGAN GYRE. HE'LL MAKE A FINE DUKE--
NO, THE SETHI.
LOOKS LIKE AN ADVISOR. HAVEN'T SEEN HIM BEFORE.
AZOTH, GO TO THAT BOY AND START A FIGHT. DISTRACT THE SETHI UNTIL I CAN GET OUT.
SUDDENLY HIS MASTER'S GONE. BUT NOT HIS ORDER.

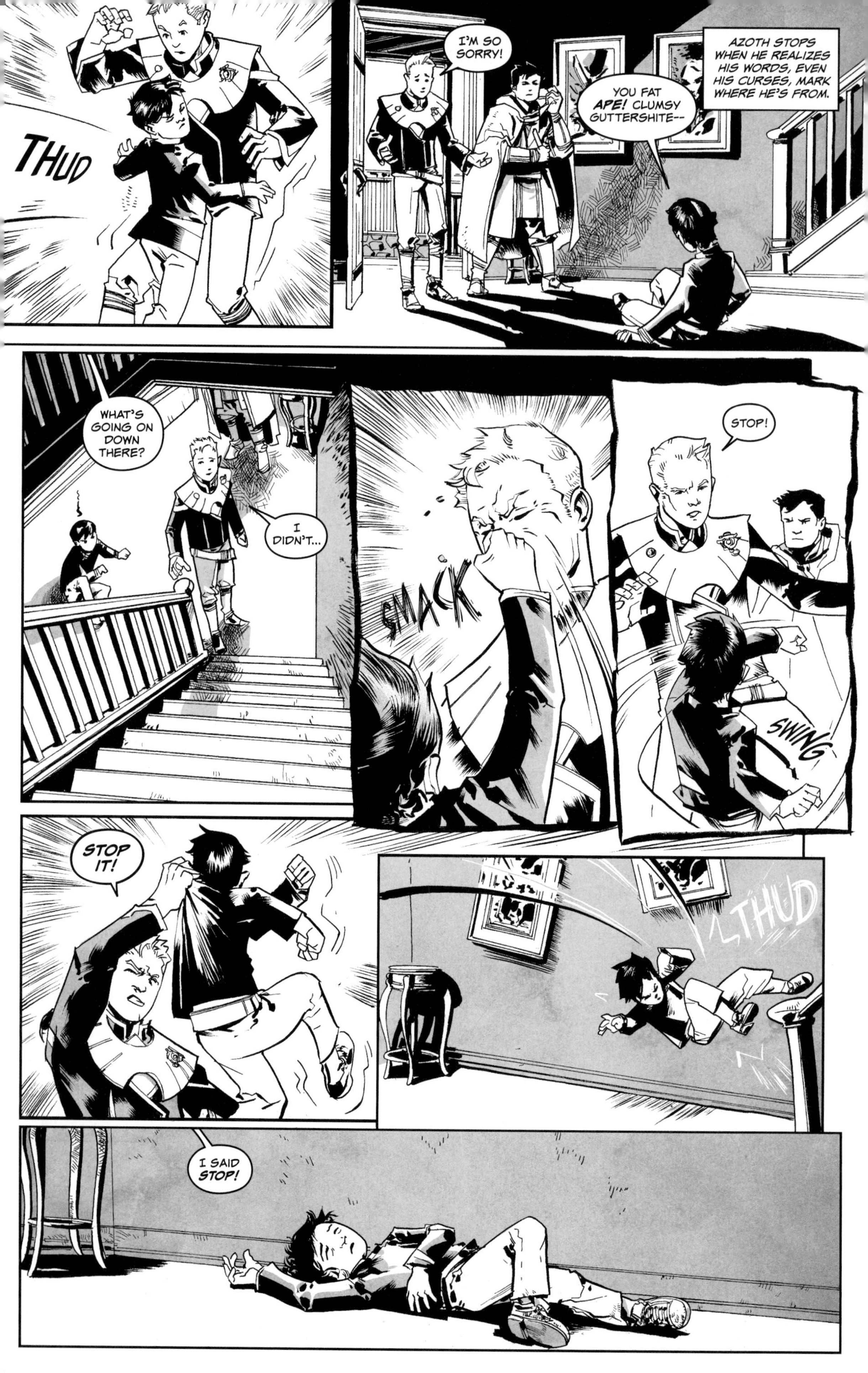
THUD
I'M SO SORRY!
YOU FAT APE! CLUMSY GUTTERSHITE--
AZOTH STOPS WHEN HE REALIZES HIS WORDS, EVEN HIS CURSES, MARK WHERE HE'S FROM.
WHAT'S GOING ON DOWN THERE?
I DIDN'T...
SMACK
STOP!
SWING
STOP IT!
THUD
I SAID STOP!

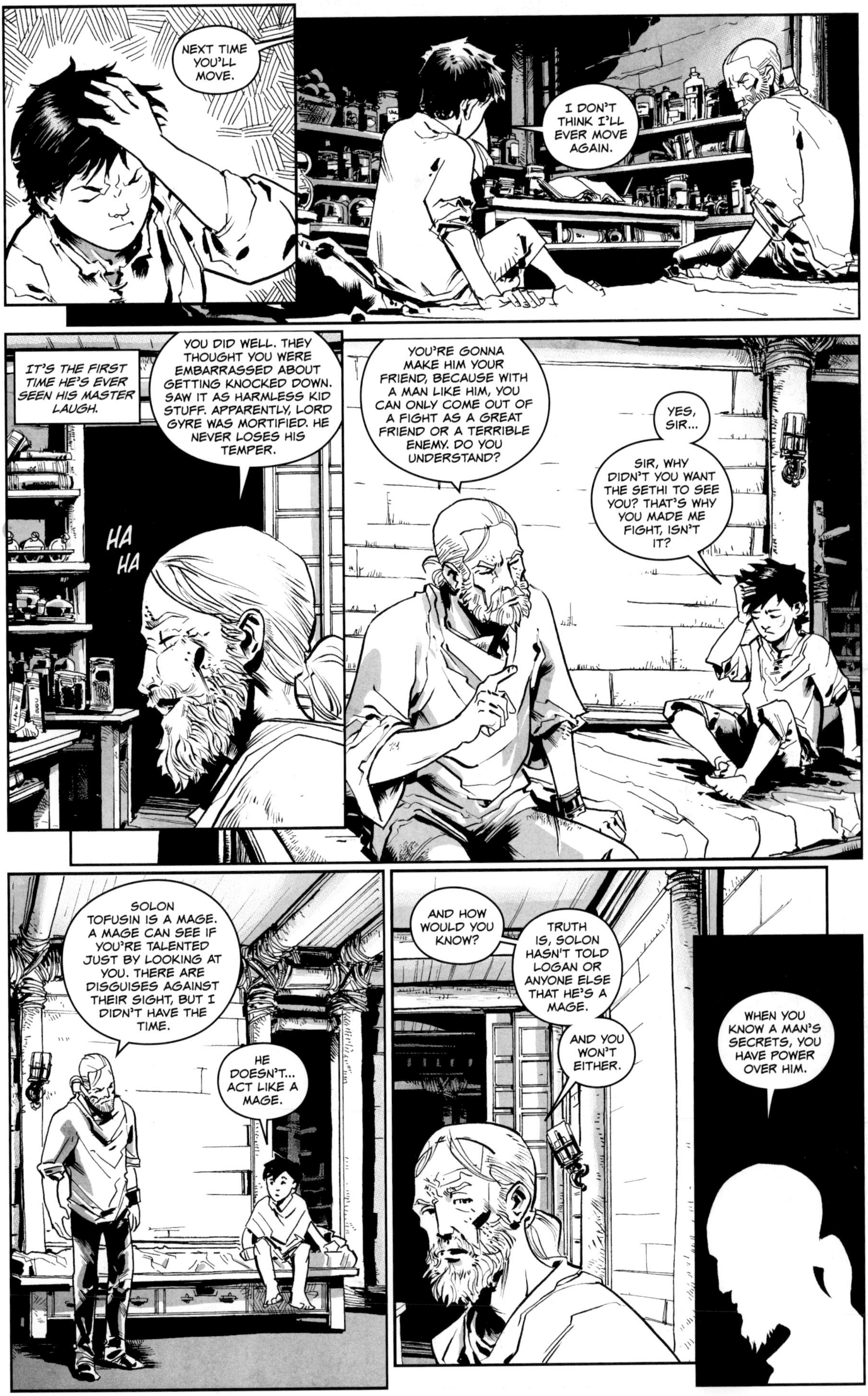
NEXT TIME YOU'LL MOVE.
I DON'T THINK I'LL EVER MOVE AGAIN.
IT'S THE FIRST TIME HE'S EVER SEEN HIS MASTER LAUGH.
YOU DID WELL. THEY THOUGHT YOU WERE EMBARRASSED ABOUT GETTING KNOCKED DOWN. SAW IT AS HARMLESS KID STUFF. APPARENTLY, LORD GYRE WAS MORTIFIED. HE NEVER LOSES HIS TEMPER.
HA HA
YOU'RE GONNA MAKE HIM YOUR FRIEND, BECAUSE WITH A MAN LIKE HIM, YOU CAN ONLY COME OUT OF A FIGHT AS A GREAT FRIEND OR A TERRIBLE ENEMY. DO YOU UNDERSTAND?
YES, SIR...
SIR, WHY DIDN'T YOU WANT THE SETHI TO SEE YOU? THAT'S WHY YOU MADE ME FIGHT, ISN'T IT?
SOLON TOFUSIN IS A MAGE. A MAGE CAN SEE IF YOU'RE TALENTED JUST BY LOOKING AT YOU. THERE ARE DISGUISES AGAINST THEIR SIGHT, BUT I DIDN'T HAVE THE TIME.
HE DOESN'T... ACT LIKE A MAGE.
AND HOW WOULD YOU KNOW?
TRUTH IS, SOLON HASN'T TOLD LOGAN OR ANYONE ELSE THAT HE'S A MAGE.
AND YOU WON'T EITHER.
WHEN YOU KNOW A MAN'S SECRETS, YOU HAVE POWER OVER HIM.

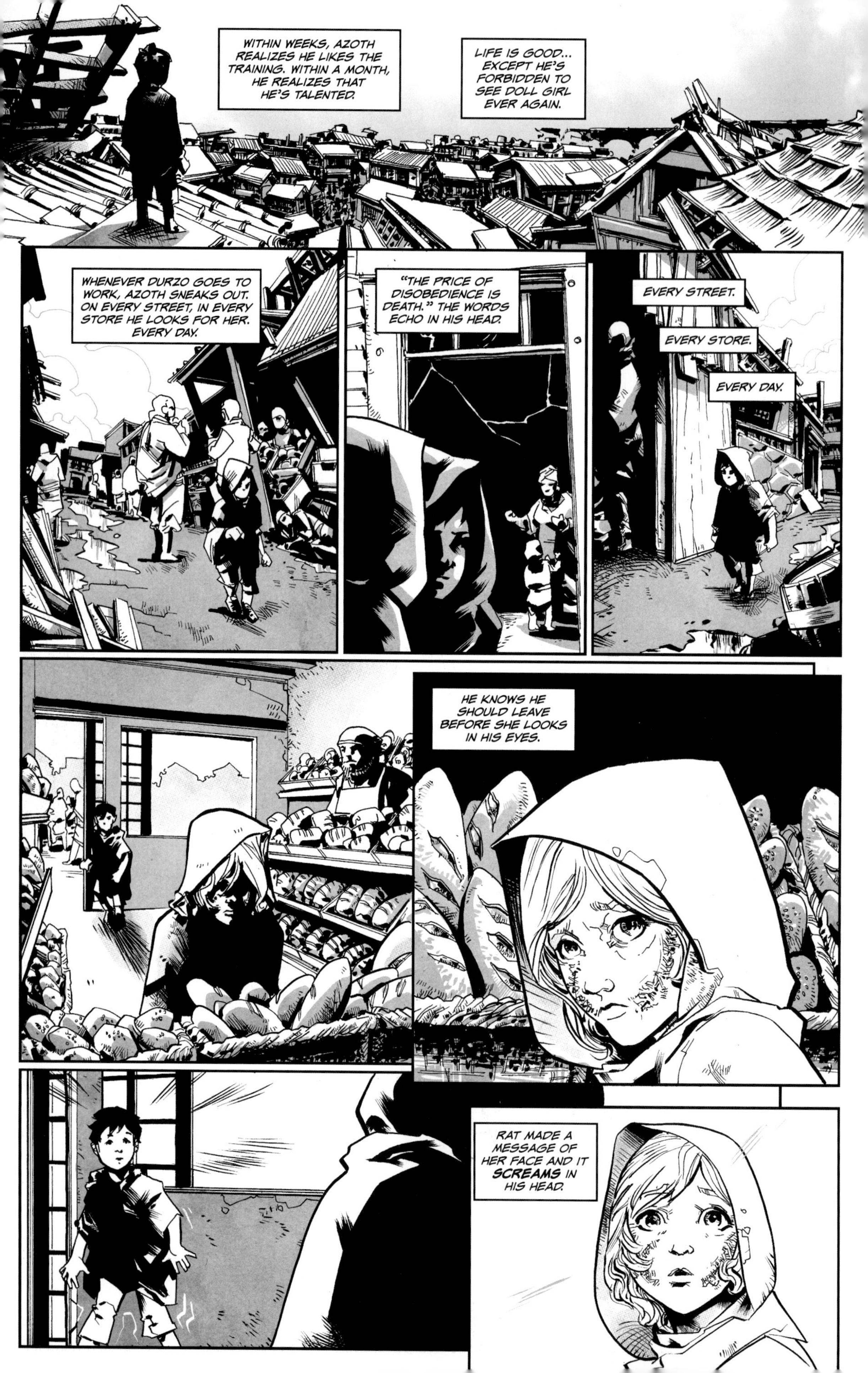
WITHIN WEEKS, AZOTH REALIZES HE LIKES THE TRAINING. WITHIN A MONTH, HE REALIZES THAT HE'S TALENTED.
LIFE IS GOOD... EXCEPT HE'S FORBIDDEN TO SEE DOLL GIRL EVER AGAIN.
WHENEVER DURZO GOES TO WORK, AZOTH SNEAKS OUT. ON EVERY STREET, IN EVERY STORE HE LOOKS FOR HER. EVERY DAY.
"THE PRICE OF DISOBEDIENCE IS DEATH." THE WORDS ECHO IN HIS HEAD.
EVERY STREET.
EVERY STORE.
EVERY DAY.
HE KNOWS HE SHOULD LEAVE BEFORE SHE LOOKS IN HIS EYES.
RAT MADE A MESSAGE OF HER FACE AND IT SCREAMS IN HIS HEAD.

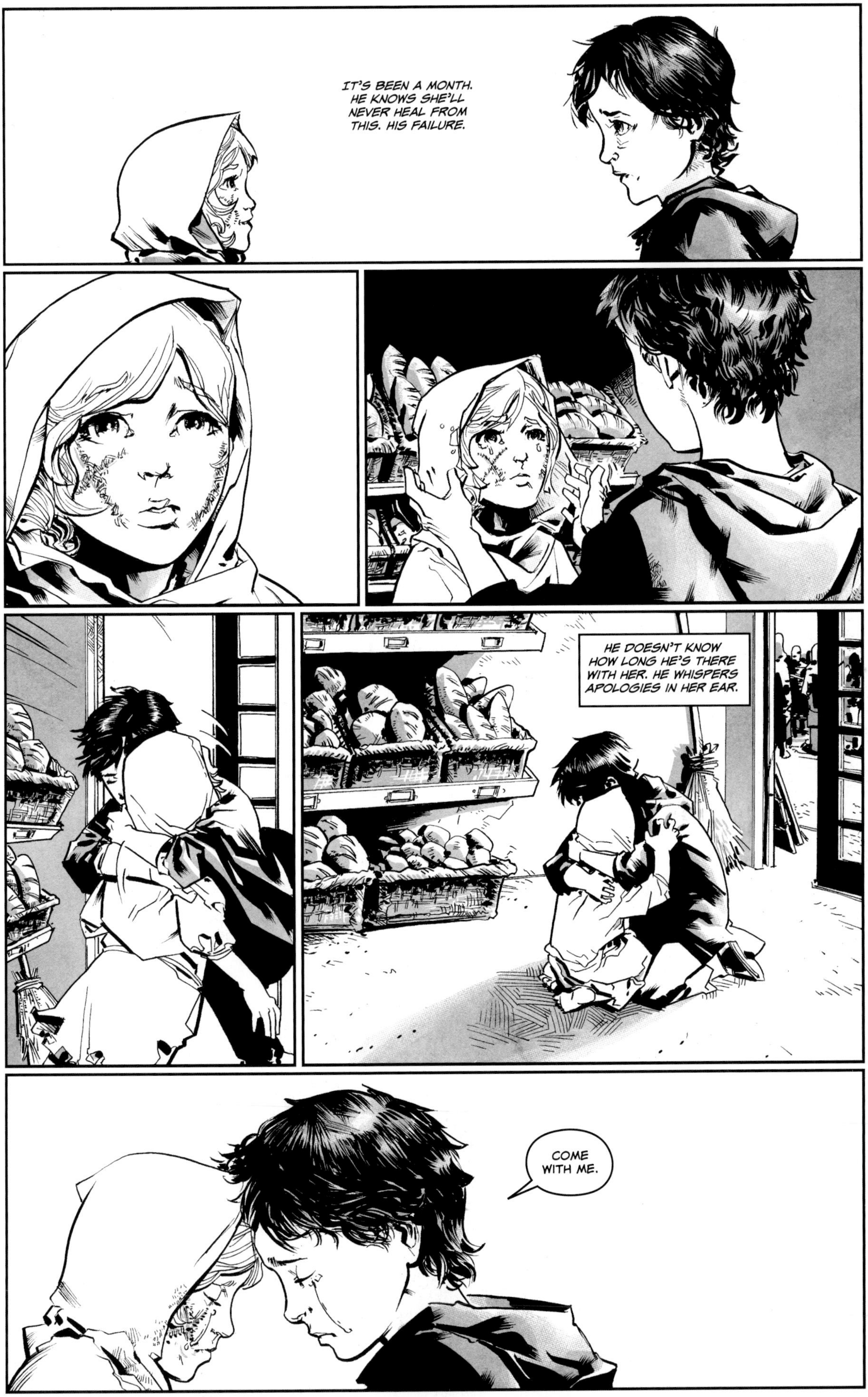
IT'S BEEN A MONTH. HE KNOWS SHE'LL NEVER HEAL FROM THIS. HIS FAILURE.
HE DOESN'T KNOW HOW LONG HE'S THERE WITH HER. HE WHISPERS APOLOGIES IN HER EAR.
COME WITH ME.

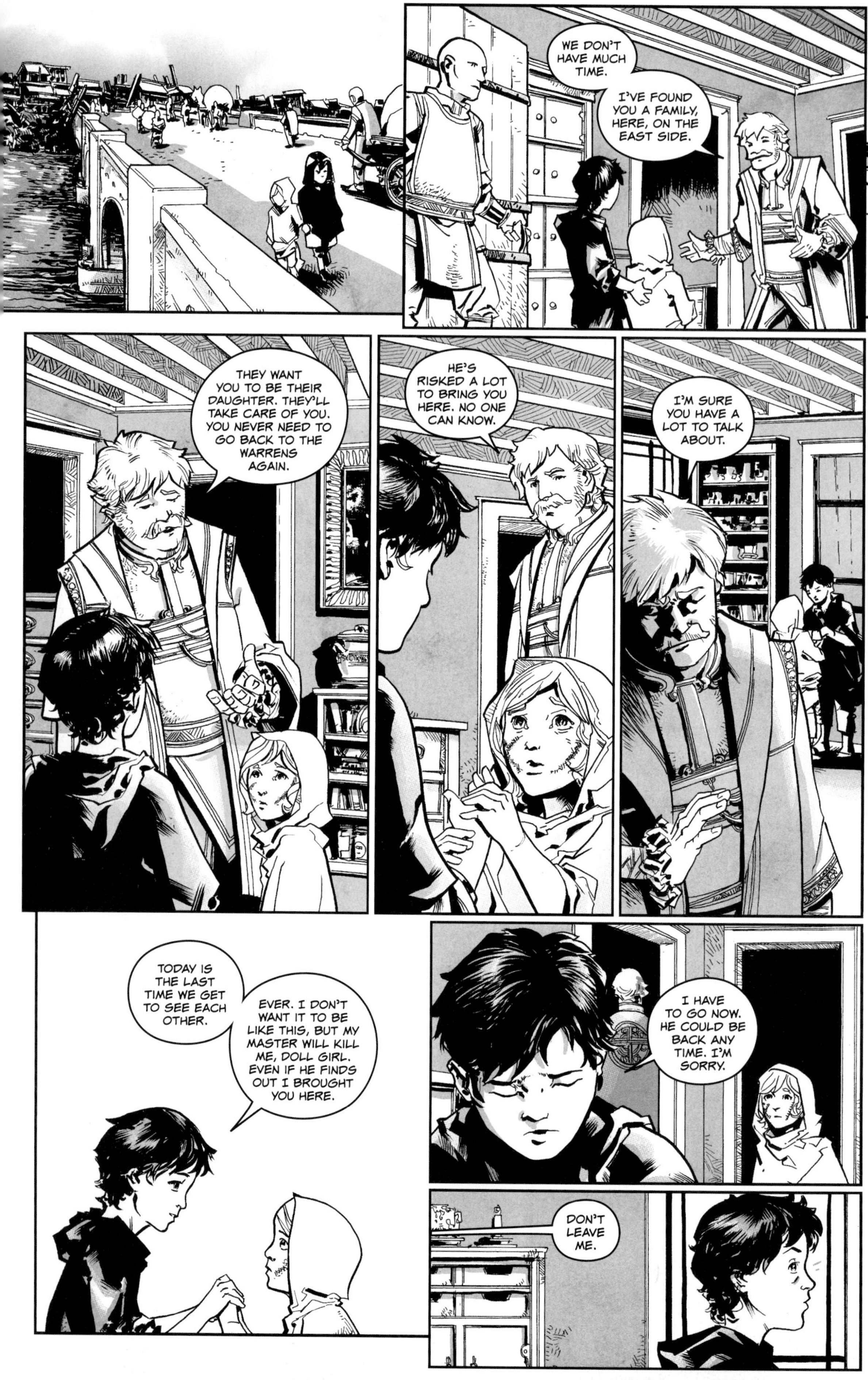
WE DON'T HAVE MUCH TIME.
I'VE FOUND YOU A FAMILY, HERE, ON THE EAST SIDE.
THEY WANT YOU TO BE THEIR DAUGHTER. THEY'LL TAKE CARE OF YOU. YOU NEVER NEED TO GO BACK TO THE WARRENS AGAIN.
HE'S RISKED A LOT TO BRING YOU HERE. NO ONE CAN KNOW.
I'M SURE YOU HAVE A LOT TO TALK ABOUT.
TODAY IS THE LAST TIME WE GET TO SEE EACH OTHER.
EVER. I DON'T WANT IT TO BE LIKE THIS, BUT MY MASTER WILL KILL ME, DOLL GIRL. EVEN IF HE FINDS OUT I BROUGHT YOU HERE.
I HAVE TO GO NOW. HE COULD BE BACK ANY TIME. I'M SORRY.
DON'T LEAVE ME.

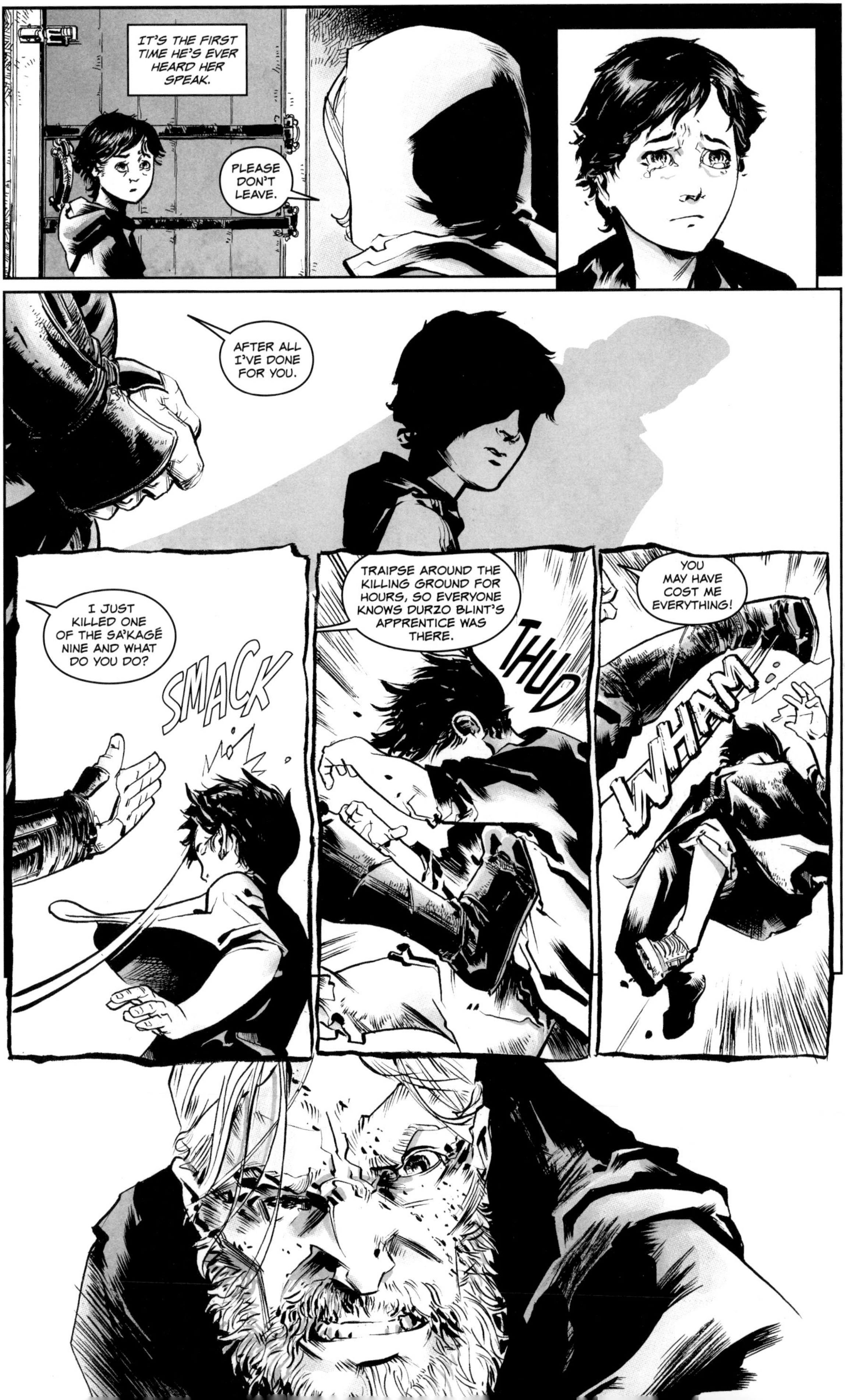
IT'S THE FIRST TIME HE'S EVER HEARD HER SPEAK.
PLEASE DON'T LEAVE.
AFTER ALL I'VE DONE FOR YOU.
I JUST KILLED ONE OF THE SA'KAGÉ NINE AND WHAT DO YOU DO?
SMACK
TRAIPSE AROUND THE KILLING GROUND FOR HOURS, SO EVERYONE KNOWS DURZO BLINT'S APPRENTICE WAS THERE.
THUD
YOU MAY HAVE COST ME EVERYTHING!
WHAM

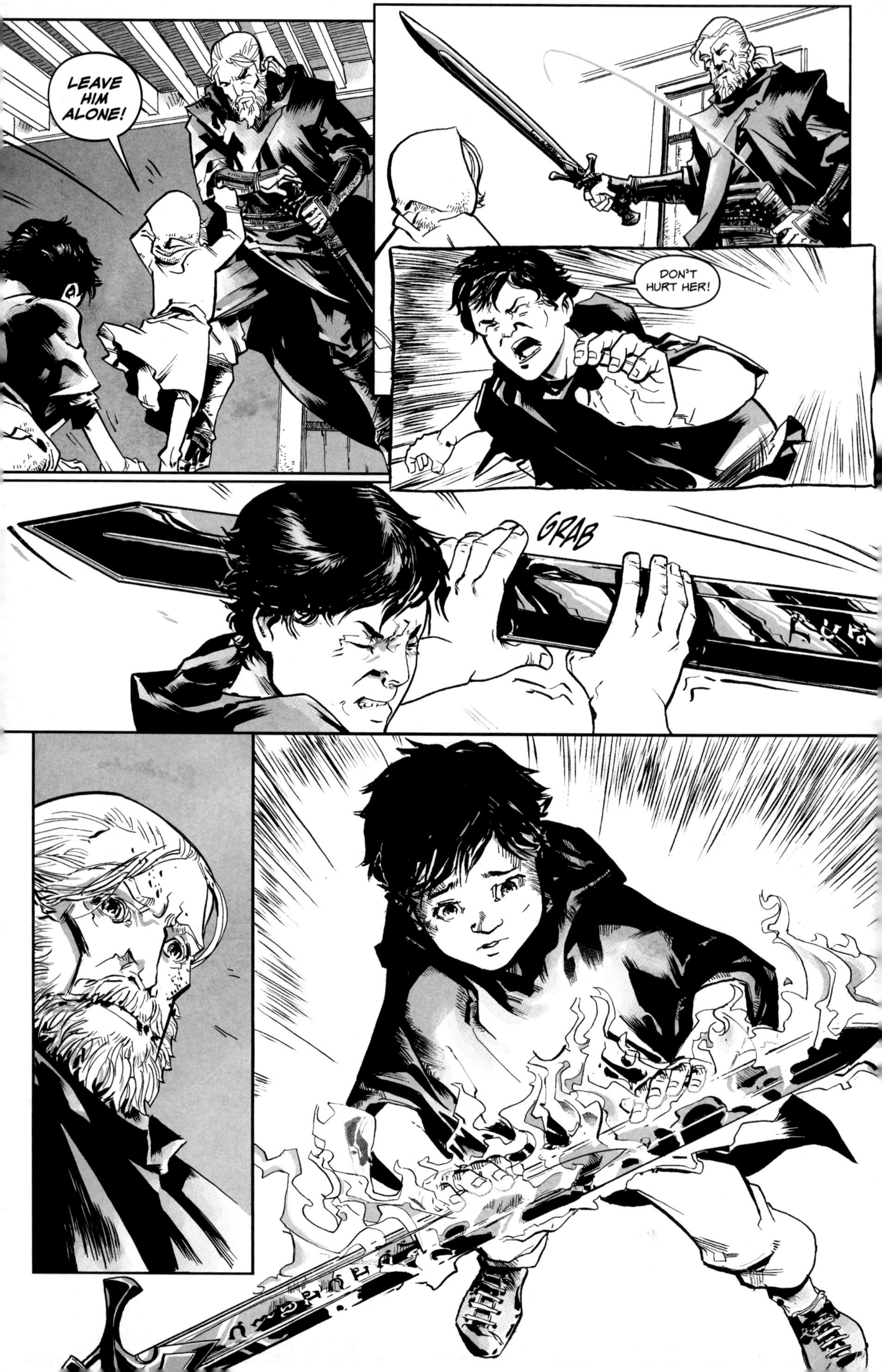
LEAVE HIM ALONE!
DON'T HURT HER!
GRAB

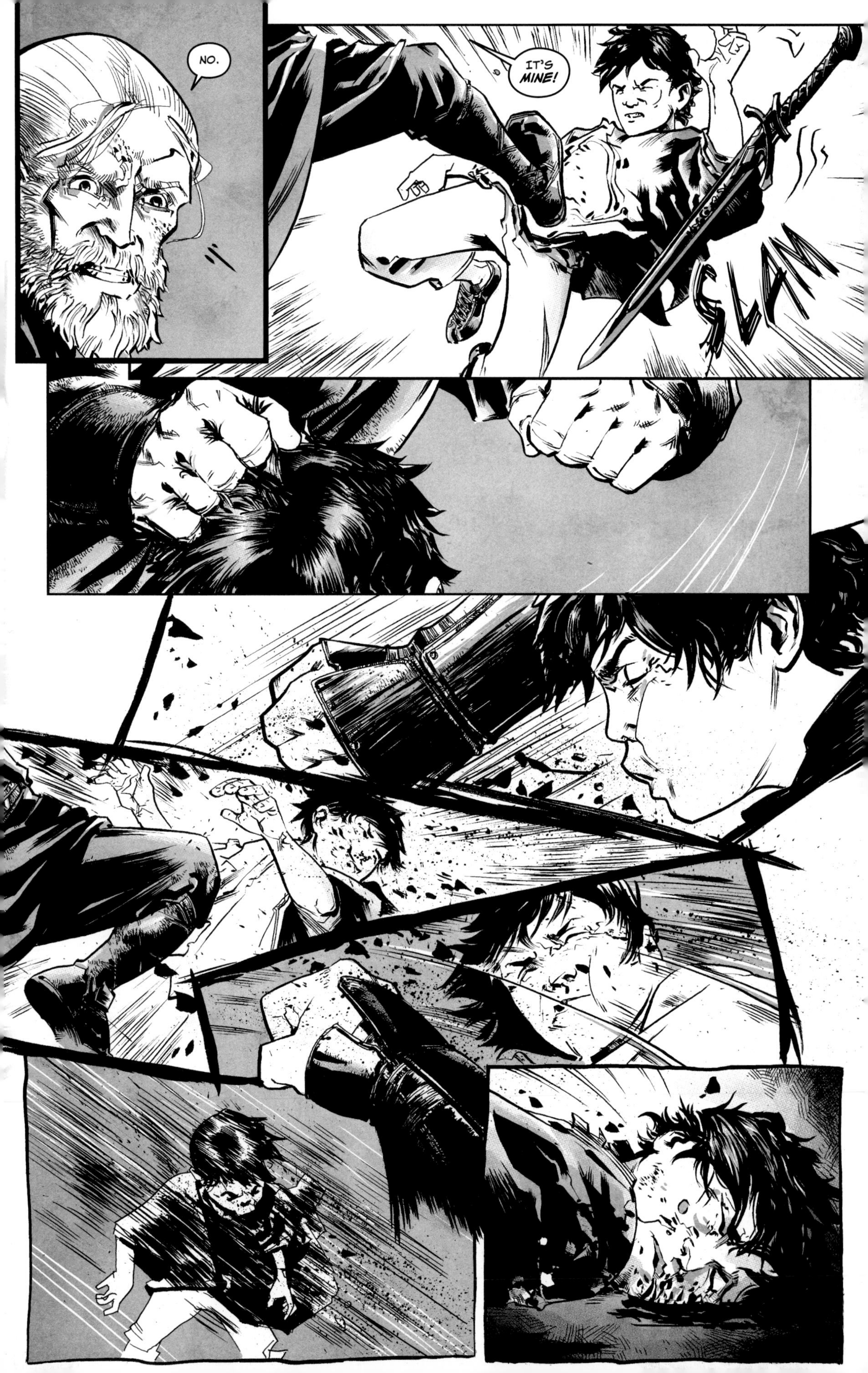
NO.
IT'S MINE!
SLAM

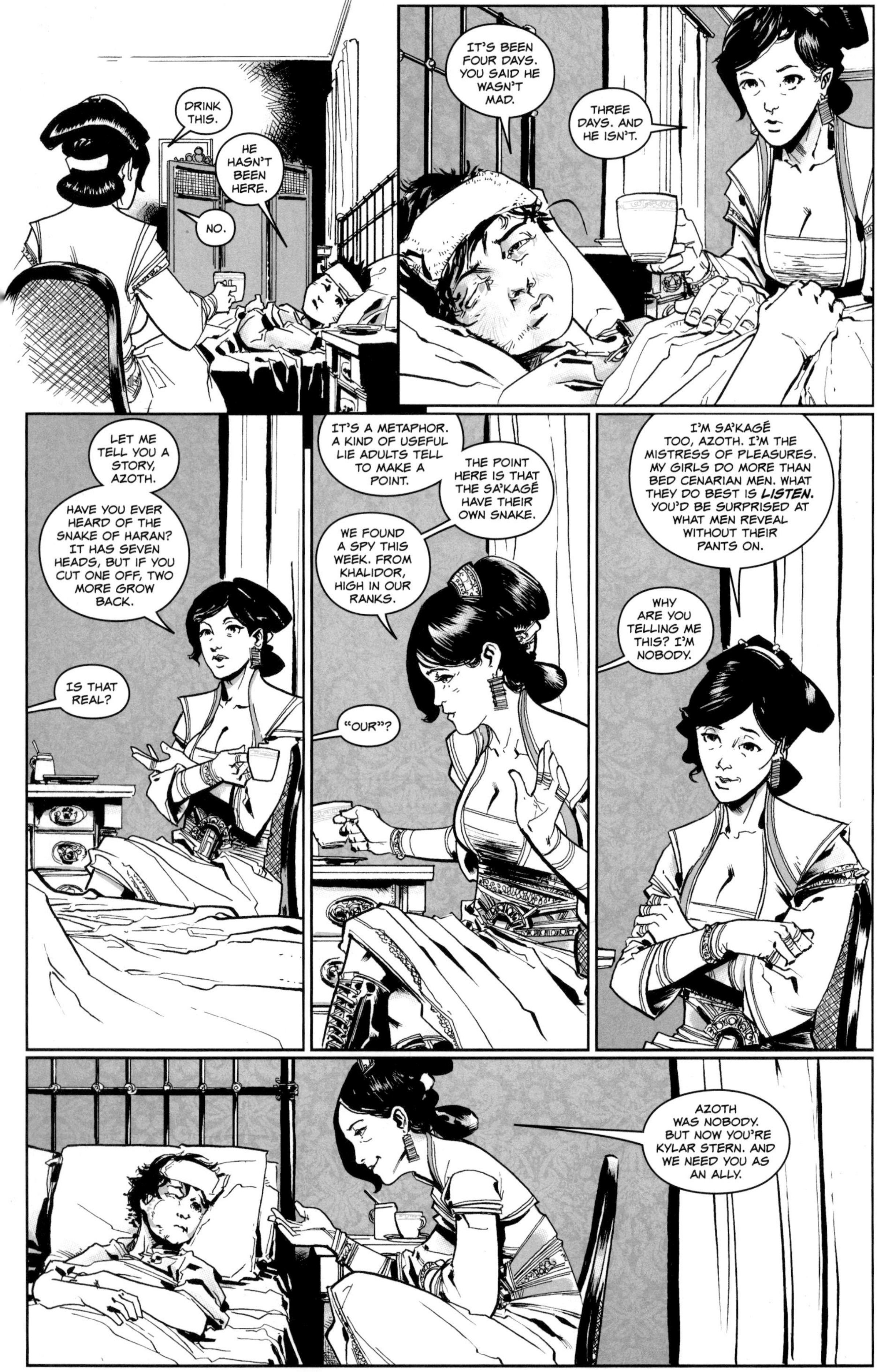
DRINK THIS.
HE HASN'T BEEN HERE.
NO.
IT'S BEEN FOUR DAYS. YOU SAID HE WASN'T MAD.
THREE DAYS. AND HE ISN'T.
LET ME TELL YOU A STORY, AZOTH.
HAVE YOU EVER HEARD OF THE SNAKE OF HARAN? IT HAS SEVEN HEADS, BUT IF YOU CUT ONE OFF, TWO MORE GROW BACK.
IS THAT REAL?
IT'S A METAPHOR. A KIND OF USEFUL LIE ADULTS TELL TO MAKE A POINT.
THE POINT HERE IS THAT THE SA'KAGÉ HAVE THEIR OWN SNAKE.
WE FOUND A SPY THIS WEEK. FROM KHALIDOR, HIGH IN OUR RANKS.
"OUR"?
I'M SA'KAGÉ TOO, AZOTH. I'M THE MISTRESS OF PLEASURES. MY GIRLS DO MORE THAN BED CENARIAN MEN. WHAT THEY DO BEST IS ***LISTEN.*** YOU'D BE SURPRISED AT WHAT MEN REVEAL WITHOUT THEIR PANTS ON.
WHY ARE YOU TELLING ME THIS? I'M NOBODY.
AZOTH WAS NOBODY. BUT NOW YOU'RE KYLAR STERN. AND WE NEED YOU AS AN ALLY.

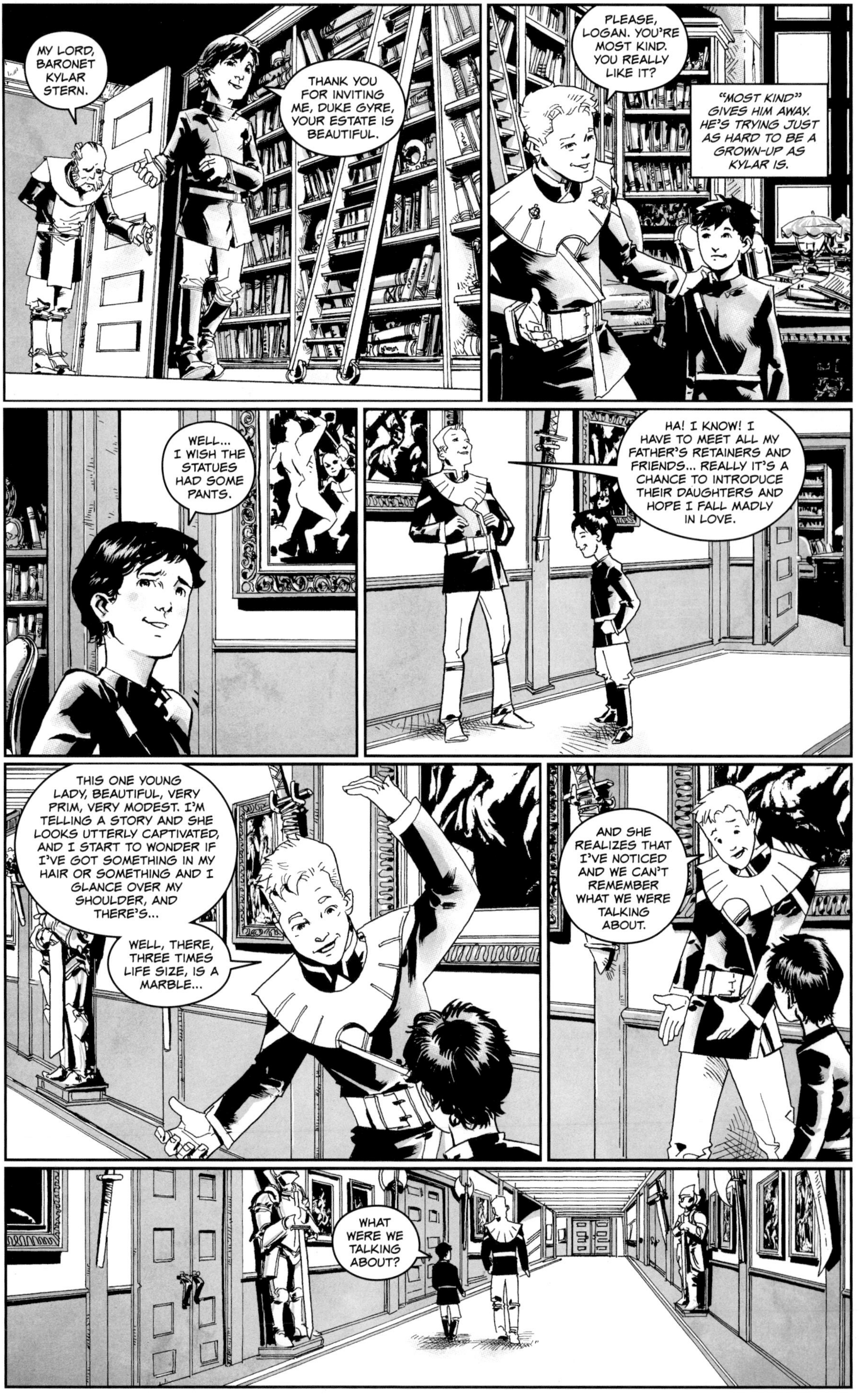
MY LORD, BARONET KYLAR STERN.
THANK YOU FOR INVITING ME, DUKE GYRE, YOUR ESTATE IS BEAUTIFUL.
PLEASE, LOGAN. YOU'RE MOST KIND. YOU REALLY LIKE IT?
"MOST KIND" GIVES HIM AWAY. HE'S TRYING JUST AS HARD TO BE A GROWN-UP AS KYLAR IS.
WELL... I WISH THE STATUES HAD SOME PANTS.
HA! I KNOW! I HAVE TO MEET ALL MY FATHER'S RETAINERS AND FRIENDS... REALLY IT'S A CHANCE TO INTRODUCE THEIR DAUGHTERS AND HOPE I FALL MADLY IN LOVE.
THIS ONE YOUNG LADY, BEAUTIFUL, VERY PRIM, VERY MODEST. I'M TELLING A STORY AND SHE LOOKS UTTERLY CAPTIVATED, AND I START TO WONDER IF I'VE GOT SOMETHING IN MY HAIR OR SOMETHING AND I GLANCE OVER MY SHOULDER, AND THERE'S...
WELL, THERE, THREE TIMES LIFE SIZE, IS A MARBLE...
AND SHE REALIZES THAT I'VE NOTICED AND WE CAN'T REMEMBER WHAT WE WERE TALKING ABOUT.
WHAT WERE WE TALKING ABOUT?

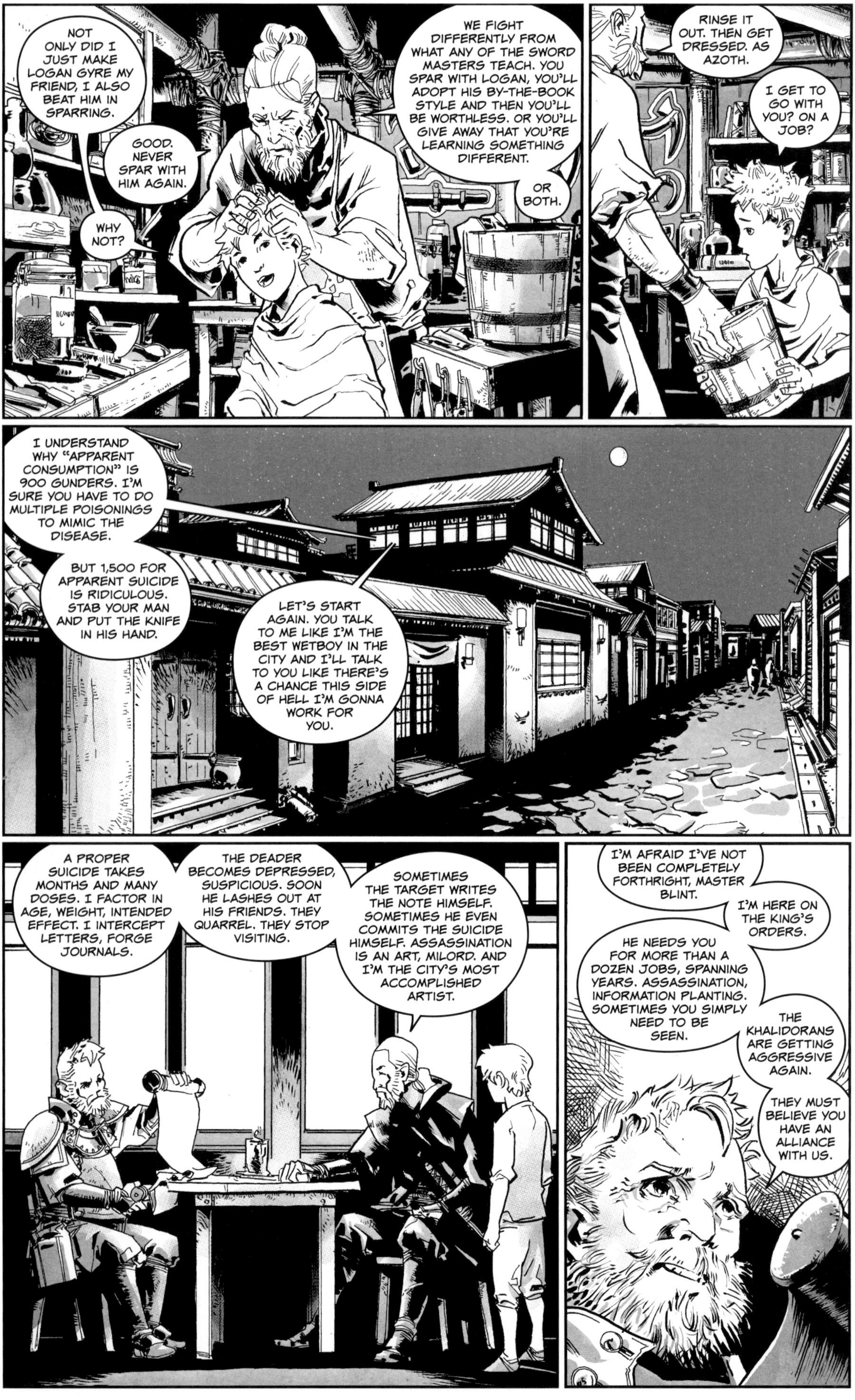
NOT ONLY DID I JUST MAKE LOGAN GYRE MY FRIEND, I ALSO BEAT HIM IN SPARRING.
GOOD. NEVER SPAR WITH HIM AGAIN.
WHY NOT?
WE FIGHT DIFFERENTLY FROM WHAT ANY OF THE SWORD MASTERS TEACH. YOU SPAR WITH LOGAN, YOU'LL ADOPT HIS BY-THE-BOOK STYLE AND THEN YOU'LL BE WORTHLESS. OR YOU'LL GIVE AWAY THAT YOU'RE LEARNING SOMETHING DIFFERENT.
OR BOTH.
RINSE IT OUT. THEN GET DRESSED. AS AZOTH.
I GET TO GO WITH YOU? ON A JOB?
I UNDERSTAND WHY "APPARENT CONSUMPTION" IS 900 GUNDERS. I'M SURE YOU HAVE TO DO MULTIPLE POISONINGS TO MIMIC THE DISEASE.
BUT 1,500 FOR APPARENT SUICIDE IS RIDICULOUS. STAB YOUR MAN AND PUT THE KNIFE IN HIS HAND.
LET'S START AGAIN. YOU TALK TO ME LIKE I'M THE BEST WETBOY IN THE CITY AND I'LL TALK TO YOU LIKE THERE'S A CHANCE THIS SIDE OF HELL I'M GONNA WORK FOR YOU.
A PROPER SUICIDE TAKES MONTHS AND MANY DOSES. I FACTOR IN AGE, WEIGHT, INTENDED EFFECT. I INTERCEPT LETTERS, FORGE JOURNALS.
THE DEADER BECOMES DEPRESSED, SUSPICIOUS. SOON HE LASHES OUT AT HIS FRIENDS. THEY QUARREL. THEY STOP VISITING.
SOMETIMES THE TARGET WRITES THE NOTE HIMSELF. SOMETIMES HE EVEN COMMITS THE SUICIDE HIMSELF. ASSASSINATION IS AN ART, MILORD. AND I'M THE CITY'S MOST ACCOMPLISHED ARTIST.
I'M AFRAID I'VE NOT BEEN COMPLETELY FORTHRIGHT, MASTER BLINT.
I'M HERE ON THE KING'S ORDERS.
HE NEEDS YOU FOR MORE THAN A DOZEN JOBS, SPANNING YEARS. ASSASSINATION, INFORMATION PLANTING. SOMETIMES YOU SIMPLY NEED TO BE SEEN.
THE KHALIDORANS ARE GETTING AGGRESSIVE AGAIN.
THEY MUST BELIEVE YOU HAVE AN ALLIANCE WITH US.

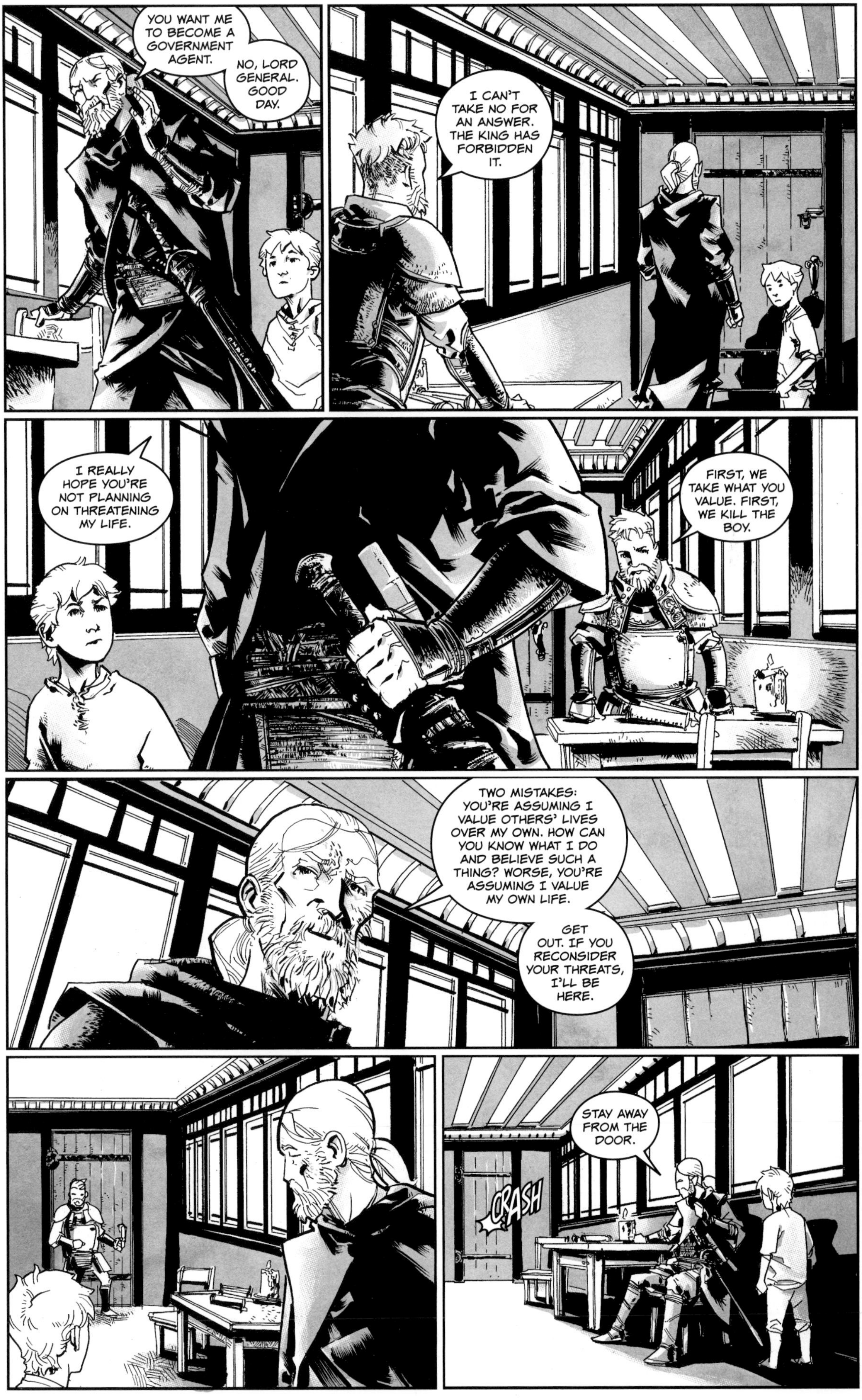
YOU WANT ME TO BECOME A GOVERNMENT AGENT.
NO, LORD GENERAL. GOOD DAY.
I CAN'T TAKE NO FOR AN ANSWER. THE KING HAS FORBIDDEN IT.
I REALLY HOPE YOU'RE NOT PLANNING ON THREATENING MY LIFE.
FIRST, WE TAKE WHAT YOU VALUE. FIRST, WE KILL THE BOY.
TWO MISTAKES: YOU'RE ASSUMING I VALUE OTHERS' LIVES OVER MY OWN. HOW CAN YOU KNOW WHAT I DO AND BELIEVE SUCH A THING? WORSE, YOU'RE ASSUMING I VALUE MY OWN LIFE.
GET OUT. IF YOU RECONSIDER YOUR THREATS, I'LL BE HERE.
STAY AWAY FROM THE DOOR.
CRASH

WHAT... HAVE... YOU...

SLAM

CONTACT POISON ON THE DOOR LATCH. IF WE'D MADE A DEAL, I'D HAVE OPENED THE DOOR IT FOR YOU.

I WANT YOU TO LISTEN TO ME CLOSELY.

YOUR KING'S AN INCOMPETENT, TREACHEROUS, FOUL-MOUTHED CHILD, SO I'M GOING TO MAKE THIS VERY CLEAR. I'M A FIRST-RATE WETBOY. HE'S A SECOND-RATE KING.

I'LL NEVER WORK FOR HIM. IF YOU WANT, YOU CAN HIRE ME YOURSELF: I'LL KILL THE KING, BUT I WON'T KILL FOR HIM.

THERE'S NO WAY YOU OR HE CAN PRESSURE ME. I KNOW HE WON'T BELIEVE THAT, BECAUSE ALEINE GUNDER BELIEVES HE CAN GET WHATEVER HE WANTS.

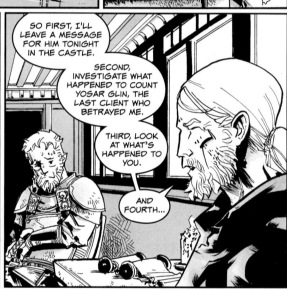

SO FIRST, I'LL LEAVE A MESSAGE FOR HIM TONIGHT IN THE CASTLE.

SECOND, INVESTIGATE WHAT HAPPENED TO COUNT YOSAR GLIN, THE LAST CLIENT WHO BETRAYED ME.

THIRD, LOOK AT WHAT'S HAPPENED TO YOU.

AND FOURTH...

LORD GENERAL, I DON'T CARE WHO HE KILLS. I KNOW THIS PLACE IS SURROUNDED. I KNOW YOU HAVE CROSSSBOWS COVERING THE WINDOWS OF THIS ROOM. THEY DON'T MATTER.

CLINK

AZOTH HERE IS MY BEST APPRENTICE. AGILE, SMART. HE LEARNS FAST, WORKS TIRELESSLY.

AZOTH, TELL THE GENERAL WHAT YOU'VE LEARNED ABOUT LIFE.

AZOTH WONDERS WHY DURZO HAS TOLD THE GENERAL HIS NAME.

LIFE IS EMPTY. LIFE IS MEANINGLESS. WHEN WE TAKE A LIFE, WE AREN'T TAKING ANYTHING OF VALUE.

WETBOYS ARE KILLERS. THAT'S ALL WE DO. THAT'S ALL WE ARE.

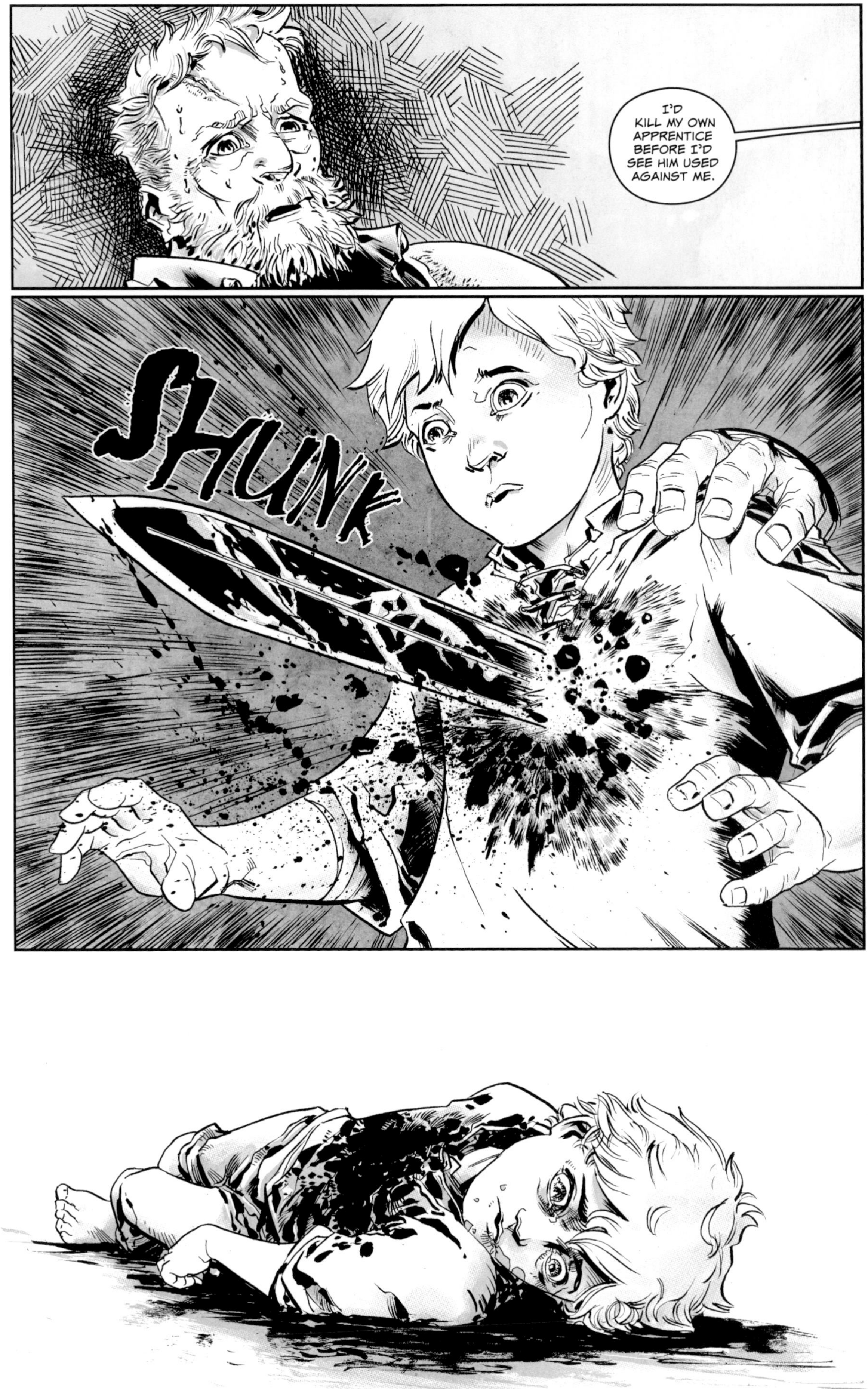
I'D KILL MY OWN APPRENTICE BEFORE I'D SEE HIM USED AGAINST ME.
SHUNK

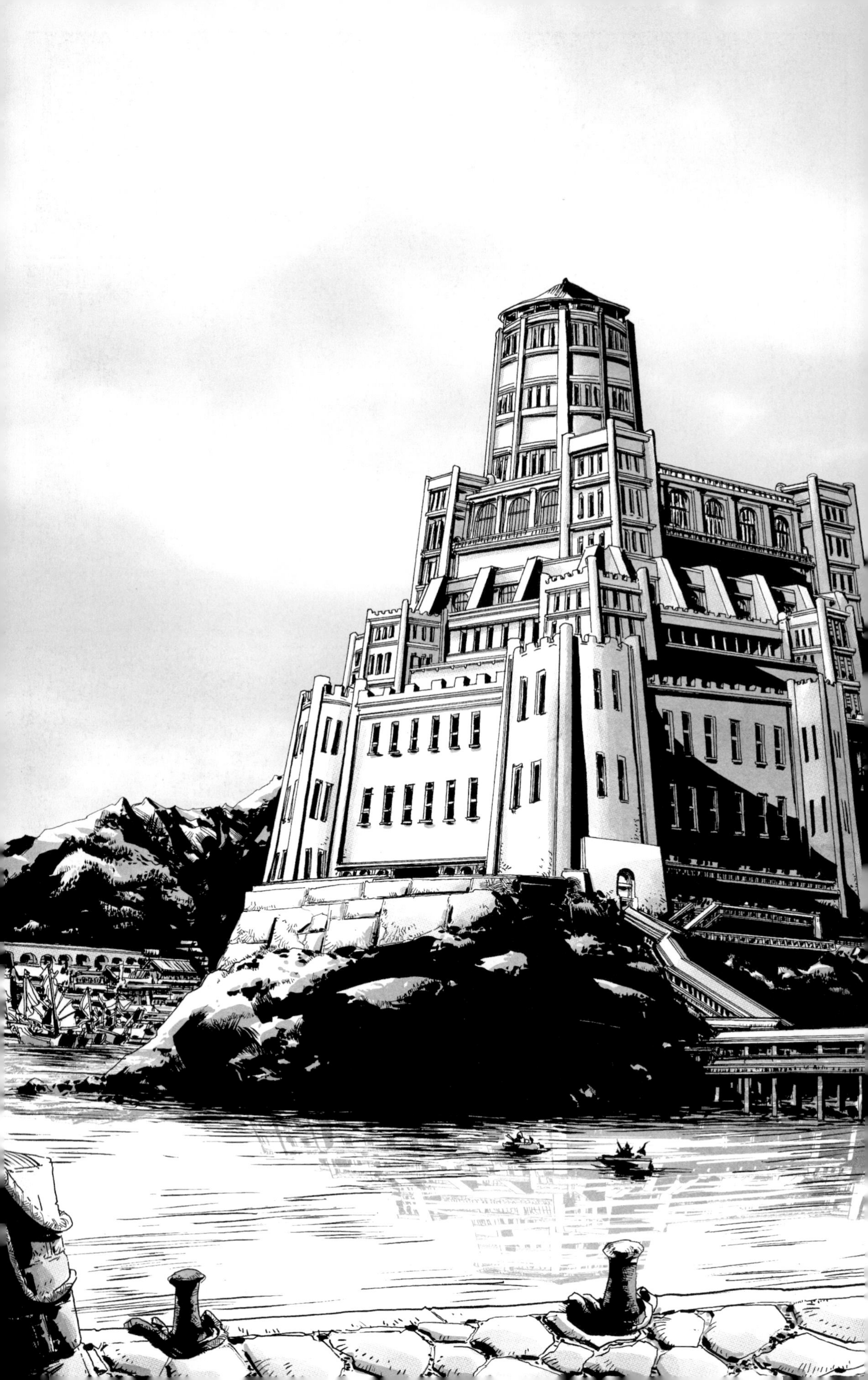

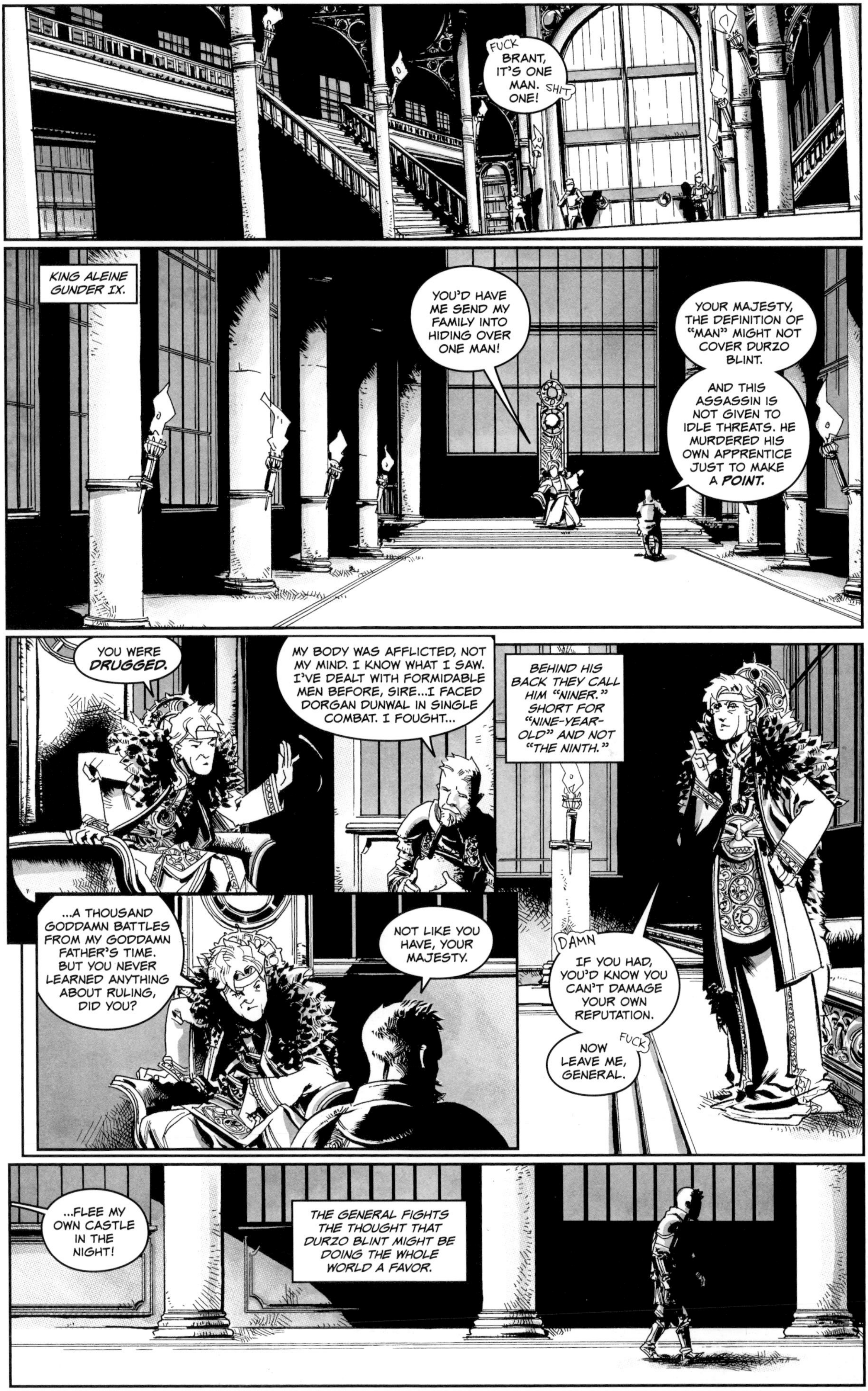
FUCK
BRANT, IT'S ONE MAN. ONE!
SHIT
KING ALEINE GUNDER IX.
YOU'D HAVE ME SEND MY FAMILY INTO HIDING OVER ONE MAN!
YOUR MAJESTY, THE DEFINITION OF "MAN" MIGHT NOT COVER DURZO BLINT.
AND THIS ASSASSIN IS NOT GIVEN TO IDLE THREATS. HE MURDERED HIS OWN APPRENTICE JUST TO MAKE A POINT.
YOU WERE DRUGGED.
MY BODY WAS AFFLICTED, NOT MY MIND. I KNOW WHAT I SAW. I'VE DEALT WITH FORMIDABLE MEN BEFORE, SIRE...I FACED DORGAN DUNWAL IN SINGLE COMBAT. I FOUGHT...
BEHIND HIS BACK THEY CALL HIM "NINER." SHORT FOR "NINE-YEAR-OLD" AND NOT "THE NINTH."
...A THOUSAND GODDAMN BATTLES FROM MY GODDAMN FATHER'S TIME. BUT YOU NEVER LEARNED ANYTHING ABOUT RULING, DID YOU?
NOT LIKE YOU HAVE, YOUR MAJESTY.
DAMN
IF YOU HAD, YOU'D KNOW YOU CAN'T DAMAGE YOUR OWN REPUTATION.
FUCK
NOW LEAVE ME, GENERAL.
...FLEE MY OWN CASTLE IN THE NIGHT!
THE GENERAL FIGHTS THE THOUGHT THAT DURZO BLINT MIGHT BE DOING THE WHOLE WORLD A FAVOR.

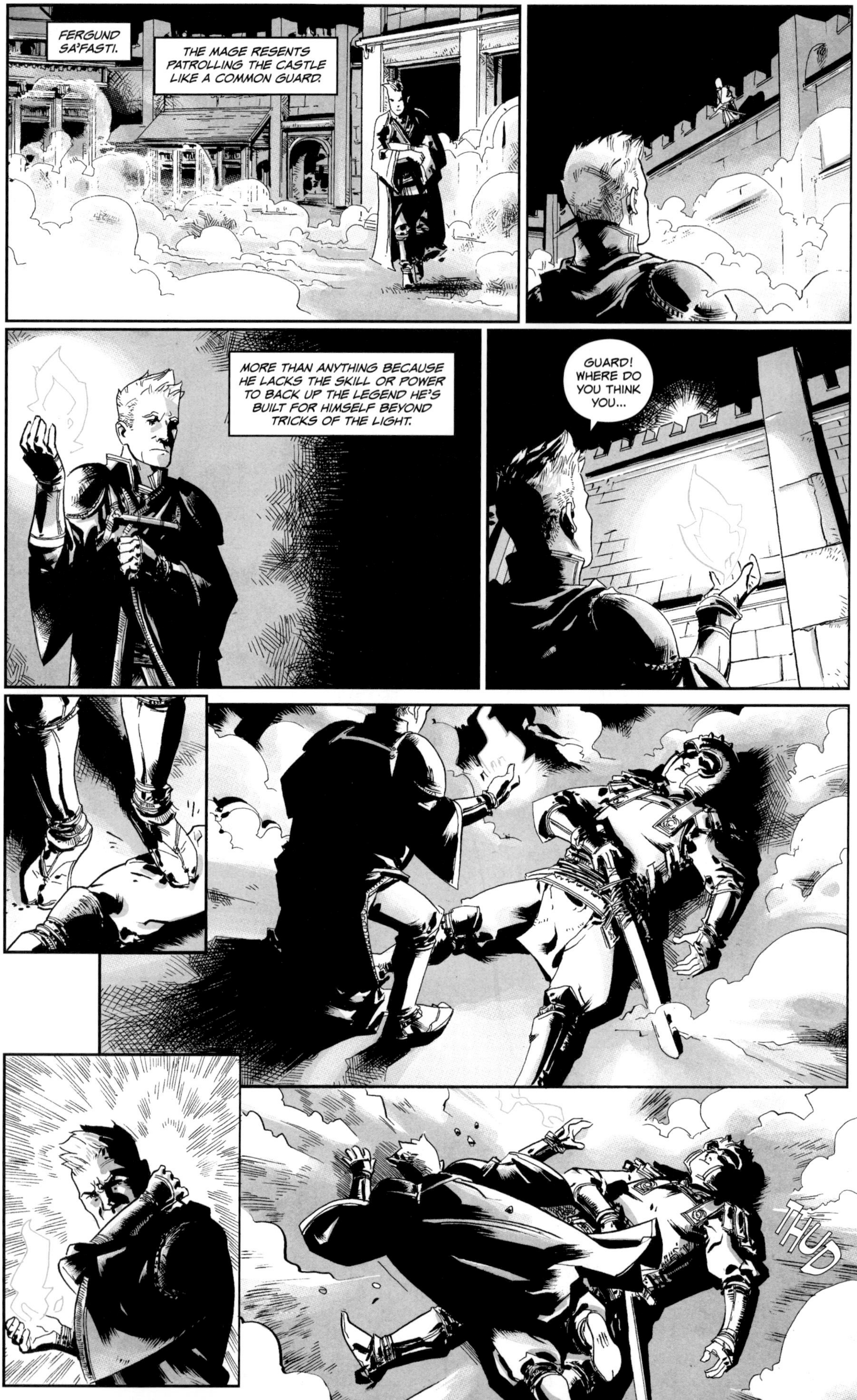
FERGUND SA'FASTI.
THE MAGE RESENTS PATROLLING THE CASTLE LIKE A COMMON GUARD.
MORE THAN ANYTHING BECAUSE HE LACKS THE SKILL OR POWER TO BACK UP THE LEGEND HE'S BUILT FOR HIMSELF BEYOND TRICKS OF THE LIGHT.
GUARD! WHERE DO YOU THINK YOU...
THUD

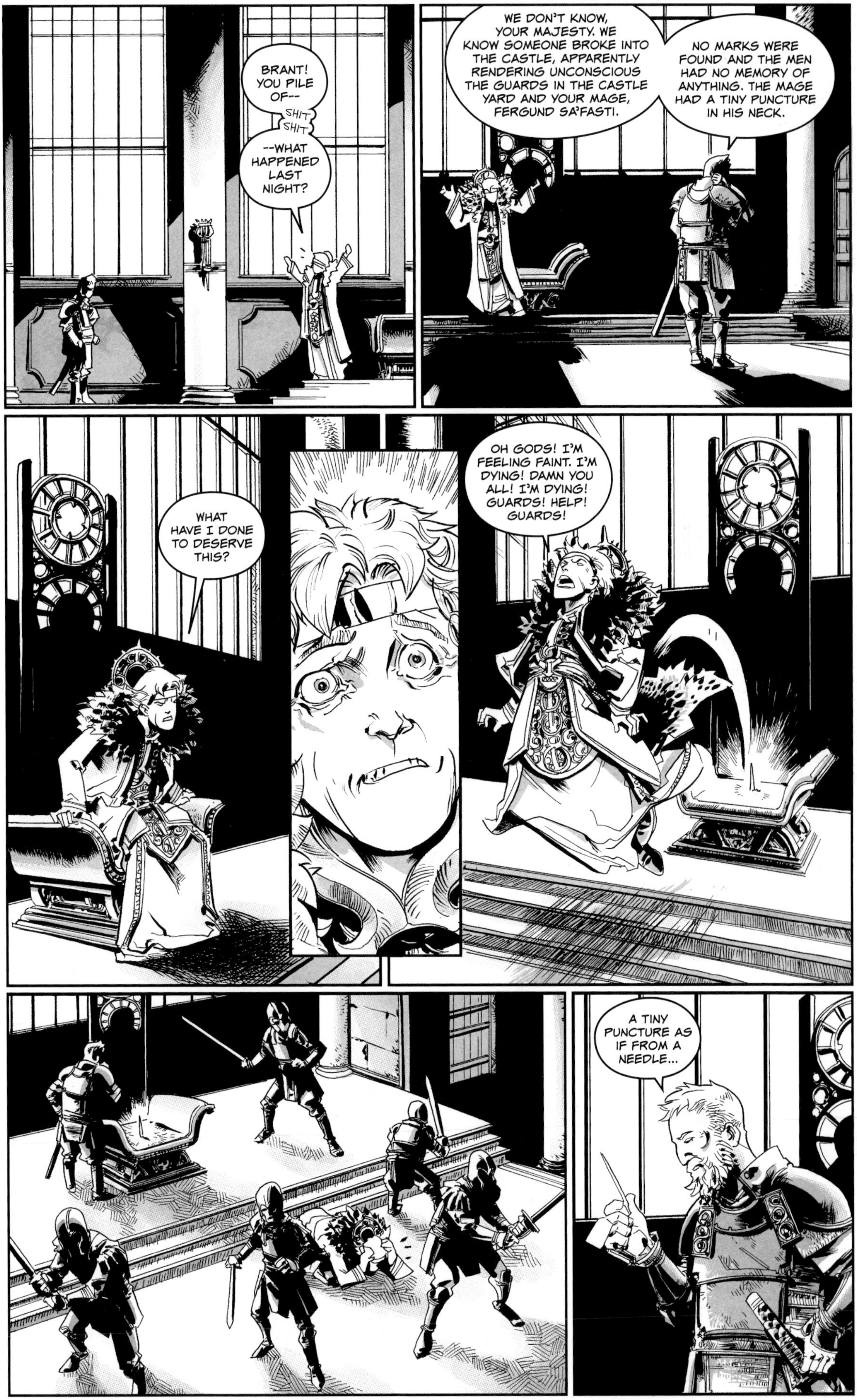
BRANT! YOU PILE OF--
SHIT SHIT
--WHAT HAPPENED LAST NIGHT?
WE DON'T KNOW, YOUR MAJESTY. WE KNOW SOMEONE BROKE INTO THE CASTLE, APPARENTLY RENDERING UNCONSCIOUS THE GUARDS IN THE CASTLE YARD AND YOUR MAGE, FERGUND SA'FASTI.
NO MARKS WERE FOUND AND THE MEN HAD NO MEMORY OF ANYTHING. THE MAGE HAD A TINY PUNCTURE IN HIS NECK.
WHAT HAVE I DONE TO DESERVE THIS?
OH GODS! I'M FEELING FAINT. I'M DYING! DAMN YOU ALL! I'M DYING! GUARDS! HELP! GUARDS!
A TINY PUNCTURE AS IF FROM A NEEDLE...

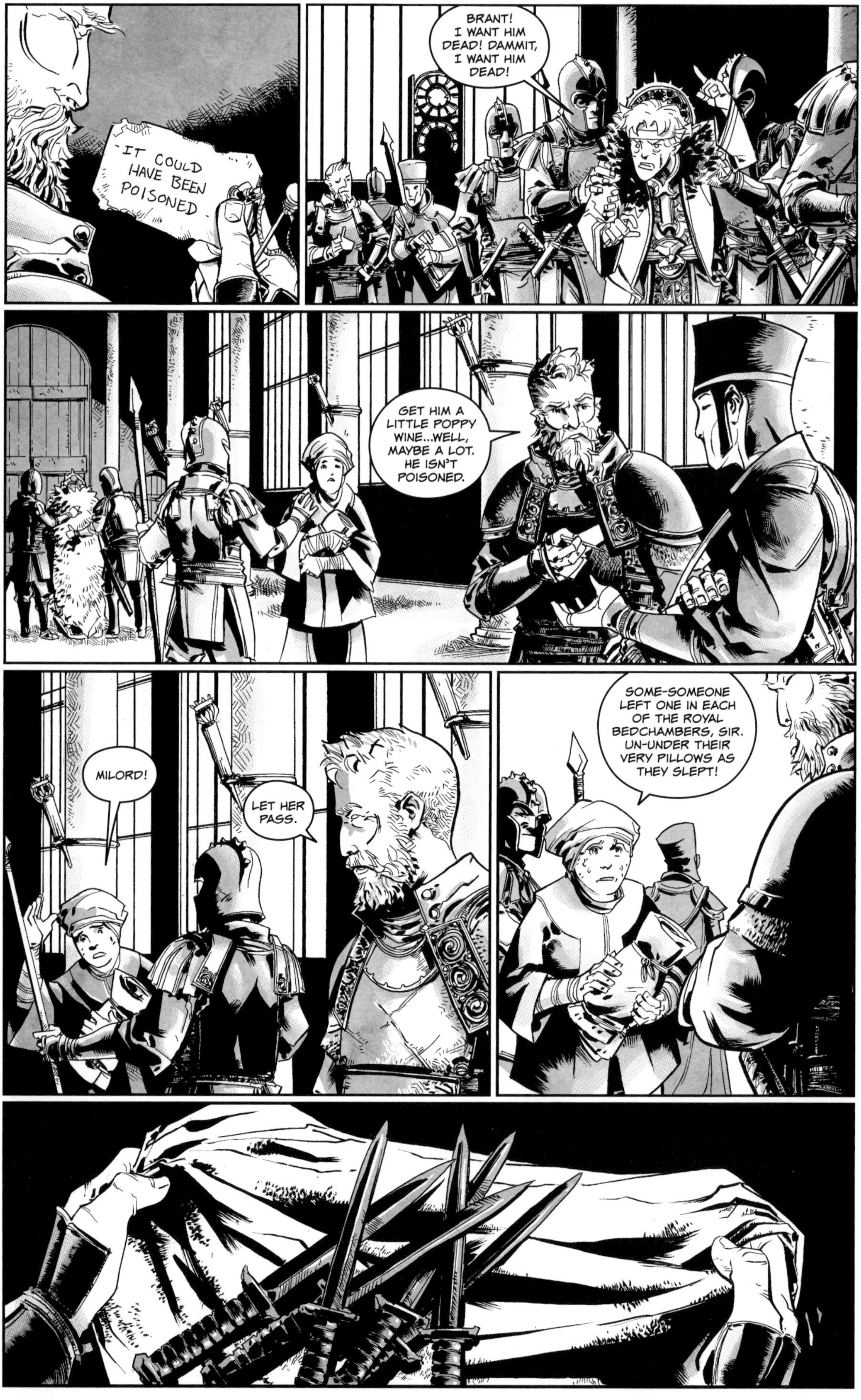
-IT COULD HAVE BEEN POISONED-
BRANT! I WANT HIM DEAD! DAMMIT, I WANT HIM DEAD!
GET HIM A LITTLE POPPY WINE...WELL, MAYBE A LOT. HE ISN'T POISONED.
MILORD!
LET HER PASS.
SOME-SOMEONE LEFT ONE IN EACH OF THE ROYAL BEDCHAMBERS, SIR. UN-UNDER THEIR VERY PILLOWS AS THEY SLEPT!

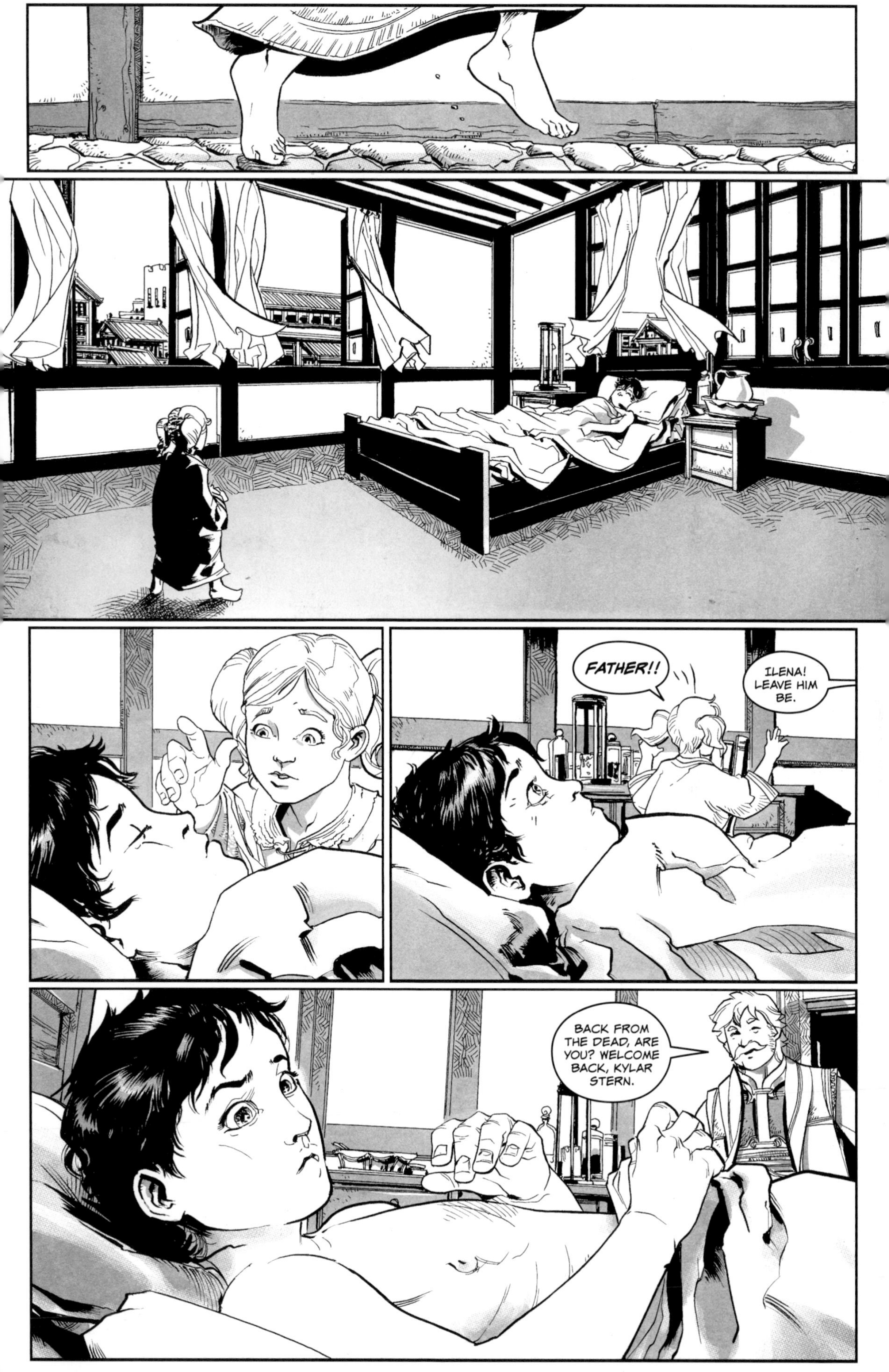
FATHER!!
ILENA! LEAVE HIM BE.
BACK FROM THE DEAD, ARE YOU? WELCOME BACK, KYLAR STERN.

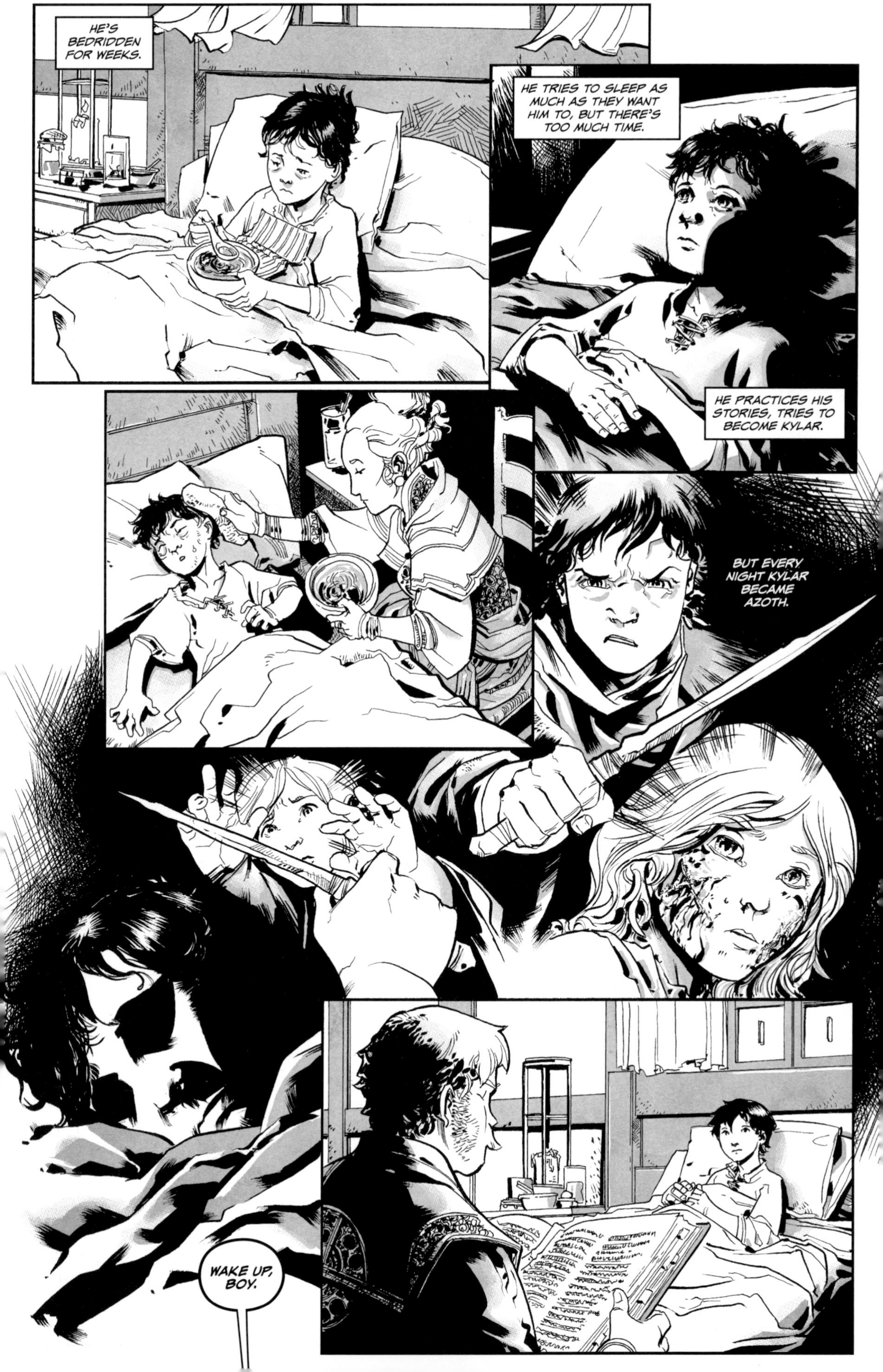
HE'S BEDRIDDEN FOR WEEKS.
HE TRIES TO SLEEP AS MUCH AS THEY WANT HIM TO, BUT THERE'S TOO MUCH TIME.
HE PRACTICES HIS STORIES, TRIES TO BECOME KYLAR.
BUT EVERY NIGHT KYLAR BECAME AZOTH.
WAKE UP, BOY.

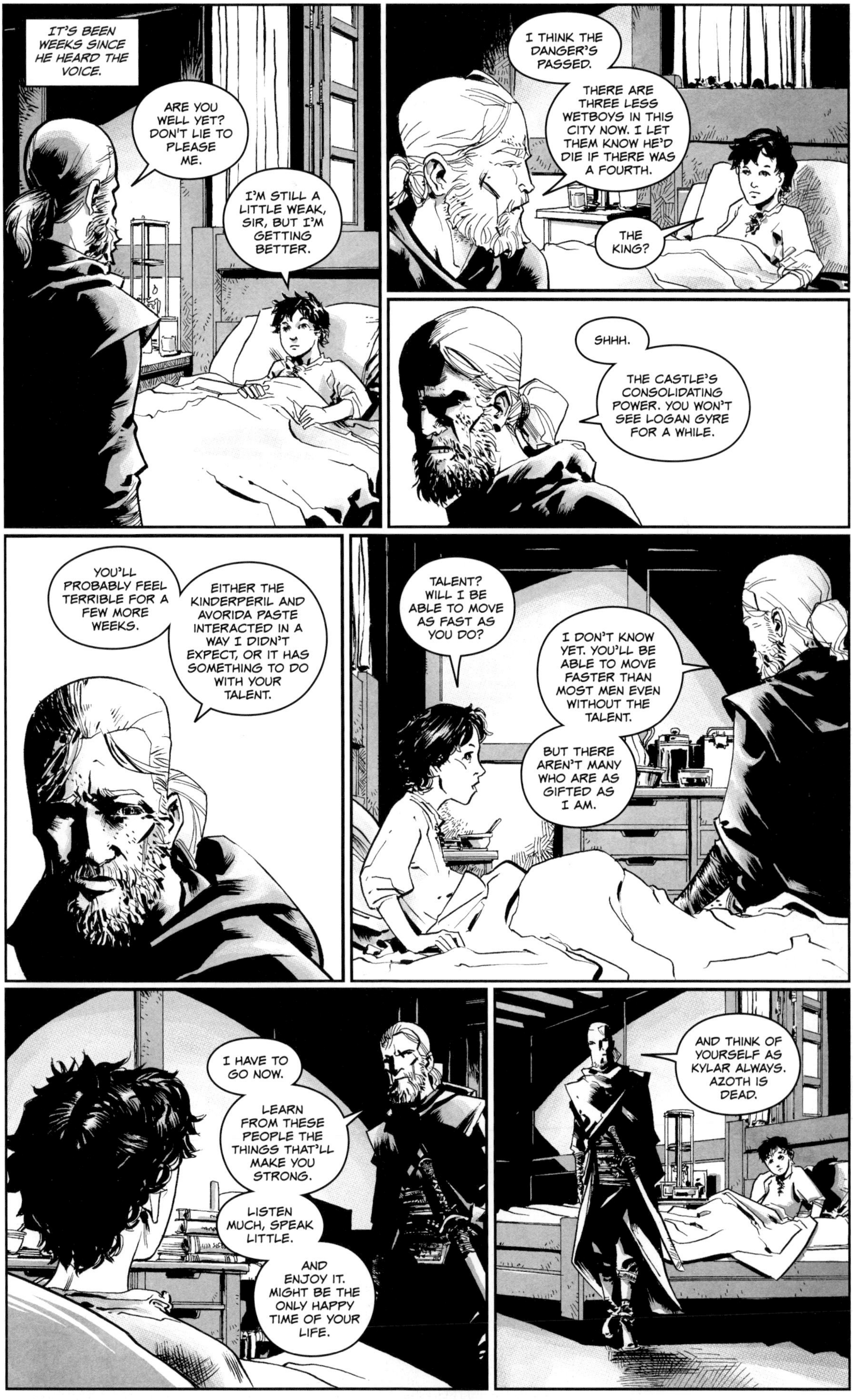
IT'S BEEN WEEKS SINCE HE HEARD THE VOICE.
ARE YOU WELL YET? DON'T LIE TO PLEASE ME.
I'M STILL A LITTLE WEAK, SIR, BUT I'M GETTING BETTER.
I THINK THE DANGER'S PASSED.
THERE ARE THREE LESS WETBOYS IN THIS CITY NOW. I LET THEM KNOW HE'D DIE IF THERE WAS A FOURTH.
THE KING?
SHHH.
THE CASTLE'S CONSOLIDATING POWER. YOU WON'T SEE LOGAN GYRE FOR A WHILE.
YOU'LL PROBABLY FEEL TERRIBLE FOR A FEW MORE WEEKS.
EITHER THE KINDERPERIL AND AVORIDA PASTE INTERACTED IN A WAY I DIDN'T EXPECT, OR IT HAS SOMETHING TO DO WITH YOUR TALENT.
TALENT? WILL I BE ABLE TO MOVE AS FAST AS YOU DO?
I DON'T KNOW YET. YOU'LL BE ABLE TO MOVE FASTER THAN MOST MEN EVEN WITHOUT THE TALENT.
BUT THERE AREN'T MANY WHO ARE AS GIFTED AS I AM.
I HAVE TO GO NOW.
LEARN FROM THESE PEOPLE THE THINGS THAT'LL MAKE YOU STRONG.
LISTEN MUCH, SPEAK LITTLE.
AND ENJOY IT. MIGHT BE THE ONLY HAPPY TIME OF YOUR LIFE.
AND THINK OF YOURSELF AS KYLAR ALWAYS. AZOTH IS DEAD.

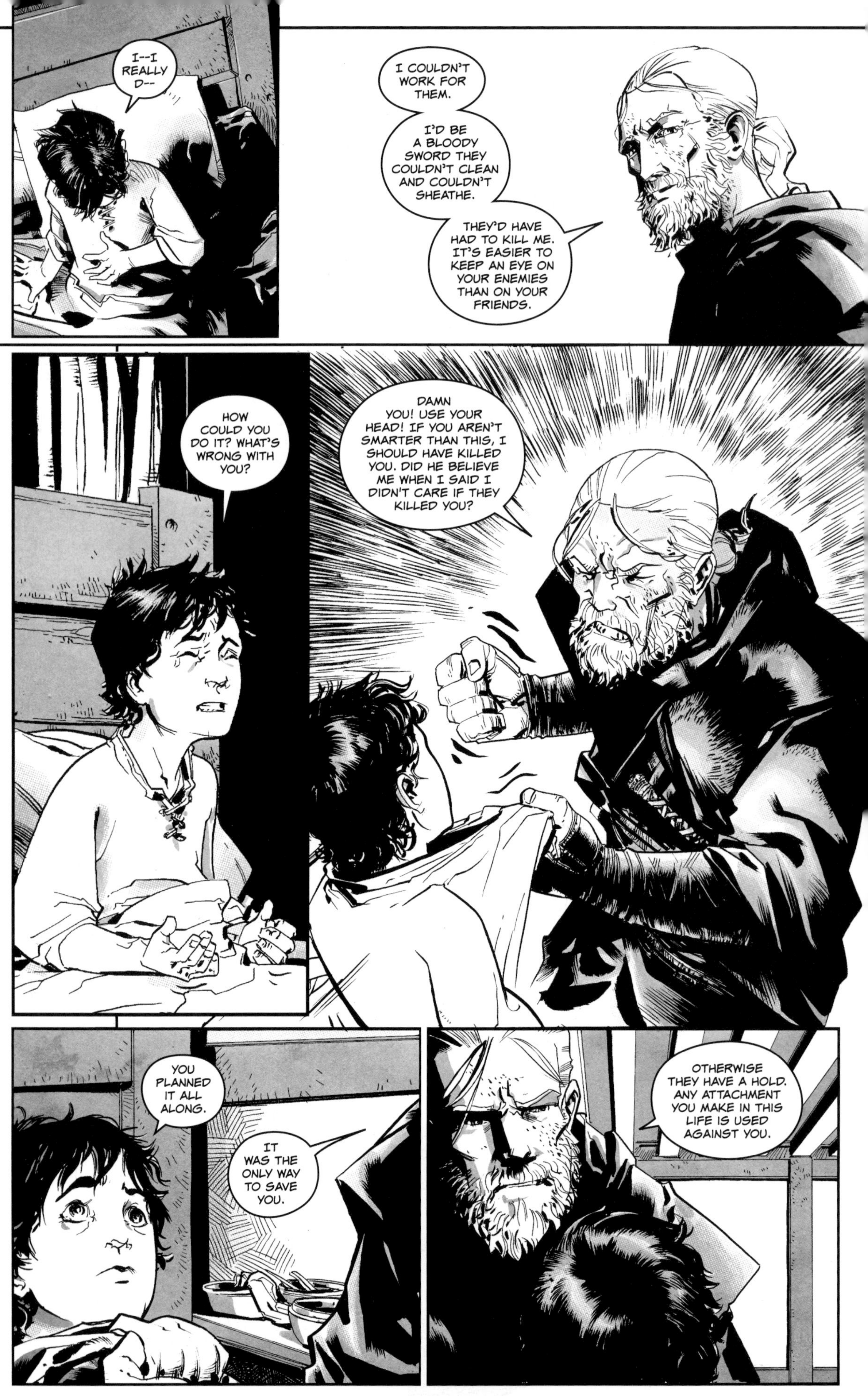
I--I REALLY D--
I COULDN'T WORK FOR THEM.
I'D BE A BLOODY SWORD THEY COULDN'T CLEAN AND COULDN'T SHEATHE.
THEY'D HAVE HAD TO KILL ME. IT'S EASIER TO KEEP AN EYE ON YOUR ENEMIES THAN ON YOUR FRIENDS.
HOW COULD YOU DO IT? WHAT'S WRONG WITH YOU?
DAMN YOU! USE YOUR HEAD! IF YOU AREN'T SMARTER THAN THIS, I SHOULD HAVE KILLED YOU. DID HE BELIEVE ME WHEN I SAID I DIDN'T CARE IF THEY KILLED YOU?
YOU PLANNED IT ALL ALONG.
IT WAS THE ONLY WAY TO SAVE YOU.
OTHERWISE THEY HAVE A HOLD. ANY ATTACHMENT YOU MAKE IN THIS LIFE IS USED AGAINST YOU.

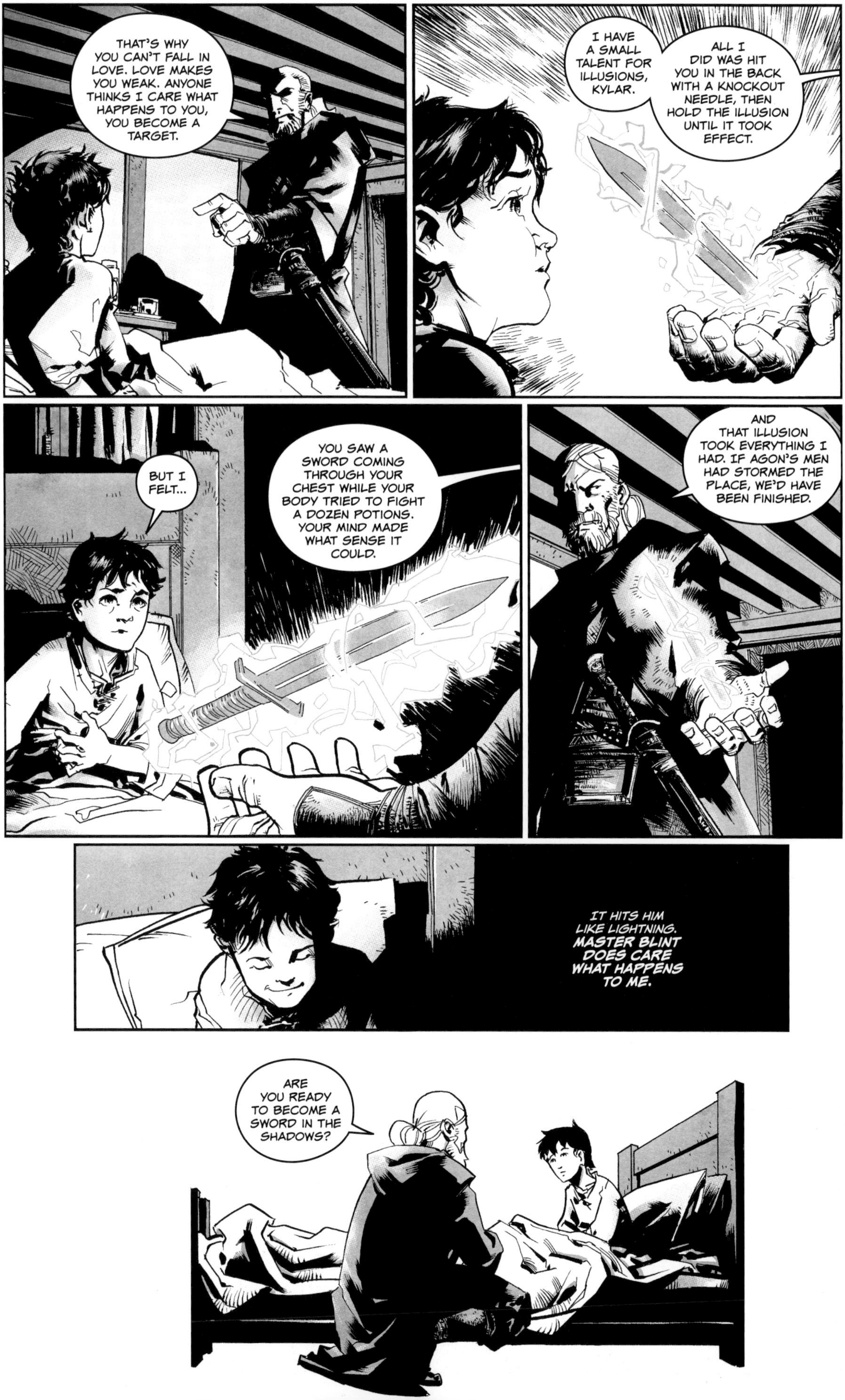
THAT'S WHY YOU CAN'T FALL IN LOVE. LOVE MAKES YOU WEAK. ANYONE THINKS I CARE WHAT HAPPENS TO YOU, YOU BECOME A TARGET.
I HAVE A SMALL TALENT FOR ILLUSIONS, KYLAR.
ALL I DID WAS HIT YOU IN THE BACK WITH A KNOCKOUT NEEDLE, THEN HOLD THE ILLUSION UNTIL IT TOOK EFFECT.
BUT I FELT...
YOU SAW A SWORD COMING THROUGH YOUR CHEST WHILE YOUR BODY TRIED TO FIGHT A DOZEN POTIONS. YOUR MIND MADE WHAT SENSE IT COULD.
AND THAT ILLUSION TOOK EVERYTHING I HAD. IF AGON'S MEN HAD STORMED THE PLACE, WE'D HAVE BEEN FINISHED.
IT HITS HIM LIKE LIGHTNING. MASTER BLINT DOES CARE WHAT HAPPENS TO ME.
ARE YOU READY TO BECOME A SWORD IN THE SHADOWS?

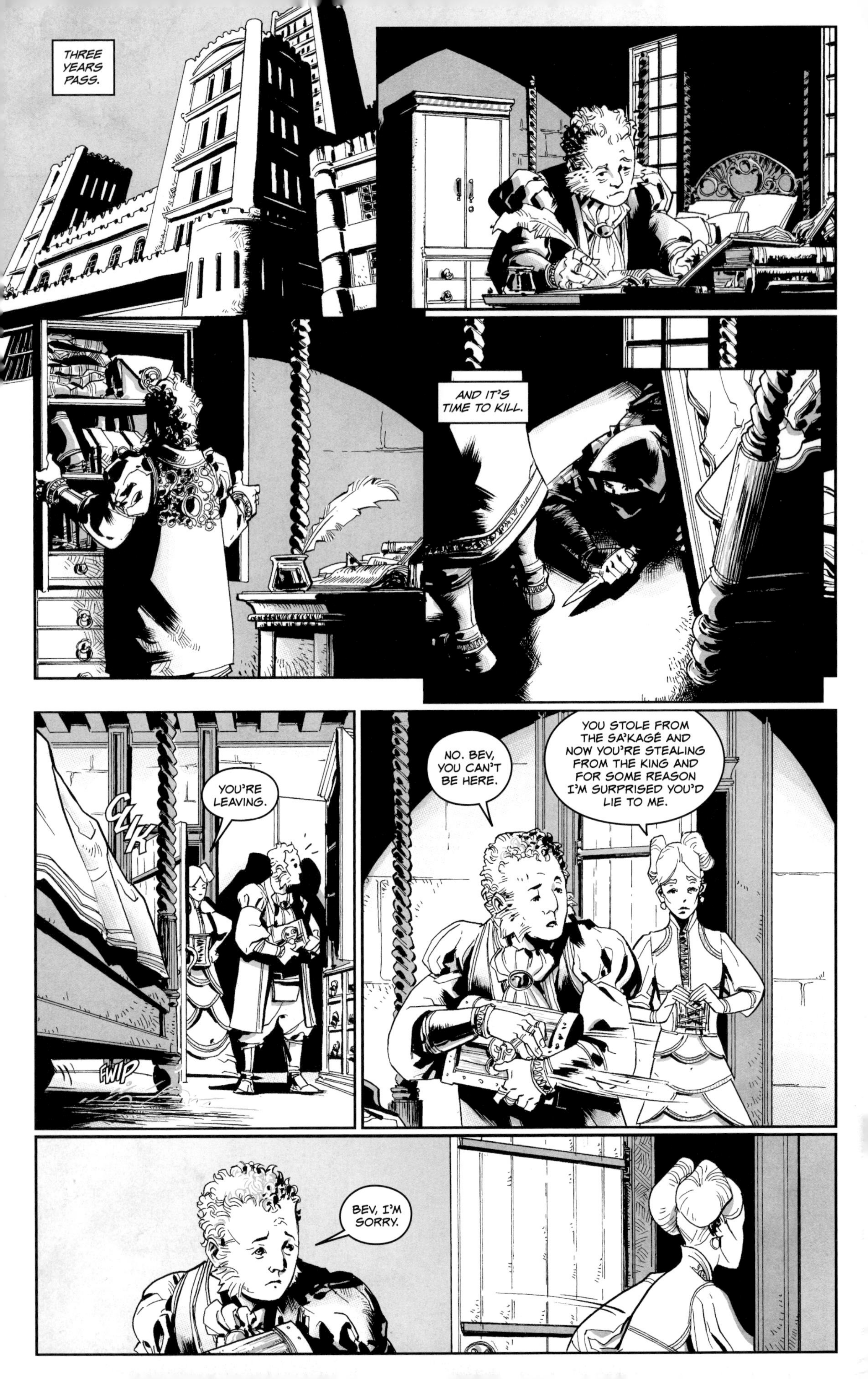
THREE YEARS PASS.
AND IT'S TIME TO KILL.
CLIK
FWIP
YOU'RE LEAVING.
NO. BEV, YOU CAN'T BE HERE.
YOU STOLE FROM THE SA'KAGÉ AND NOW YOU'RE STEALING FROM THE KING AND FOR SOME REASON I'M SURPRISED YOU'D LIE TO ME.
BEV, I'M SORRY.

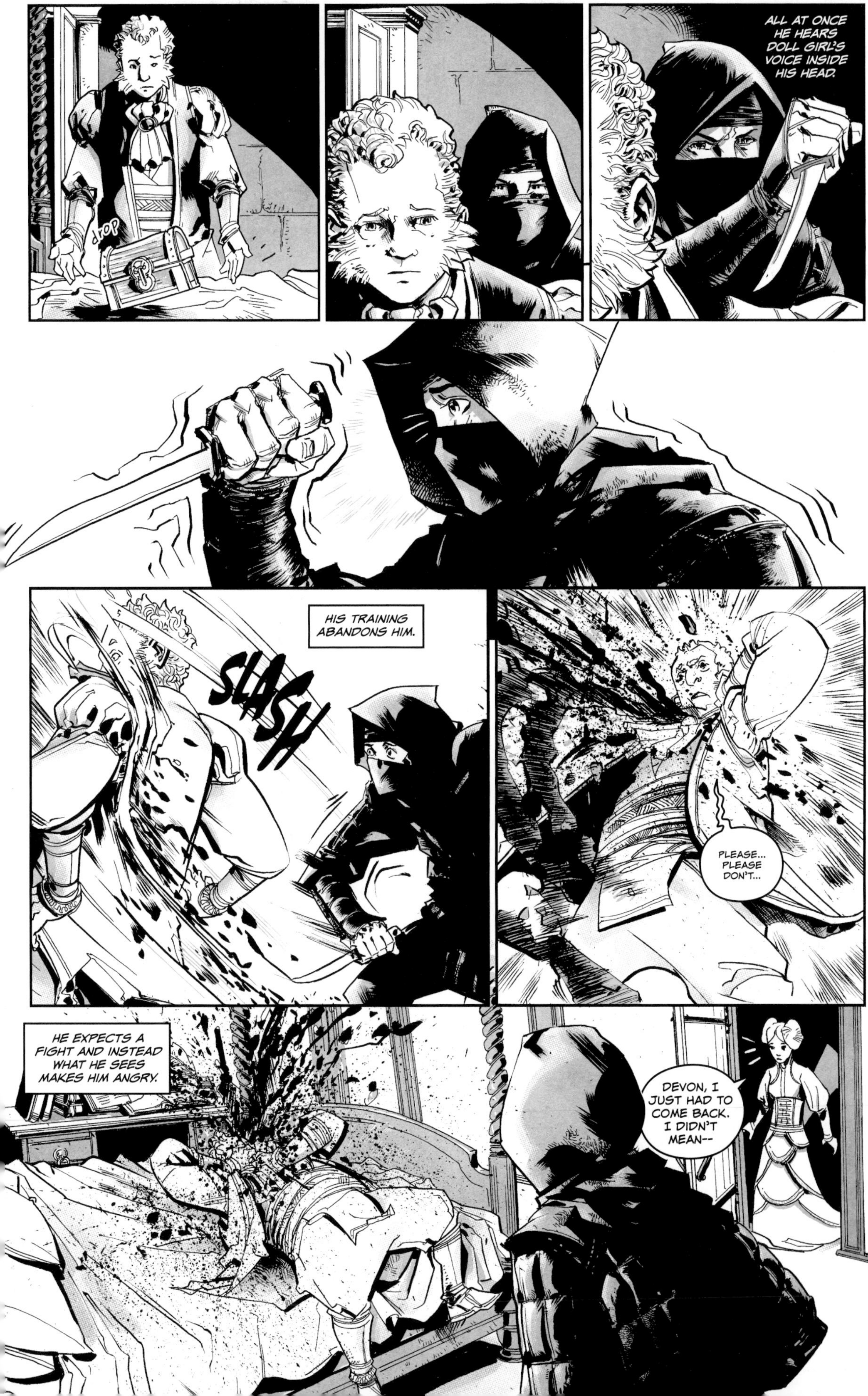
drop
ALL AT ONCE HE HEARS DOLL GIRL'S VOICE INSIDE HIS HEAD.
HIS TRAINING ABANDONS HIM.
SLASH
PLEASE... PLEASE DON'T...
HE EXPECTS A FIGHT AND INSTEAD WHAT HE SEES MAKES HIM ANGRY.
DEVON, I JUST HAD TO COME BACK. I DIDN'T MEAN--

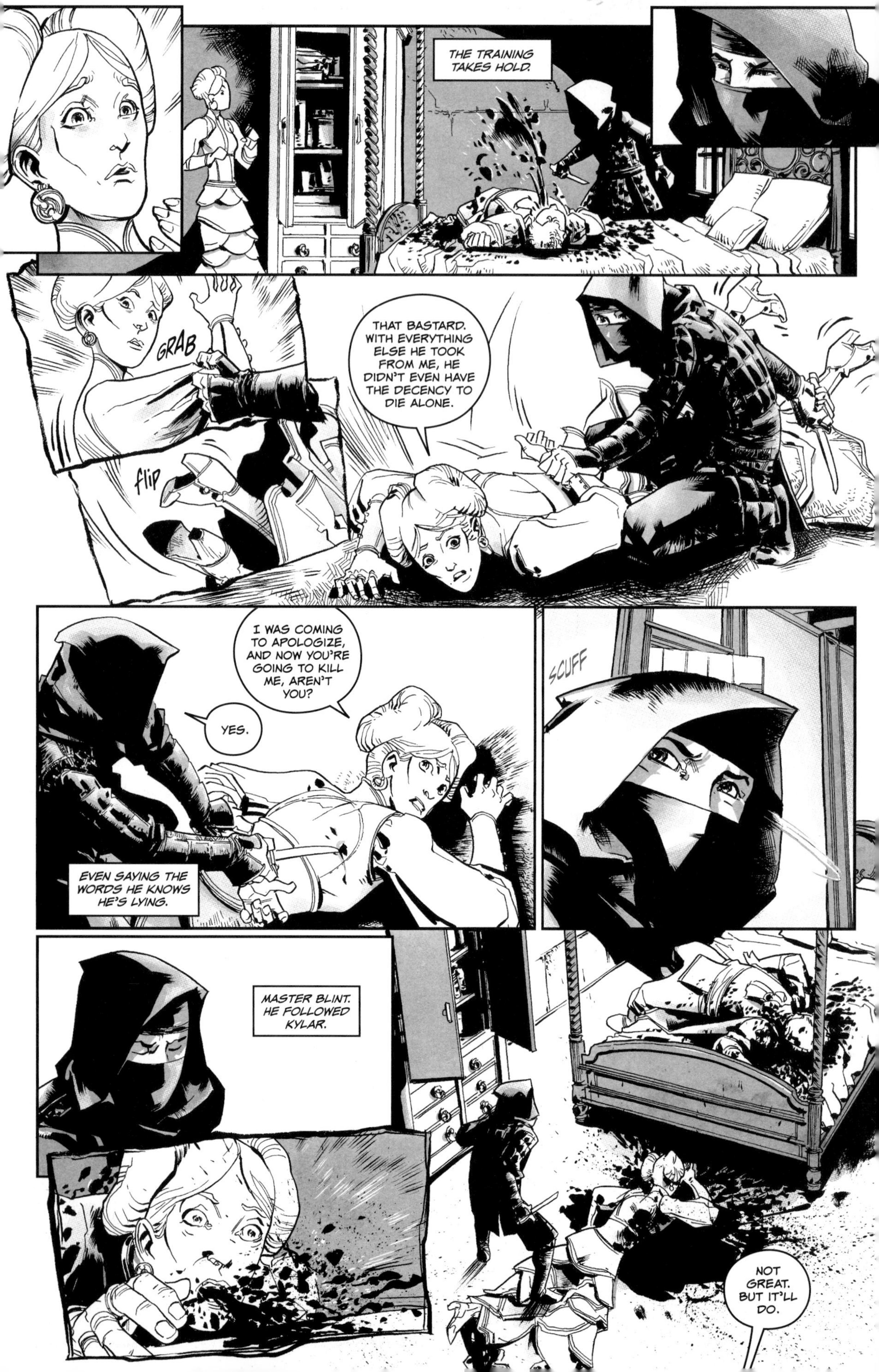
THE TRAINING TAKES HOLD.
GRAB
flip
THAT BASTARD. WITH EVERYTHING ELSE HE TOOK FROM ME, HE DIDN'T EVEN HAVE THE DECENCY TO DIE ALONE.
I WAS COMING TO APOLOGIZE, AND NOW YOU'RE GOING TO KILL ME, AREN'T YOU?
YES.
EVEN SAYING THE WORDS HE KNOWS HE'S LYING.
SCUFF
MASTER BLINT. HE FOLLOWED KYLAR.
NOT GREAT. BUT IT'LL DO.

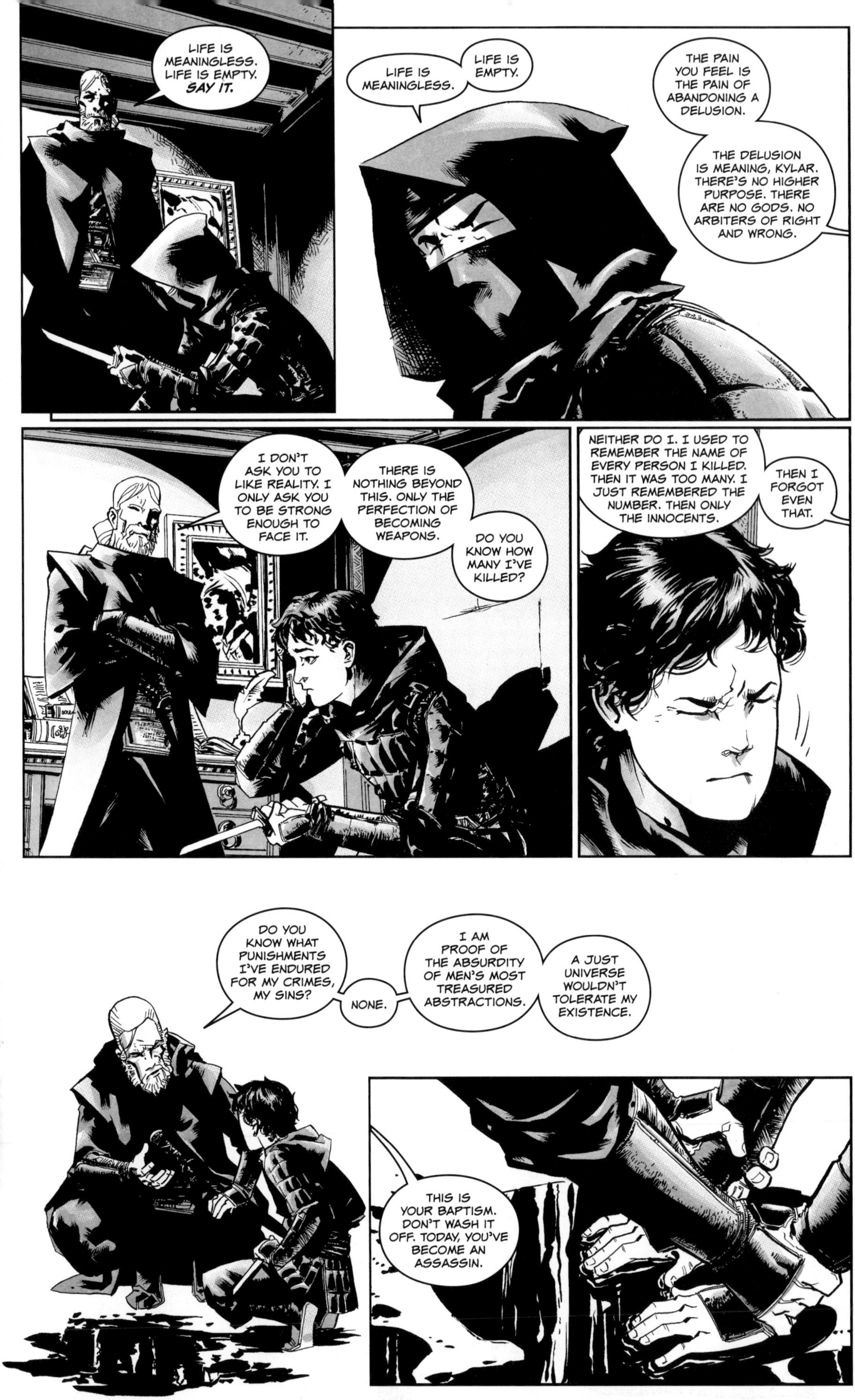
LIFE IS MEANINGLESS. LIFE IS EMPTY. *SAY IT.*
LIFE IS MEANINGLESS.
LIFE IS EMPTY.
THE PAIN YOU FEEL IS THE PAIN OF ABANDONING A DELUSION.
THE DELUSION IS MEANING, KYLAR. THERE'S NO HIGHER PURPOSE. THERE ARE NO GODS. NO ARBITERS OF RIGHT AND WRONG.
I DON'T ASK YOU TO LIKE REALITY. I ONLY ASK YOU TO BE STRONG ENOUGH TO FACE IT.
THERE IS NOTHING BEYOND THIS. ONLY THE PERFECTION OF BECOMING WEAPONS.
DO YOU KNOW HOW MANY I'VE KILLED?
NEITHER DO I. I USED TO REMEMBER THE NAME OF EVERY PERSON I KILLED. THEN IT WAS TOO MANY. I JUST REMEMBERED THE NUMBER. THEN ONLY THE INNOCENTS.
THEN I FORGOT EVEN THAT.
DO YOU KNOW WHAT PUNISHMENTS I'VE ENDURED FOR MY CRIMES, MY SINS?
NONE.
I AM PROOF OF THE ABSURDITY OF MEN'S MOST TREASURED ABSTRACTIONS.
A JUST UNIVERSE WOULDN'T TOLERATE MY EXISTENCE.
THIS IS YOUR BAPTISM. DON'T WASH IT OFF. TODAY, YOU'VE BECOME AN ASSASSIN.

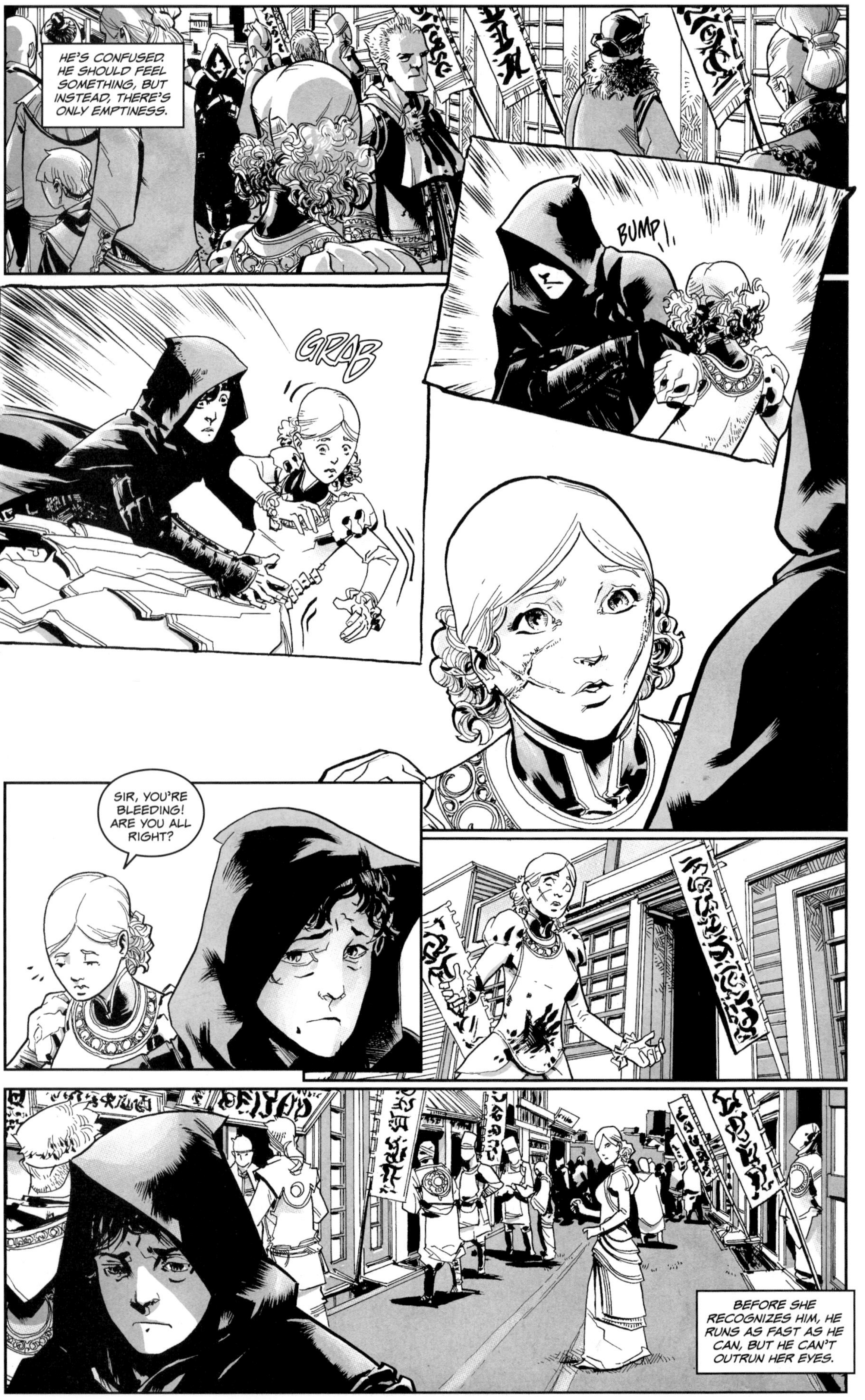
HE'S CONFUSED. HE SHOULD FEEL SOMETHING, BUT INSTEAD, THERE'S ONLY EMPTINESS.
BUMP
GRAB
SIR, YOU'RE BLEEDING! ARE YOU ALL RIGHT?
BEFORE SHE RECOGNIZES HIM, HE RUNS AS FAST AS HE CAN, BUT HE CAN'T OUTRUN HER EYES.

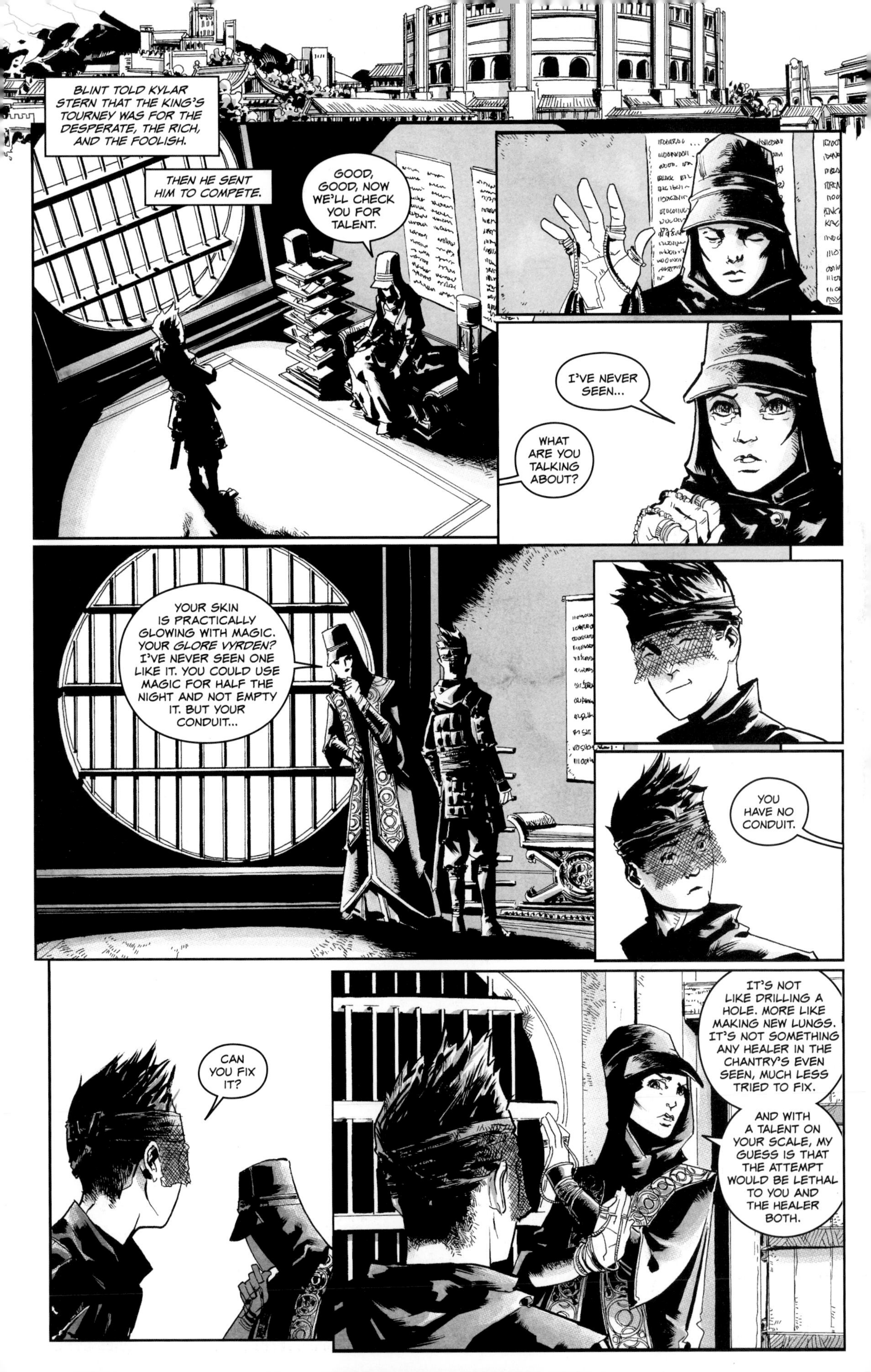
BLINT TOLD KYLAR STERN THAT THE KING'S TOURNEY WAS FOR THE DESPERATE, THE RICH, AND THE FOOLISH.
THEN HE SENT HIM TO COMPETE.
GOOD, GOOD, NOW WE'LL CHECK YOU FOR TALENT.
I'VE NEVER SEEN...
WHAT ARE YOU TALKING ABOUT?
YOUR SKIN IS PRACTICALLY GLOWING WITH MAGIC. YOUR GLORE VYRDEN? I'VE NEVER SEEN ONE LIKE IT. YOU COULD USE MAGIC FOR HALF THE NIGHT AND NOT EMPTY IT. BUT YOUR CONDUIT...
YOU HAVE NO CONDUIT.
CAN YOU FIX IT?
IT'S NOT LIKE DRILLING A HOLE. MORE LIKE MAKING NEW LUNGS. IT'S NOT SOMETHING ANY HEALER IN THE CHANTRY'S EVEN SEEN, MUCH LESS TRIED TO FIX.
AND WITH A TALENT ON YOUR SCALE, MY GUESS IS THAT THE ATTEMPT WOULD BE LETHAL TO YOU AND THE HEALER BOTH.

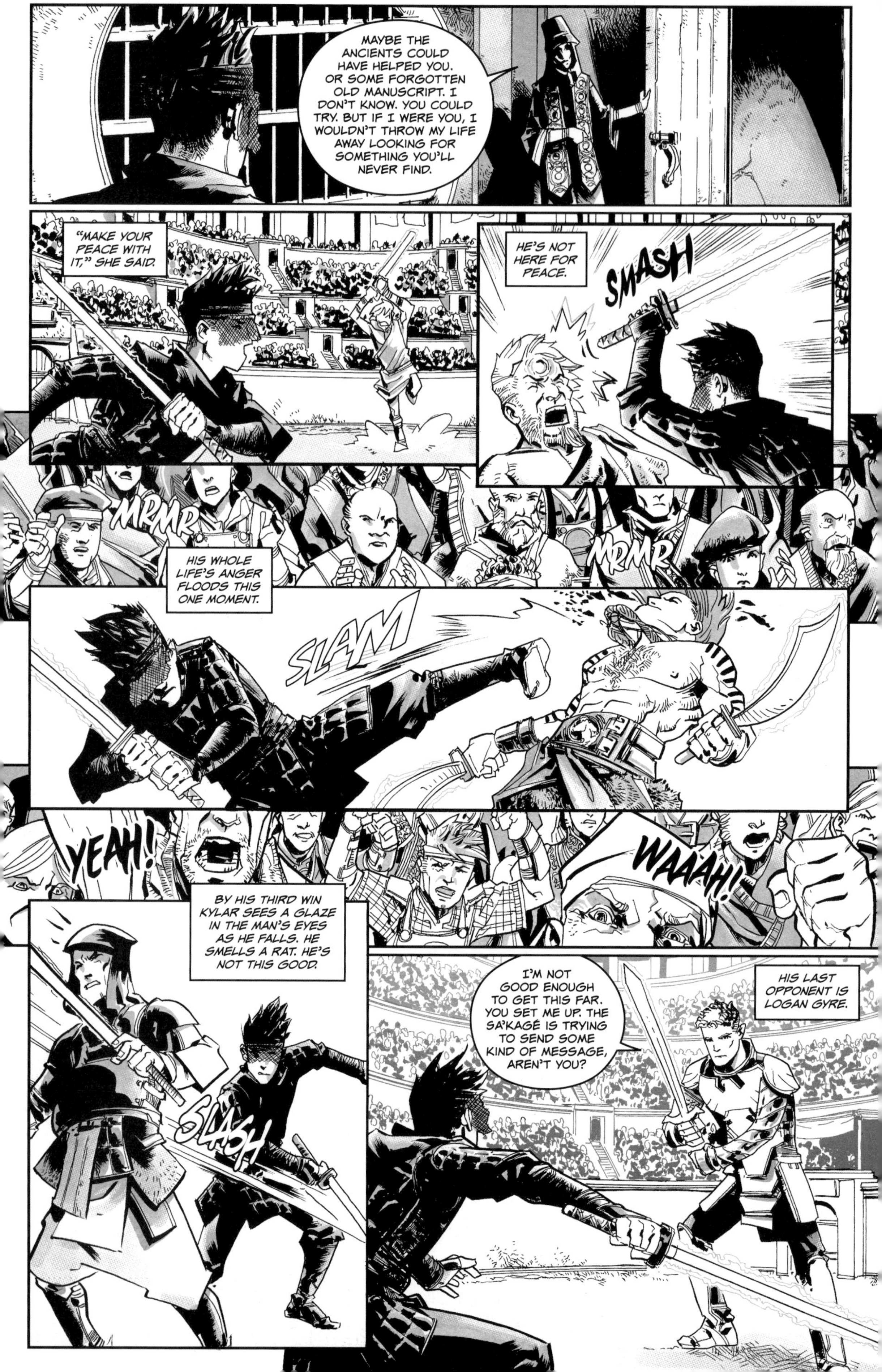
MAYBE THE ANCIENTS COULD HAVE HELPED YOU. OR SOME FORGOTTEN OLD MANUSCRIPT. I DON'T KNOW. YOU COULD TRY. BUT IF I WERE YOU, I WOULDN'T THROW MY LIFE AWAY LOOKING FOR SOMETHING YOU'LL NEVER FIND.
"MAKE YOUR PEACE WITH IT," SHE SAID.
HE'S NOT HERE FOR PEACE.
SMASH
MRMR
MRMR
HIS WHOLE LIFE'S ANGER FLOODS THIS ONE MOMENT.
SLAM
YEAH!
WAAAH!
BY HIS THIRD WIN KYLAR SEES A GLAZE IN THE MAN'S EYES AS HE FALLS. HE SMELLS A RAT. HE'S NOT THIS GOOD.
SLASH
I'M NOT GOOD ENOUGH TO GET THIS FAR. YOU SET ME UP. THE SA'KAGÉ IS TRYING TO SEND SOME KIND OF MESSAGE, AREN'T YOU?
HIS LAST OPPONENT IS LOGAN GYRE.

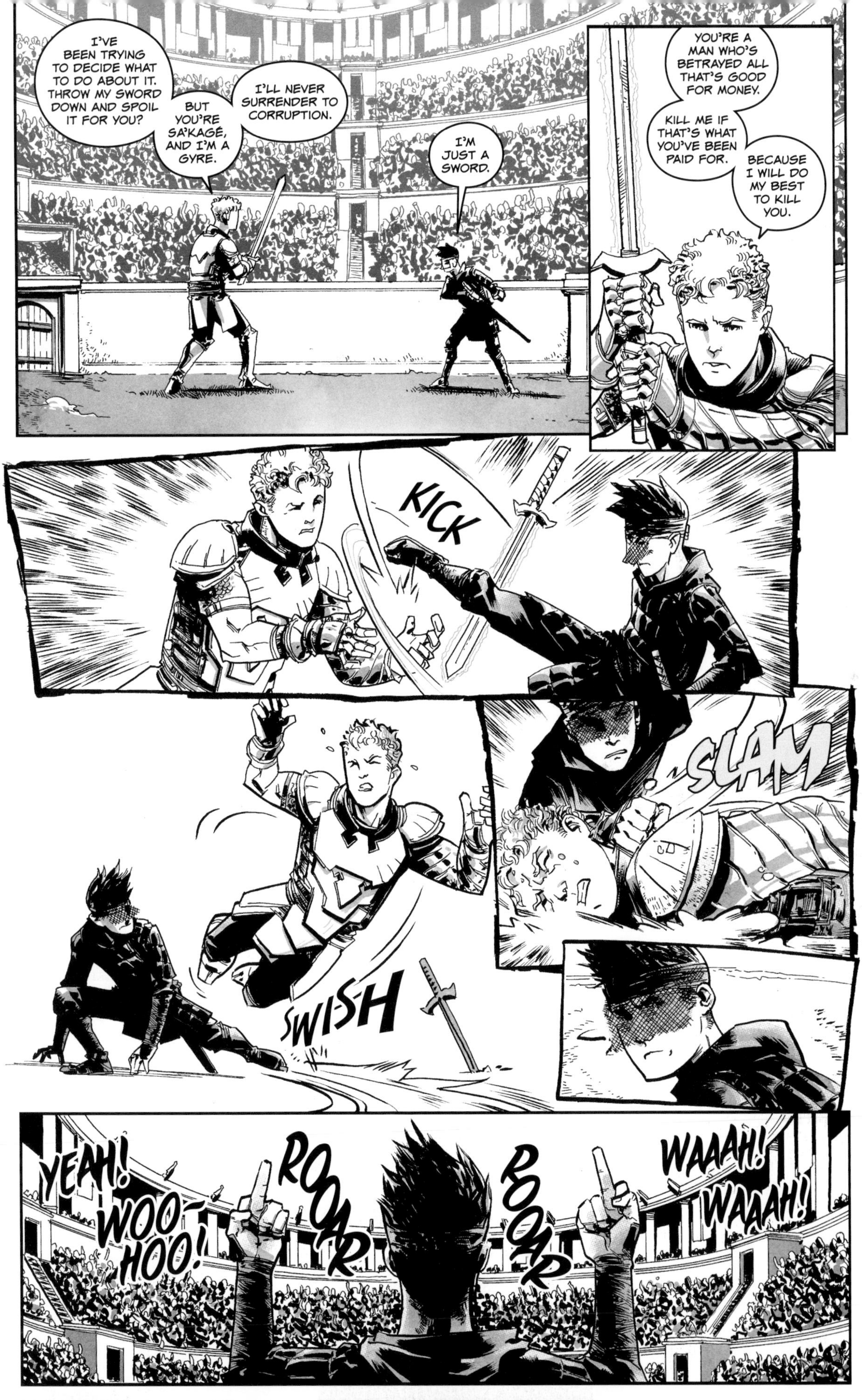
I'VE BEEN TRYING TO DECIDE WHAT TO DO ABOUT IT. THROW MY SWORD DOWN AND SPOIL IT FOR YOU?
BUT YOU'RE SA'KAGÉ, AND I'M A GYRE.
I'LL NEVER SURRENDER TO CORRUPTION.
I'M JUST A SWORD.
YOU'RE A MAN WHO'S BETRAYED ALL THAT'S GOOD FOR MONEY.
KILL ME IF THAT'S WHAT YOU'VE BEEN PAID FOR.
BECAUSE I WILL DO MY BEST TO KILL YOU.
KICK
SLAM
SWISH
YEAH!
WOO-HOO!
ROOOAR
ROOOAR
WAAAH!
WAAAH!

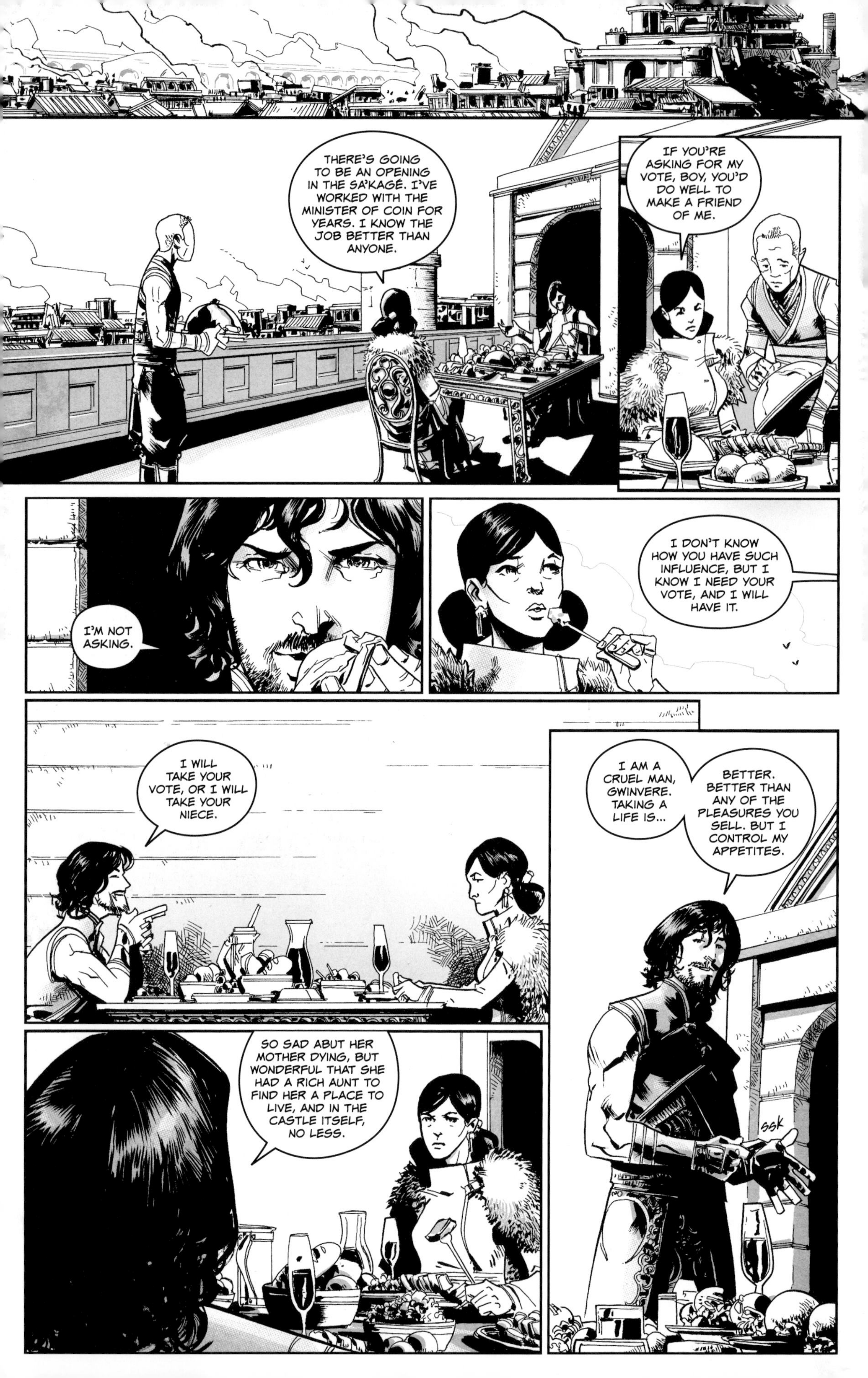

THERE'S GOING TO BE AN OPENING IN THE SA'KAGÉ. I'VE WORKED WITH THE MINISTER OF COIN FOR YEARS. I KNOW THE JOB BETTER THAN ANYONE.
IF YOU'RE ASKING FOR MY VOTE, BOY, YOU'D DO WELL TO MAKE A FRIEND OF ME.
I'M NOT ASKING.
I DON'T KNOW HOW YOU HAVE SUCH INFLUENCE, BUT I KNOW I NEED YOUR VOTE, AND I WILL HAVE IT.
I WILL TAKE YOUR VOTE, OR I WILL TAKE YOUR NIECE.
SO SAD ABUT HER MOTHER DYING, BUT WONDERFUL THAT SHE HAD A RICH AUNT TO FIND HER A PLACE TO LIVE, AND IN THE CASTLE ITSELF, NO LESS.
I AM A CRUEL MAN, GWINVERE. TAKING A LIFE IS...
BETTER. BETTER THAN ANY OF THE PLEASURES YOU SELL. BUT I CONTROL MY APPETITES.
SSK

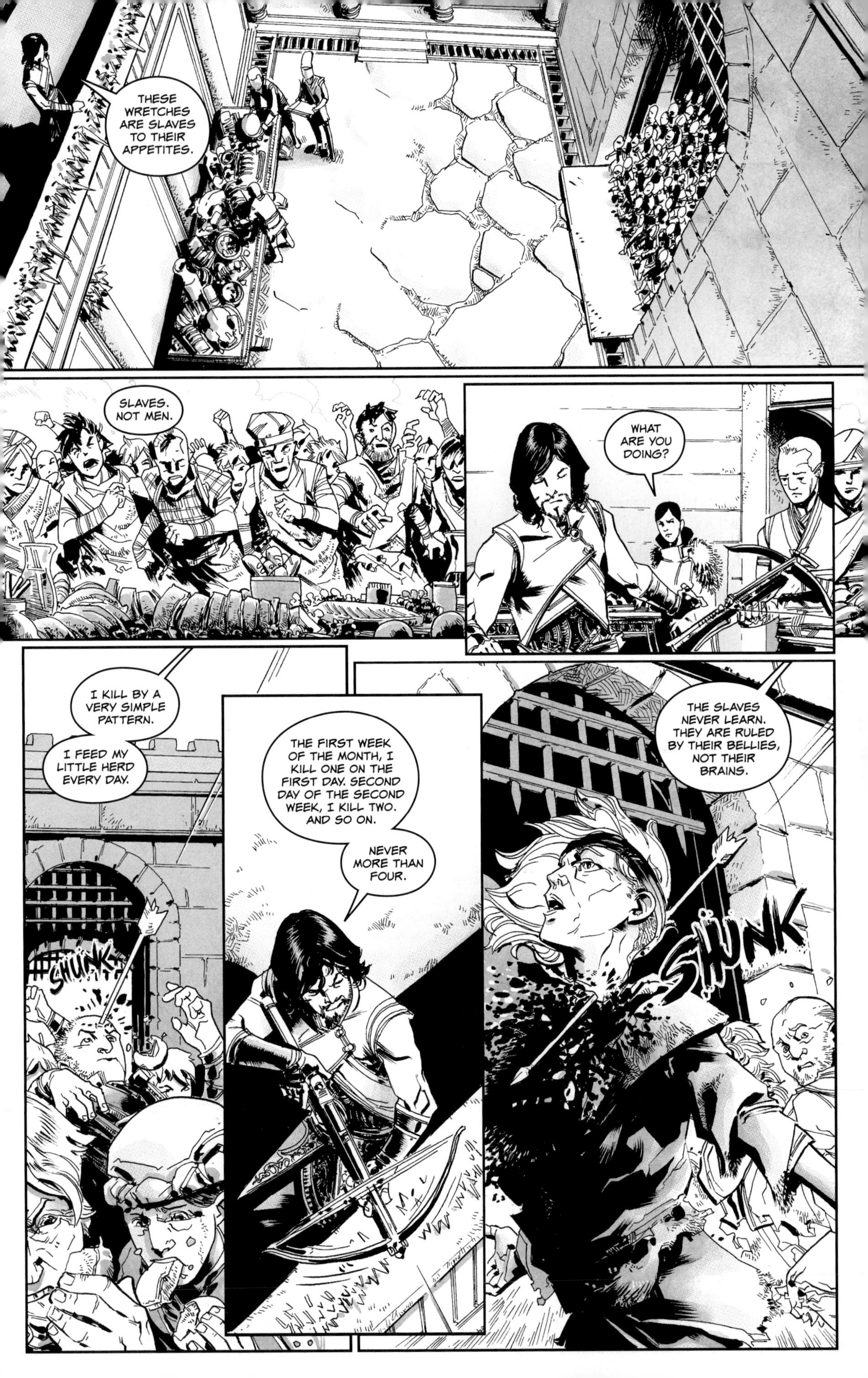
THESE WRETCHES ARE SLAVES TO THEIR APPETITES.
SLAVES. NOT MEN.
WHAT ARE YOU DOING?
I KILL BY A VERY SIMPLE PATTERN.
I FEED MY LITTLE HERD EVERY DAY.
SHUNK
THE FIRST WEEK OF THE MONTH, I KILL ONE ON THE FIRST DAY. SECOND DAY OF THE SECOND WEEK, I KILL TWO. AND SO ON.
NEVER MORE THAN FOUR.
THE SLAVES NEVER LEARN. THEY ARE RULED BY THEIR BELLIES, NOT THEIR BRAINS.
SHUNK

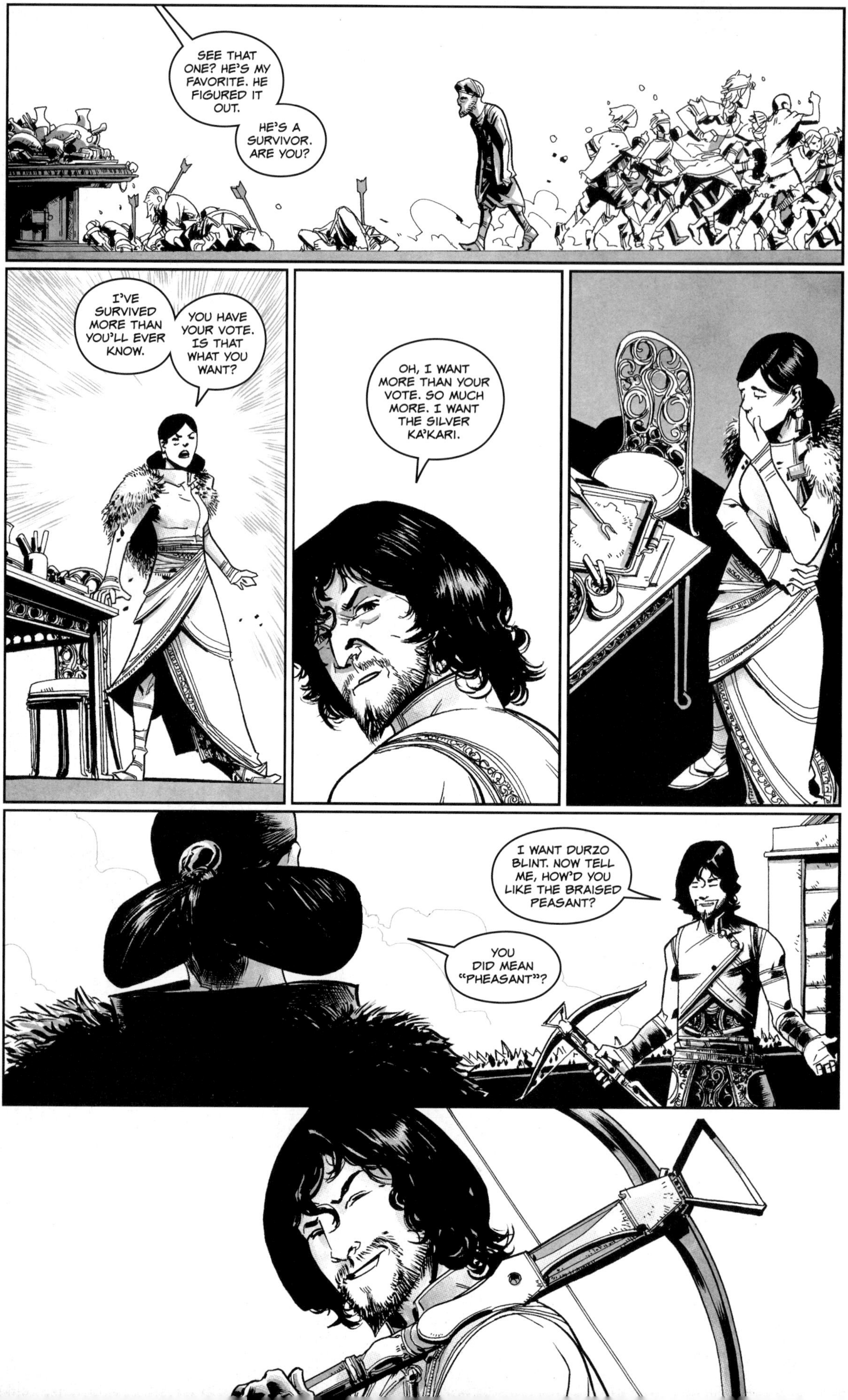
SEE THAT ONE? HE'S MY FAVORITE. HE FIGURED IT OUT.
HE'S A SURVIVOR. ARE YOU?
I'VE SURVIVED MORE THAN YOU'LL EVER KNOW.
YOU HAVE YOUR VOTE. IS THAT WHAT YOU WANT?
OH, I WANT MORE THAN YOUR VOTE. SO MUCH MORE. I WANT THE SILVER KA'KARI.
I WANT DURZO BLINT. NOW TELL ME, HOW'D YOU LIKE THE BRAISED PEASANT?
YOU DID MEAN "PHEASANT"?

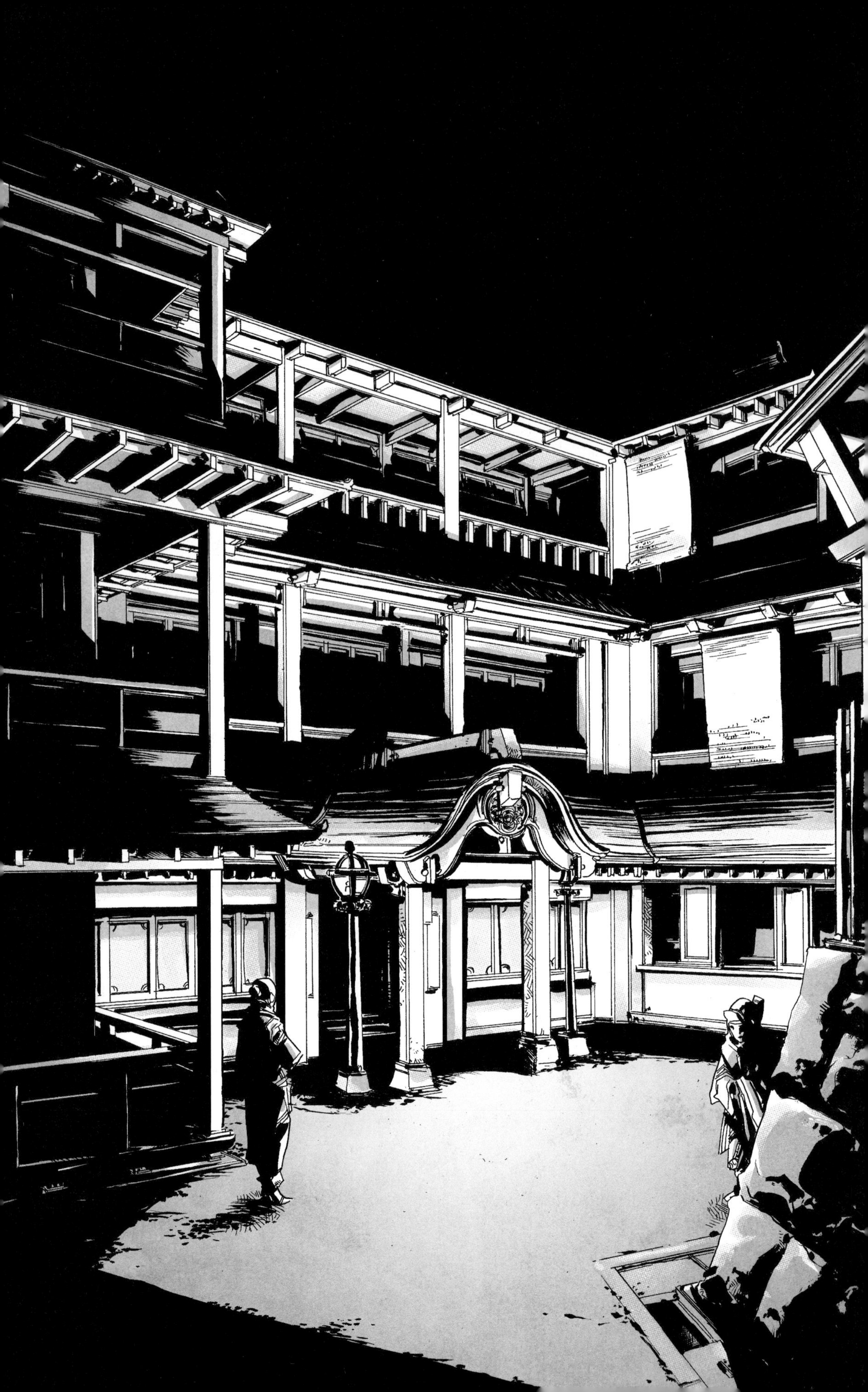

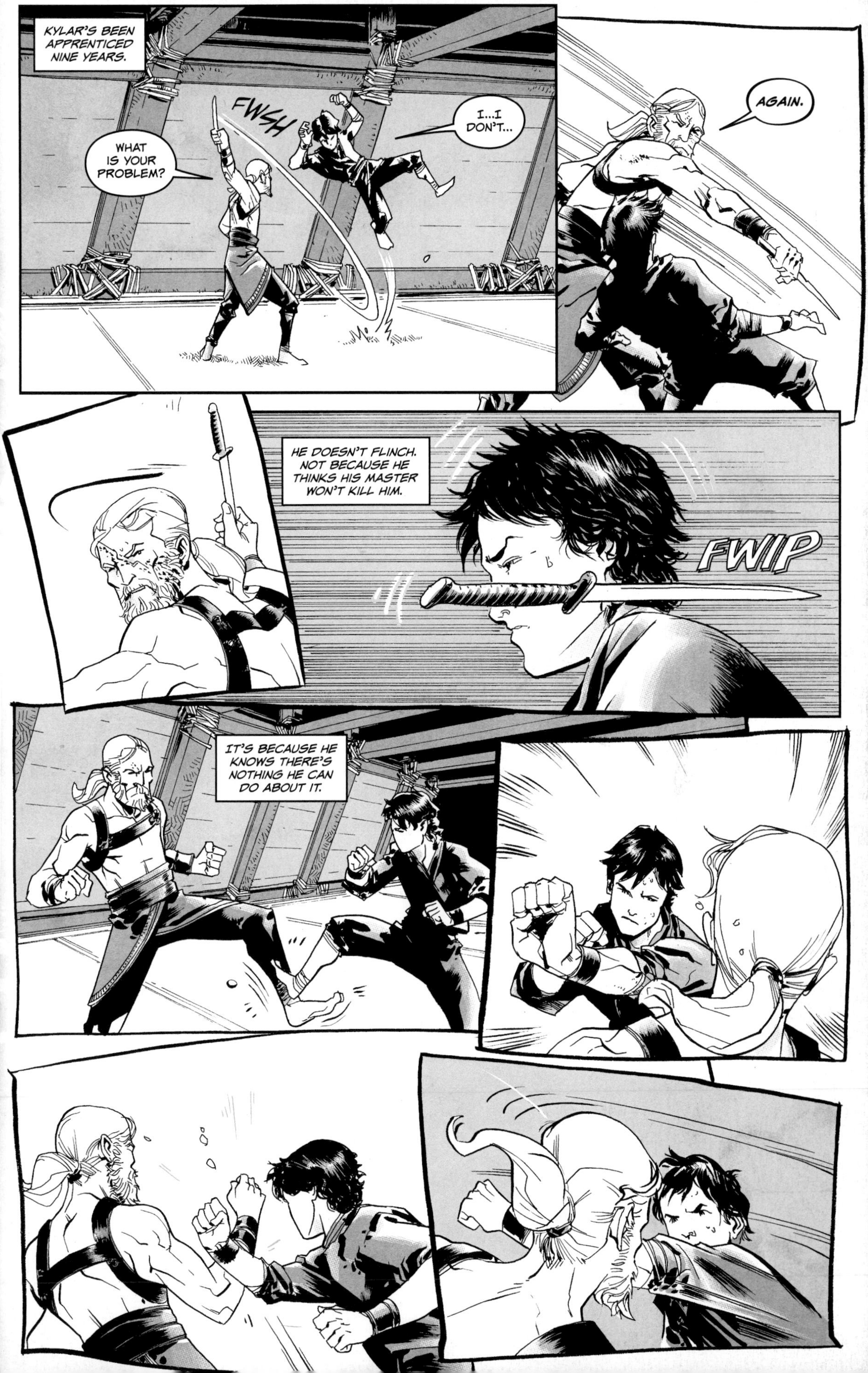
KYLAR'S BEEN APPRENTICED NINE YEARS.
FWSH
WHAT IS YOUR PROBLEM?
I...I DON'T...
AGAIN.
HE DOESN'T FLINCH. NOT BECAUSE HE THINKS HIS MASTER WON'T KILL HIM.
FWIP
IT'S BECAUSE HE KNOWS THERE'S NOTHING HE CAN DO ABOUT IT.

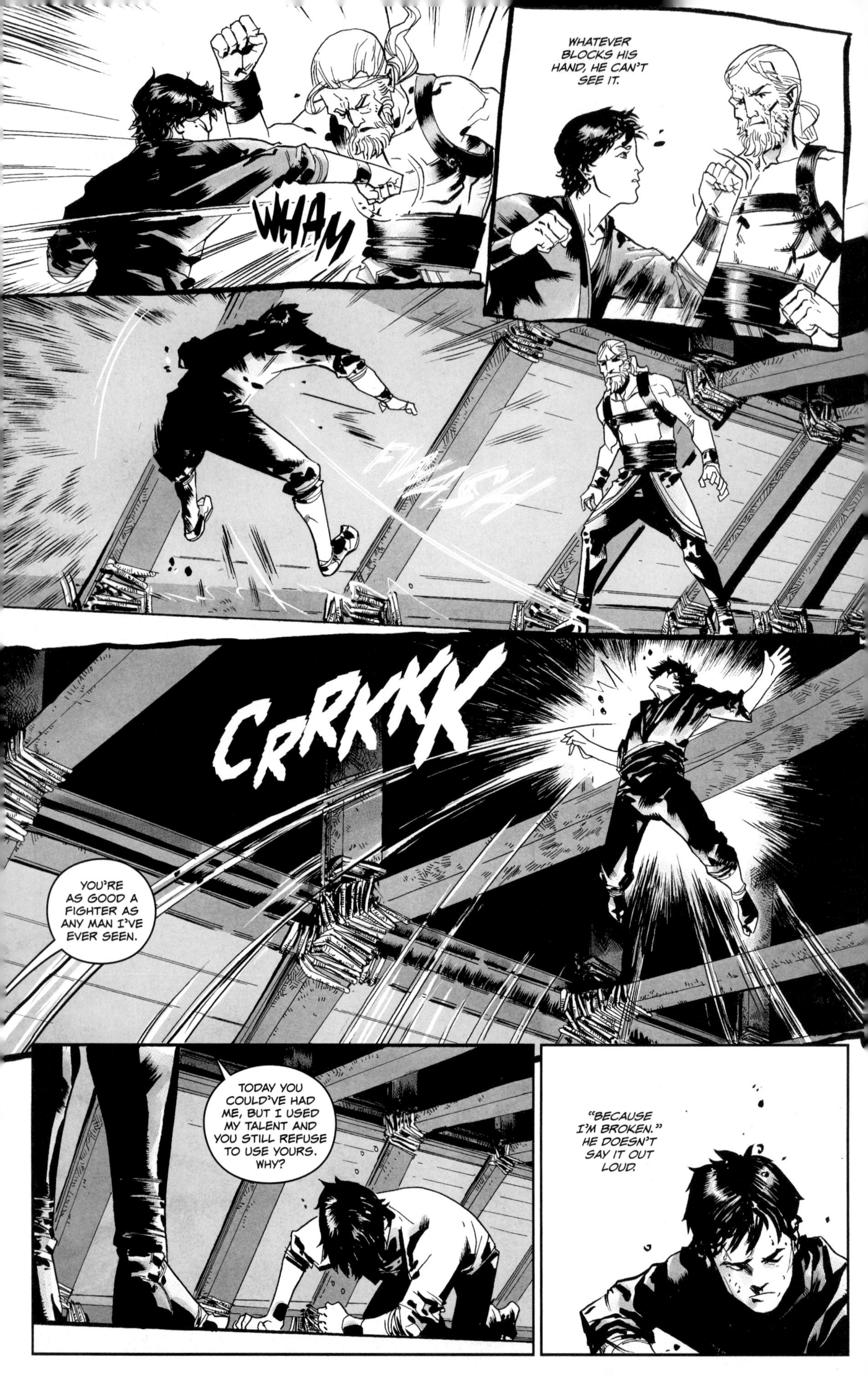
WHAM
WHATEVER BLOCKS HIS HAND, HE CAN'T SEE IT.
FWASH
CRKKK
YOU'RE AS GOOD A FIGHTER AS ANY MAN I'VE EVER SEEN.
TODAY YOU COULD'VE HAD ME, BUT I USED MY TALENT AND YOU STILL REFUSE TO USE YOURS. WHY?
"BECAUSE I'M BROKEN." HE DOESN'T SAY IT OUT LOUD.

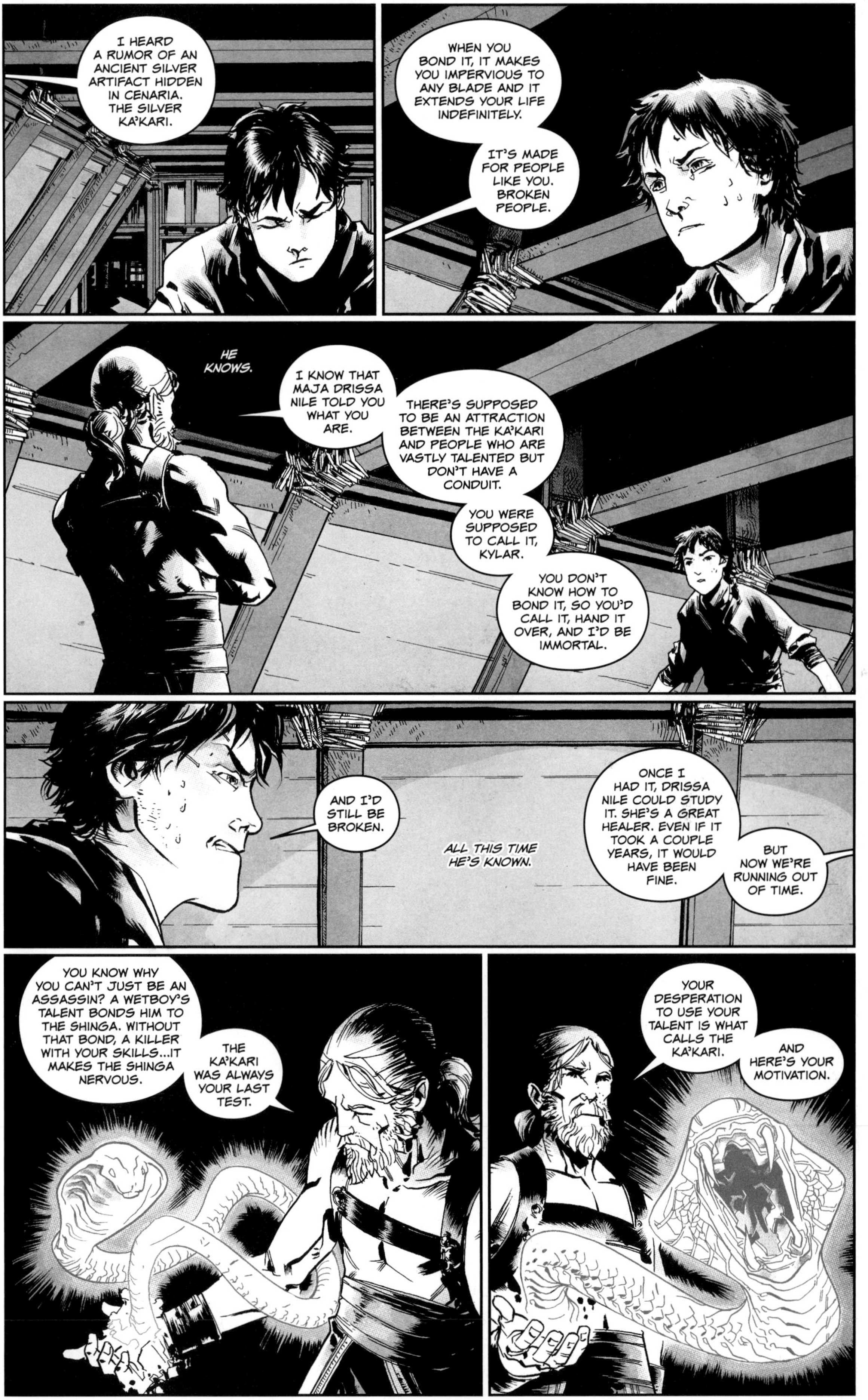
I HEARD A RUMOR OF AN ANCIENT SILVER ARTIFACT HIDDEN IN CENARIA. THE SILVER KA'KARI.
WHEN YOU BOND IT, IT MAKES YOU IMPERVIOUS TO ANY BLADE AND IT EXTENDS YOUR LIFE INDEFINITELY.
IT'S MADE FOR PEOPLE LIKE YOU. BROKEN PEOPLE.
HE KNOWS.
I KNOW THAT MAJA DRISSA NILE TOLD YOU WHAT YOU ARE.
THERE'S SUPPOSED TO BE AN ATTRACTION BETWEEN THE KA'KARI AND PEOPLE WHO ARE VASTLY TALENTED BUT DON'T HAVE A CONDUIT.
YOU WERE SUPPOSED TO CALL IT, KYLAR.
YOU DON'T KNOW HOW TO BOND IT, SO YOU'D CALL IT, HAND IT OVER, AND I'D BE IMMORTAL.
AND I'D STILL BE BROKEN.
ALL THIS TIME HE'S KNOWN.
ONCE I HAD IT, DRISSA NILE COULD STUDY IT. SHE'S A GREAT HEALER. EVEN IF IT TOOK A COUPLE YEARS, IT WOULD HAVE BEEN FINE.
BUT NOW WE'RE RUNNING OUT OF TIME.
YOU KNOW WHY YOU CAN'T JUST BE AN ASSASSIN? A WETBOY'S TALENT BONDS HIM TO THE SHINGA. WITHOUT THAT BOND, A KILLER WITH YOUR SKILLS...IT MAKES THE SHINGA NERVOUS.
THE KA'KARI WAS ALWAYS YOUR LAST TEST.
YOUR DESPERATION TO USE YOUR TALENT IS WHAT CALLS THE KA'KARI.
AND HERE'S YOUR MOTIVATION.

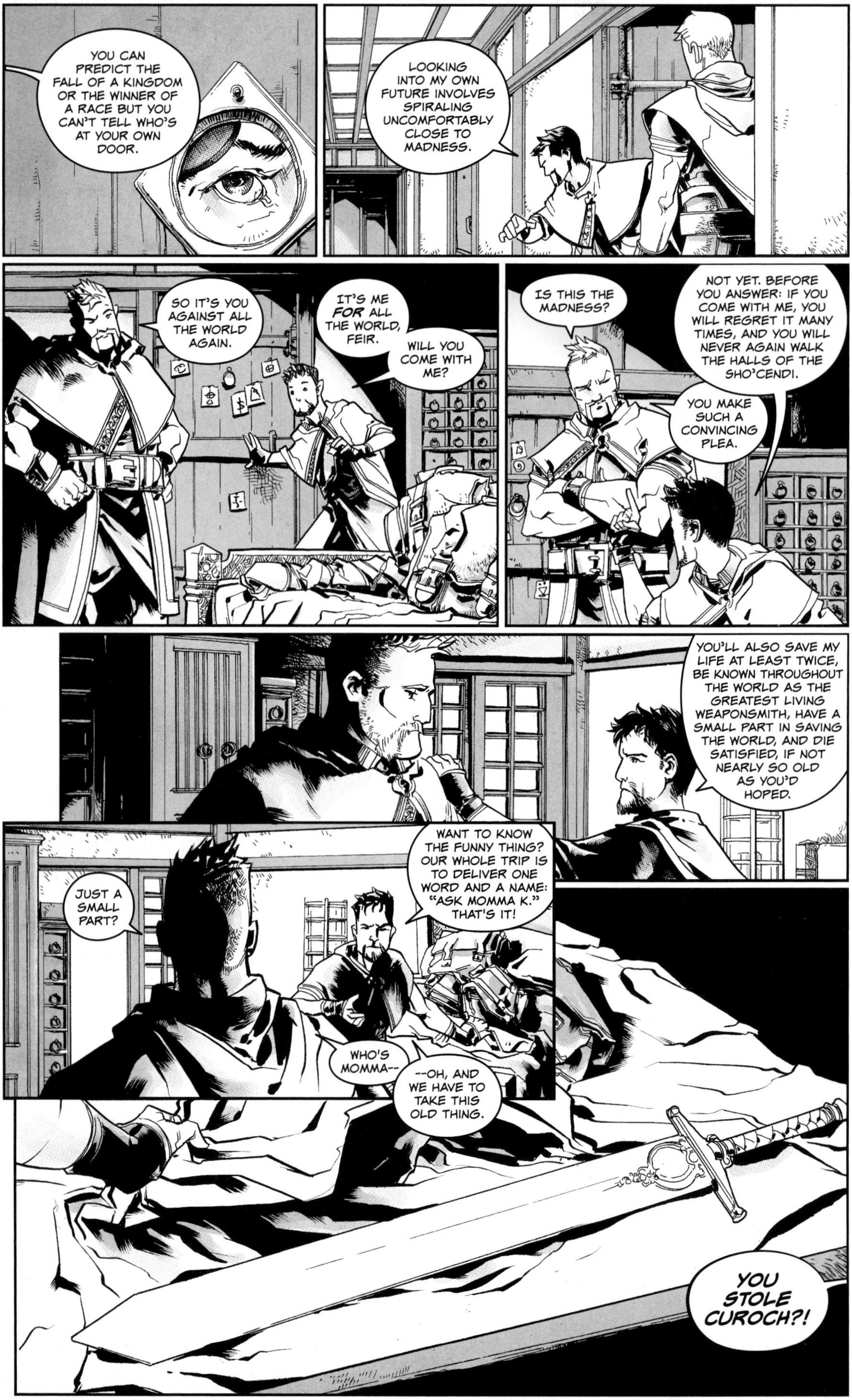
YOU CAN PREDICT THE FALL OF A KINGDOM OR THE WINNER OF A RACE BUT YOU CAN'T TELL WHO'S AT YOUR OWN DOOR.
LOOKING INTO MY OWN FUTURE INVOLVES SPIRALING UNCOMFORTABLY CLOSE TO MADNESS.
SO IT'S YOU AGAINST ALL THE WORLD AGAIN.
IT'S ME FOR ALL THE WORLD, FEIR.
WILL YOU COME WITH ME?
IS THIS THE MADNESS?
NOT YET. BEFORE YOU ANSWER: IF YOU COME WITH ME, YOU WILL REGRET IT MANY TIMES, AND YOU WILL NEVER AGAIN WALK THE HALLS OF THE SHO'CENDI.
YOU MAKE SUCH A CONVINCING PLEA.
YOU'LL ALSO SAVE MY LIFE AT LEAST TWICE, BE KNOWN THROUGHOUT THE WORLD AS THE GREATEST LIVING WEAPONSMITH, HAVE A SMALL PART IN SAVING THE WORLD, AND DIE SATISFIED, IF NOT NEARLY SO OLD AS YOU'D HOPED.
JUST A SMALL PART?
WANT TO KNOW THE FUNNY THING? OUR WHOLE TRIP IS TO DELIVER ONE WORD AND A NAME: "ASK MOMMA K." THAT'S IT!
WHO'S MOMMA--
--OH, AND WE HAVE TO TAKE THIS OLD THING.
YOU STOLE CUROCH?!

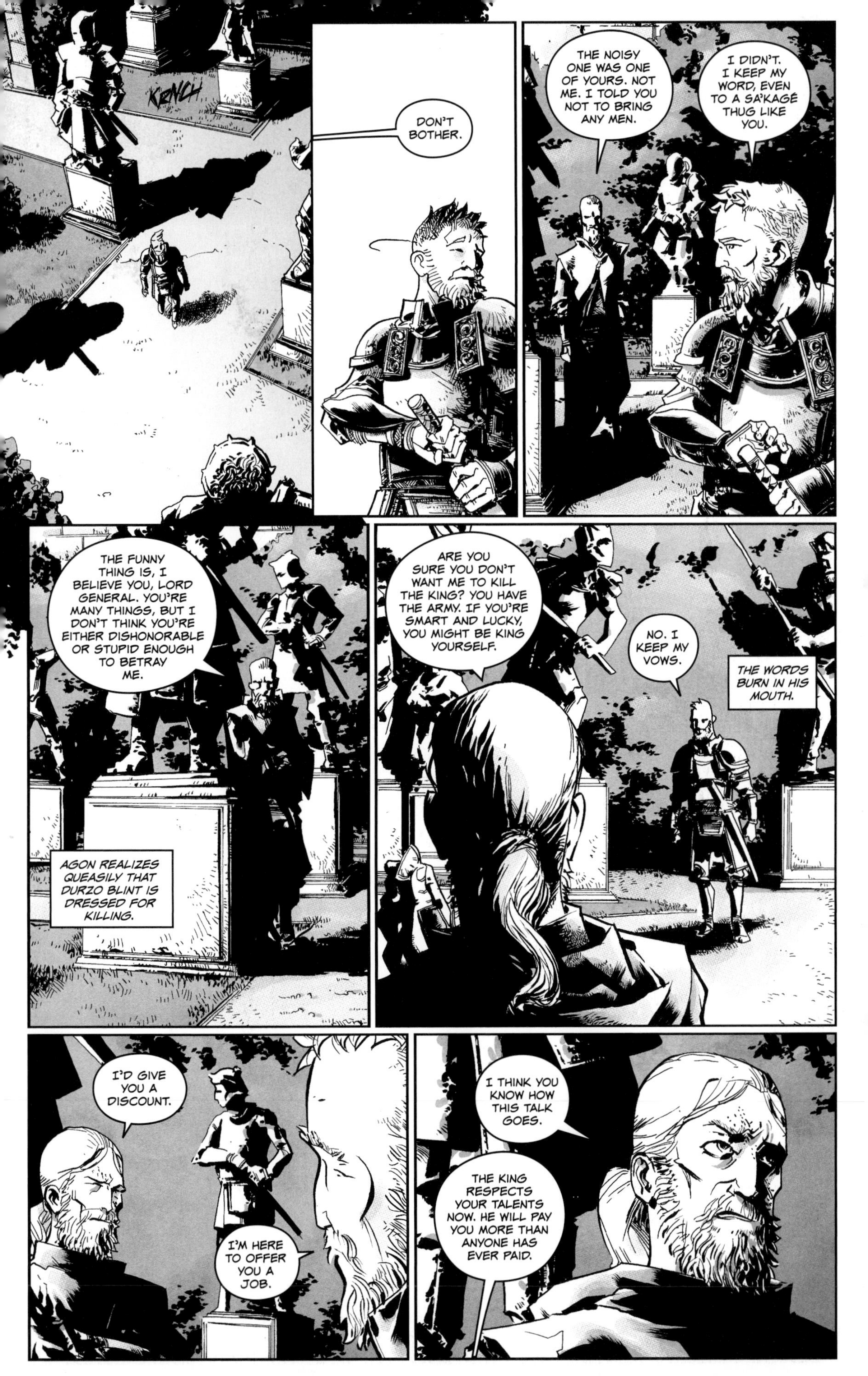
KRNCH
DON'T BOTHER.
THE NOISY ONE WAS ONE OF YOURS. NOT ME. I TOLD YOU NOT TO BRING ANY MEN.
I DIDN'T. I KEEP MY WORD, EVEN TO A SA'KAGÉ THUG LIKE YOU.
THE FUNNY THING IS, I BELIEVE YOU, LORD GENERAL. YOU'RE MANY THINGS, BUT I DON'T THINK YOU'RE EITHER DISHONORABLE OR STUPID ENOUGH TO BETRAY ME.
AGON REALIZES QUEASILY THAT DURZO BLINT IS DRESSED FOR KILLING.
ARE YOU SURE YOU DON'T WANT ME TO KILL THE KING? YOU HAVE THE ARMY. IF YOU'RE SMART AND LUCKY, YOU MIGHT BE KING YOURSELF.
NO. I KEEP MY VOWS.
THE WORDS BURN IN HIS MOUTH.
I'D GIVE YOU A DISCOUNT.
I'M HERE TO OFFER YOU A JOB.
I THINK YOU KNOW HOW THIS TALK GOES.
THE KING RESPECTS YOUR TALENTS NOW. HE WILL PAY YOU MORE THAN ANYONE HAS EVER PAID.

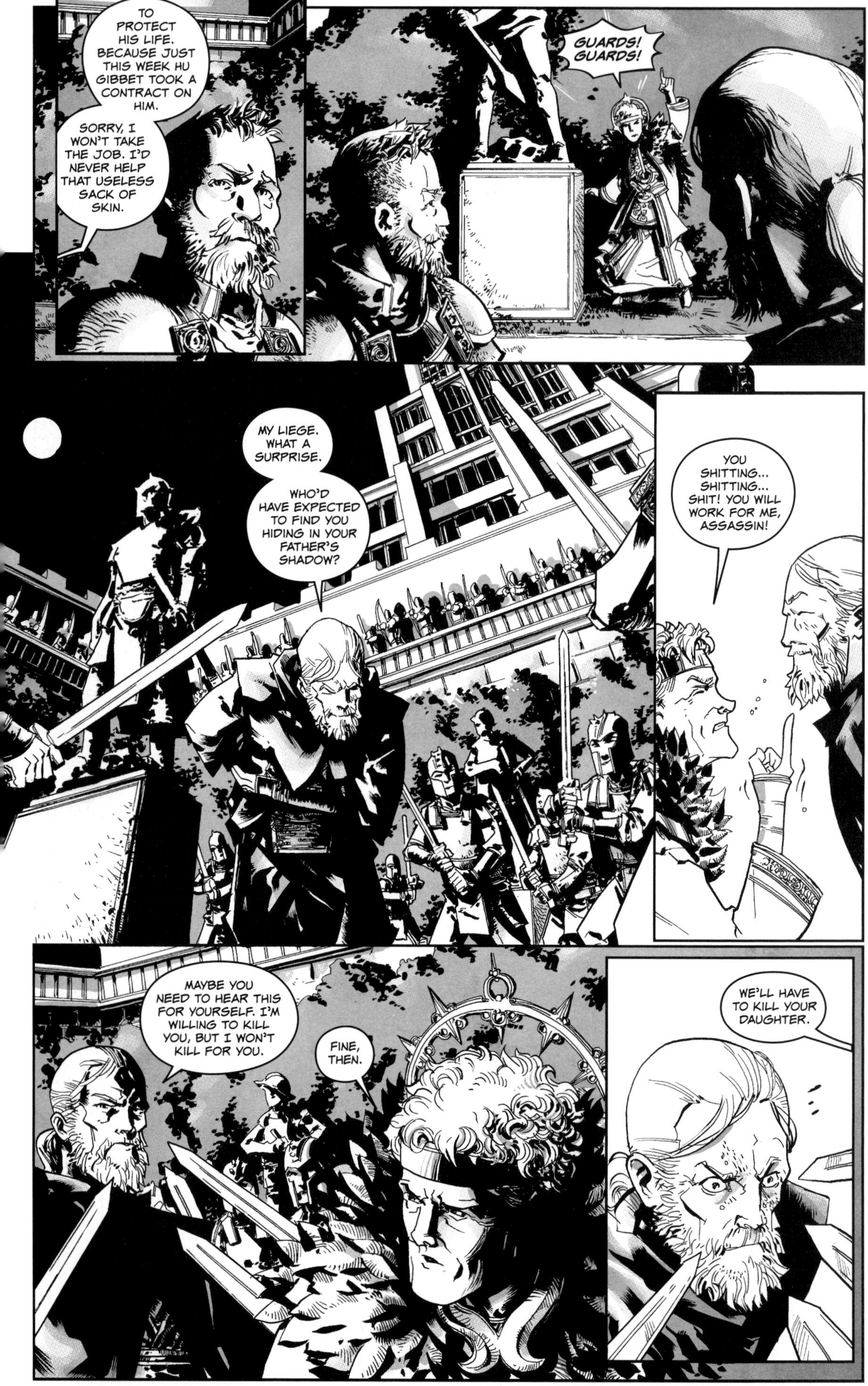
TO PROTECT HIS LIFE. BECAUSE JUST THIS WEEK HU GIBBET TOOK A CONTRACT ON HIM.
SORRY, I WON'T TAKE THE JOB. I'D NEVER HELP THAT USELESS SACK OF SKIN.
GUARDS! GUARDS!
MY LIEGE. WHAT A SURPRISE.
WHO'D HAVE EXPECTED TO FIND YOU HIDING IN YOUR FATHER'S SHADOW?
YOU SHITTING... SHITTING... SHIT! YOU WILL WORK FOR ME, ASSASSIN!
MAYBE YOU NEED TO HEAR THIS FOR YOURSELF. I'M WILLING TO KILL YOU, BUT I WON'T KILL FOR YOU.
FINE, THEN.
WE'LL HAVE TO KILL YOUR DAUGHTER.

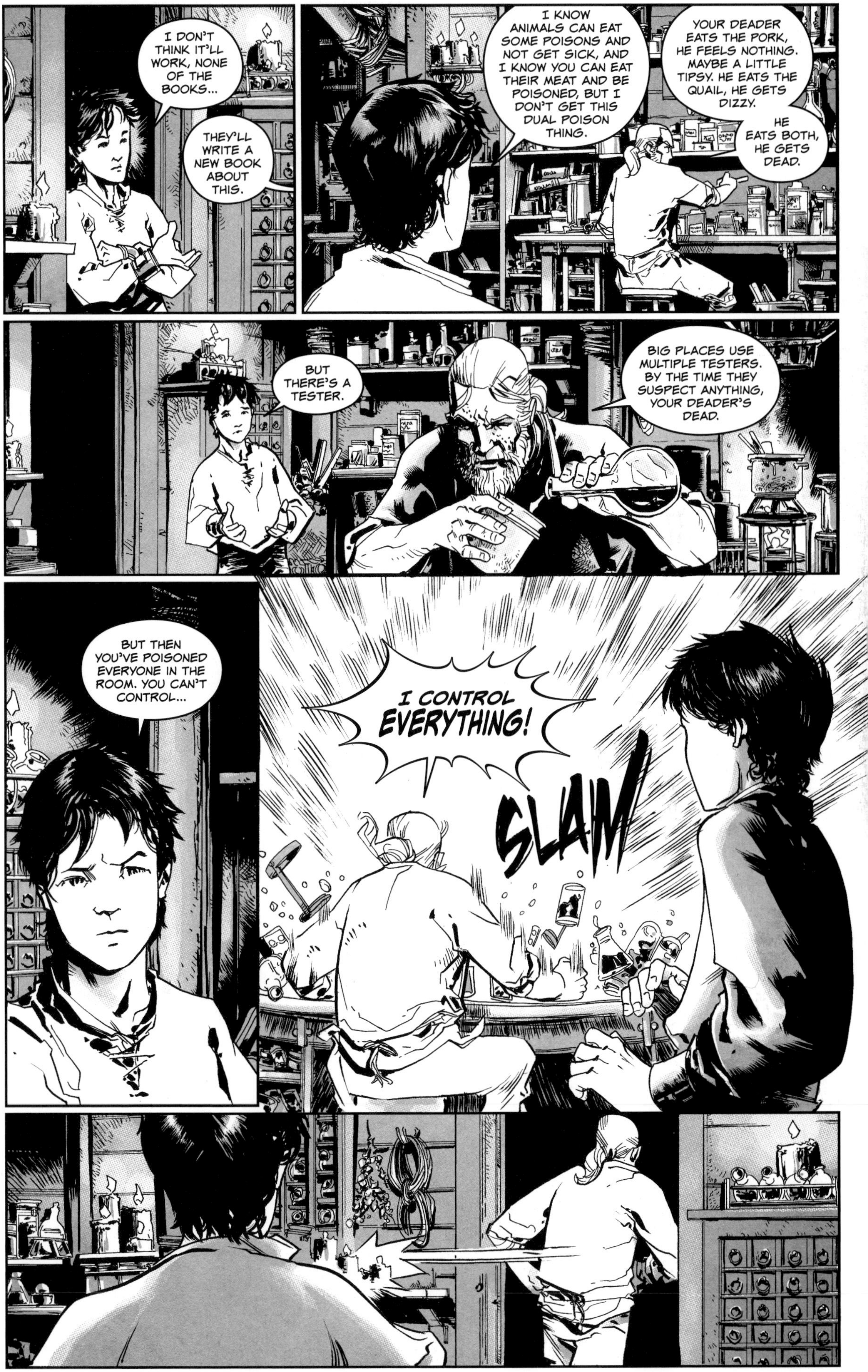
I DON'T THINK IT'LL WORK, NONE OF THE BOOKS...
THEY'LL WRITE A NEW BOOK ABOUT THIS.
I KNOW ANIMALS CAN EAT SOME POISONS AND NOT GET SICK, AND I KNOW YOU CAN EAT THEIR MEAT AND BE POISONED, BUT I DON'T GET THIS DUAL POISON THING.
YOUR DEADER EATS THE PORK, HE FEELS NOTHING. MAYBE A LITTLE TIPSY. HE EATS THE QUAIL, HE GETS DIZZY.
HE EATS BOTH, HE GETS DEAD.
BUT THERE'S A TESTER.
BIG PLACES USE MULTIPLE TESTERS. BY THE TIME THEY SUSPECT ANYTHING, YOUR DEADER'S DEAD.
BUT THEN YOU'VE POISONED EVERYONE IN THE ROOM. YOU CAN'T CONTROL...
I CONTROL EVERYTHING!
SLAM

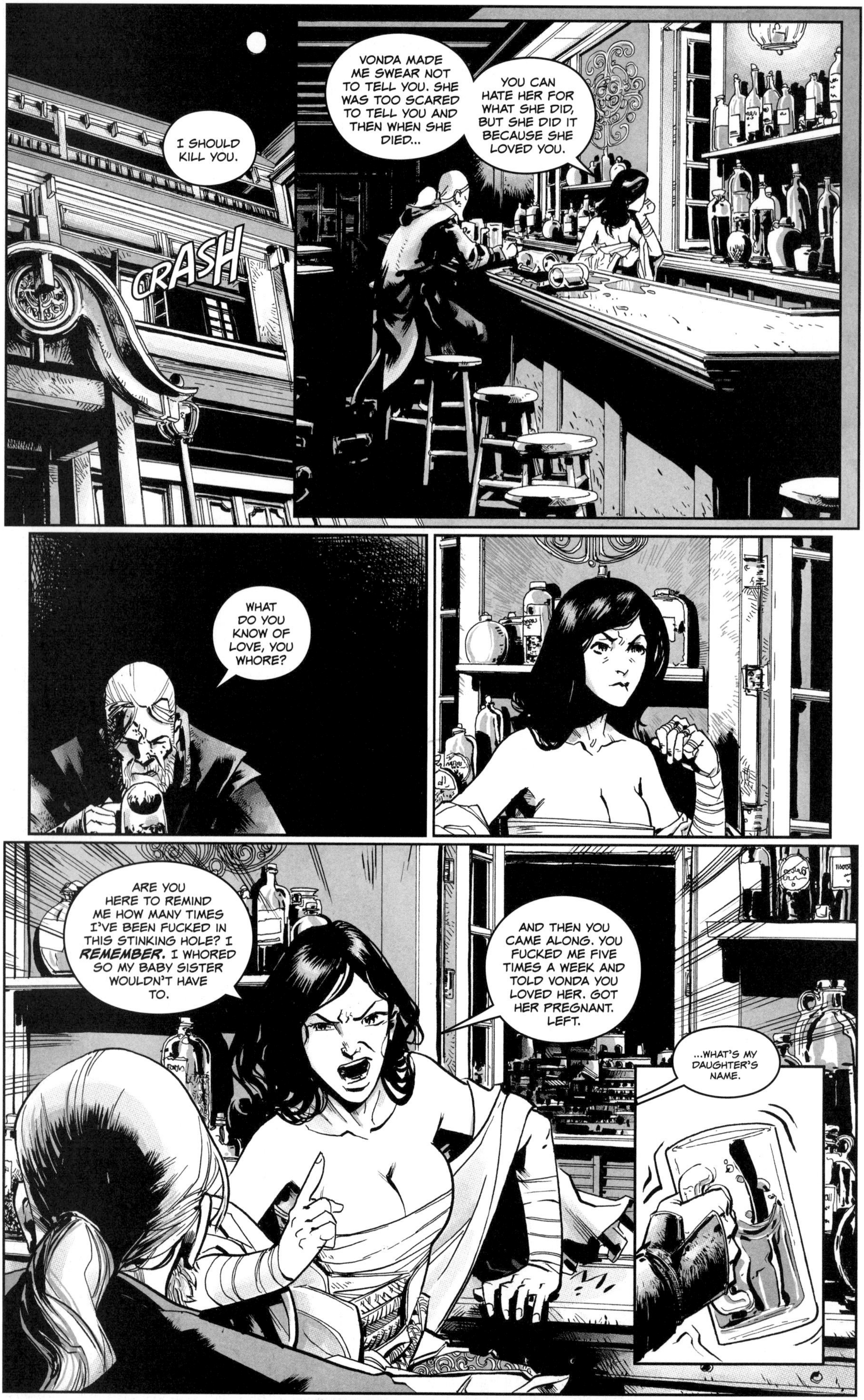
I SHOULD KILL YOU.
CRASH
VONDA MADE ME SWEAR NOT TO TELL YOU. SHE WAS TOO SCARED TO TELL YOU AND THEN WHEN SHE DIED...
YOU CAN HATE HER FOR WHAT SHE DID, BUT SHE DID IT BECAUSE SHE LOVED YOU.
WHAT DO YOU KNOW OF LOVE, YOU WHORE?
ARE YOU HERE TO REMIND ME HOW MANY TIMES I'VE BEEN FUCKED IN THIS STINKING HOLE? I ***REMEMBER.*** I WHORED SO MY BABY SISTER WOULDN'T HAVE TO.
AND THEN YOU CAME ALONG. YOU FUCKED ME FIVE TIMES A WEEK AND TOLD VONDA YOU LOVED HER. GOT HER PREGNANT. LEFT.
...WHAT'S MY DAUGHTER'S NAME.

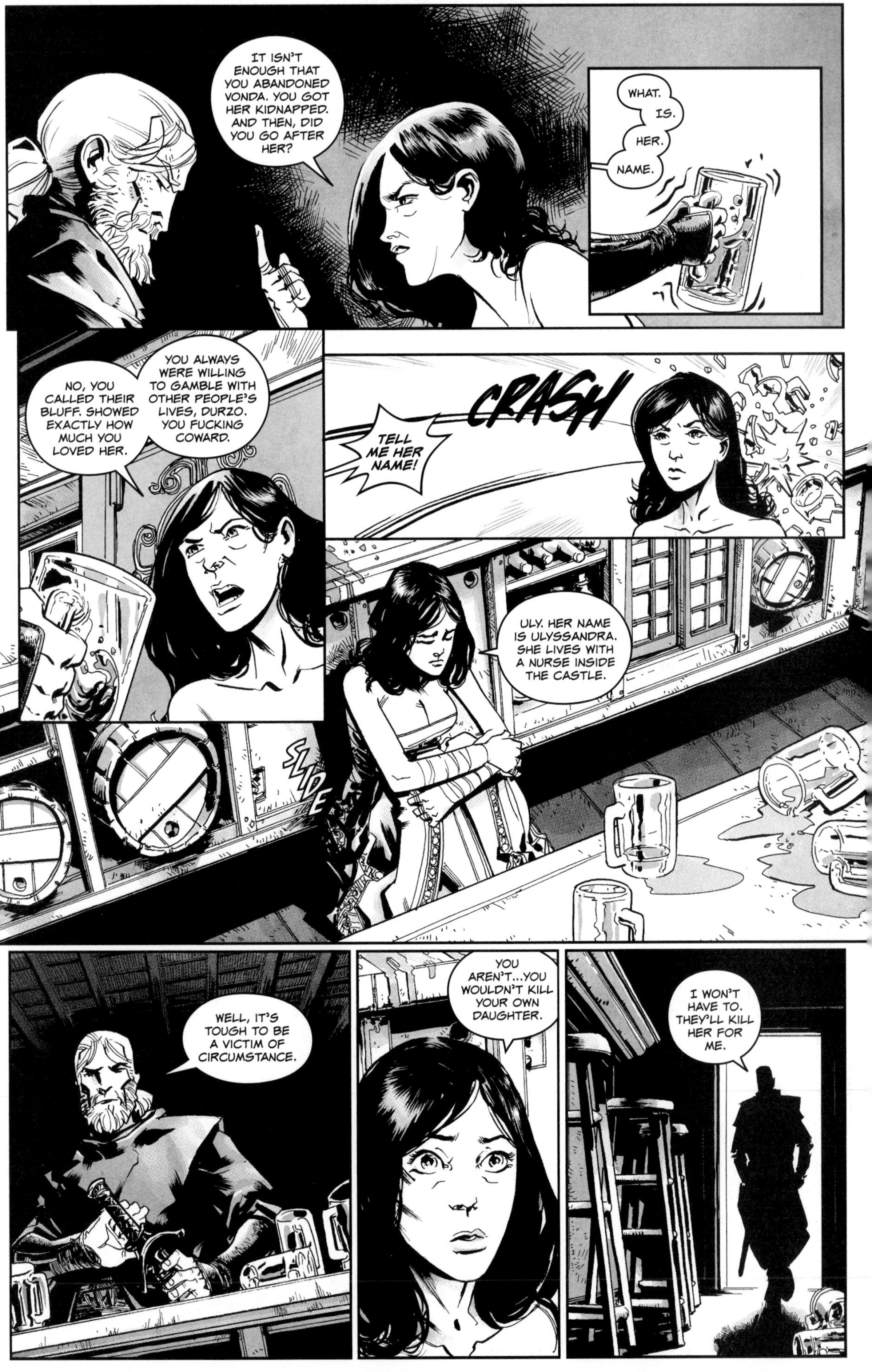
IT ISN'T ENOUGH THAT YOU ABANDONED VONDA. YOU GOT HER KIDNAPPED. AND THEN, DID YOU GO AFTER HER?
WHAT.
IS.
HER.
NAME.
NO, YOU CALLED THEIR BLUFF. SHOWED EXACTLY HOW MUCH YOU LOVED HER.
YOU ALWAYS WERE WILLING TO GAMBLE WITH OTHER PEOPLE'S LIVES, DURZO. YOU FUCKING COWARD.
CRASH
TELL ME HER NAME!
ULY. HER NAME IS ULYSSANDRA. SHE LIVES WITH A NURSE INSIDE THE CASTLE.
SLIDE
WELL, IT'S TOUGH TO BE A VICTIM OF CIRCUMSTANCE.
YOU AREN'T...YOU WOULDN'T KILL YOUR OWN DAUGHTER.
I WON'T HAVE TO. THEY'LL KILL HER FOR ME.

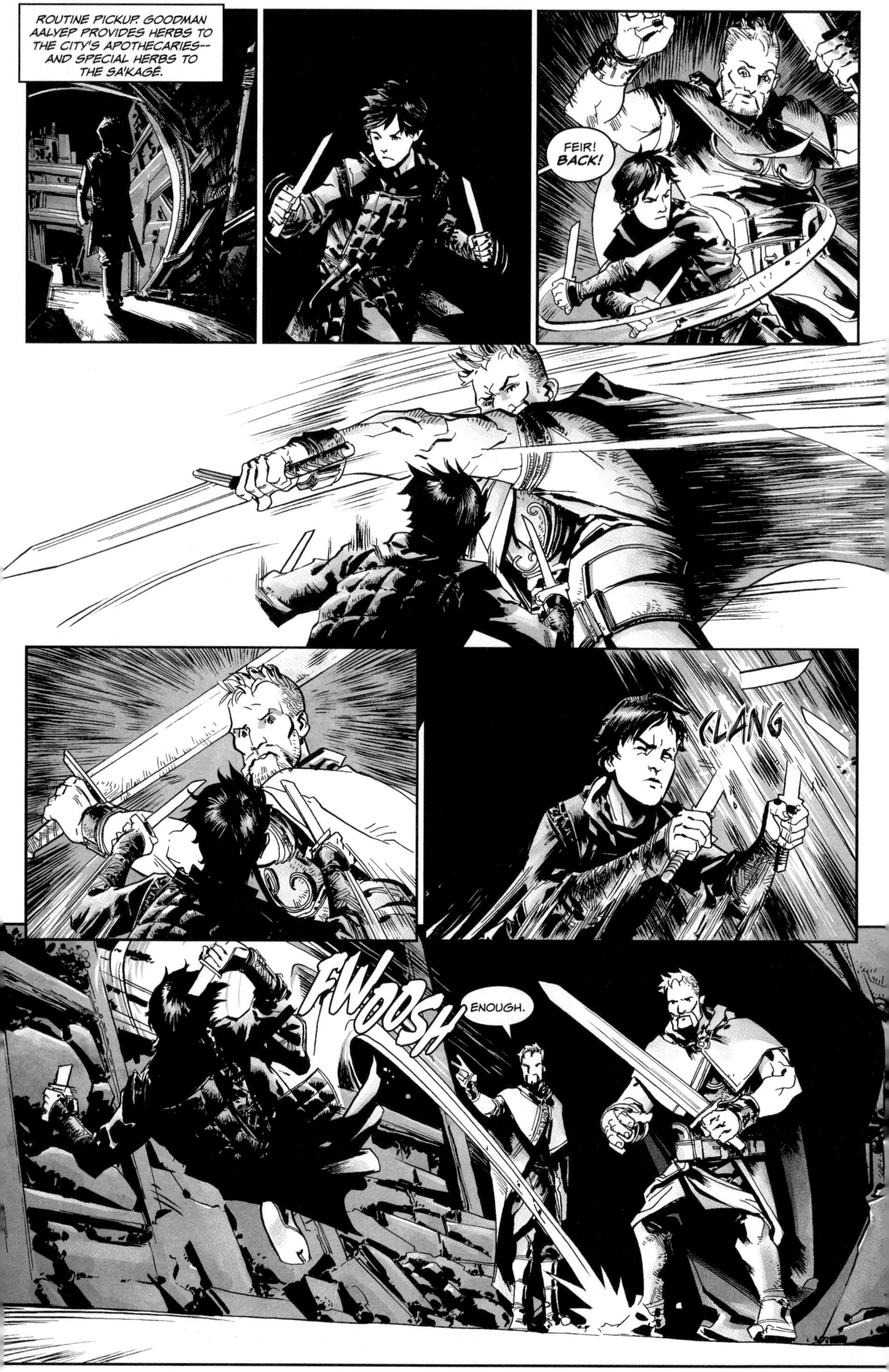
ROUTINE PICKUP. GOODMAN AALYEP PROVIDES HERBS TO THE CITY'S APOTHECARIES--AND SPECIAL HERBS TO THE SA'KAGÉ.
FEIR! BACK!
CLANG
FWOOSH
ENOUGH.

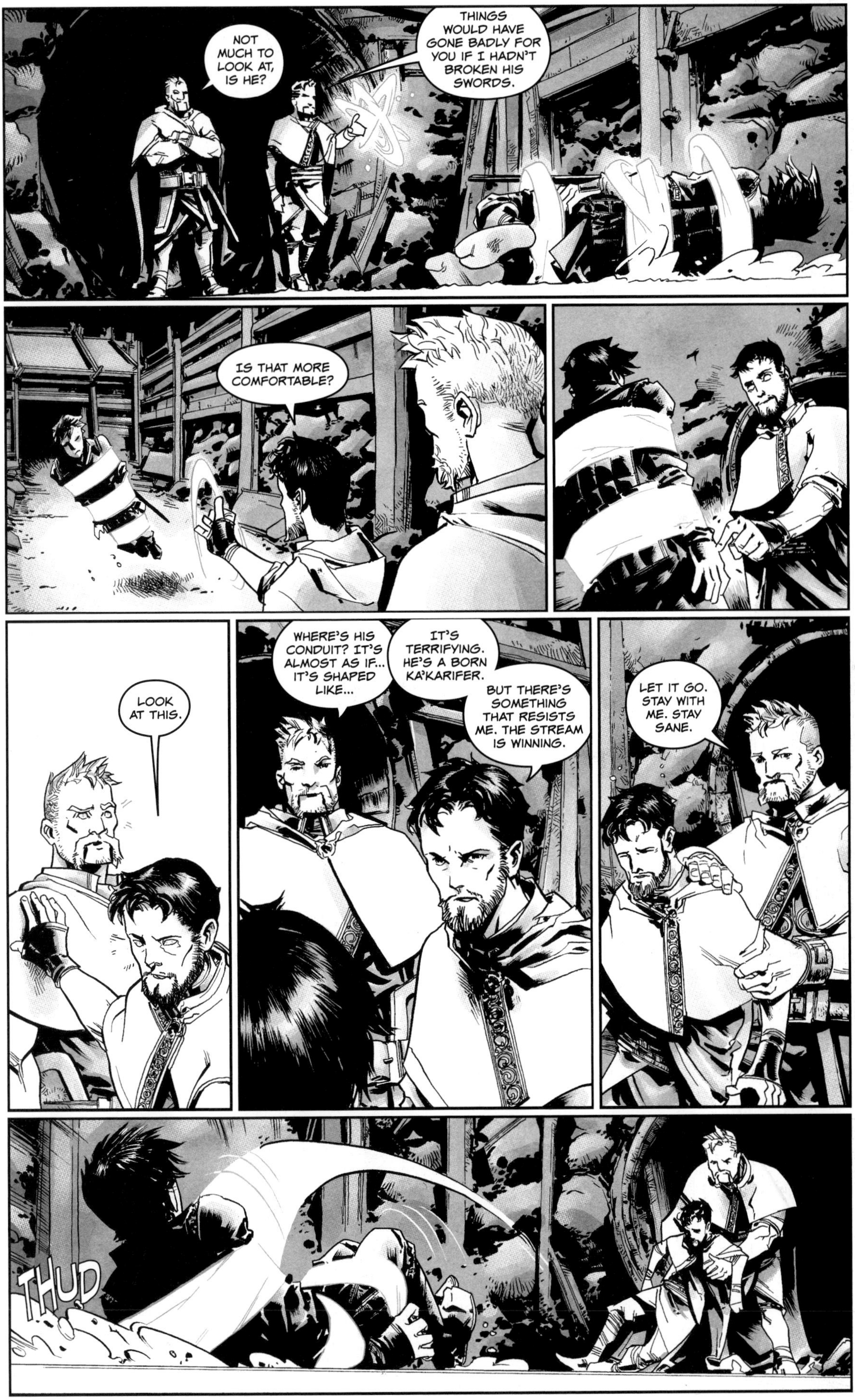
NOT MUCH TO LOOK AT, IS HE?
THINGS WOULD HAVE GONE BADLY FOR YOU IF I HADN'T BROKEN HIS SWORDS.
IS THAT MORE COMFORTABLE?
LOOK AT THIS.
WHERE'S HIS CONDUIT? IT'S ALMOST AS IF... IT'S SHAPED LIKE...
IT'S TERRIFYING. HE'S A BORN KA'KARIFER.
BUT THERE'S SOMETHING THAT RESISTS ME. THE STREAM IS WINNING.
LET IT GO. STAY WITH ME. STAY SANE.
THUD

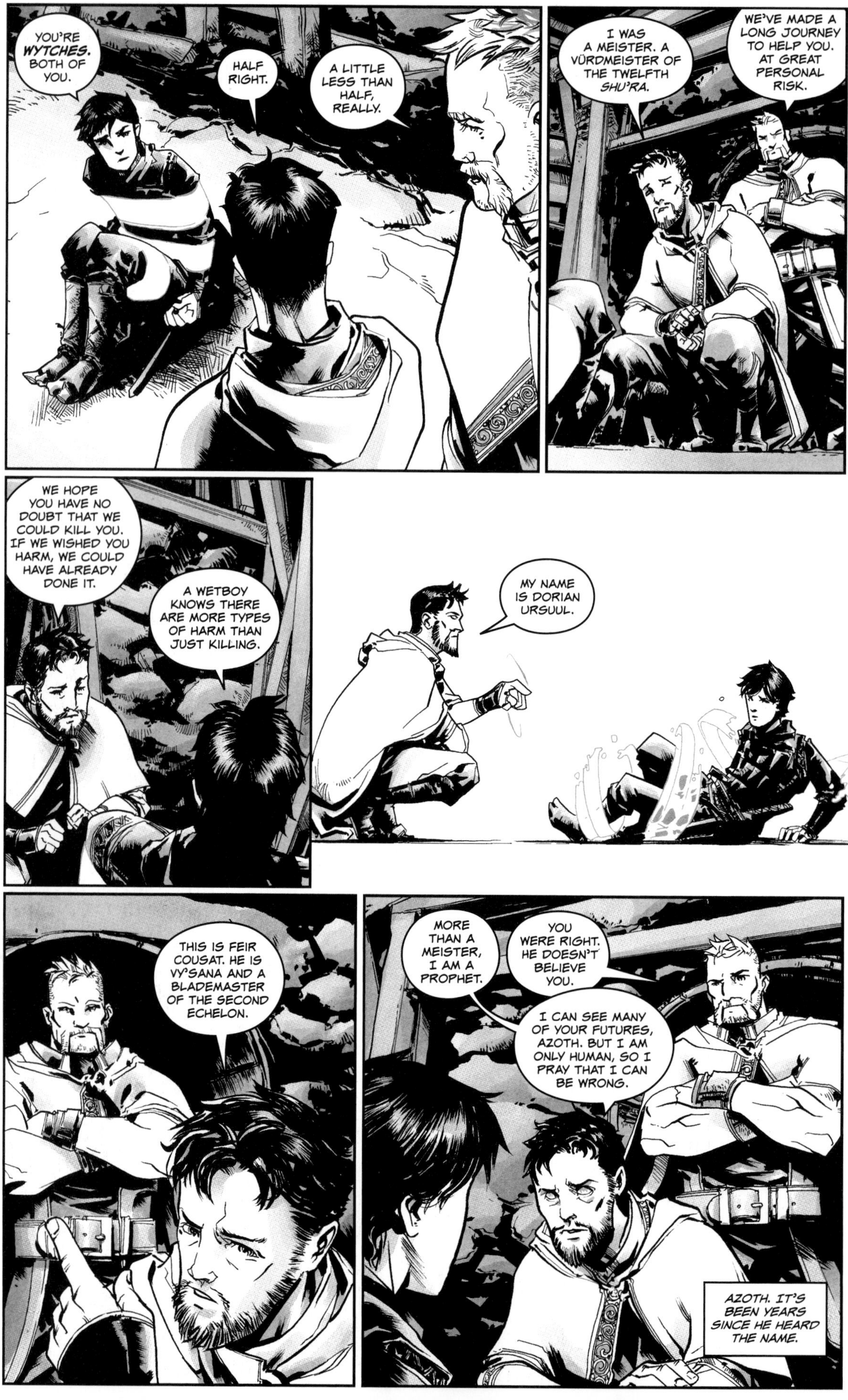
YOU'RE **WYTCHES.** BOTH OF YOU.
HALF RIGHT.
A LITTLE LESS THAN HALF, REALLY.
I WAS A MEISTER. A VÜRDMEISTER OF THE TWELFTH *SHU'RA.*
WE'VE MADE A LONG JOURNEY TO HELP YOU. AT GREAT PERSONAL RISK.
WE HOPE YOU HAVE NO DOUBT THAT WE COULD KILL YOU. IF WE WISHED YOU HARM, WE COULD HAVE ALREADY DONE IT.
A WETBOY KNOWS THERE ARE MORE TYPES OF HARM THAN JUST KILLING.
MY NAME IS DORIAN URSUUL.
THIS IS FEIR COUSAT. HE IS VY'SANA AND A BLADEMASTER OF THE SECOND ECHELON.
MORE THAN A MEISTER, I AM A PROPHET.
YOU WERE RIGHT. HE DOESN'T BELIEVE YOU.
I CAN SEE MANY OF YOUR FUTURES, AZOTH. BUT I AM ONLY HUMAN, SO I PRAY THAT I CAN BE WRONG.
AZOTH. IT'S BEEN YEARS SINCE HE HEARD THE NAME.

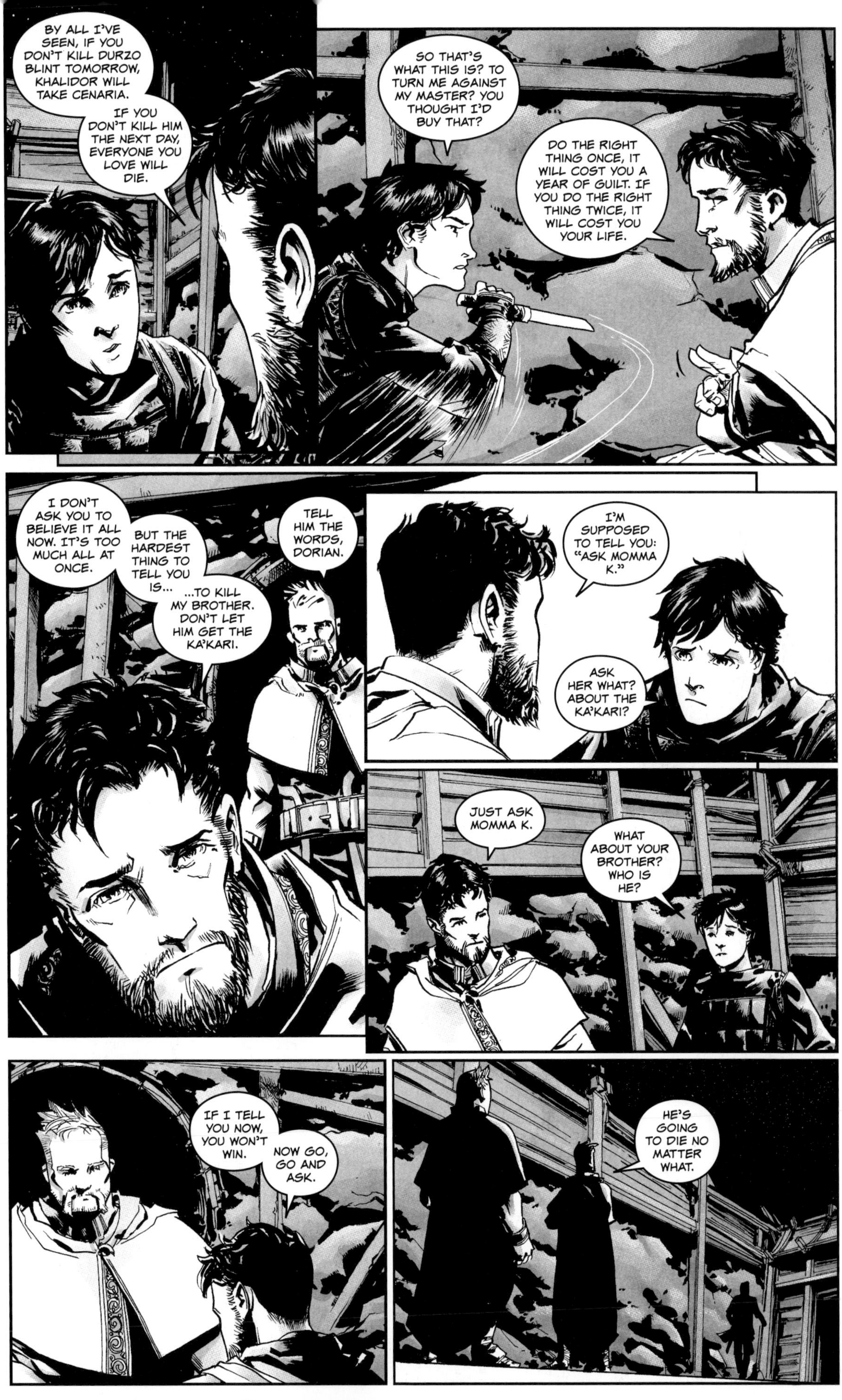
BY ALL I'VE SEEN, IF YOU DON'T KILL DURZO BLINT TOMORROW, KHALIDOR WILL TAKE CENARIA.
IF YOU DON'T KILL HIM THE NEXT DAY, EVERYONE YOU LOVE WILL DIE.
SO THAT'S WHAT THIS IS? TO TURN ME AGAINST MY MASTER? YOU THOUGHT I'D BUY THAT?
DO THE RIGHT THING ONCE, IT WILL COST YOU A YEAR OF GUILT. IF YOU DO THE RIGHT THING TWICE, IT WILL COST YOU YOUR LIFE.
I DON'T ASK YOU TO BELIEVE IT ALL NOW. IT'S TOO MUCH ALL AT ONCE.
BUT THE HARDEST THING TO TELL YOU IS...
...TO KILL MY BROTHER. DON'T LET HIM GET THE KA'KARI.
TELL HIM THE WORDS, DORIAN.
I'M SUPPOSED TO TELL YOU: "ASK MOMMA K."
ASK HER WHAT? ABOUT THE KA'KARI?
JUST ASK MOMMA K.
WHAT ABOUT YOUR BROTHER? WHO IS HE?
IF I TELL YOU NOW, YOU WON'T WIN.
NOW GO, GO AND ASK.
HE'S GOING TO DIE NO MATTER WHAT.

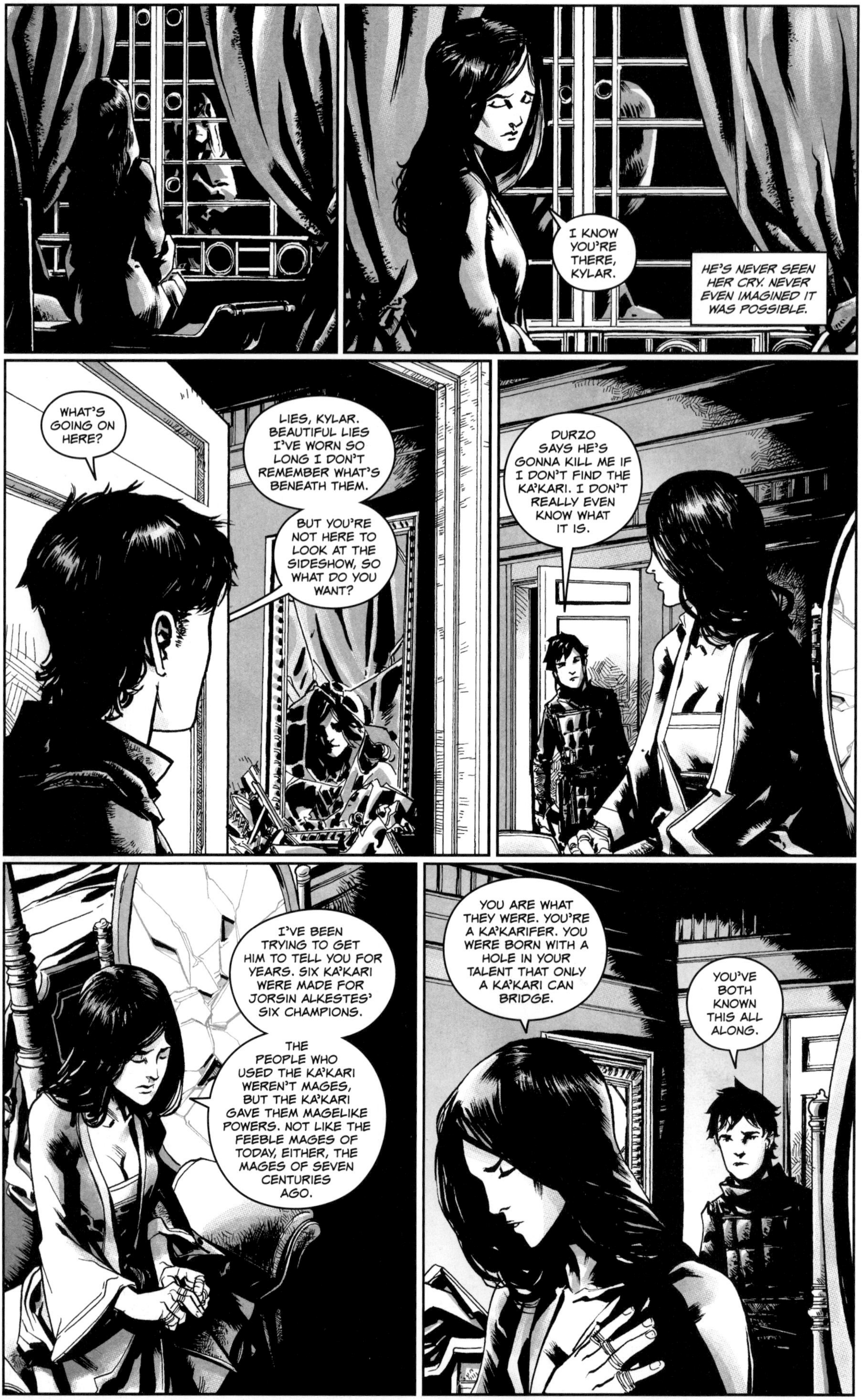
I KNOW YOU'RE THERE, KYLAR.
HE'S NEVER SEEN HER CRY. NEVER EVEN IMAGINED IT WAS POSSIBLE.
WHAT'S GOING ON HERE?
LIES, KYLAR. BEAUTIFUL LIES I'VE WORN SO LONG I DON'T REMEMBER WHAT'S BENEATH THEM.
BUT YOU'RE NOT HERE TO LOOK AT THE SIDESHOW, SO WHAT DO YOU WANT?
DURZO SAYS HE'S GONNA KILL ME IF I DON'T FIND THE KA'KARI. I DON'T REALLY EVEN KNOW WHAT IT IS.
I'VE BEEN TRYING TO GET HIM TO TELL YOU FOR YEARS. SIX KA'KARI WERE MADE FOR JORSIN ALKESTES' SIX CHAMPIONS.
THE PEOPLE WHO USED THE KA'KARI WEREN'T MAGES, BUT THE KA'KARI GAVE THEM MAGELIKE POWERS. NOT LIKE THE FEEBLE MAGES OF TODAY, EITHER, THE MAGES OF SEVEN CENTURIES AGO.
YOU ARE WHAT THEY WERE. YOU'RE A KA'KARIFER. YOU WERE BORN WITH A HOLE IN YOUR TALENT THAT ONLY A KA'KARI CAN BRIDGE.
YOU'VE BOTH KNOWN THIS ALL ALONG.

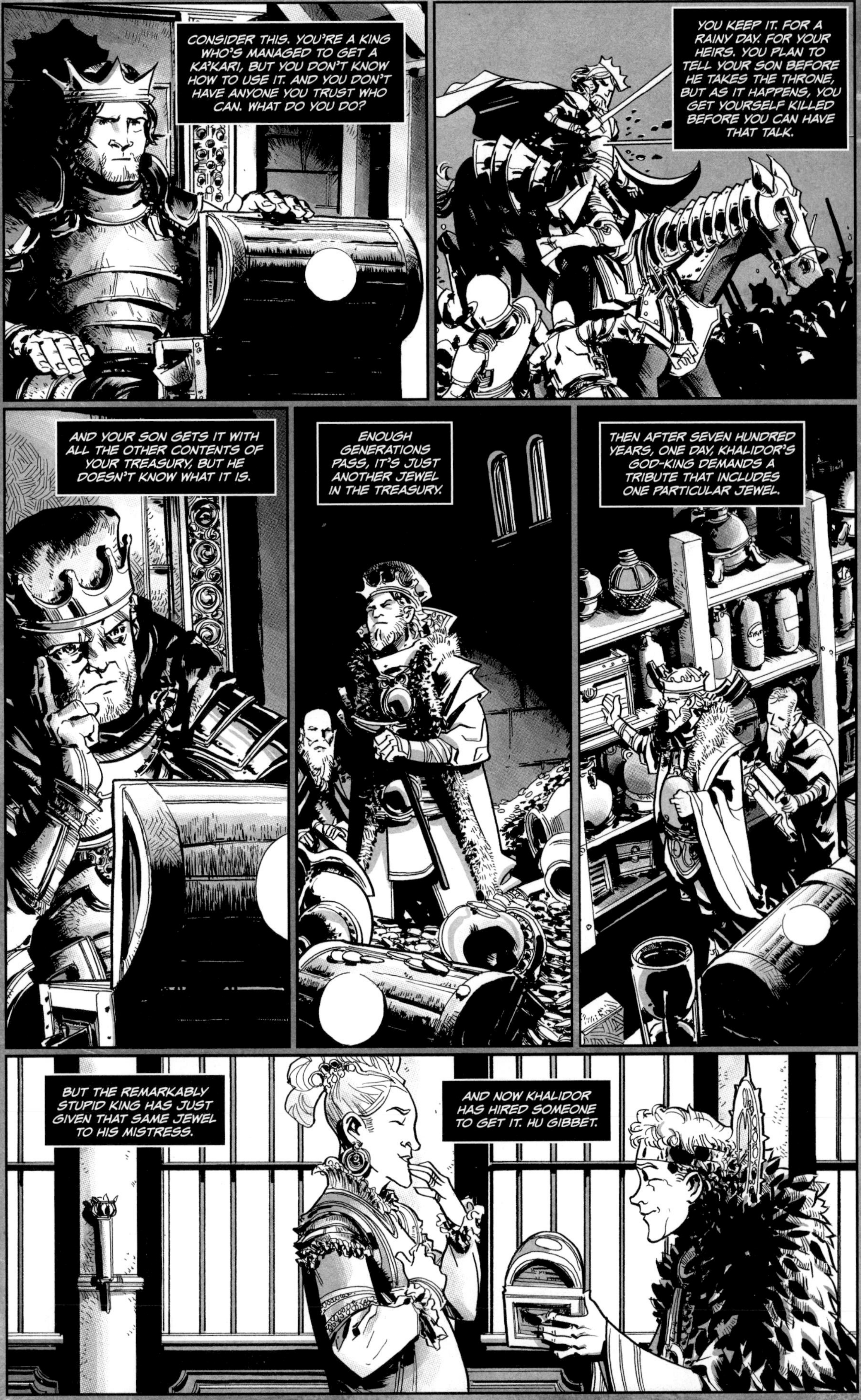
CONSIDER THIS. YOU'RE A KING WHO'S MANAGED TO GET A KA'KARI, BUT YOU DON'T KNOW HOW TO USE IT. AND YOU DON'T HAVE ANYONE YOU TRUST WHO CAN. WHAT DO YOU DO?
YOU KEEP IT. FOR A RAINY DAY. FOR YOUR HEIRS. YOU PLAN TO TELL YOUR SON BEFORE HE TAKES THE THRONE, BUT AS IT HAPPENS, YOU GET YOURSELF KILLED BEFORE YOU CAN HAVE THAT TALK.
AND YOUR SON GETS IT WITH ALL THE OTHER CONTENTS OF YOUR TREASURY, BUT HE DOESN'T KNOW WHAT IT IS.
ENOUGH GENERATIONS PASS, IT'S JUST ANOTHER JEWEL IN THE TREASURY.
THEN AFTER SEVEN HUNDRED YEARS, ONE DAY, KHALIDOR'S GOD-KING DEMANDS A TRIBUTE THAT INCLUDES ONE PARTICULAR JEWEL.
BUT THE REMARKABLY STUPID KING HAS JUST GIVEN THAT SAME JEWEL TO HIS MISTRESS.
AND NOW KHALIDOR HAS HIRED SOMEONE TO GET IT. HU GIBBET.

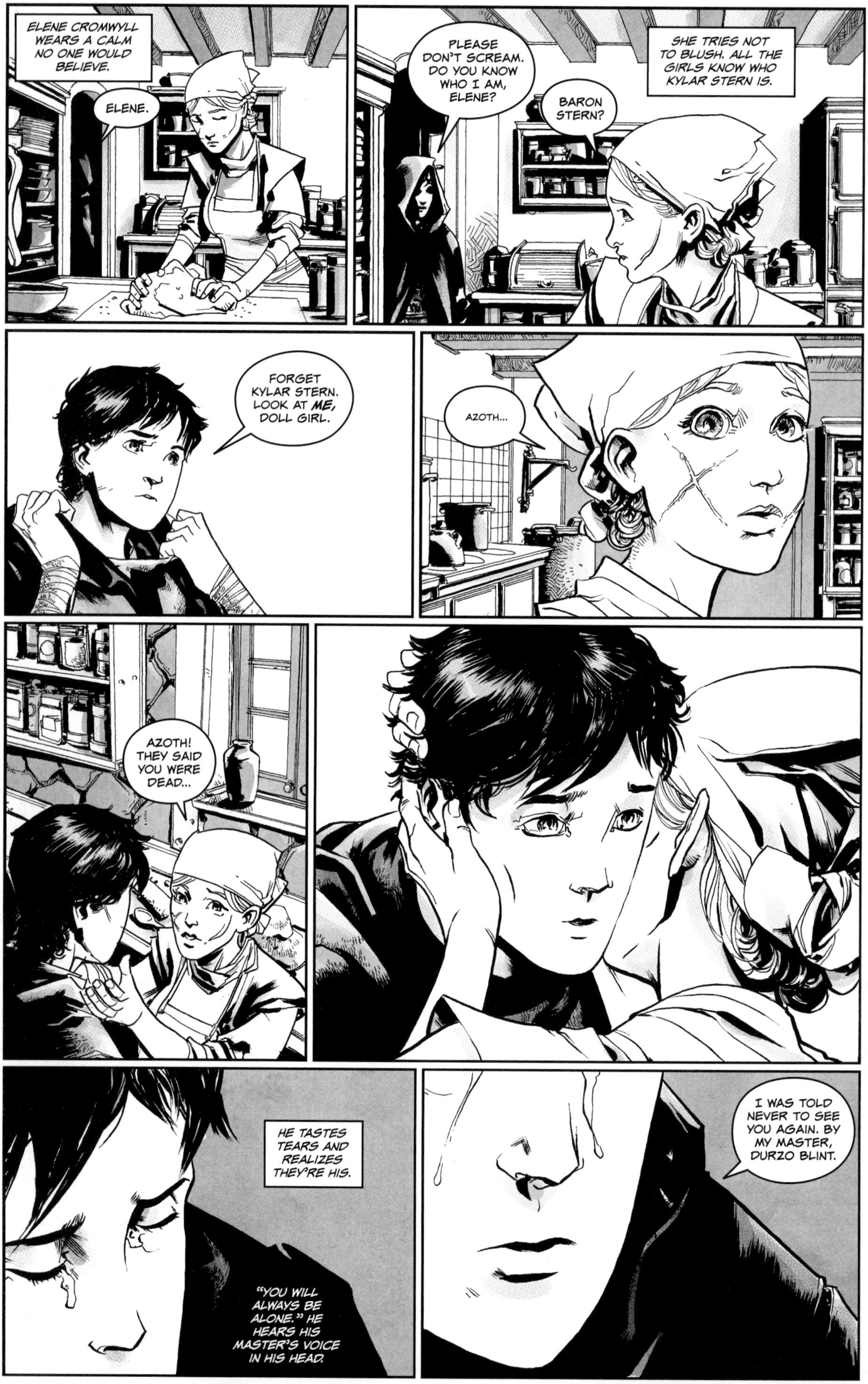
ELENE CROMWYLL WEARS A CALM NO ONE WOULD BELIEVE.
ELENE.
PLEASE DON'T SCREAM. DO YOU KNOW WHO I AM, ELENE?
SHE TRIES NOT TO BLUSH. ALL THE GIRLS KNOW WHO KYLAR STERN IS.
BARON STERN?
FORGET KYLAR STERN. LOOK AT *ME,* DOLL GIRL.
AZOTH...
AZOTH! THEY SAID YOU WERE DEAD...
HE TASTES TEARS AND REALIZES THEY'RE HIS.
"YOU WILL ALWAYS BE ALONE." HE HEARS HIS MASTER'S VOICE IN HIS HEAD.
I WAS TOLD NEVER TO SEE YOU AGAIN. BY MY MASTER, DURZO BLINT.

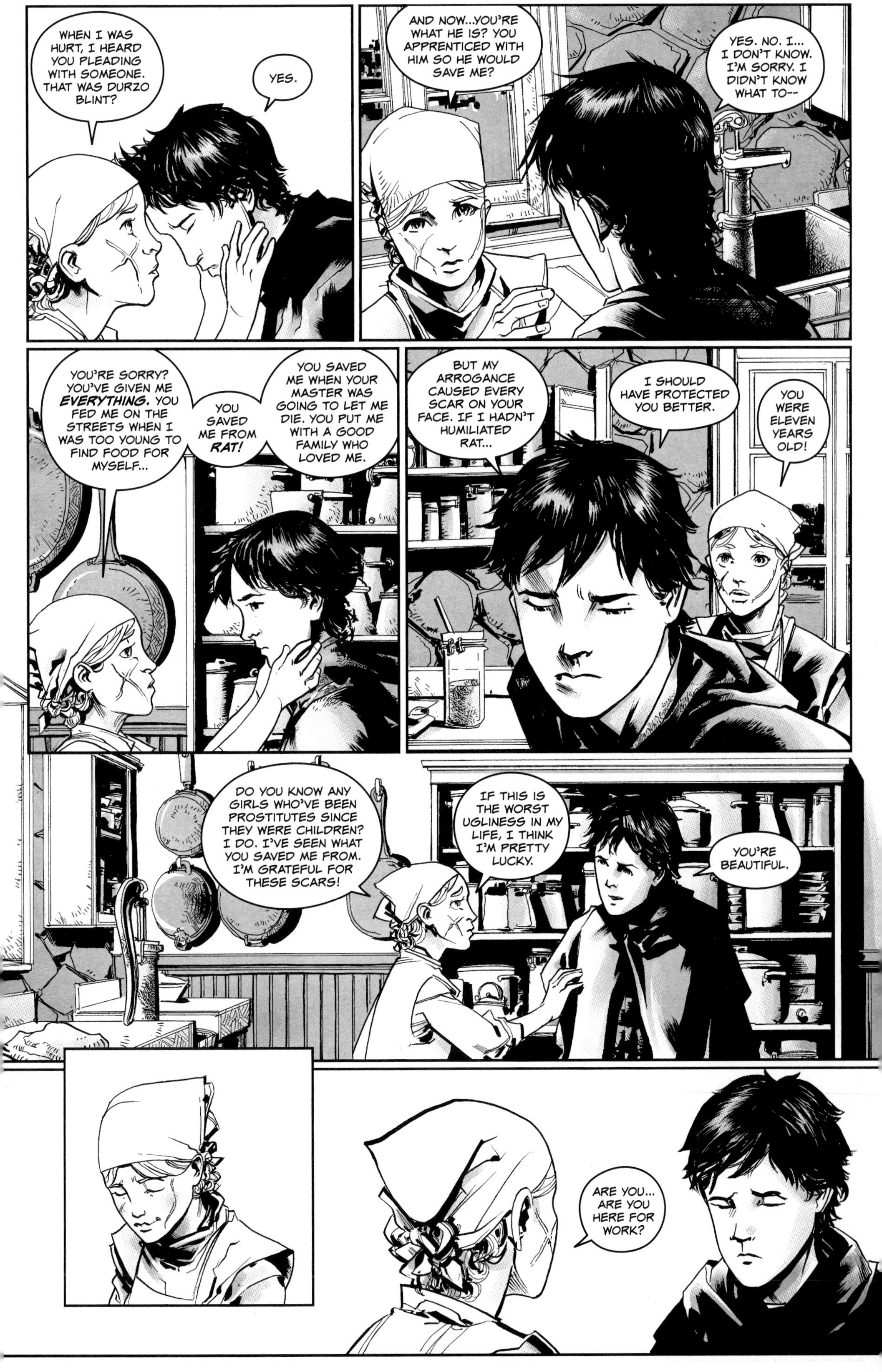

WHEN I WAS HURT, I HEARD YOU PLEADING WITH SOMEONE. THAT WAS DURZO BLINT?
YES.
AND NOW...YOU'RE WHAT HE IS? YOU APPRENTICED WITH HIM SO HE WOULD SAVE ME?
YES. NO. I... I DON'T KNOW. I'M SORRY. I DIDN'T KNOW WHAT TO--
YOU'RE SORRY? YOU'VE GIVEN ME EVERYTHING. YOU FED ME ON THE STREETS WHEN I WAS TOO YOUNG TO FIND FOOD FOR MYSELF...
YOU SAVED ME FROM RAT!
YOU SAVED ME WHEN YOUR MASTER WAS GOING TO LET ME DIE. YOU PUT ME WITH A GOOD FAMILY WHO LOVED ME.
BUT MY ARROGANCE CAUSED EVERY SCAR ON YOUR FACE. IF I HADN'T HUMILIATED RAT...
I SHOULD HAVE PROTECTED YOU BETTER.
YOU WERE ELEVEN YEARS OLD!
DO YOU KNOW ANY GIRLS WHO'VE BEEN PROSTITUTES SINCE THEY WERE CHILDREN? I DO. I'VE SEEN WHAT YOU SAVED ME FROM. I'M GRATEFUL FOR THESE SCARS!
IF THIS IS THE WORST UGLINESS IN MY LIFE, I THINK I'M PRETTY LUCKY.
YOU'RE BEAUTIFUL.
ARE YOU... ARE YOU HERE FOR WORK?

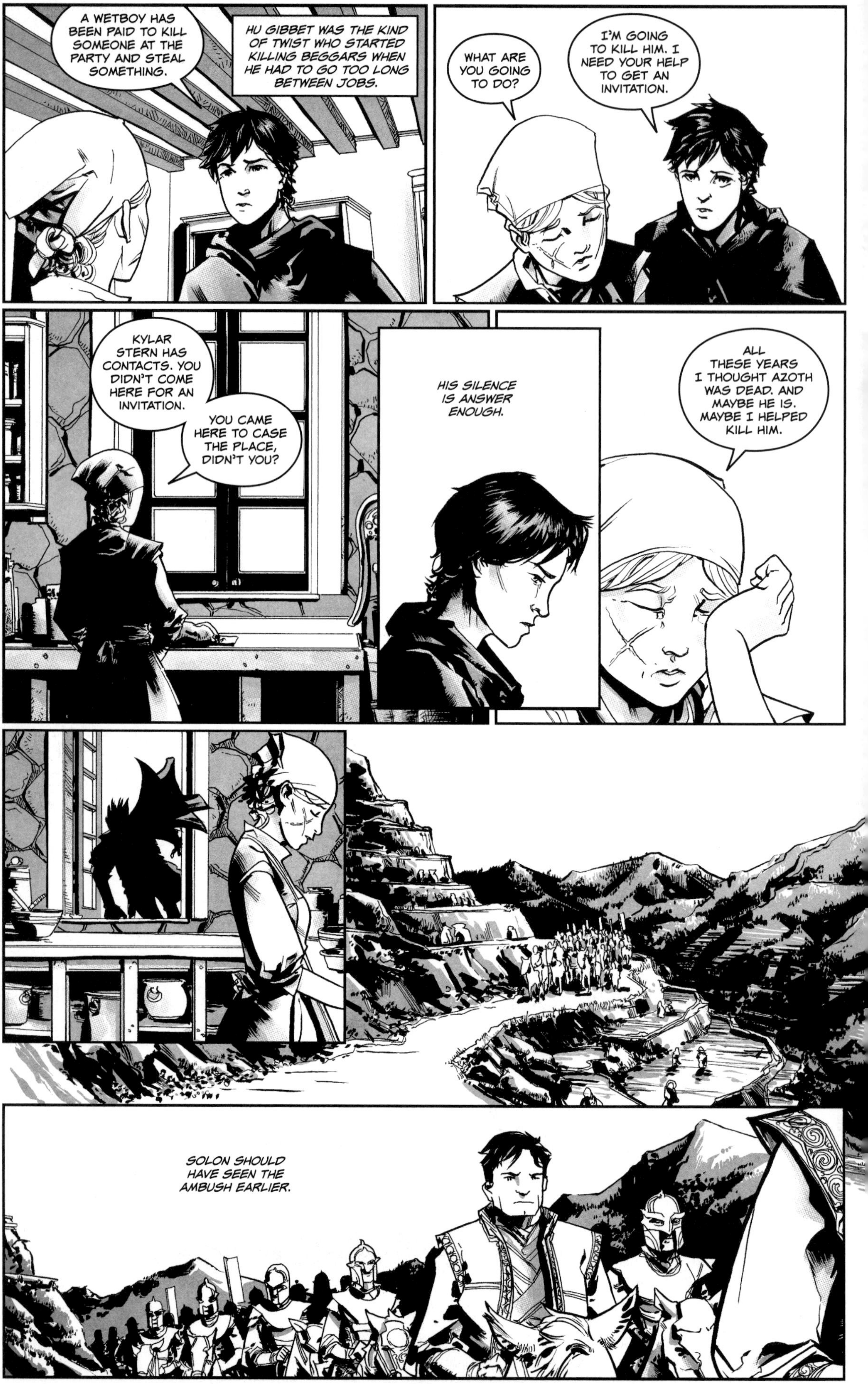
A WETBOY HAS BEEN PAID TO KILL SOMEONE AT THE PARTY AND STEAL SOMETHING.
HU GIBBET WAS THE KIND OF TWIST WHO STARTED KILLING BEGGARS WHEN HE HAD TO GO TOO LONG BETWEEN JOBS.
WHAT ARE YOU GOING TO DO?
I'M GOING TO KILL HIM. I NEED YOUR HELP TO GET AN INVITATION.
KYLAR STERN HAS CONTACTS. YOU DIDN'T COME HERE FOR AN INVITATION.
YOU CAME HERE TO CASE THE PLACE, DIDN'T YOU?
HIS SILENCE IS ANSWER ENOUGH.
ALL THESE YEARS I THOUGHT AZOTH WAS DEAD. AND MAYBE HE IS. MAYBE I HELPED KILL HIM.
SOLON SHOULD HAVE SEEN THE AMBUSH EARLIER.

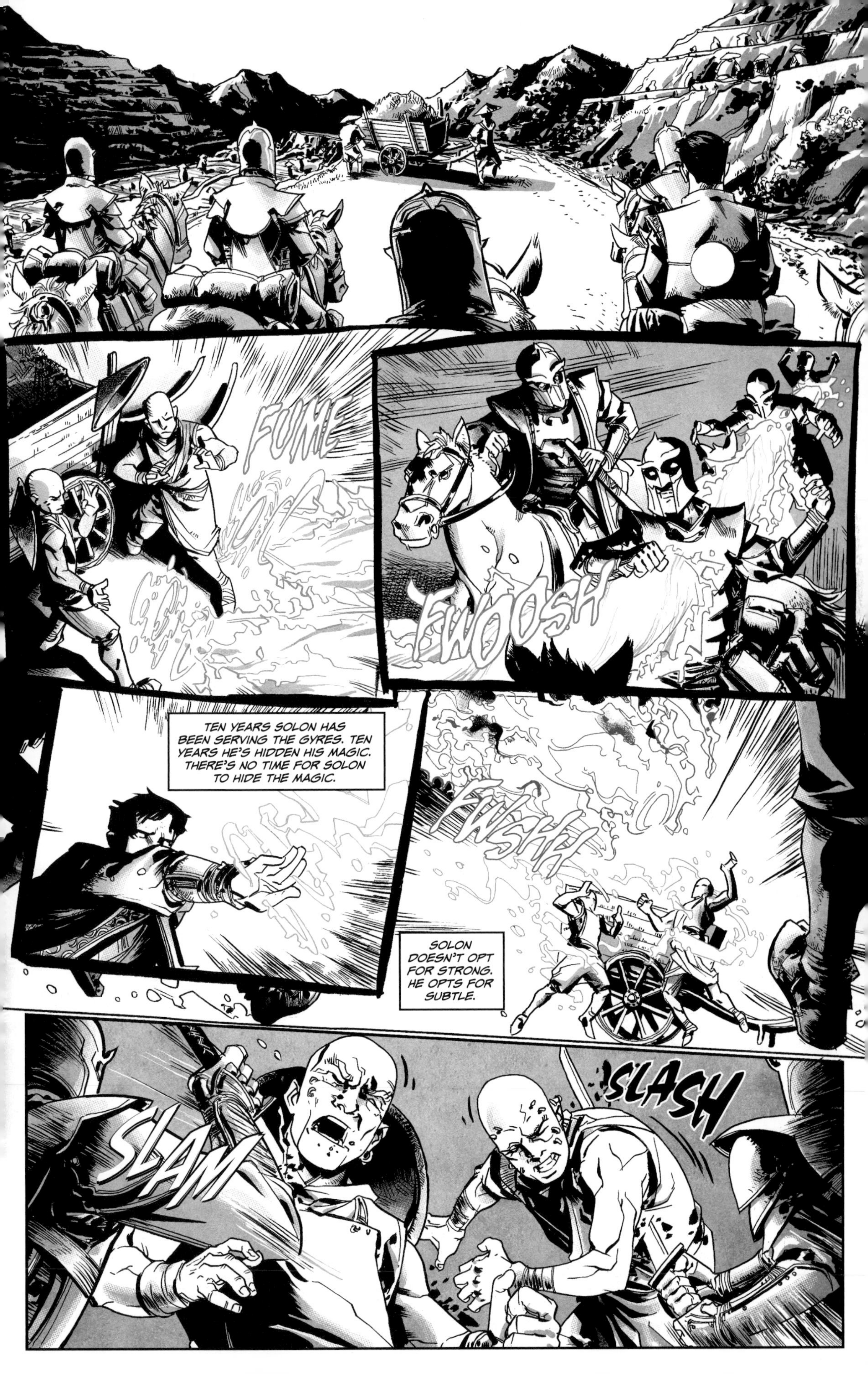
FUME
FWOOSH
TEN YEARS SOLON HAS BEEN SERVING THE GYRES. TEN YEARS HE'S HIDDEN HIS MAGIC. THERE'S NO TIME FOR SOLON TO HIDE THE MAGIC.
FWSHH
SOLON DOESN'T OPT FOR STRONG. HE OPTS FOR SUBTLE.
SLAM
SLASH

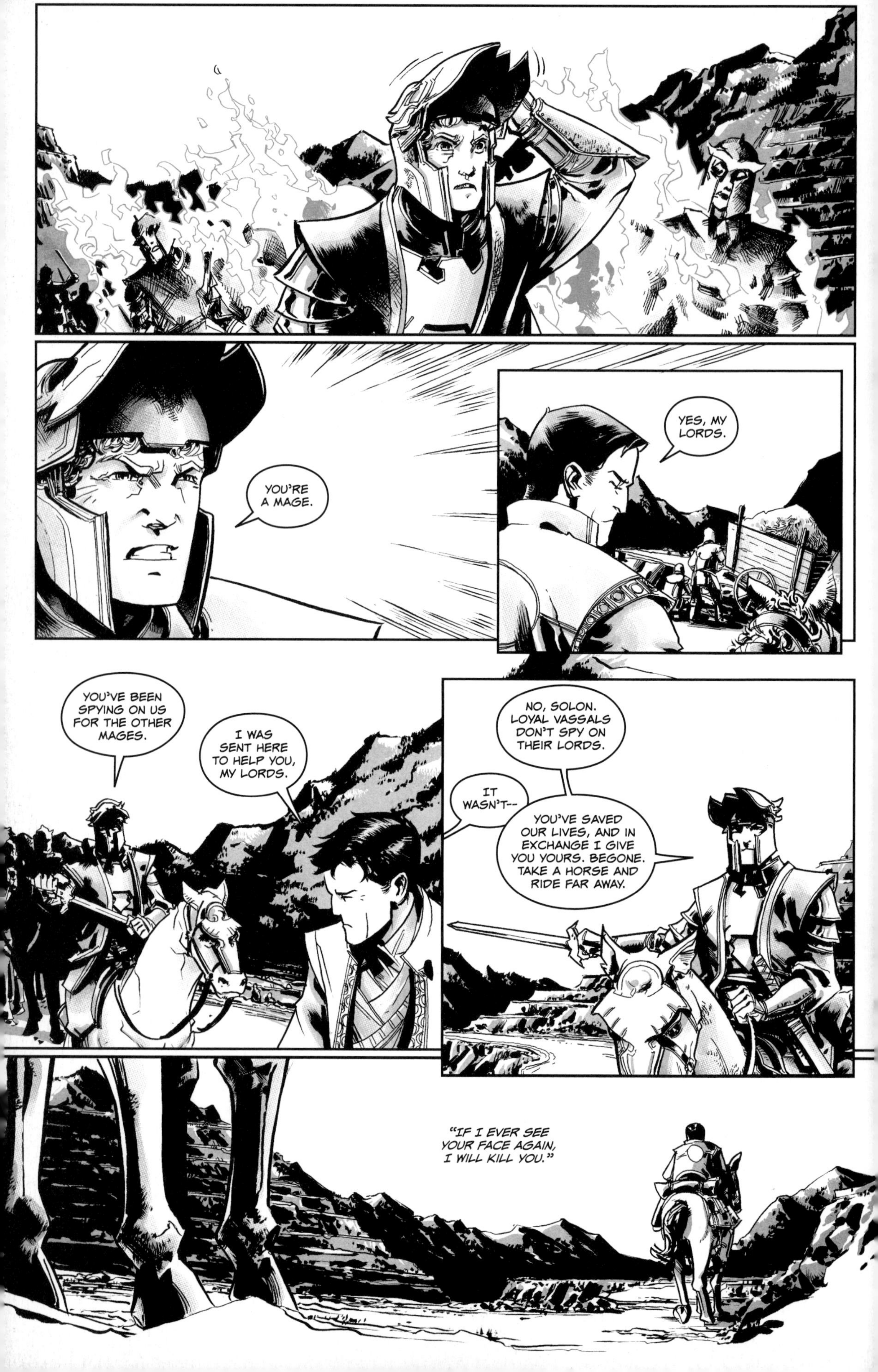
YOU'RE A MAGE.
YES, MY LORDS.
YOU'VE BEEN SPYING ON US FOR THE OTHER MAGES.
I WAS SENT HERE TO HELP YOU, MY LORDS.
NO, SOLON. LOYAL VASSALS DON'T SPY ON THEIR LORDS.
IT WASN'T--
YOU'VE SAVED OUR LIVES, AND IN EXCHANGE I GIVE YOU YOURS. BEGONE. TAKE A HORSE AND RIDE FAR AWAY.
"IF I EVER SEE YOUR FACE AGAIN, I WILL KILL YOU."

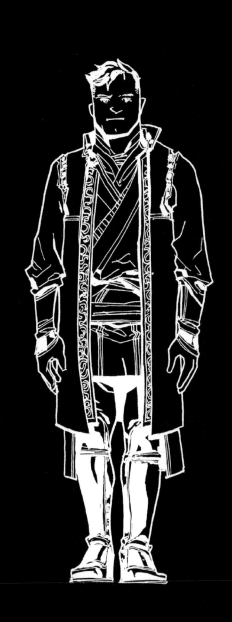

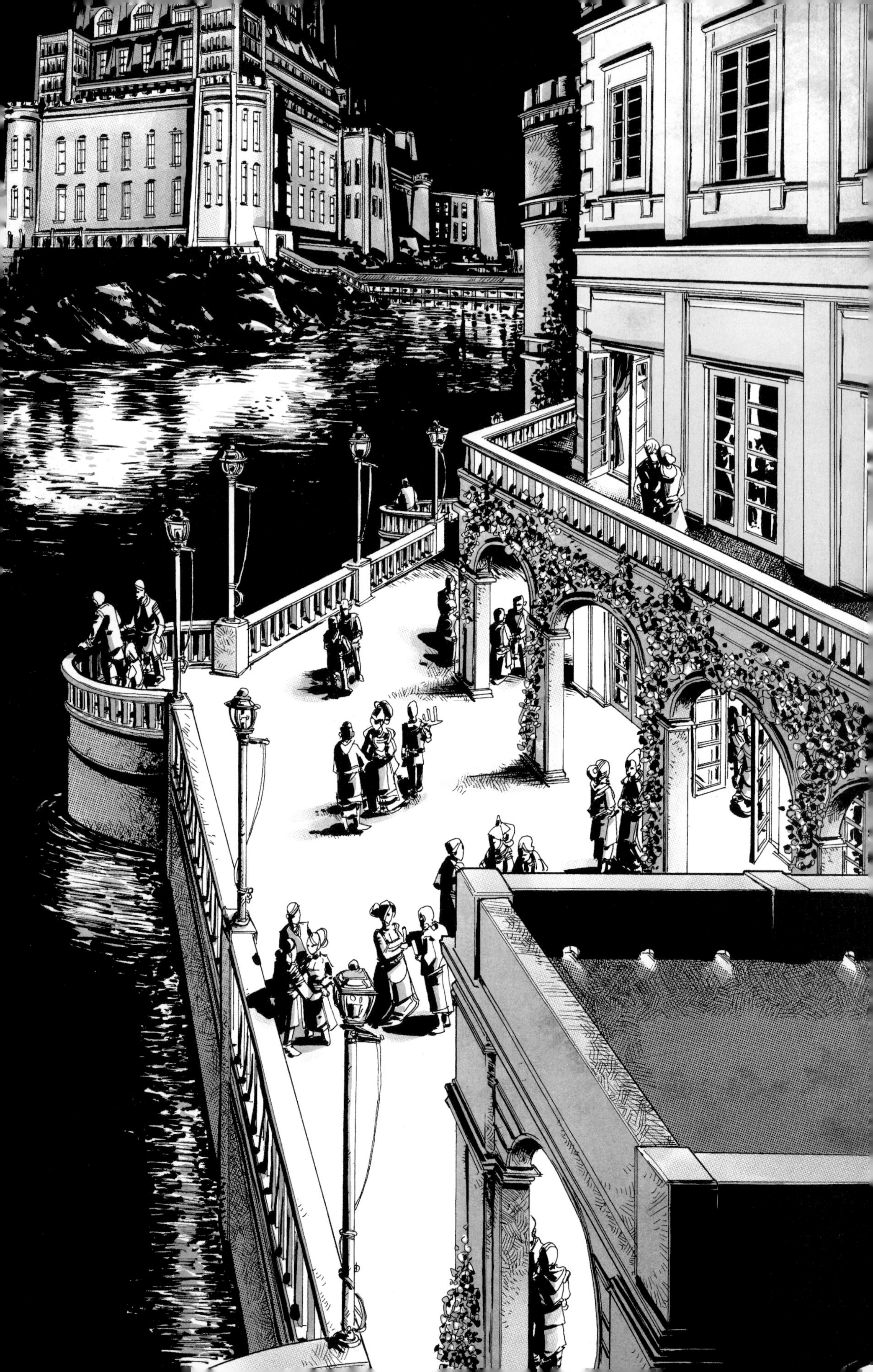

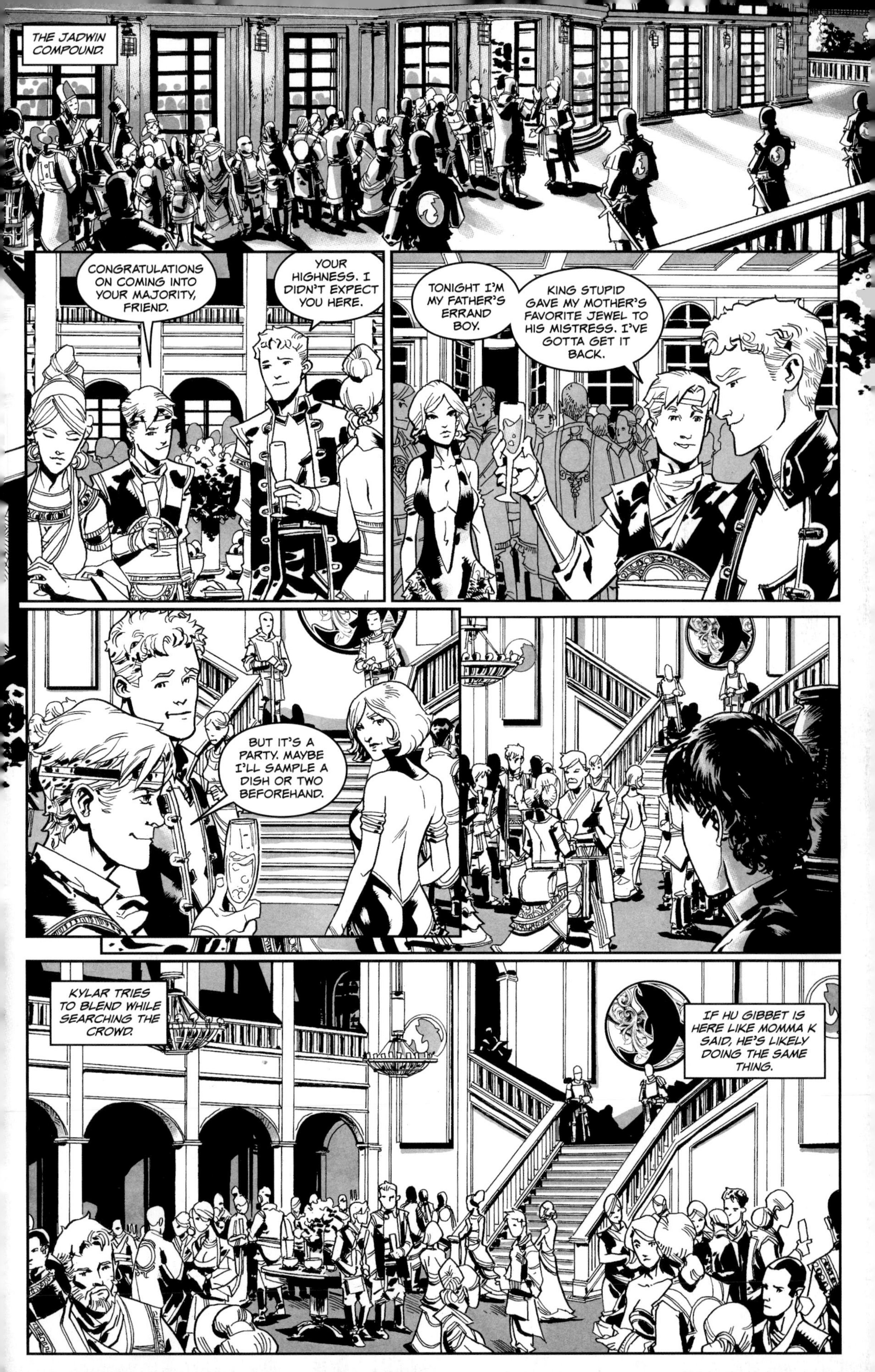
THE JADWIN COMPOUND.
CONGRATULATIONS ON COMING INTO YOUR MAJORITY, FRIEND.
YOUR HIGHNESS. I DIDN'T EXPECT YOU HERE.
TONIGHT I'M MY FATHER'S ERRAND BOY.
KING STUPID GAVE MY MOTHER'S FAVORITE JEWEL TO HIS MISTRESS. I'VE GOTTA GET IT BACK.
BUT IT'S A PARTY. MAYBE I'LL SAMPLE A DISH OR TWO BEFOREHAND.
KYLAR TRIES TO BLEND WHILE SEARCHING THE CROWD.
IF HU GIBBET IS HERE LIKE MOMMA K SAID, HE'S LIKELY DOING THE SAME THING.

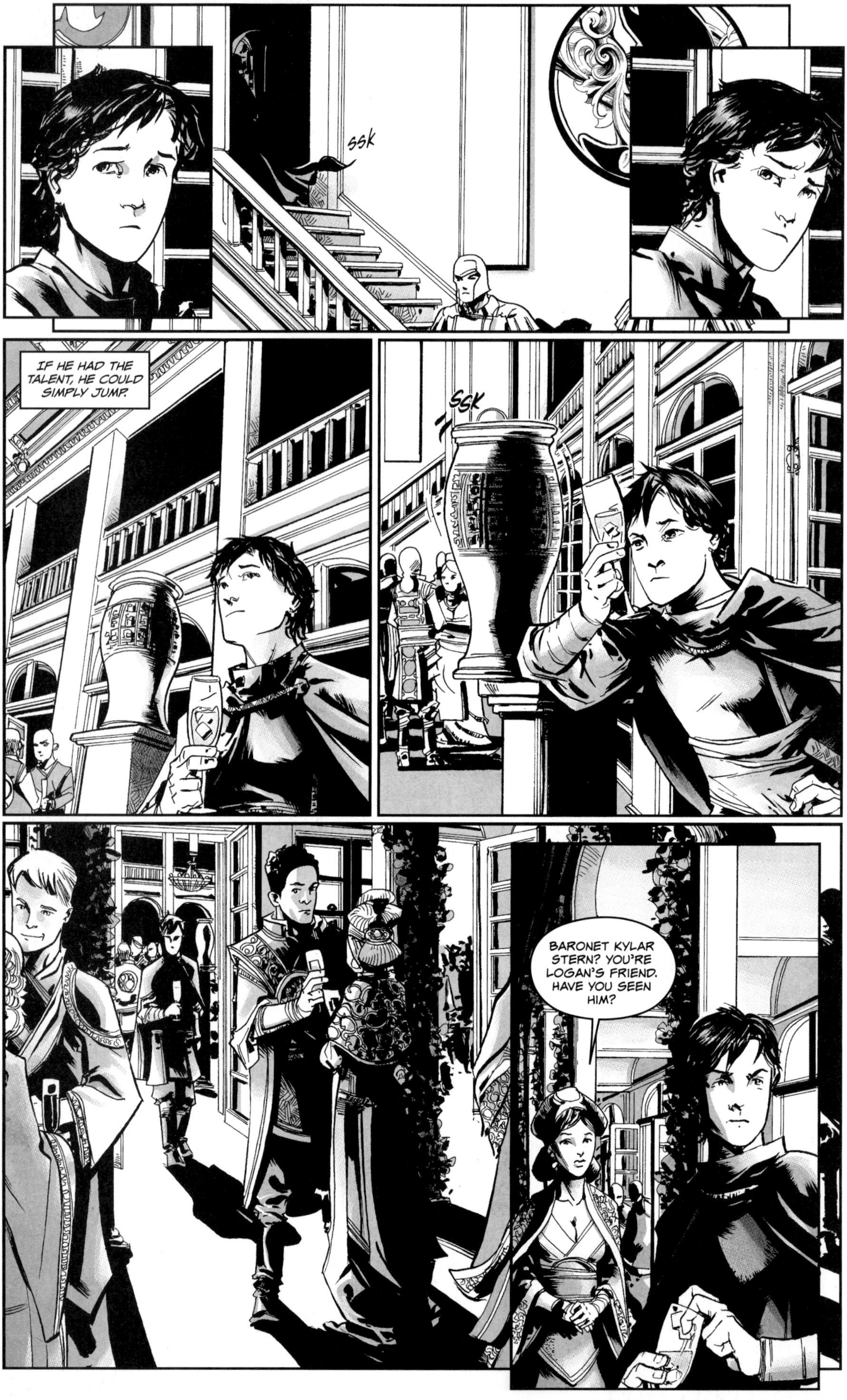
SSK
IF HE HAD THE TALENT, HE COULD SIMPLY JUMP.
SSK
BARONET KYLAR STERN? YOU'RE LOGAN'S FRIEND. HAVE YOU SEEN HIM?

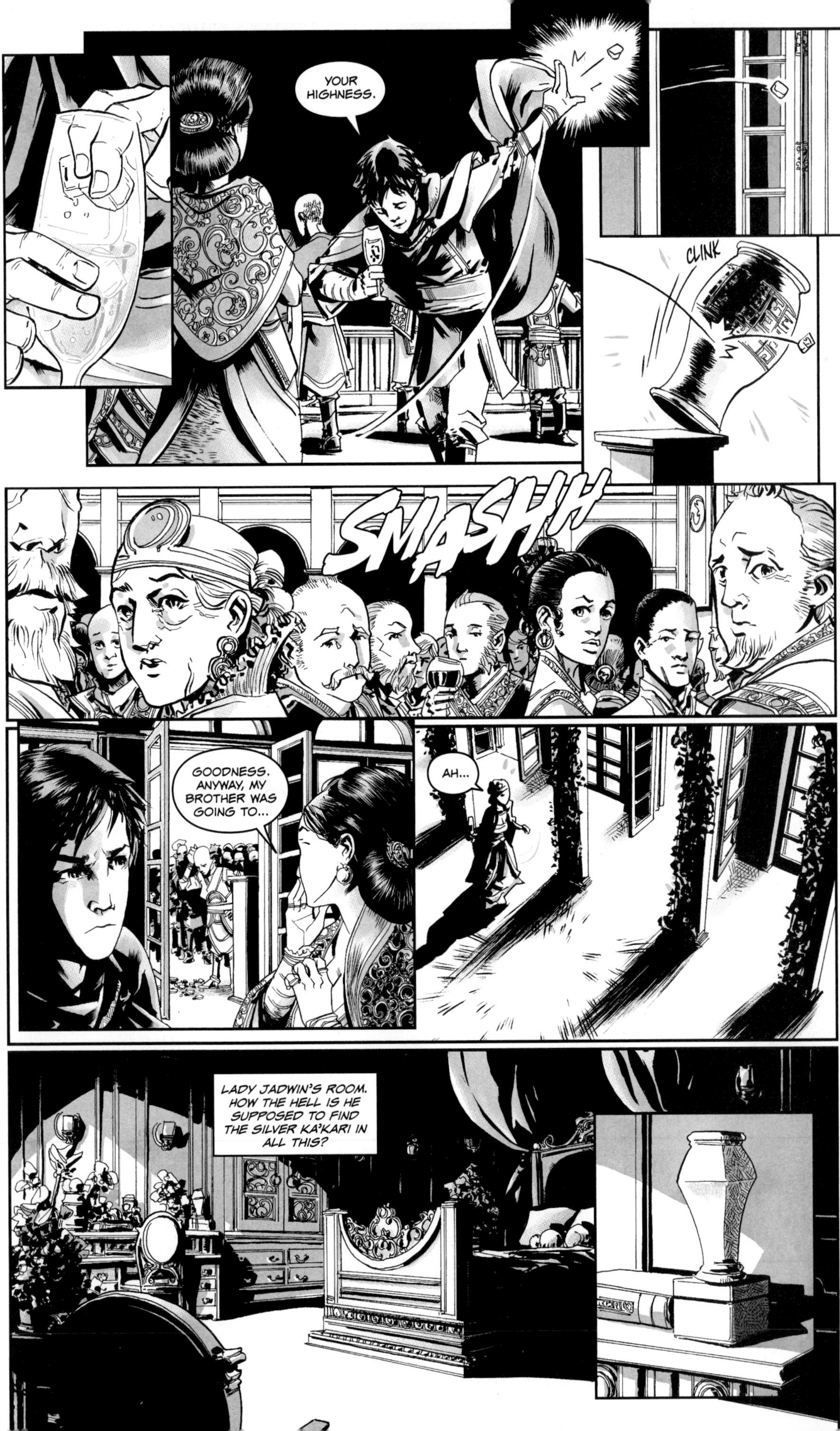
YOUR HIGHNESS.
CLINK
SMASHH
GOODNESS. ANYWAY, MY BROTHER WAS GOING TO...
AH...
LADY JADWIN'S ROOM. HOW THE HELL IS HE SUPPOSED TO FIND THE SILVER KA'KARI IN ALL THIS?

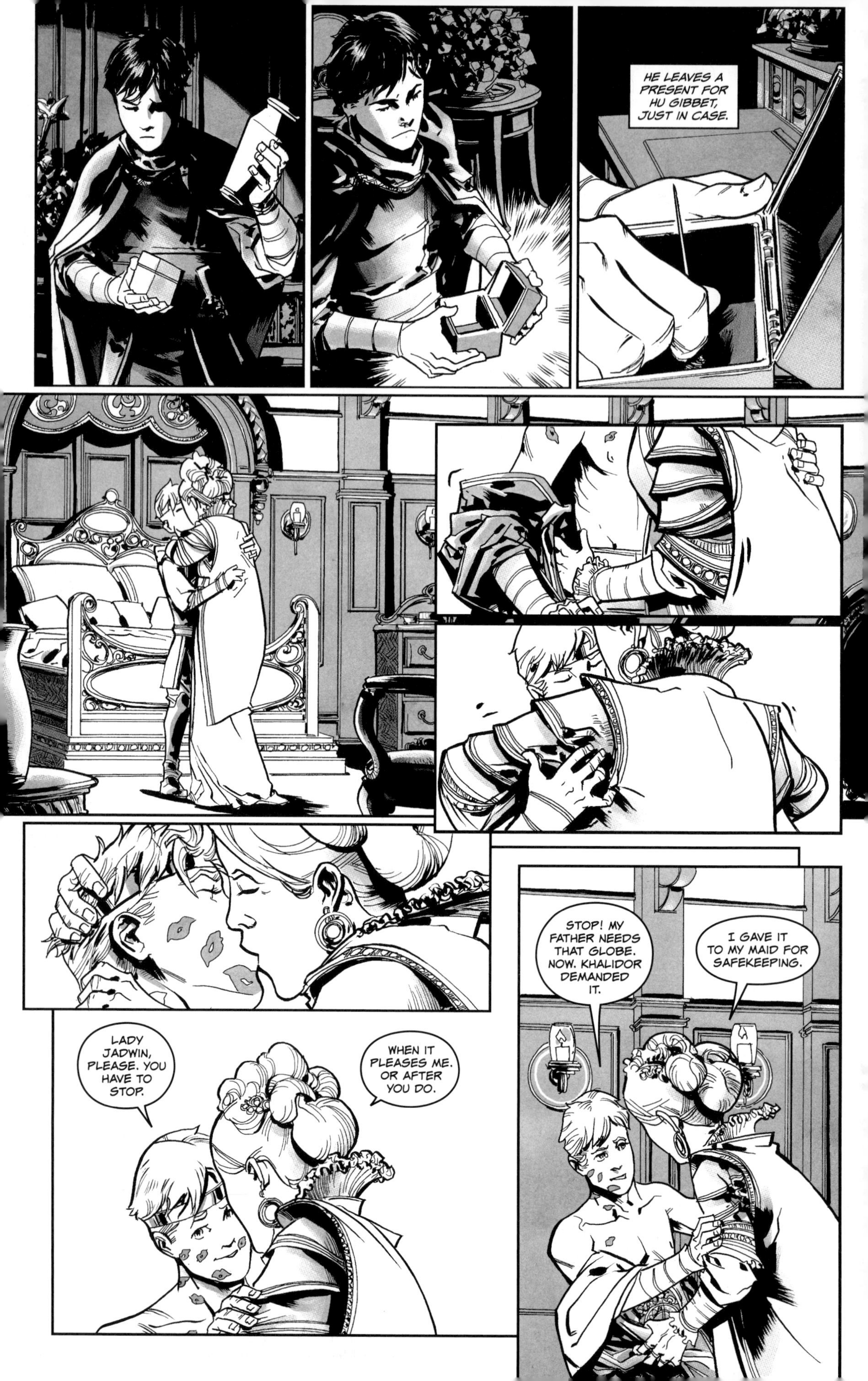
HE LEAVES A PRESENT FOR HU GIBBET, JUST IN CASE.
LADY JADWIN, PLEASE. YOU HAVE TO STOP.
WHEN IT PLEASES ME. OR AFTER YOU DO.
STOP! MY FATHER NEEDS THAT GLOBE. NOW. KHALIDOR DEMANDED IT.
I GAVE IT TO MY MAID FOR SAFEKEEPING.

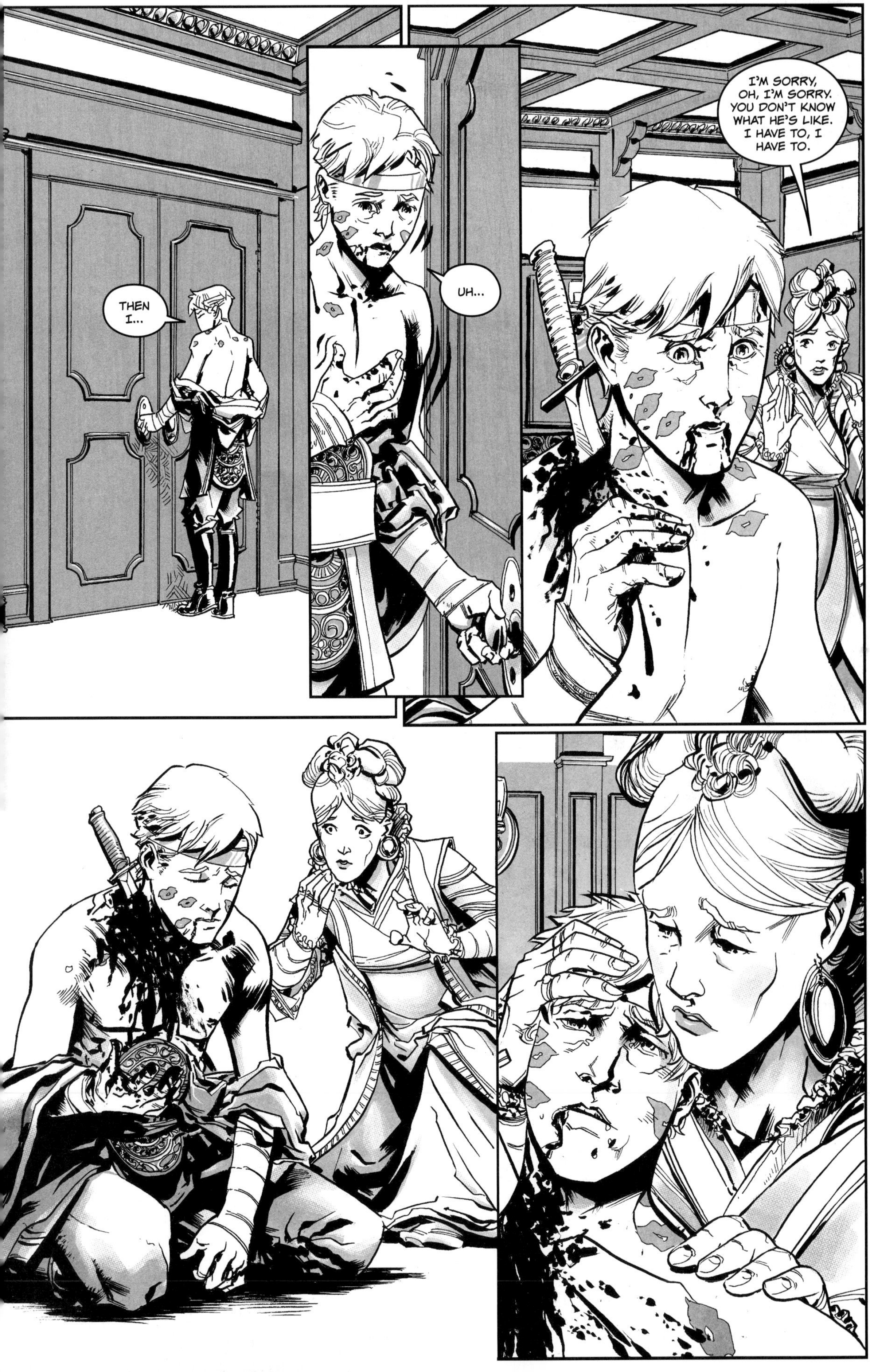
THEN I...
UH...
I'M SORRY, OH, I'M SORRY. YOU DON'T KNOW WHAT HE'S LIKE. I HAVE TO, I HAVE TO.

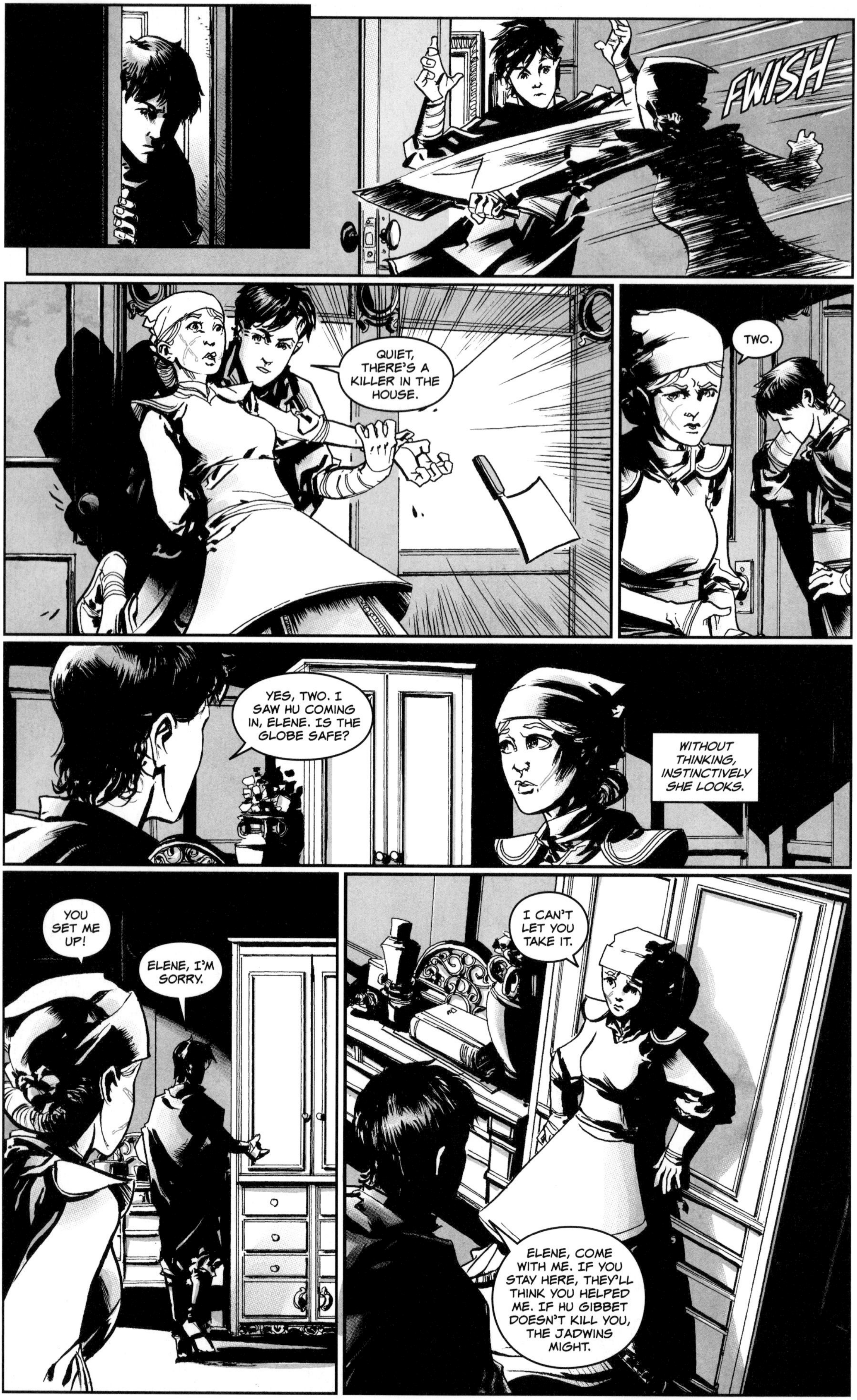
FWISH
QUIET, THERE'S A KILLER IN THE HOUSE.
TWO.
YES, TWO. I SAW HU COMING IN, ELENE. IS THE GLOBE SAFE?
WITHOUT THINKING, INSTINCTIVELY SHE LOOKS.
YOU SET ME UP!
ELENE, I'M SORRY.
I CAN'T LET YOU TAKE IT.
ELENE, COME WITH ME. IF YOU STAY HERE, THEY'LL THINK YOU HELPED ME. IF HU GIBBET DOESN'T KILL YOU, THE JADWINS MIGHT.

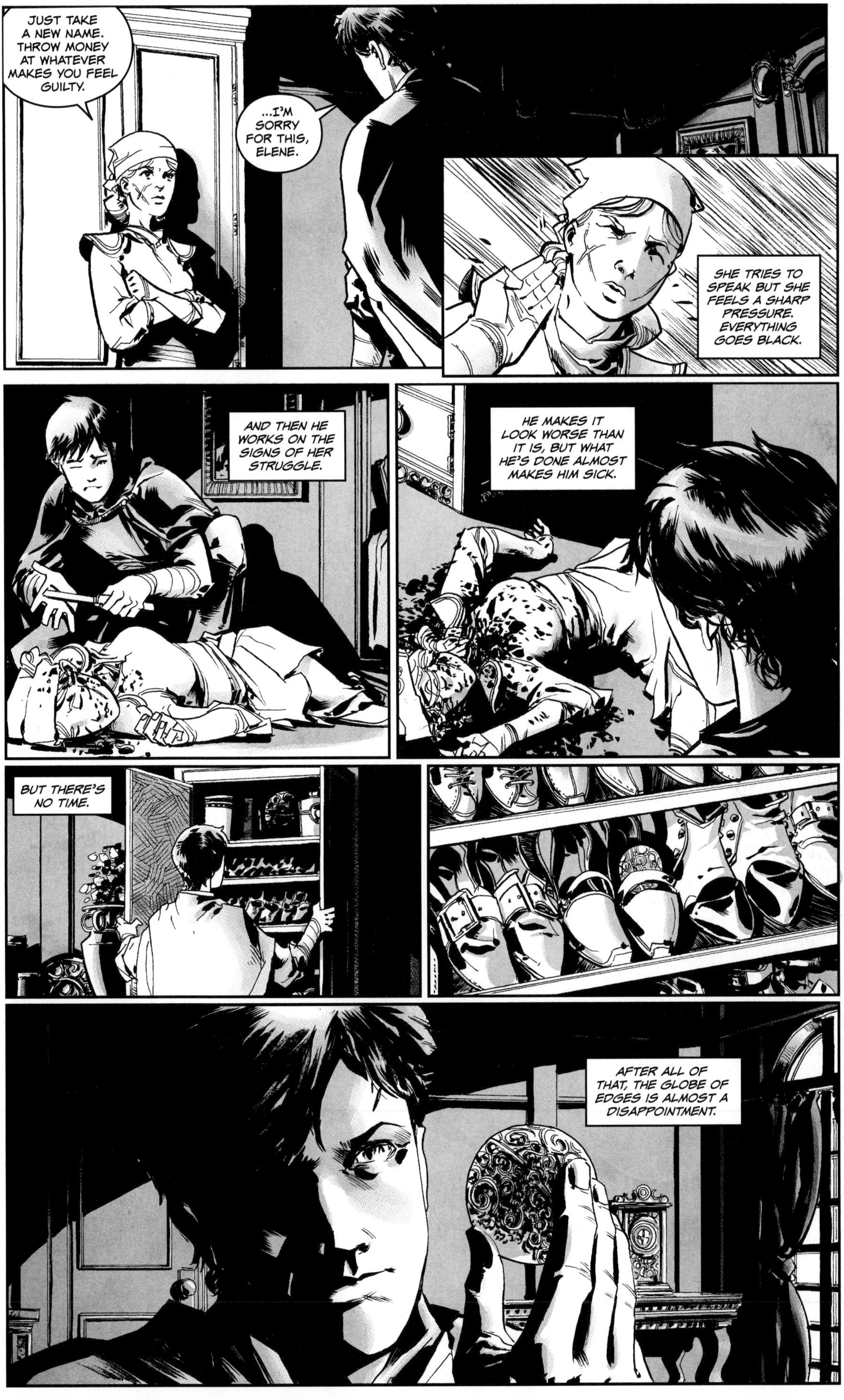
JUST TAKE A NEW NAME. THROW MONEY AT WHATEVER MAKES YOU FEEL GUILTY.
...I'M SORRY FOR THIS, ELENE.
SHE TRIES TO SPEAK BUT SHE FEELS A SHARP PRESSURE. EVERYTHING GOES BLACK.
AND THEN HE WORKS ON THE SIGNS OF HER STRUGGLE.
HE MAKES IT LOOK WORSE THAN IT IS, BUT WHAT HE'S DONE ALMOST MAKES HIM SICK.
BUT THERE'S NO TIME.
AFTER ALL OF THAT, THE GLOBE OF EDGES IS ALMOST A DISAPPOINTMENT.

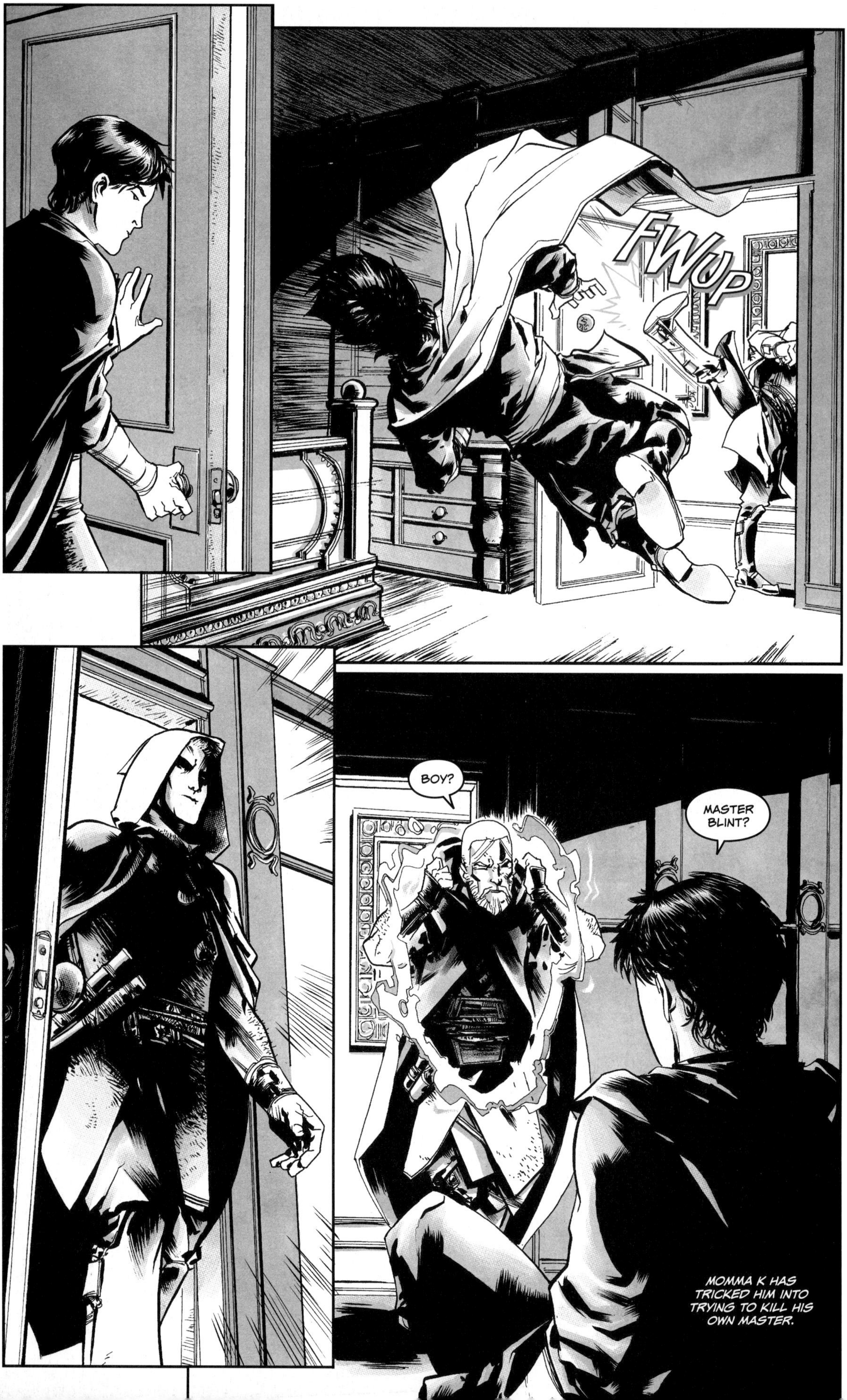
FWUP
BOY?
MASTER BLINT?
MOMMA K HAS TRICKED HIM INTO TRYING TO KILL HIS OWN MASTER.

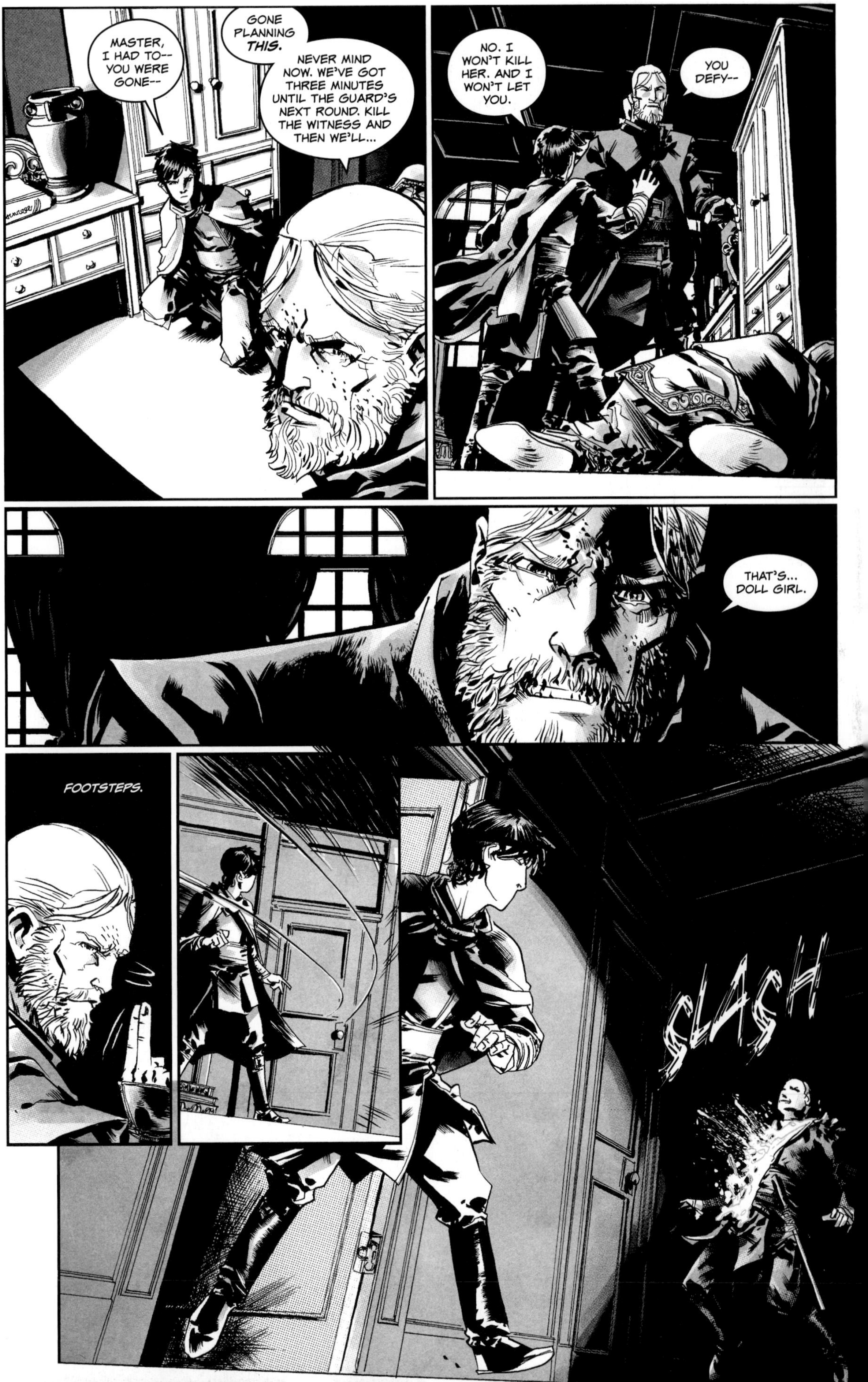

MASTER, I HAD TO-- YOU WERE GONE--
GONE PLANNING THIS.
NEVER MIND NOW. WE'VE GOT THREE MINUTES UNTIL THE GUARD'S NEXT ROUND. KILL THE WITNESS AND THEN WE'LL...
NO. I WON'T KILL HER. AND I WON'T LET YOU.
YOU DEFY--
THAT'S... DOLL GIRL.
FOOTSTEPS.
SLASH

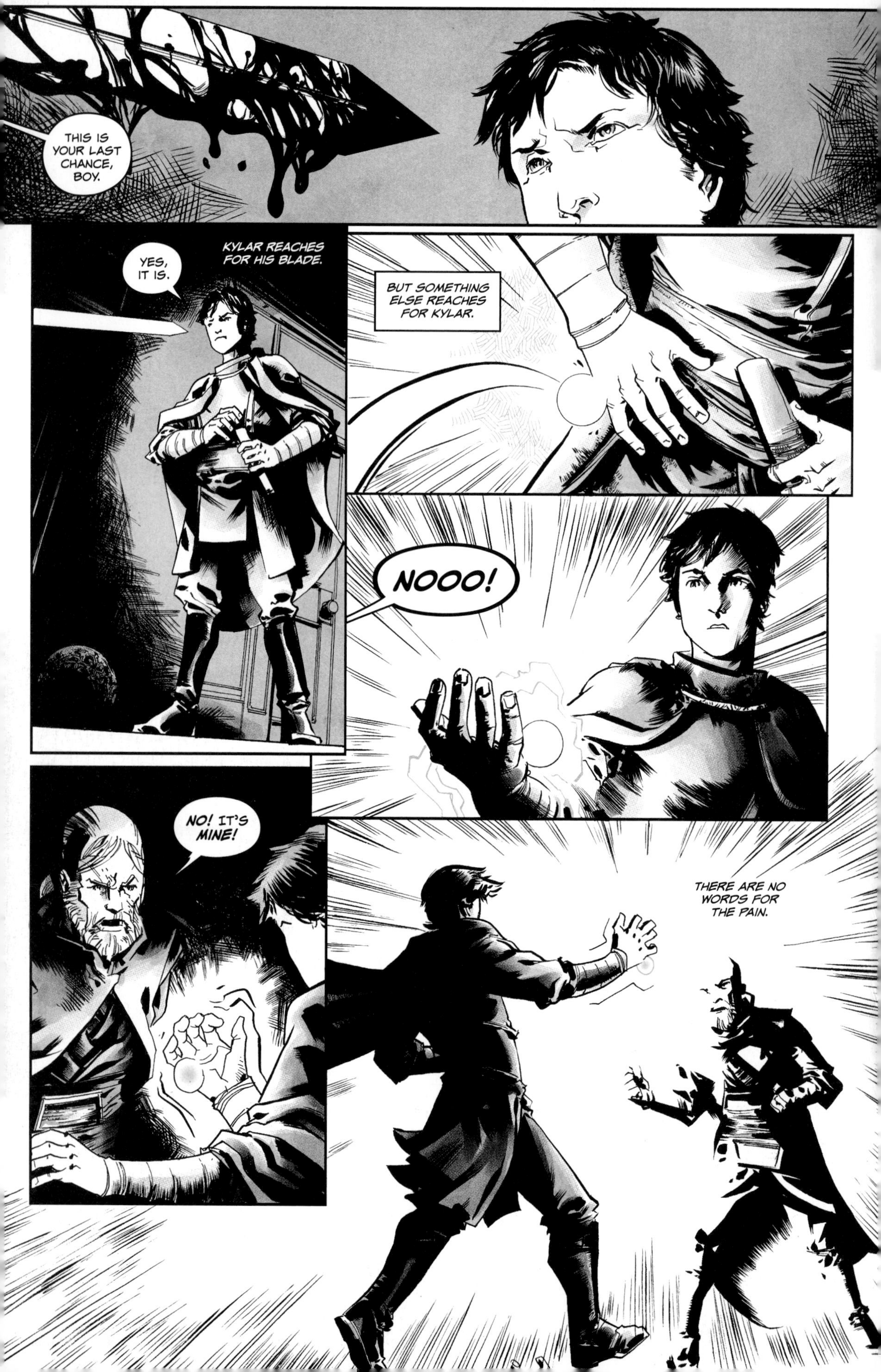
THIS IS YOUR LAST CHANCE, BOY.
YES, IT IS.
KYLAR REACHES FOR HIS BLADE.
BUT SOMETHING ELSE REACHES FOR KYLAR.
NOOO!
NO! IT'S MINE!
THERE ARE NO WORDS FOR THE PAIN.

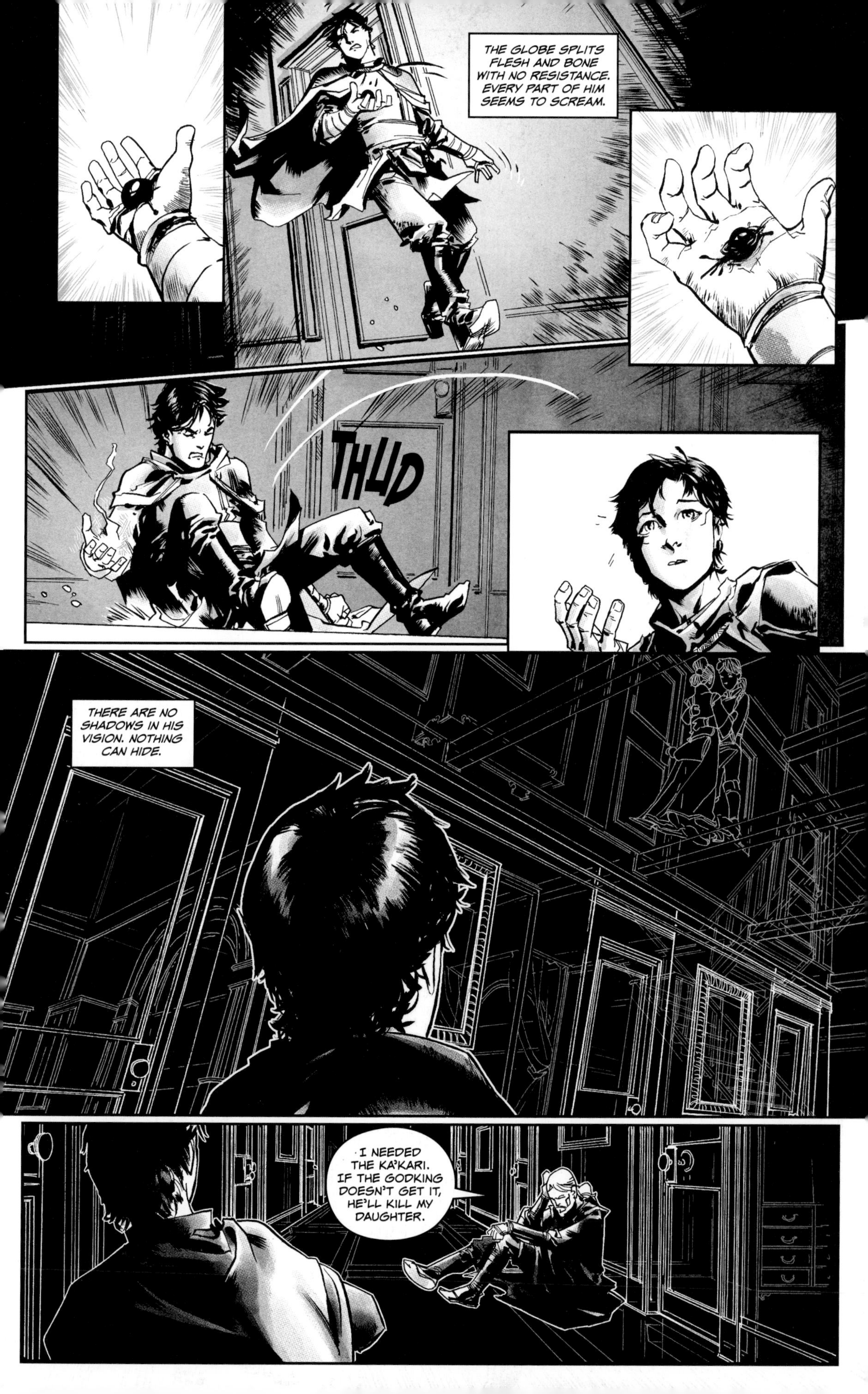
THE GLOBE SPLITS FLESH AND BONE WITH NO RESISTANCE. EVERY PART OF HIM SEEMS TO SCREAM.
THUD
THERE ARE NO SHADOWS IN HIS VISION. NOTHING CAN HIDE.
I NEEDED THE KA'KARI. IF THE GODKING DOESN'T GET IT, HE'LL KILL MY DAUGHTER.

I'M SORRY, I DIDN'T...

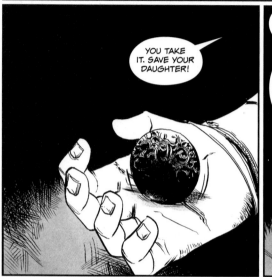

YOU TAKE IT. SAVE YOUR DAUGHTER!

YOU BONDED IT. IT BONDS FOR LIFE.

YOUR TALENT WILL WORK NOW, WHETHER YOU'RE HOLDING IT OR NOT, BUT ITS OTHER POWERS WON'T WORK FOR ANYONE ELSE UNTIL YOU'RE DEAD.

THEY'RE COMING FAST.

HE REMEMBERS THE MEISTER'S WORDS. "IF YOU DON'T KILL DURZO BLINT TOMORROW, KHALIDOR WILL TAKE CENARIA."

THIS CLOSE, NOT EVEN DURZO COULD PROTECT HIMSELF.

LIFE IS EMPTY.

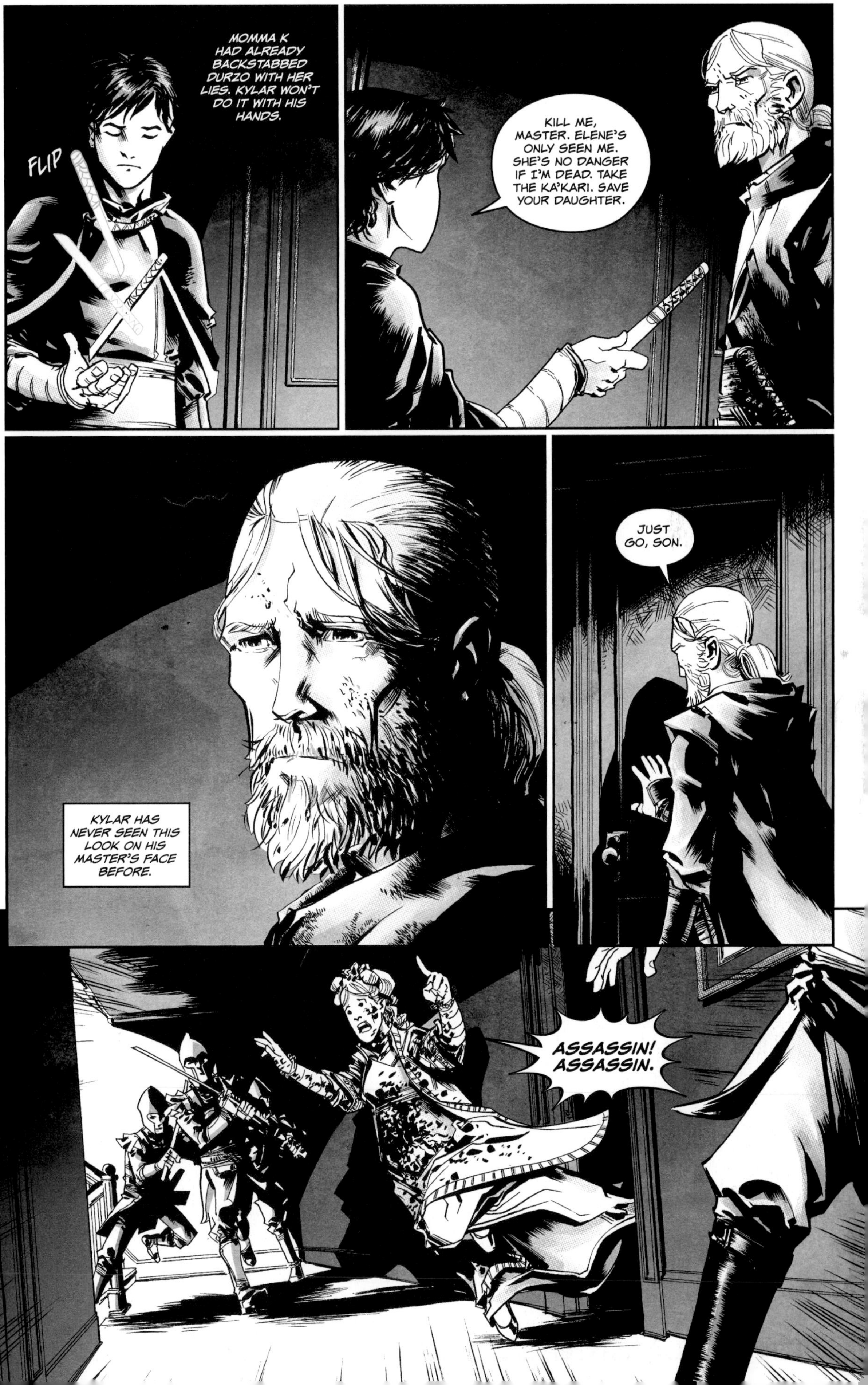
MOMMA K HAD ALREADY BACKSTABBED DURZO WITH HER LIES. KYLAR WON'T DO IT WITH HIS HANDS.
FLIP
KILL ME, MASTER. ELENE'S ONLY SEEN ME. SHE'S NO DANGER IF I'M DEAD. TAKE THE KA'KARI. SAVE YOUR DAUGHTER.
KYLAR HAS NEVER SEEN THIS LOOK ON HIS MASTER'S FACE BEFORE.
JUST GO, SON.
ASSASSIN! ASSASSIN.

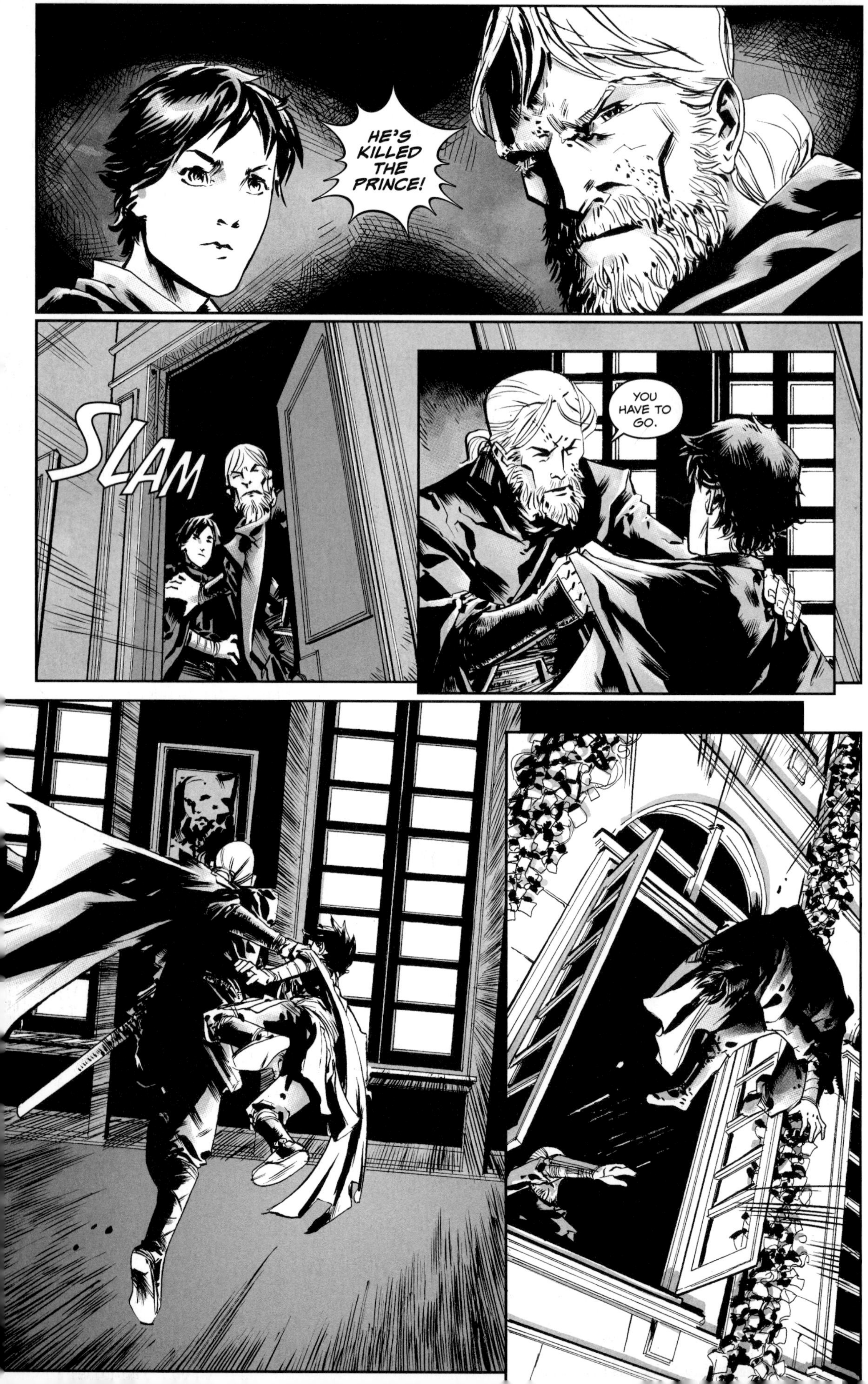
HE'S KILLED THE PRINCE!
SLAM
YOU HAVE TO GO.

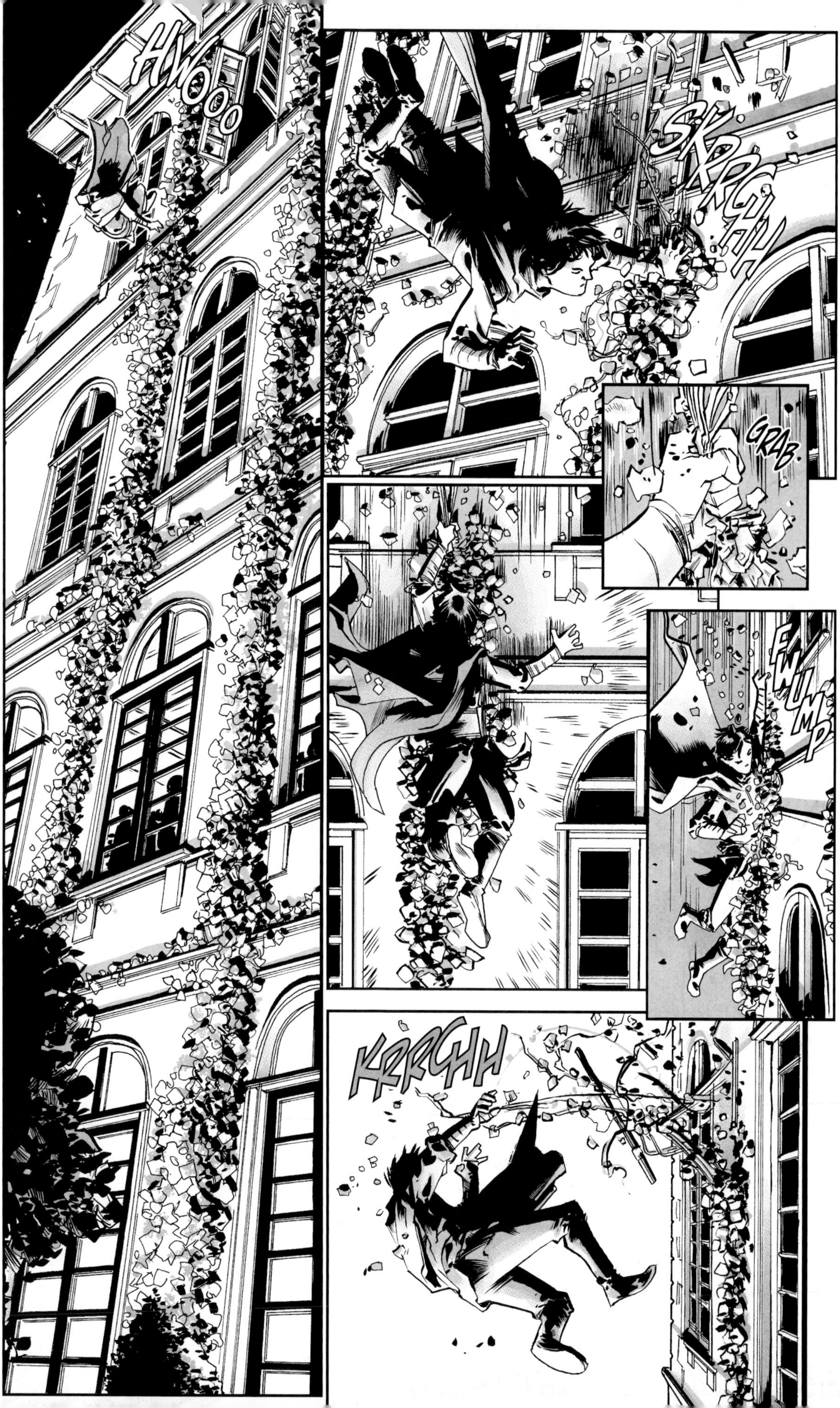
HWOOO
SKRCHH
GRAB.
FWUMP
KRRCHH

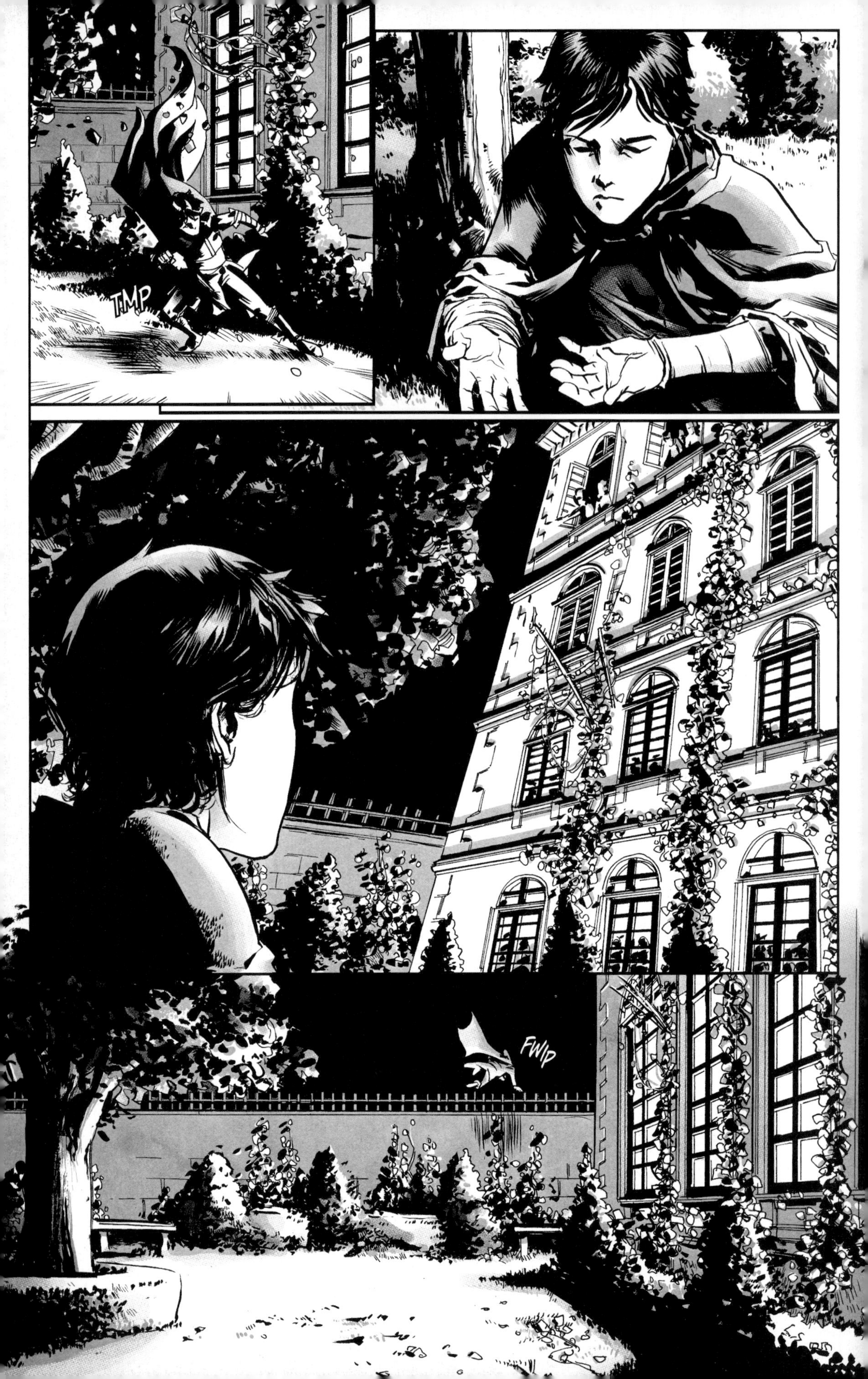
TMP
FWIP

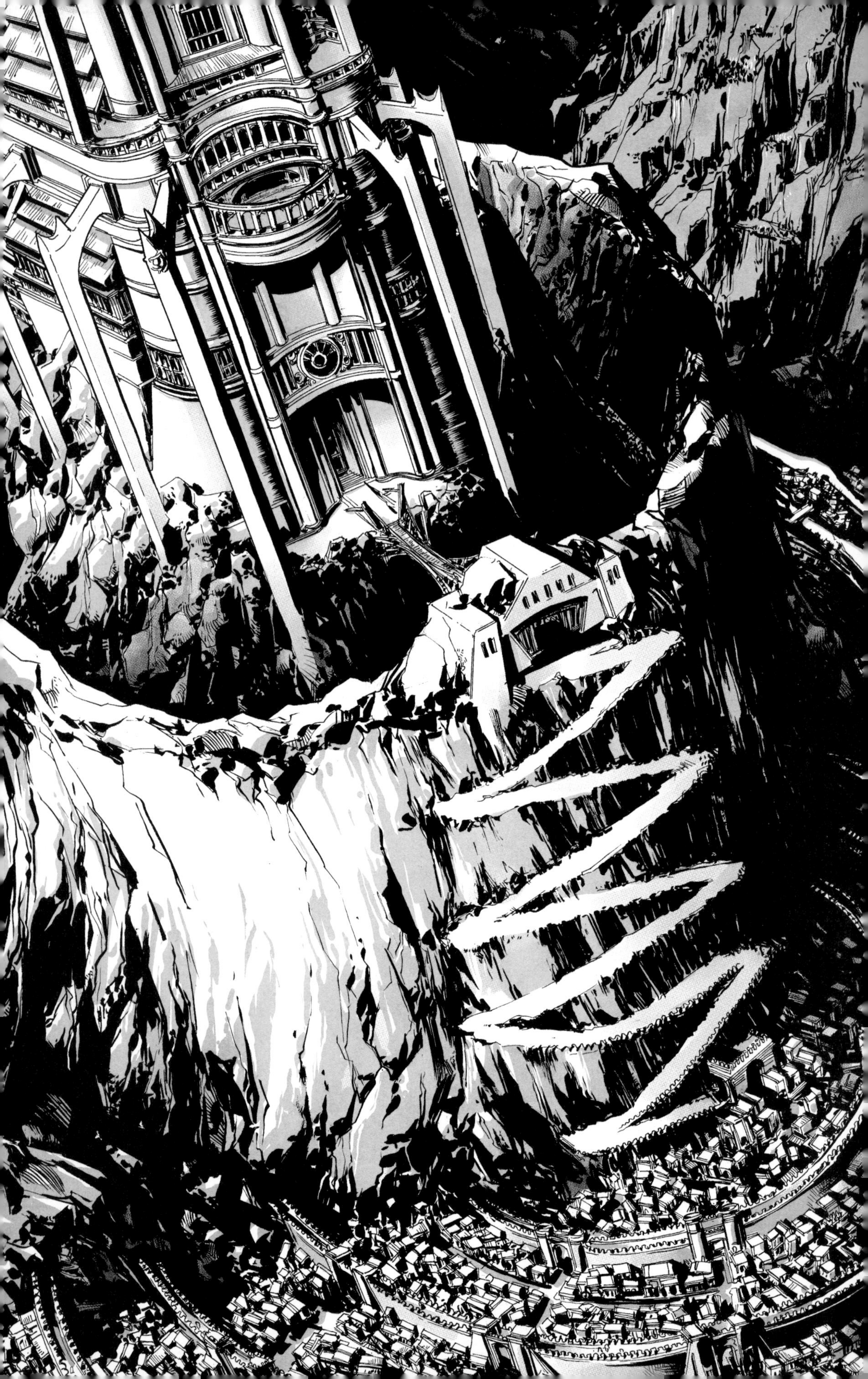

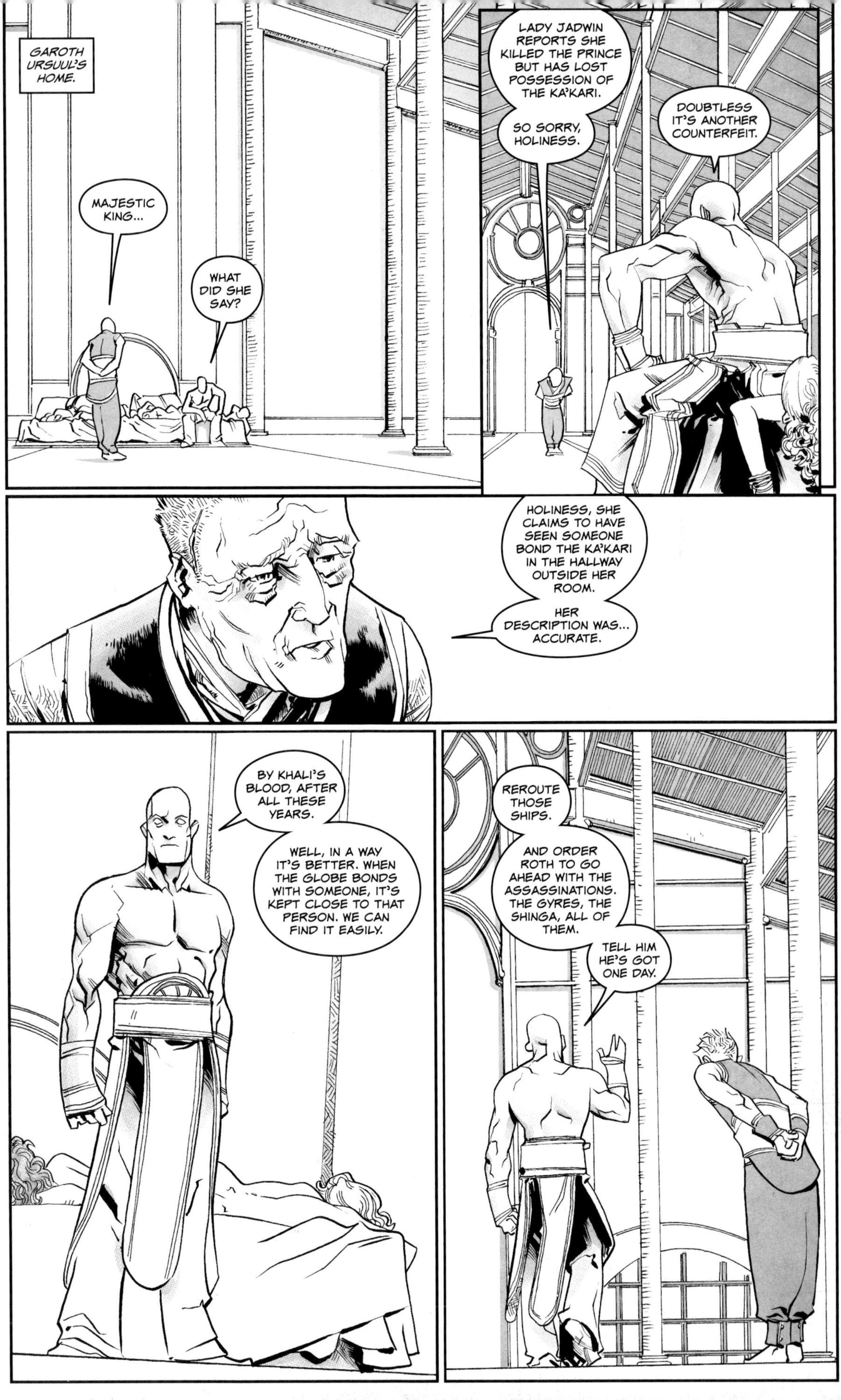
GAROTH URSUUL'S HOME.
MAJESTIC KING...
WHAT DID SHE SAY?
LADY JADWIN REPORTS SHE KILLED THE PRINCE BUT HAS LOST POSSESSION OF THE KA'KARI.
SO SORRY, HOLINESS.
DOUBTLESS IT'S ANOTHER COUNTERFEIT.
HOLINESS, SHE CLAIMS TO HAVE SEEN SOMEONE BOND THE KA'KARI IN THE HALLWAY OUTSIDE HER ROOM.
HER DESCRIPTION WAS... ACCURATE.
BY KHALI'S BLOOD, AFTER ALL THESE YEARS.
WELL, IN A WAY IT'S BETTER. WHEN THE GLOBE BONDS WITH SOMEONE, IT'S KEPT CLOSE TO THAT PERSON. WE CAN FIND IT EASILY.
REROUTE THOSE SHIPS.
AND ORDER ROTH TO GO AHEAD WITH THE ASSASSINATIONS. THE GYRES, THE SHINGA, ALL OF THEM.
TELL HIM HE'S GOT ONE DAY.

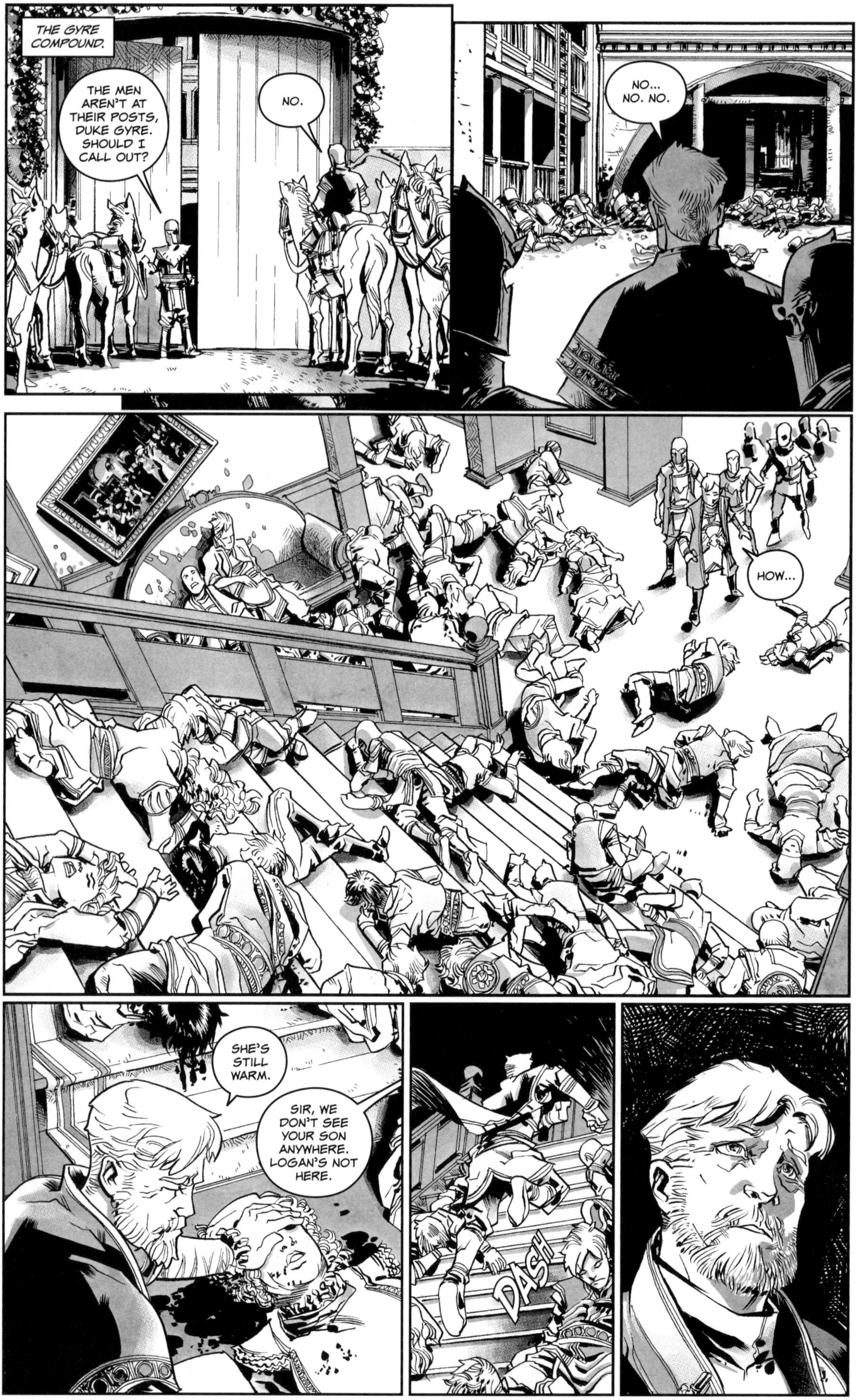
THE GYRE COMPOUND.
THE MEN AREN'T AT THEIR POSTS, DUKE GYRE. SHOULD I CALL OUT?
NO.
NO... NO. NO.
HOW...
SHE'S STILL WARM.
SIR, WE DON'T SEE YOUR SON ANYWHERE. LOGAN'S NOT HERE.
DASH

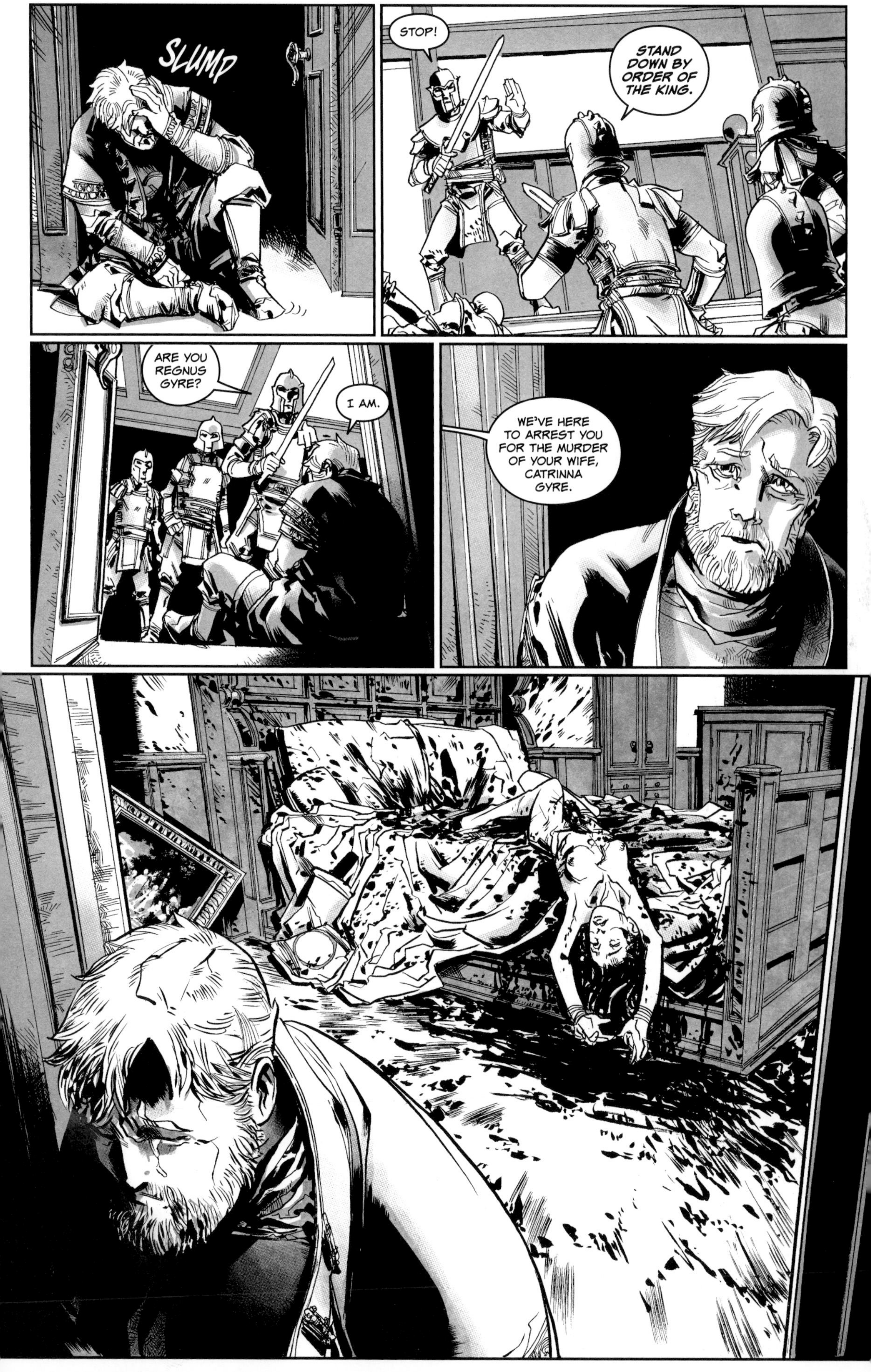
SLUMP
STOP!
STAND DOWN BY ORDER OF THE KING.
ARE YOU REGNUS GYRE?
I AM.
WE'VE HERE TO ARREST YOU FOR THE MURDER OF YOUR WIFE, CATRINNA GYRE.

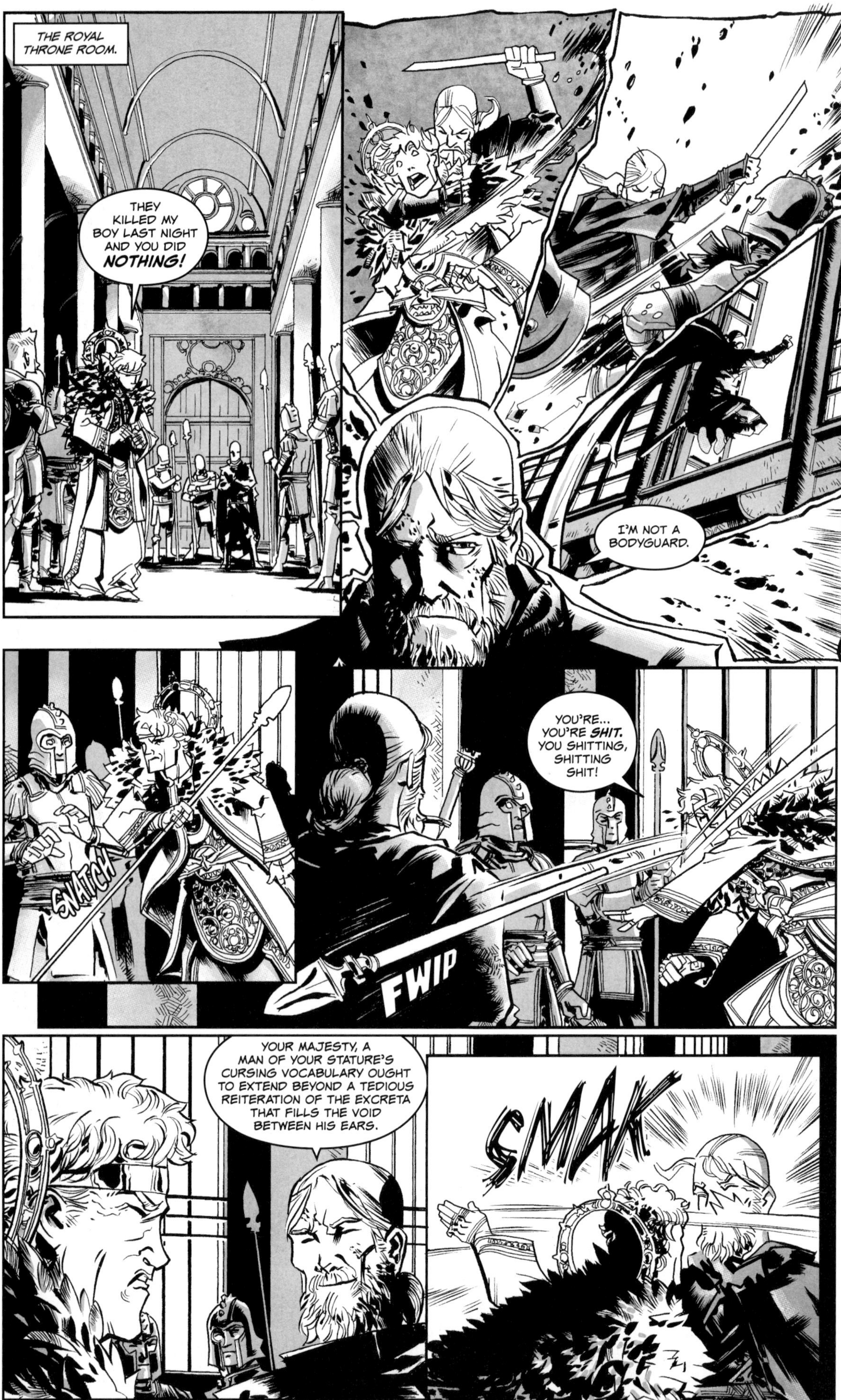
THE ROYAL THRONE ROOM.
THEY KILLED MY BOY LAST NIGHT AND YOU DID NOTHING!
I'M NOT A BODYGUARD.
SNATCH
YOU'RE... YOU'RE SHIT. YOU SHITTING, SHITTING SHIT!
FWIP
YOUR MAJESTY, A MAN OF YOUR STATURE'S CURSING VOCABULARY OUGHT TO EXTEND BEYOND A TEDIOUS REITERATION OF THE EXCRETA THAT FILLS THE VOID BETWEEN HIS EARS.
SMAK

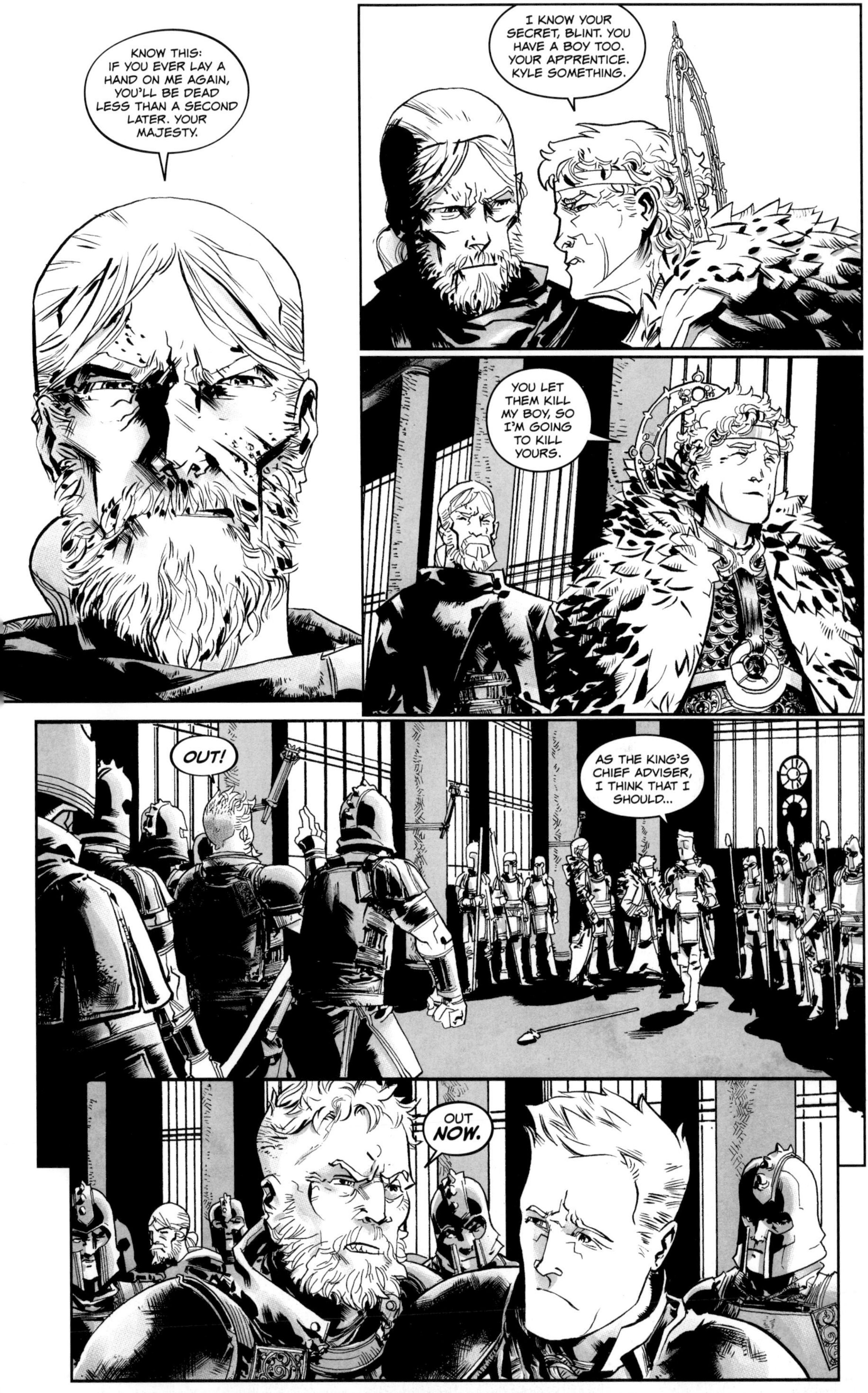
KNOW THIS: IF YOU EVER LAY A HAND ON ME AGAIN, YOU'LL BE DEAD LESS THAN A SECOND LATER. YOUR MAJESTY.
I KNOW YOUR SECRET, BLINT. YOU HAVE A BOY TOO. YOUR APPRENTICE. KYLE SOMETHING.
YOU LET THEM KILL MY BOY, SO I'M GOING TO KILL YOURS.
OUT!
AS THE KING'S CHIEF ADVISER, I THINK THAT I SHOULD...
OUT NOW.

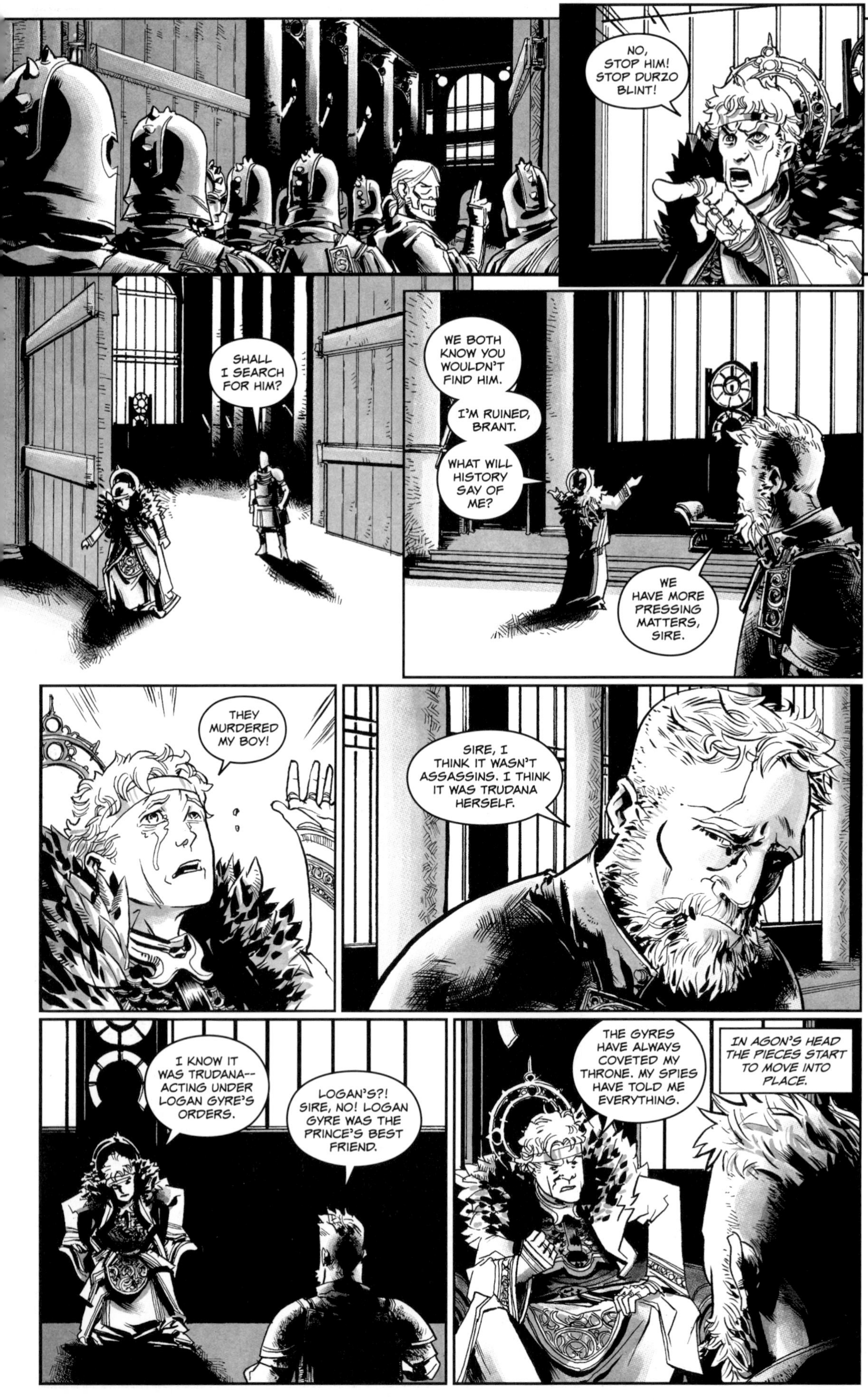
NO, STOP HIM! STOP DURZO BLINT!
SHALL I SEARCH FOR HIM?
WE BOTH KNOW YOU WOULDN'T FIND HIM.
I'M RUINED, BRANT.
WHAT WILL HISTORY SAY OF ME?
WE HAVE MORE PRESSING MATTERS, SIRE.
THEY MURDERED MY BOY!
SIRE, I THINK IT WASN'T ASSASSINS. I THINK IT WAS TRUDANA HERSELF.
I KNOW IT WAS TRUDANA-- ACTING UNDER LOGAN GYRE'S ORDERS.
LOGAN'S?! SIRE, NO! LOGAN GYRE WAS THE PRINCE'S BEST FRIEND.
THE GYRES HAVE ALWAYS COVETED MY THRONE. MY SPIES HAVE TOLD ME EVERYTHING.
IN AGON'S HEAD THE PIECES START TO MOVE INTO PLACE.

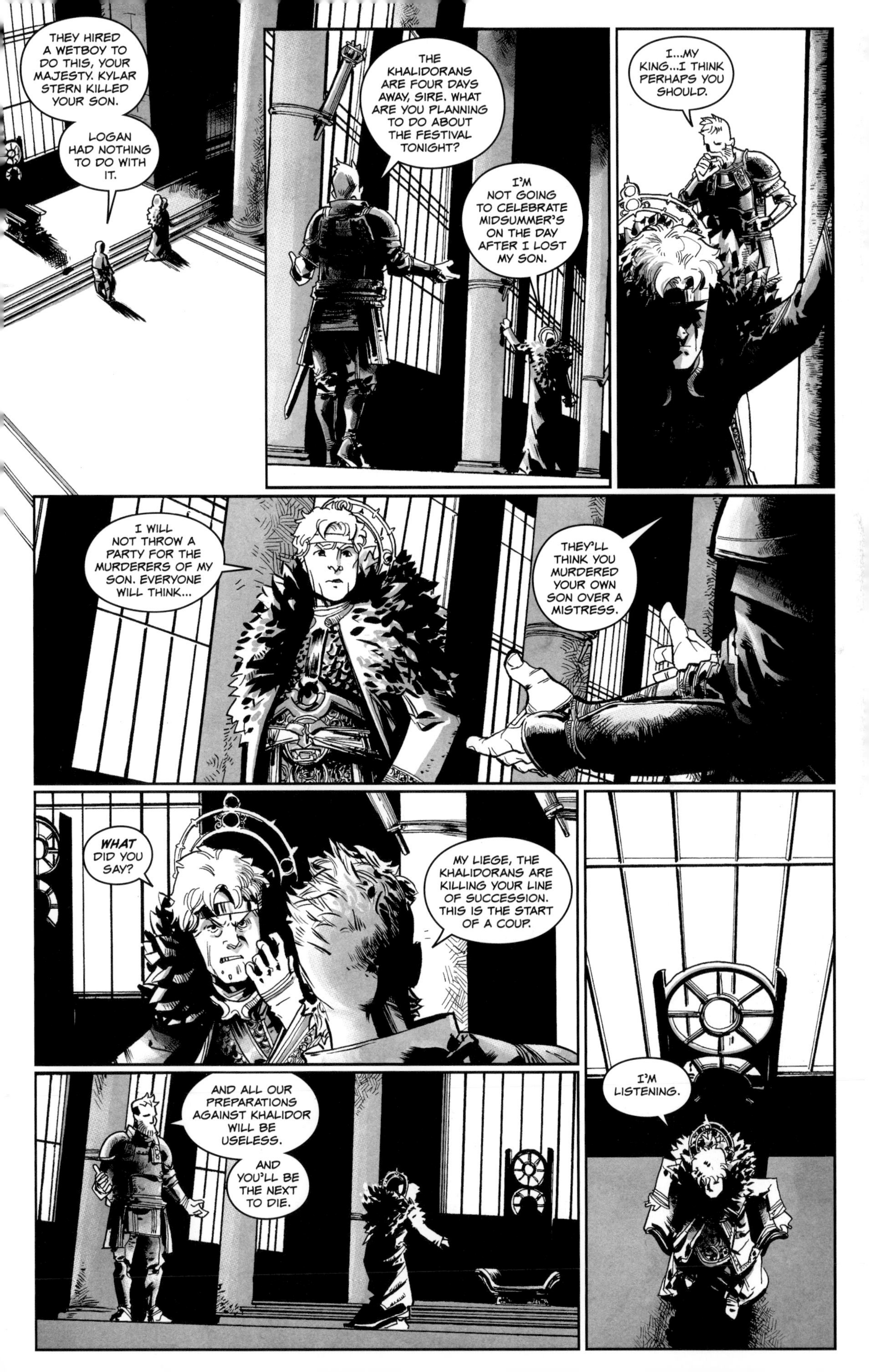
THEY HIRED A WETBOY TO DO THIS, YOUR MAJESTY. KYLAR STERN KILLED YOUR SON.
LOGAN HAD NOTHING TO DO WITH IT.
THE KHALIDORANS ARE FOUR DAYS AWAY, SIRE. WHAT ARE YOU PLANNING TO DO ABOUT THE FESTIVAL TONIGHT?
I'M NOT GOING TO CELEBRATE MIDSUMMER'S ON THE DAY AFTER I LOST MY SON.
I...MY KING...I THINK PERHAPS YOU SHOULD.
I WILL NOT THROW A PARTY FOR THE MURDERERS OF MY SON. EVERYONE WILL THINK...
THEY'LL THINK YOU MURDERED YOUR OWN SON OVER A MISTRESS.
WHAT DID YOU SAY?
MY LIEGE, THE KHALIDORANS ARE KILLING YOUR LINE OF SUCCESSION. THIS IS THE START OF A COUP.
AND ALL OUR PREPARATIONS AGAINST KHALIDOR WILL BE USELESS.
AND YOU'LL BE THE NEXT TO DIE.
I'M LISTENING.

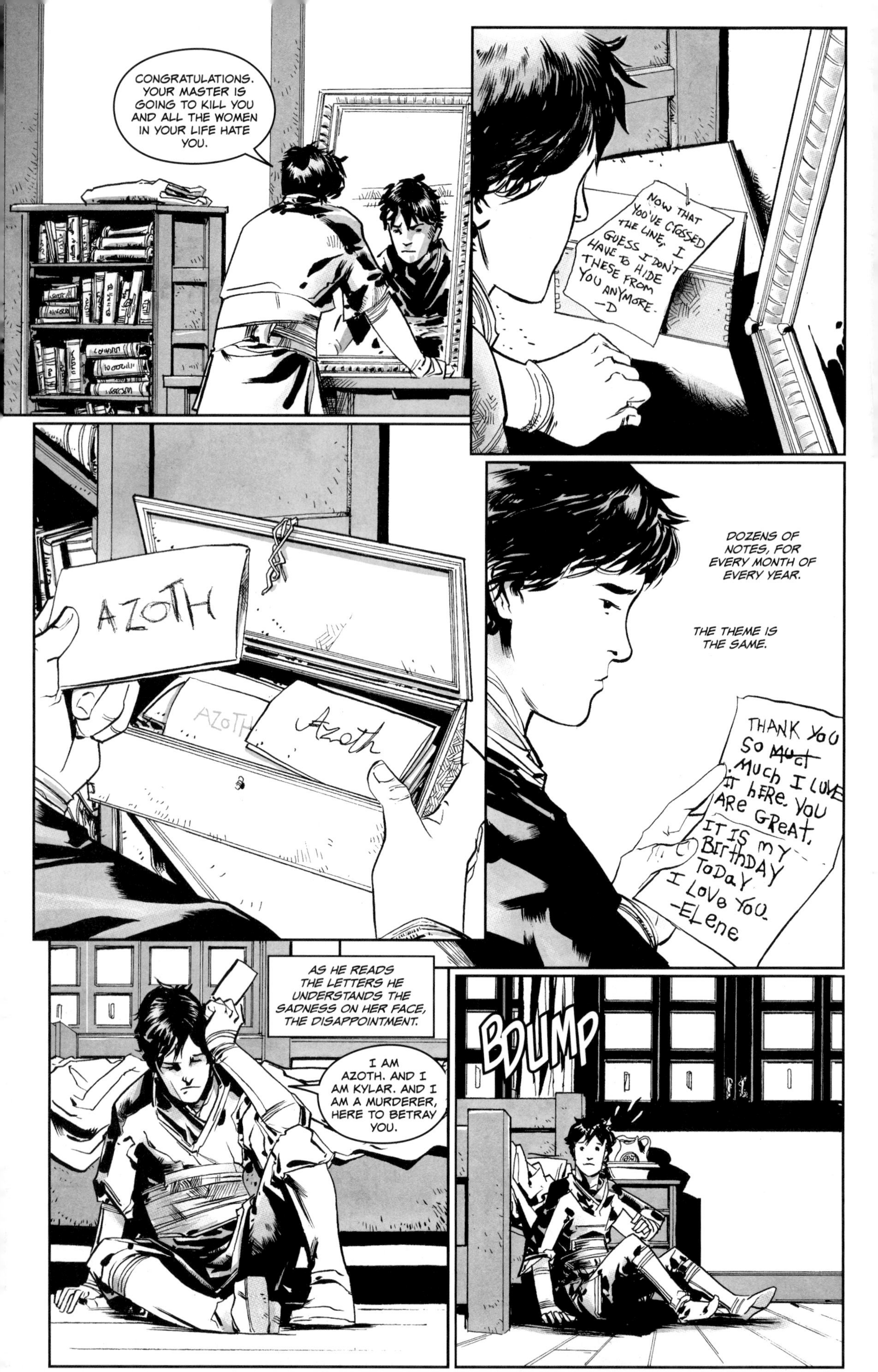
CONGRATULATIONS. YOUR MASTER IS GOING TO KILL YOU AND ALL THE WOMEN IN YOUR LIFE HATE YOU.
NOW THAT YOU'VE CROSSED THE LINE, I GUESS I DON'T HAVE TO HIDE THESE FROM YOU ANYMORE. -D
AZOTH
AZOTH
Azoth
DOZENS OF NOTES, FOR EVERY MONTH OF EVERY YEAR.
THE THEME IS THE SAME.
THANK YOU SO Muct Much I LOVE IT hERE. YOU ARE GREAT. IT IS my BirthDAY TODay I LOVE YOU. -ELene
AS HE READS THE LETTERS HE UNDERSTANDS THE SADNESS ON HER FACE, THE DISAPPOINTMENT.
I AM AZOTH. AND I AM KYLAR. AND I AM A MURDERER, HERE TO BETRAY YOU.
BDUMP

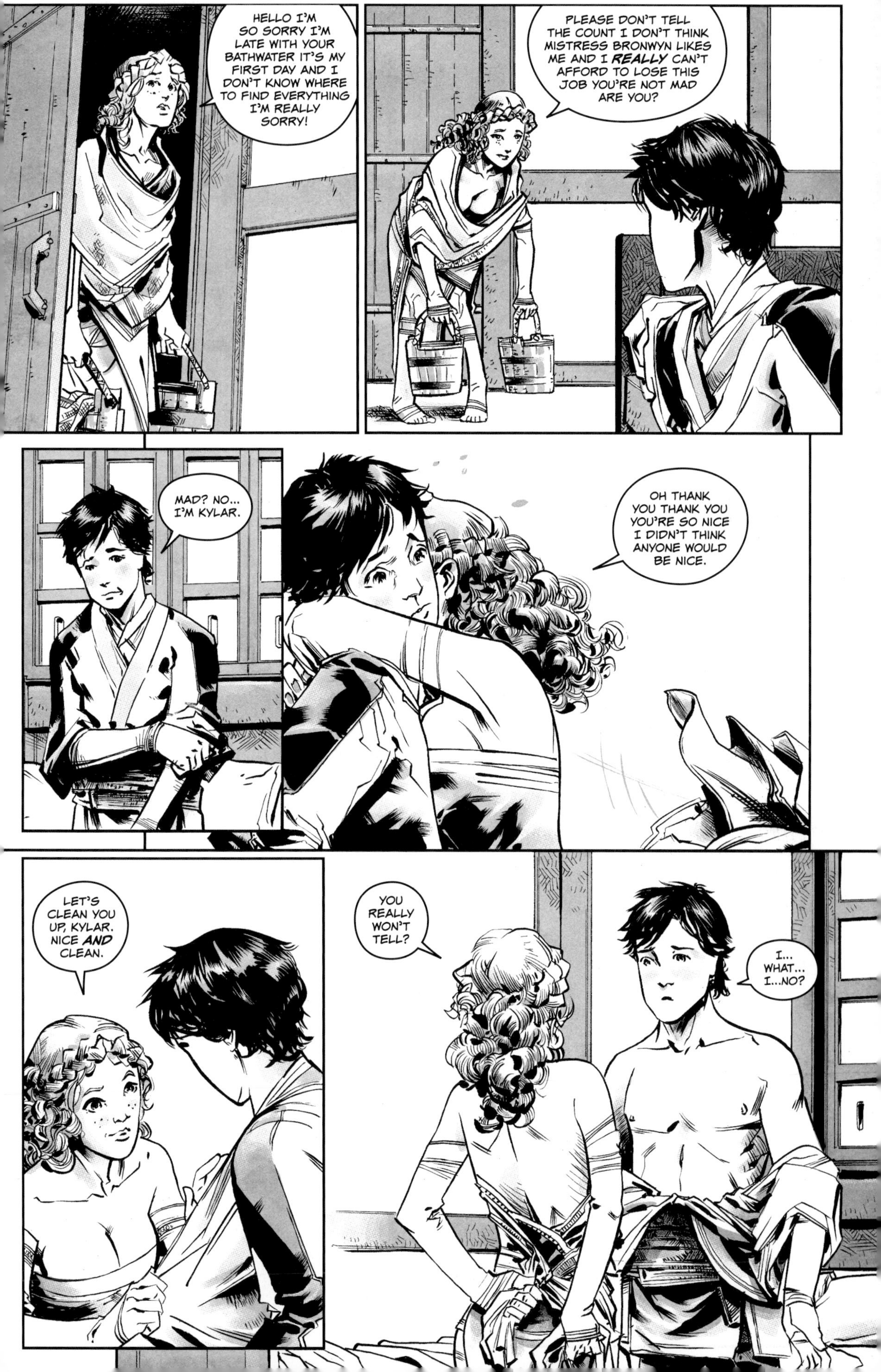
HELLO I'M SO SORRY I'M LATE WITH YOUR BATHWATER IT'S MY FIRST DAY AND I DON'T KNOW WHERE TO FIND EVERYTHING I'M REALLY SORRY!
PLEASE DON'T TELL THE COUNT I DON'T THINK MISTRESS BRONWYN LIKES ME AND I **REALLY** CAN'T AFFORD TO LOSE THIS JOB YOU'RE NOT MAD ARE YOU?
MAD? NO... I'M KYLAR.
OH THANK YOU THANK YOU YOU'RE SO NICE I DIDN'T THINK ANYONE WOULD BE NICE.
LET'S CLEAN YOU UP, KYLAR. NICE **AND** CLEAN.
YOU REALLY WON'T TELL?
I... WHAT... I...NO?

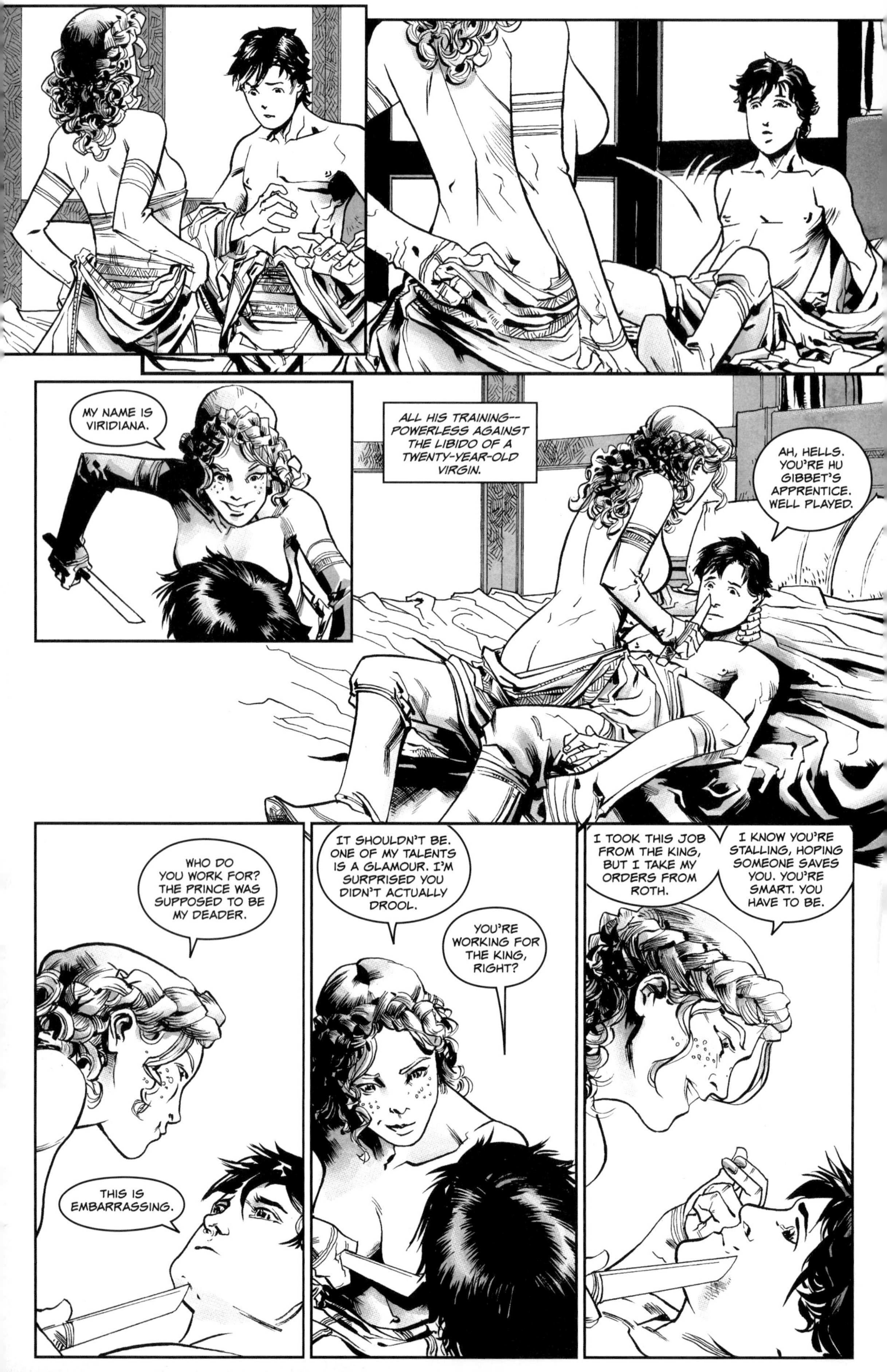
MY NAME IS VIRIDIANA.
ALL HIS TRAINING-- POWERLESS AGAINST THE LIBIDO OF A TWENTY-YEAR-OLD VIRGIN.
AH, HELLS. YOU'RE HU GIBBET'S APPRENTICE. WELL PLAYED.
WHO DO YOU WORK FOR? THE PRINCE WAS SUPPOSED TO BE MY DEADER.
THIS IS EMBARRASSING.
IT SHOULDN'T BE. ONE OF MY TALENTS IS A GLAMOUR. I'M SURPRISED YOU DIDN'T ACTUALLY DROOL.
YOU'RE WORKING FOR THE KING, RIGHT?
I TOOK THIS JOB FROM THE KING, BUT I TAKE MY ORDERS FROM ROTH.
I KNOW YOU'RE STALLING, HOPING SOMEONE SAVES YOU. YOU'RE SMART. YOU HAVE TO BE.

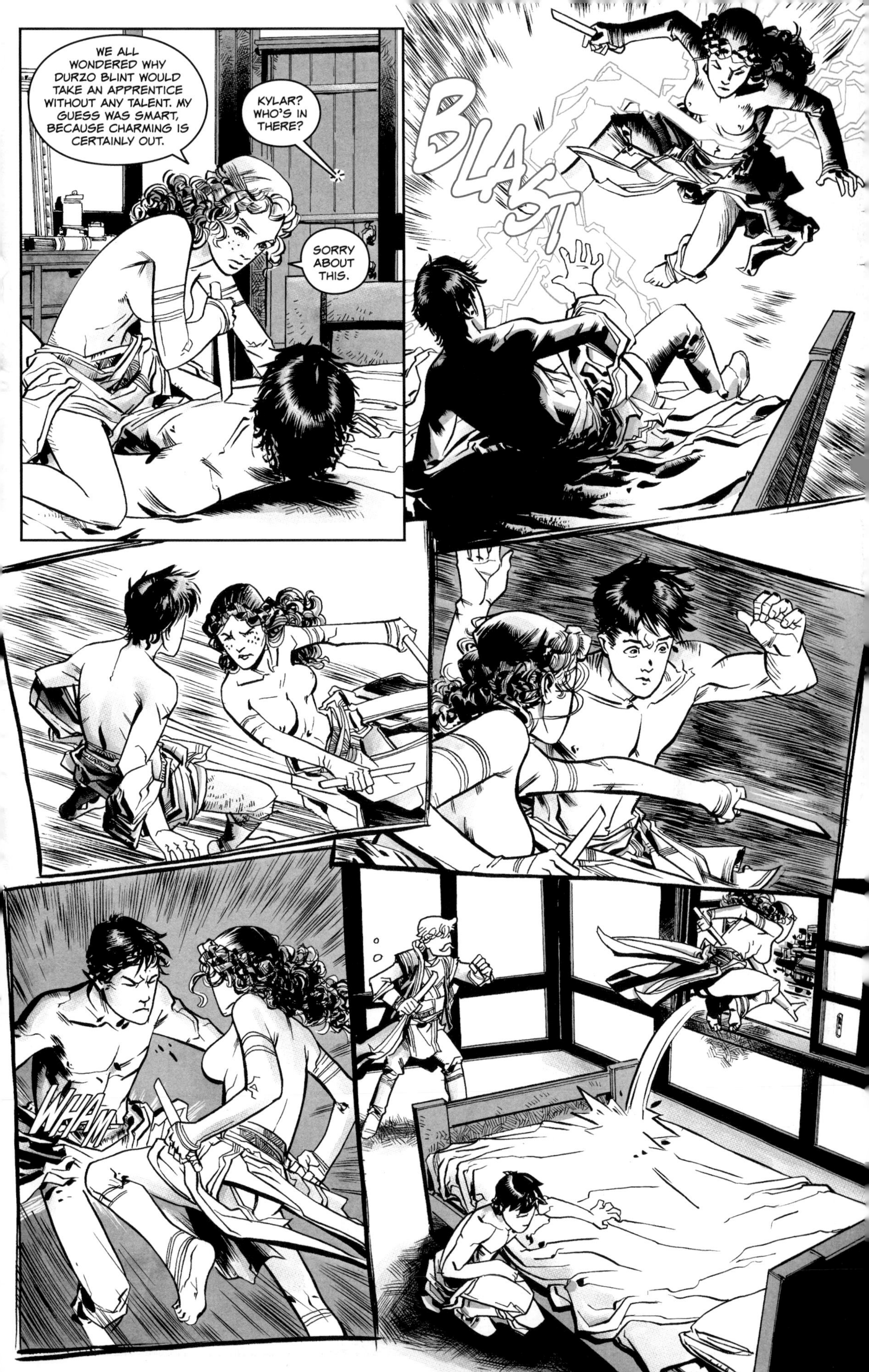
WE ALL WONDERED WHY DURZO BLINT WOULD TAKE AN APPRENTICE WITHOUT ANY TALENT. MY GUESS WAS SMART, BECAUSE CHARMING IS CERTAINLY OUT.
KYLAR? WHO'S IN THERE?
SORRY ABOUT THIS.
BLAST
WHAM

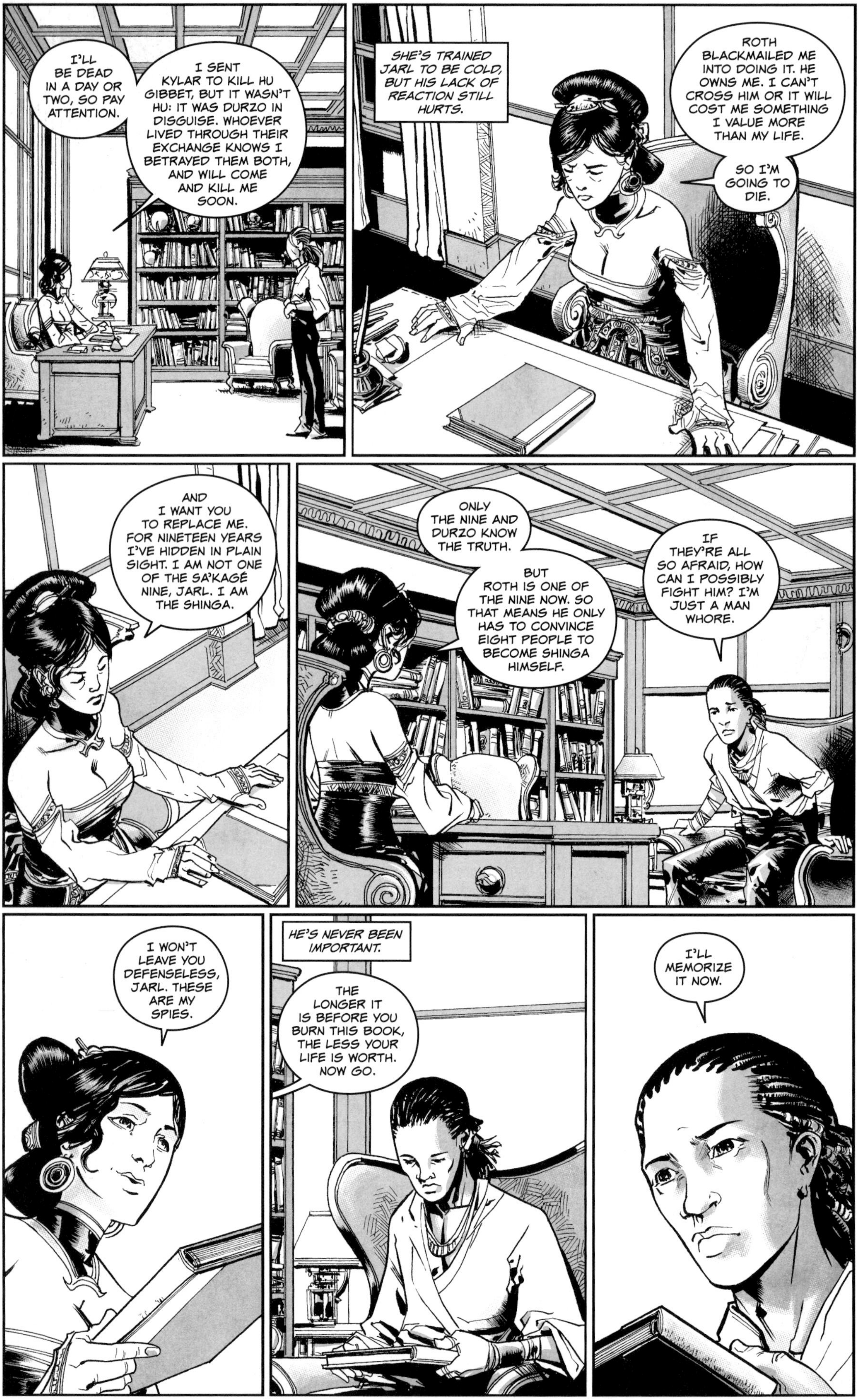

I'LL BE DEAD IN A DAY OR TWO, SO PAY ATTENTION.
I SENT KYLAR TO KILL HU GIBBET, BUT IT WASN'T HU: IT WAS DURZO IN DISGUISE. WHOEVER LIVED THROUGH THEIR EXCHANGE KNOWS I BETRAYED THEM BOTH, AND WILL COME AND KILL ME SOON.
SHE'S TRAINED JARL TO BE COLD, BUT HIS LACK OF REACTION STILL HURTS.
ROTH BLACKMAILED ME INTO DOING IT. HE OWNS ME. I CAN'T CROSS HIM OR IT WILL COST ME SOMETHING I VALUE MORE THAN MY LIFE.
SO I'M GOING TO DIE.
AND I WANT YOU TO REPLACE ME. FOR NINETEEN YEARS I'VE HIDDEN IN PLAIN SIGHT. I AM NOT ONE OF THE SA'KAGÉ NINE, JARL. I AM THE SHINGA.
ONLY THE NINE AND DURZO KNOW THE TRUTH.
BUT ROTH IS ONE OF THE NINE NOW. SO THAT MEANS HE ONLY HAS TO CONVINCE EIGHT PEOPLE TO BECOME SHINGA HIMSELF.
IF THEY'RE ALL SO AFRAID, HOW CAN I POSSIBLY FIGHT HIM? I'M JUST A MAN WHORE.
I WON'T LEAVE YOU DEFENSELESS, JARL. THESE ARE MY SPIES.
HE'S NEVER BEEN IMPORTANT.
THE LONGER IT IS BEFORE YOU BURN THIS BOOK, THE LESS YOUR LIFE IS WORTH. NOW GO.
I'LL MEMORIZE IT NOW.

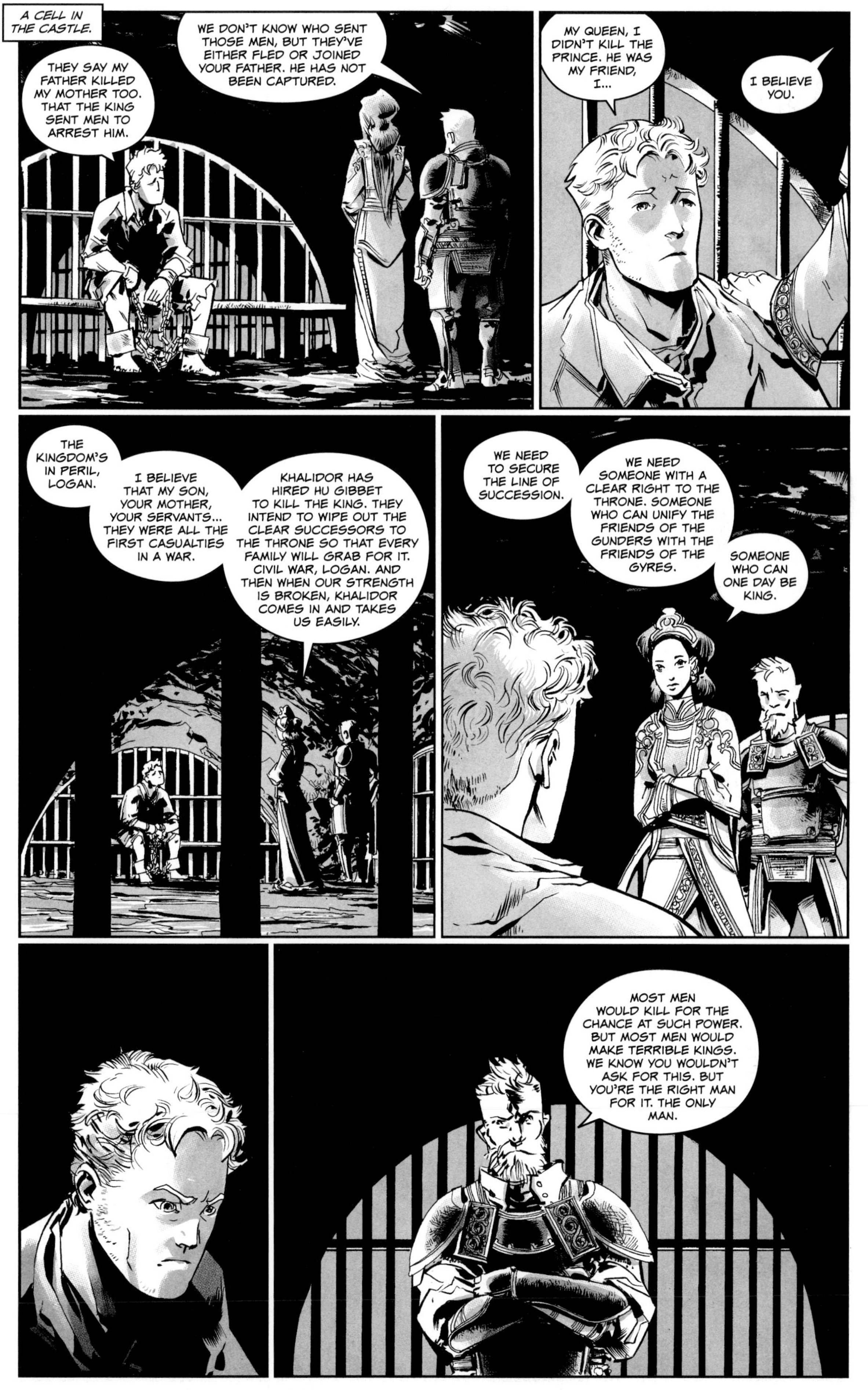
A CELL IN THE CASTLE.
THEY SAY MY FATHER KILLED MY MOTHER TOO. THAT THE KING SENT MEN TO ARREST HIM.
WE DON'T KNOW WHO SENT THOSE MEN, BUT THEY'VE EITHER FLED OR JOINED YOUR FATHER. HE HAS NOT BEEN CAPTURED.
MY QUEEN, I DIDN'T KILL THE PRINCE. HE WAS MY FRIEND, I...
I BELIEVE YOU.
THE KINGDOM'S IN PERIL, LOGAN.
I BELIEVE THAT MY SON, YOUR MOTHER, YOUR SERVANTS... THEY WERE ALL THE FIRST CASUALTIES IN A WAR.
KHALIDOR HAS HIRED HU GIBBET TO KILL THE KING. THEY INTEND TO WIPE OUT THE CLEAR SUCCESSORS TO THE THRONE SO THAT EVERY FAMILY WILL GRAB FOR IT. CIVIL WAR, LOGAN. AND THEN WHEN OUR STRENGTH IS BROKEN, KHALIDOR COMES IN AND TAKES US EASILY.
WE NEED TO SECURE THE LINE OF SUCCESSION.
WE NEED SOMEONE WITH A CLEAR RIGHT TO THE THRONE. SOMEONE WHO CAN UNIFY THE FRIENDS OF THE GUNDERS WITH THE FRIENDS OF THE GYRES.
SOMEONE WHO CAN ONE DAY BE KING.
MOST MEN WOULD KILL FOR THE CHANCE AT SUCH POWER. BUT MOST MEN WOULD MAKE TERRIBLE KINGS. WE KNOW YOU WOULDN'T ASK FOR THIS. BUT YOU'RE THE RIGHT MAN FOR IT. THE ONLY MAN.

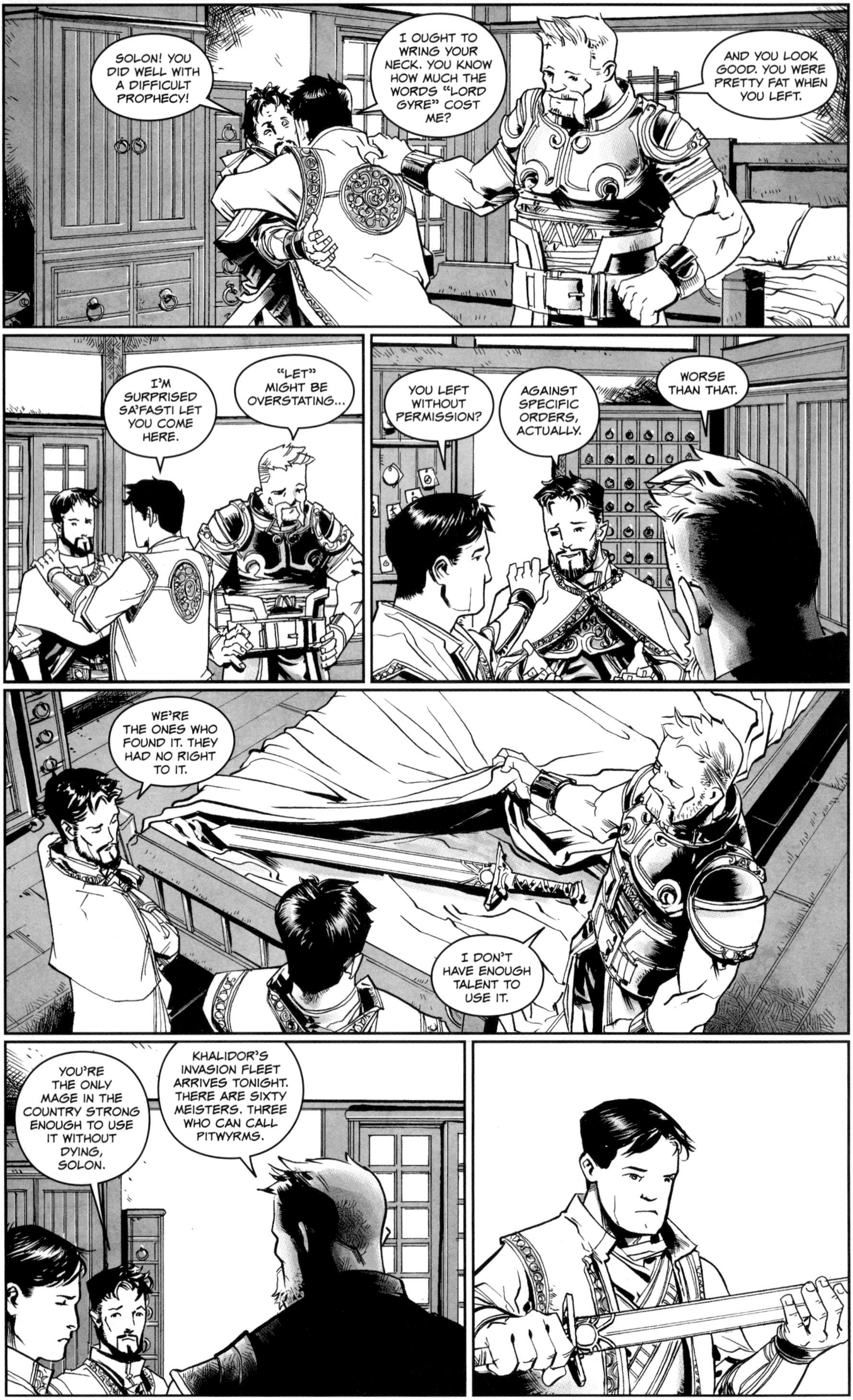
SOLON! YOU DID WELL WITH A DIFFICULT PROPHECY!
I OUGHT TO WRING YOUR NECK. YOU KNOW HOW MUCH THE WORDS "LORD GYRE" COST ME?
AND YOU LOOK GOOD. YOU WERE PRETTY FAT WHEN YOU LEFT.
I'M SURPRISED SA'FASTI LET YOU COME HERE.
"LET" MIGHT BE OVERSTATING...
YOU LEFT WITHOUT PERMISSION?
AGAINST SPECIFIC ORDERS, ACTUALLY.
WORSE THAN THAT.
WE'RE THE ONES WHO FOUND IT. THEY HAD NO RIGHT TO IT.
I DON'T HAVE ENOUGH TALENT TO USE IT.
YOU'RE THE ONLY MAGE IN THE COUNTRY STRONG ENOUGH TO USE IT WITHOUT DYING, SOLON.
KHALIDOR'S INVASION FLEET ARRIVES TONIGHT. THERE ARE SIXTY MEISTERS. THREE WHO CAN CALL PITWYRMS.

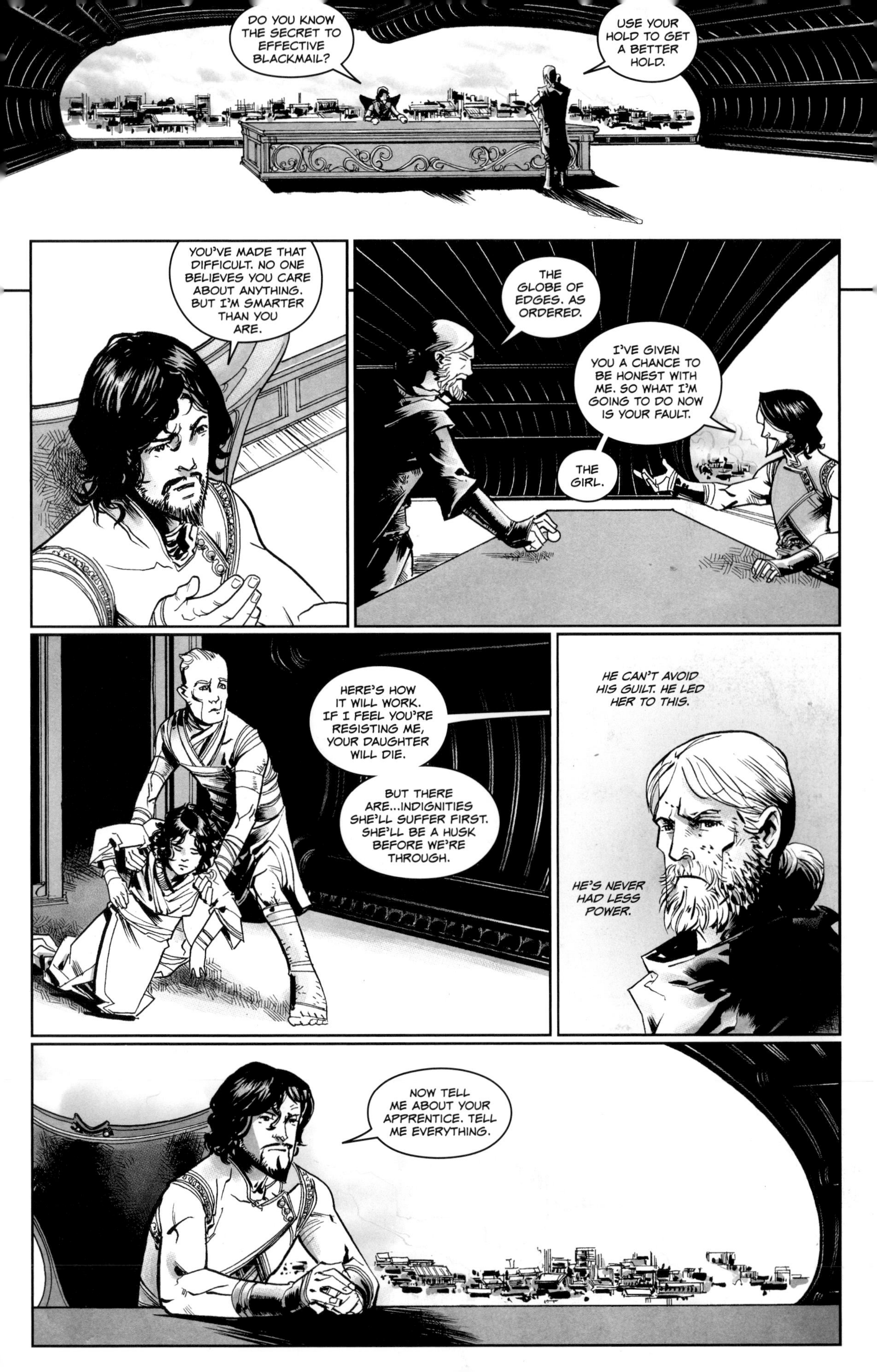
DO YOU KNOW THE SECRET TO EFFECTIVE BLACKMAIL?
USE YOUR HOLD TO GET A BETTER HOLD.
YOU'VE MADE THAT DIFFICULT. NO ONE BELIEVES YOU CARE ABOUT ANYTHING. BUT I'M SMARTER THAN YOU ARE.
THE GLOBE OF EDGES. AS ORDERED.
I'VE GIVEN YOU A CHANCE TO BE HONEST WITH ME. SO WHAT I'M GOING TO DO NOW IS YOUR FAULT.
THE GIRL.
HERE'S HOW IT WILL WORK. IF I FEEL YOU'RE RESISTING ME, YOUR DAUGHTER WILL DIE.
BUT THERE ARE...INDIGNITIES SHE'LL SUFFER FIRST. SHE'LL BE A HUSK BEFORE WE'RE THROUGH.
HE CAN'T AVOID HIS GUILT. HE LED HER TO THIS.
HE'S NEVER HAD LESS POWER.
NOW TELL ME ABOUT YOUR APPRENTICE. TELL ME EVERYTHING.

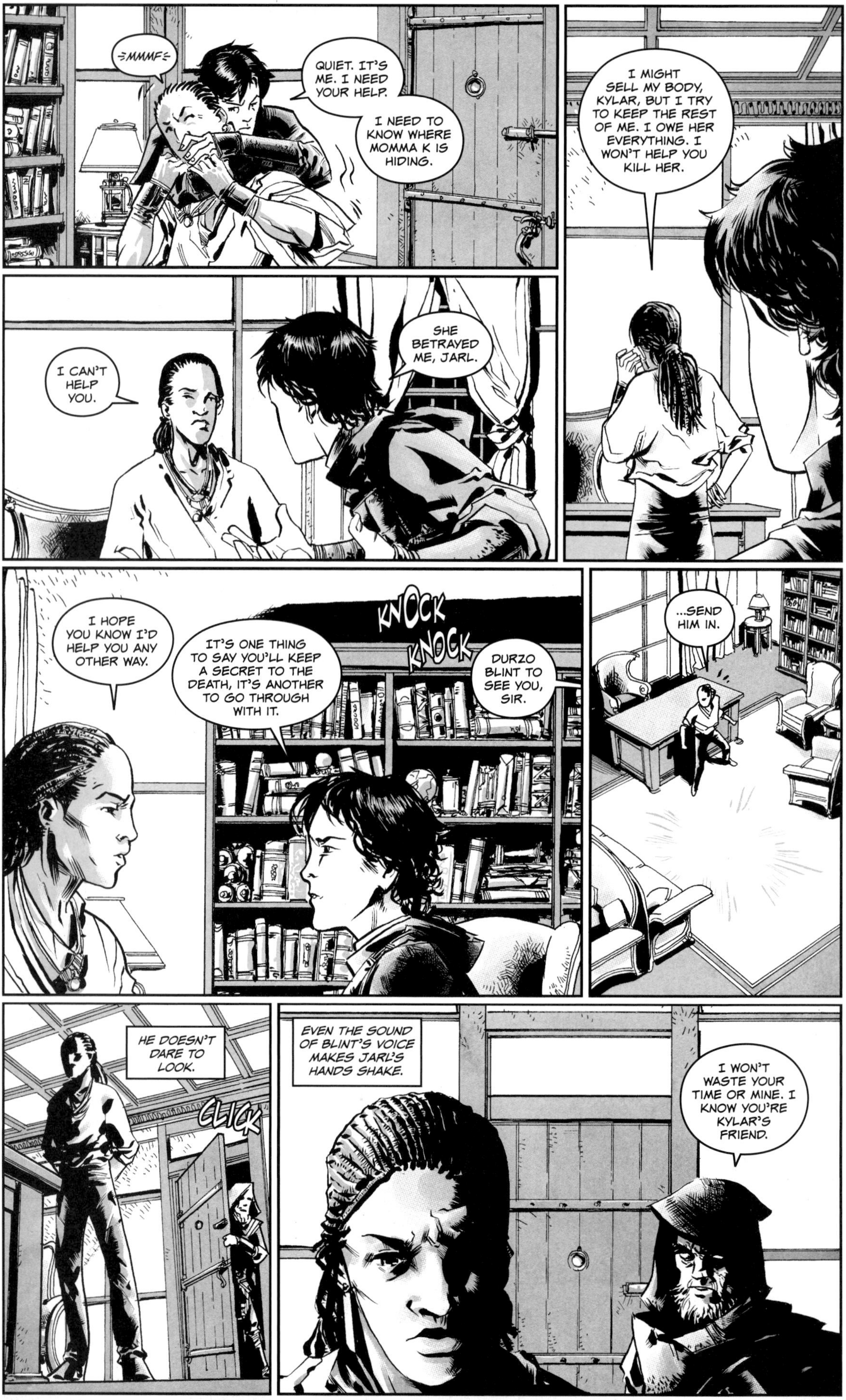

MMMF
QUIET. IT'S ME. I NEED YOUR HELP.
I NEED TO KNOW WHERE MOMMA K IS HIDING.
I MIGHT SELL MY BODY, KYLAR, BUT I TRY TO KEEP THE REST OF ME. I OWE HER EVERYTHING. I WON'T HELP YOU KILL HER.
I CAN'T HELP YOU.
SHE BETRAYED ME, JARL.
I HOPE YOU KNOW I'D HELP YOU ANY OTHER WAY.
IT'S ONE THING TO SAY YOU'LL KEEP A SECRET TO THE DEATH, IT'S ANOTHER TO GO THROUGH WITH IT.
KNOCK KNOCK
DURZO BLINT TO SEE YOU, SIR.
...SEND HIM IN.
HE DOESN'T DARE TO LOOK.
CLICK
EVEN THE SOUND OF BLINT'S VOICE MAKES JARL'S HANDS SHAKE.
I WON'T WASTE YOUR TIME OR MINE. I KNOW YOU'RE KYLAR'S FRIEND.

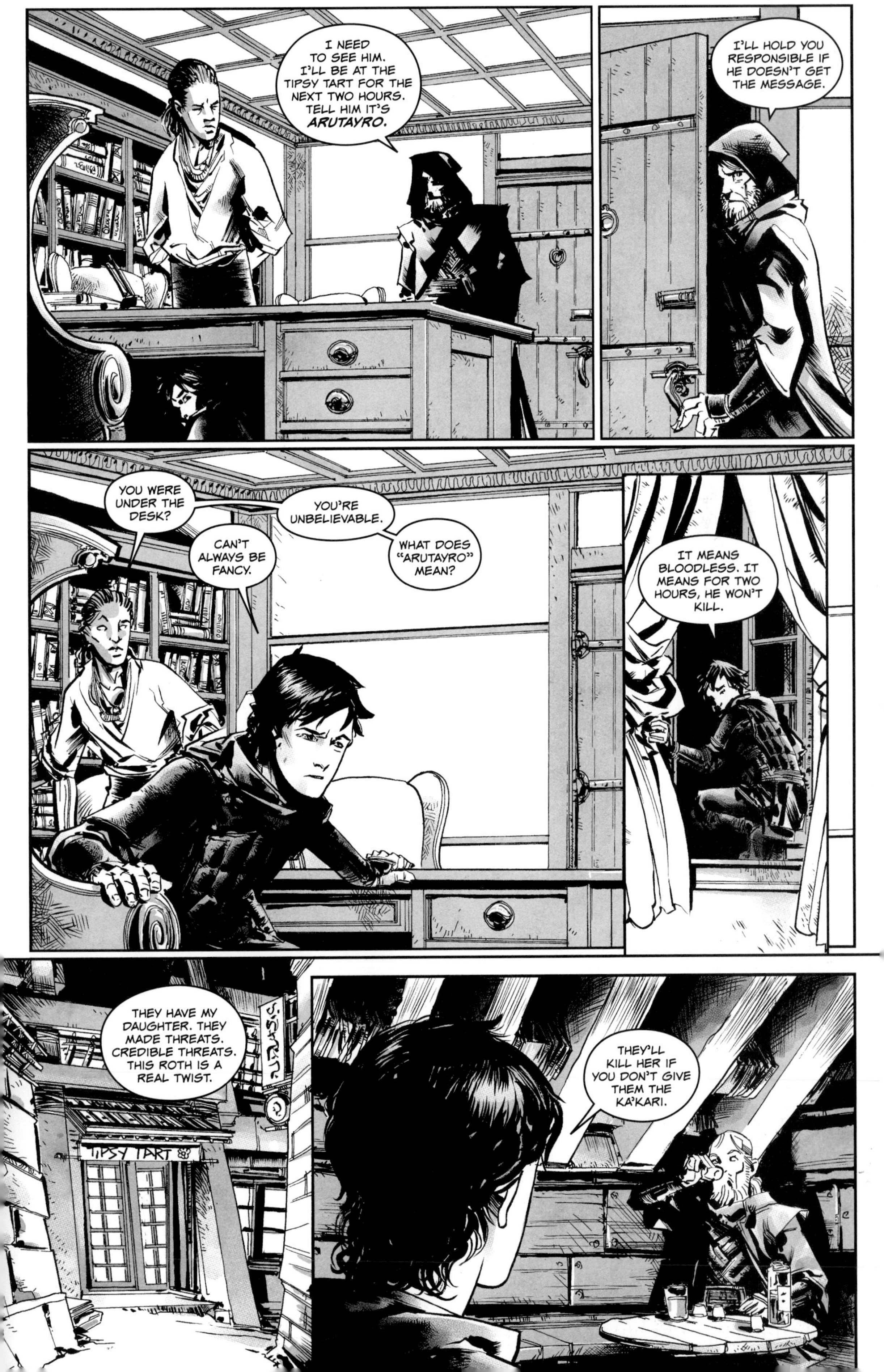

I NEED TO SEE HIM. I'LL BE AT THE TIPSY TART FOR THE NEXT TWO HOURS. TELL HIM IT'S *ARUTAYRO.*
I'LL HOLD YOU RESPONSIBLE IF HE DOESN'T GET THE MESSAGE.
YOU WERE UNDER THE DESK?
CAN'T ALWAYS BE FANCY.
YOU'RE UNBELIEVABLE.
WHAT DOES "ARUTAYRO" MEAN?
IT MEANS BLOODLESS. IT MEANS FOR TWO HOURS, HE WON'T KILL.
TIPSY TART
THEY HAVE MY DAUGHTER. THEY MADE THREATS. CREDIBLE THREATS. THIS ROTH IS A REAL TWIST.
THEY'LL KILL HER IF YOU DON'T GIVE THEM THE KA'KARI.

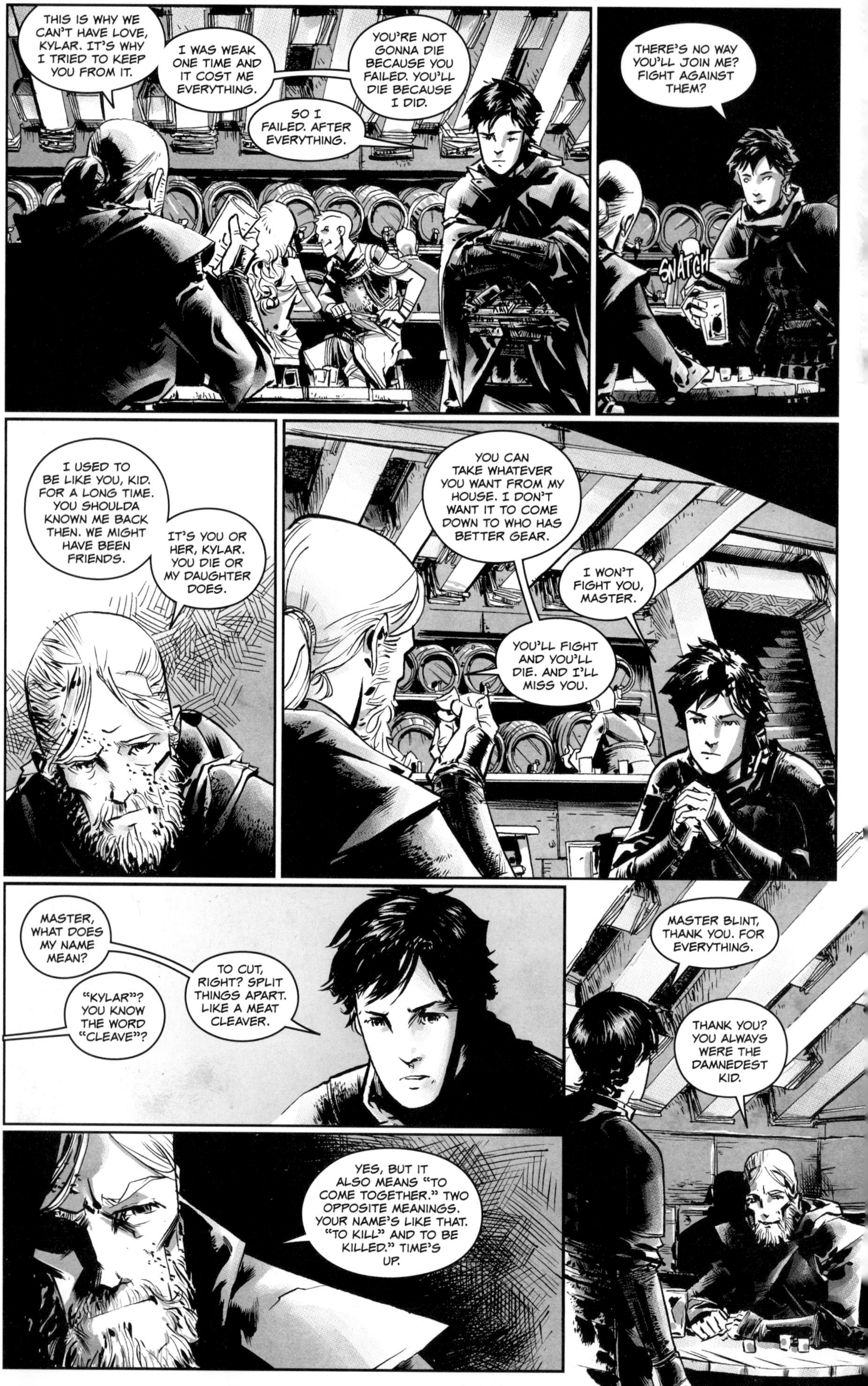
THIS IS WHY WE CAN'T HAVE LOVE, KYLAR. IT'S WHY I TRIED TO KEEP YOU FROM IT.
I WAS WEAK ONE TIME AND IT COST ME EVERYTHING.
SO I FAILED. AFTER EVERYTHING.
YOU'RE NOT GONNA DIE BECAUSE YOU FAILED. YOU'LL DIE BECAUSE I DID.
THERE'S NO WAY YOU'LL JOIN ME? FIGHT AGAINST THEM?
SNATCH
I USED TO BE LIKE YOU, KID. FOR A LONG TIME. YOU SHOULDA KNOWN ME BACK THEN. WE MIGHT HAVE BEEN FRIENDS.
IT'S YOU OR HER, KYLAR. YOU DIE OR MY DAUGHTER DOES.
YOU CAN TAKE WHATEVER YOU WANT FROM MY HOUSE. I DON'T WANT IT TO COME DOWN TO WHO HAS BETTER GEAR.
I WON'T FIGHT YOU, MASTER.
YOU'LL FIGHT AND YOU'LL DIE. AND I'LL MISS YOU.
MASTER, WHAT DOES MY NAME MEAN?
"KYLAR"? YOU KNOW THE WORD "CLEAVE"?
TO CUT, RIGHT? SPLIT THINGS APART. LIKE A MEAT CLEAVER.
YES, BUT IT ALSO MEANS "TO COME TOGETHER." TWO OPPOSITE MEANINGS. YOUR NAME'S LIKE THAT. "TO KILL" AND TO BE KILLED." TIME'S UP.
MASTER BLINT, THANK YOU. FOR EVERYTHING.
THANK YOU? YOU ALWAYS WERE THE DAMNEDEST KID.

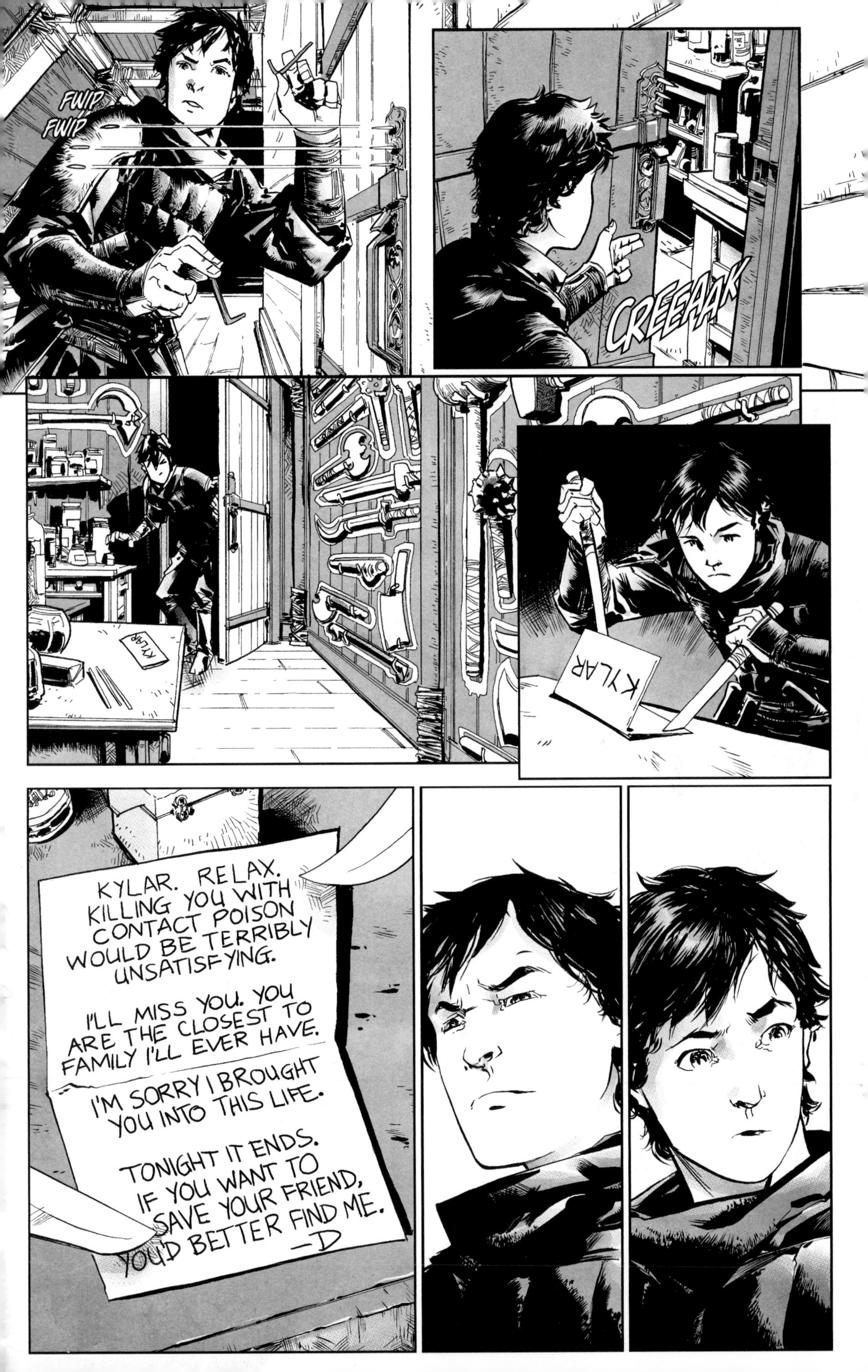
FWIP
FWIP
CREEAAK
KYLAR
KYLAR
KYLAR. RELAX. KILLING YOU WITH CONTACT POISON WOULD BE TERRIBLY UNSATISFYING.
I'LL MISS YOU. YOU ARE THE CLOSEST TO FAMILY I'LL EVER HAVE.
I'M SORRY I BROUGHT YOU INTO THIS LIFE.
TONIGHT IT ENDS. IF YOU WANT TO SAVE YOUR FRIEND, YOU'D BETTER FIND ME.
—D

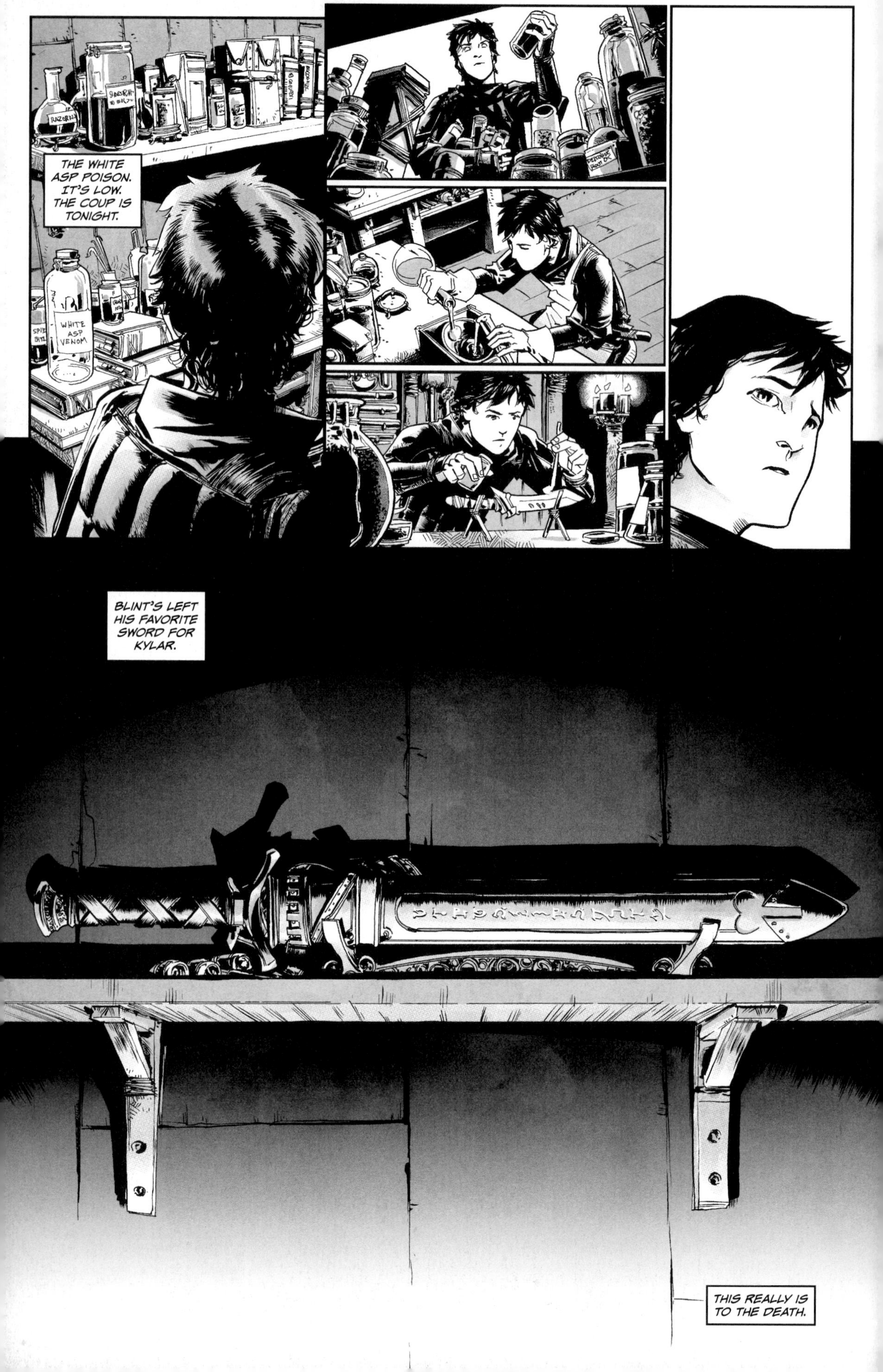
THE WHITE ASP POISON. IT'S LOW. THE COUP IS TONIGHT.
WHITE ASP VENOM
BLINT'S LEFT HIS FAVORITE SWORD FOR KYLAR.
THIS REALLY IS TO THE DEATH.

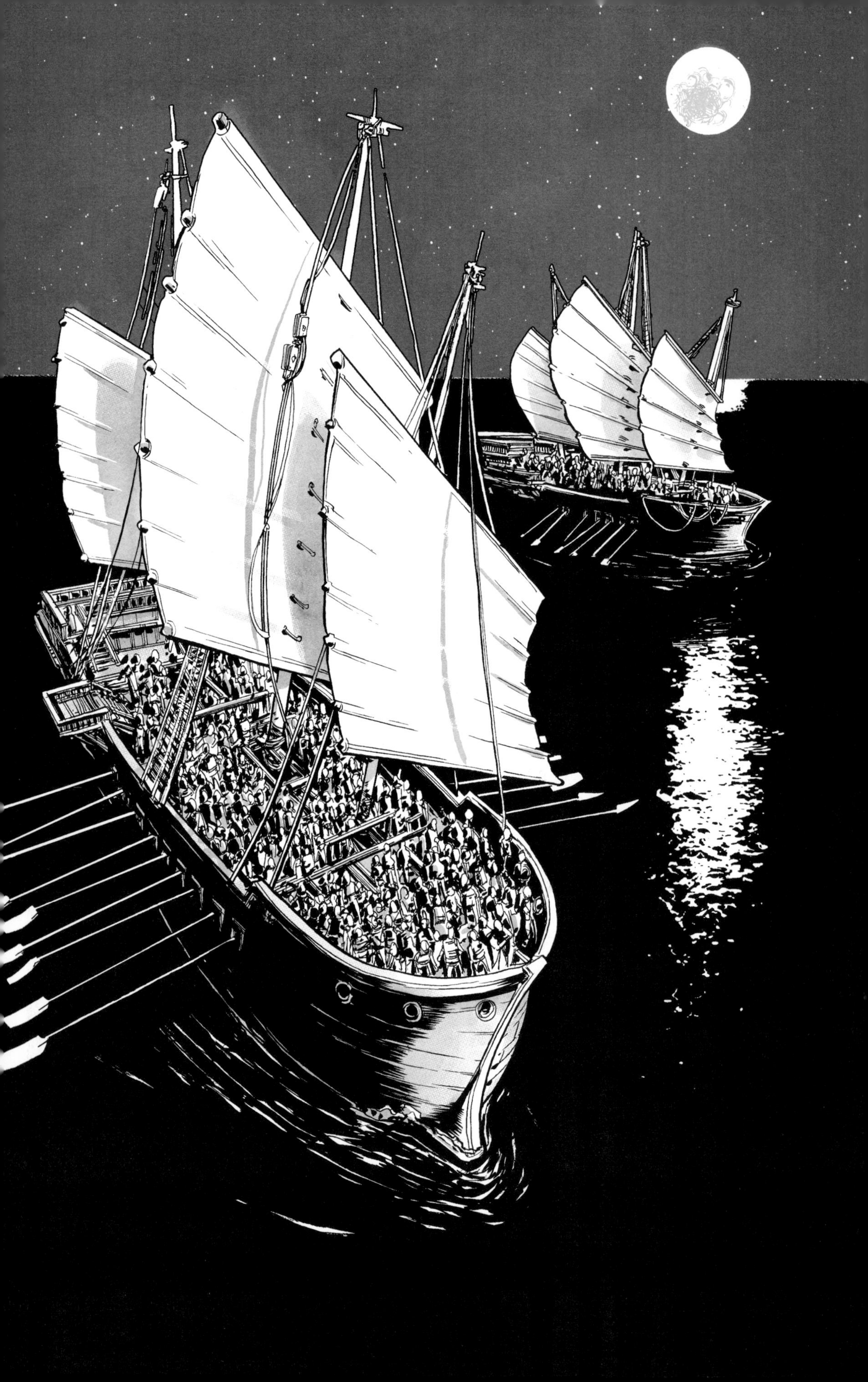

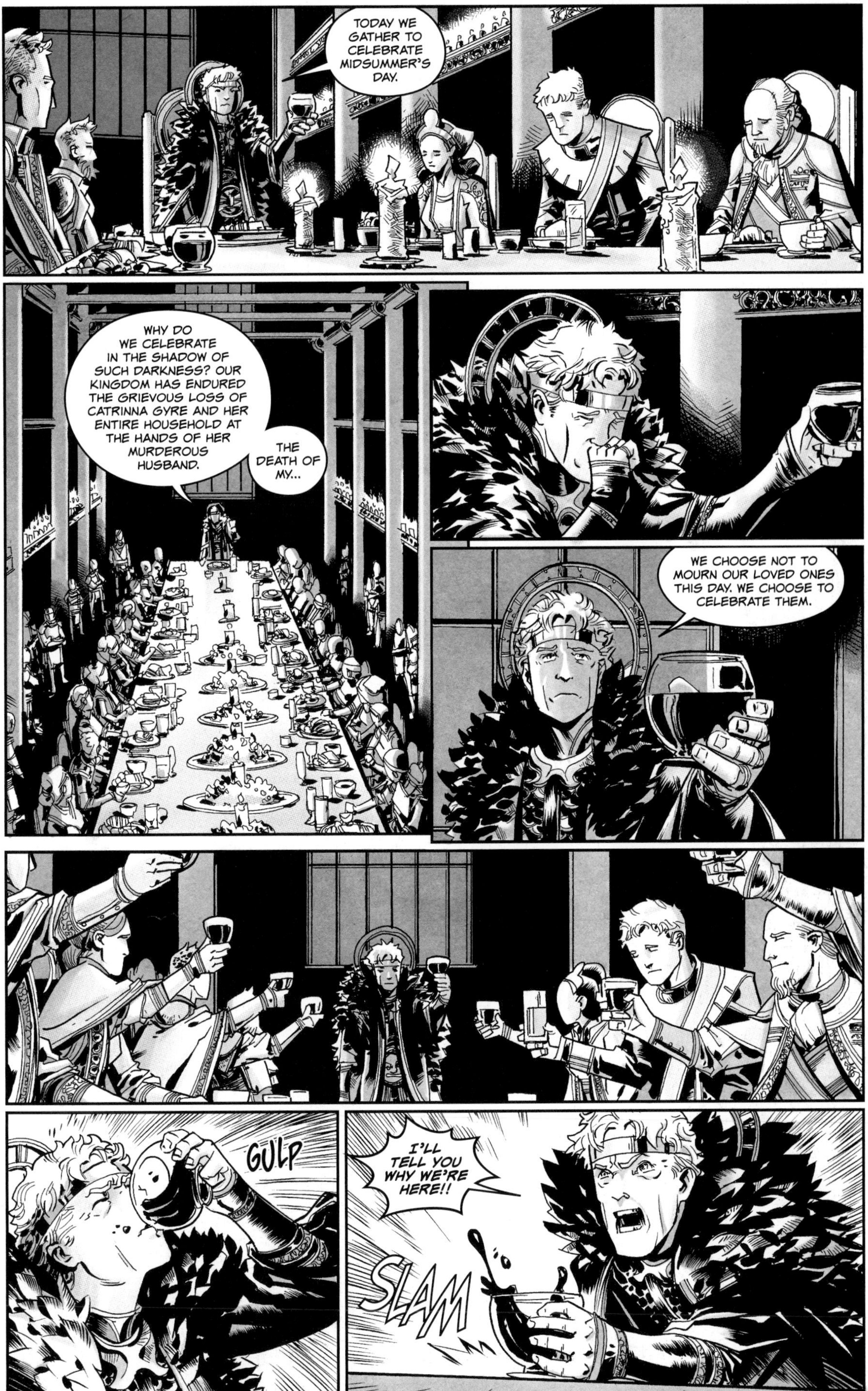
TODAY WE GATHER TO CELEBRATE MIDSUMMER'S DAY.
WHY DO WE CELEBRATE IN THE SHADOW OF SUCH DARKNESS? OUR KINGDOM HAS ENDURED THE GRIEVOUS LOSS OF CATRINNA GYRE AND HER ENTIRE HOUSEHOLD AT THE HANDS OF HER MURDEROUS HUSBAND.
THE DEATH OF MY...
WE CHOOSE NOT TO MOURN OUR LOVED ONES THIS DAY. WE CHOOSE TO CELEBRATE THEM.
GULP
I'LL TELL YOU WHY WE'RE HERE!!
SLAM

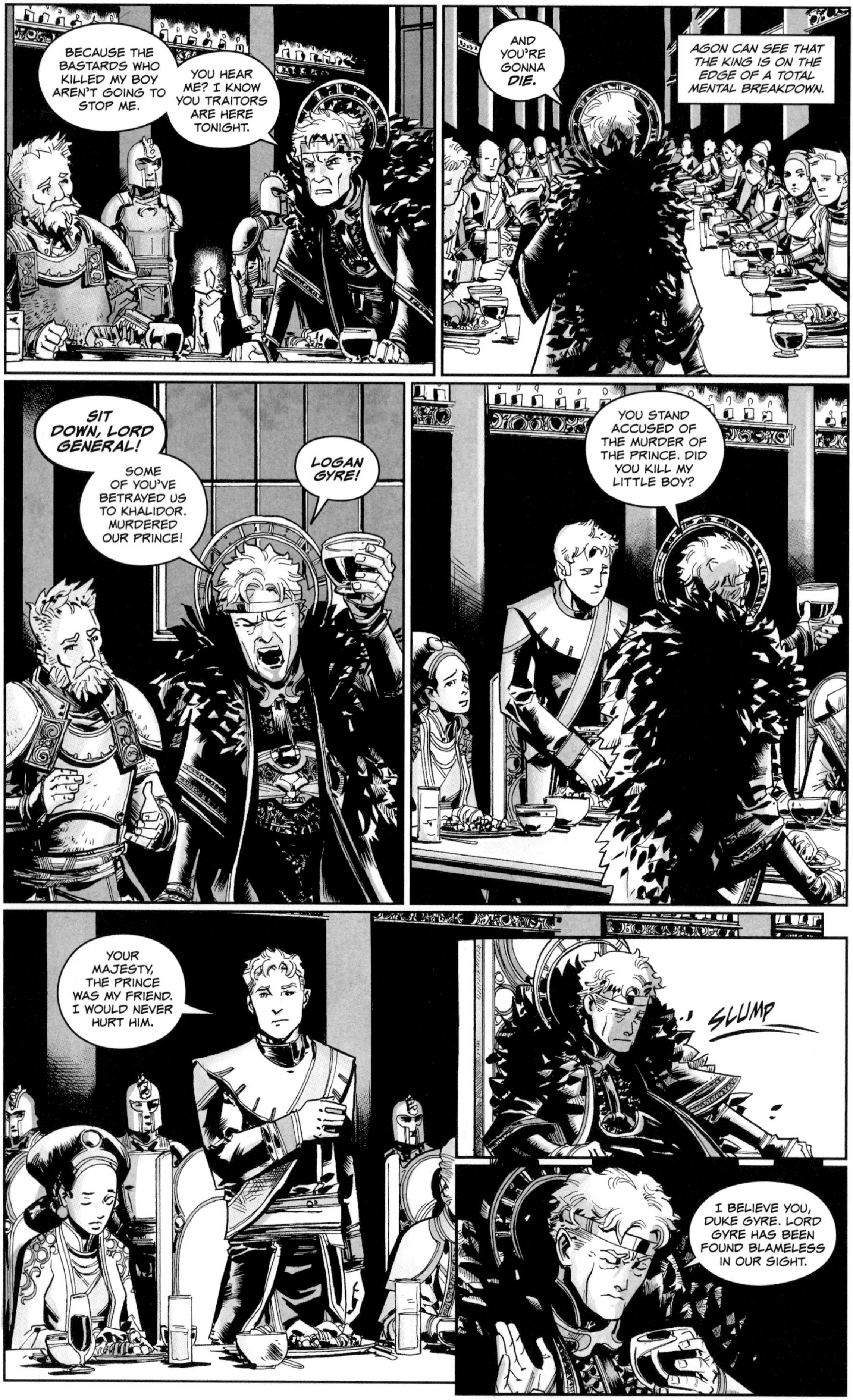
BECAUSE THE BASTARDS WHO KILLED MY BOY AREN'T GOING TO STOP ME.
YOU HEAR ME? I KNOW YOU TRAITORS ARE HERE TONIGHT.
AND YOU'RE GONNA DIE.
AGON CAN SEE THAT THE KING IS ON THE EDGE OF A TOTAL MENTAL BREAKDOWN.
SIT DOWN, LORD GENERAL!
SOME OF YOU'VE BETRAYED US TO KHALIDOR. MURDERED OUR PRINCE!
LOGAN GYRE!
YOU STAND ACCUSED OF THE MURDER OF THE PRINCE. DID YOU KILL MY LITTLE BOY?
YOUR MAJESTY, THE PRINCE WAS MY FRIEND. I WOULD NEVER HURT HIM.
SLUMP
I BELIEVE YOU, DUKE GYRE. LORD GYRE HAS BEEN FOUND BLAMELESS IN OUR SIGHT.

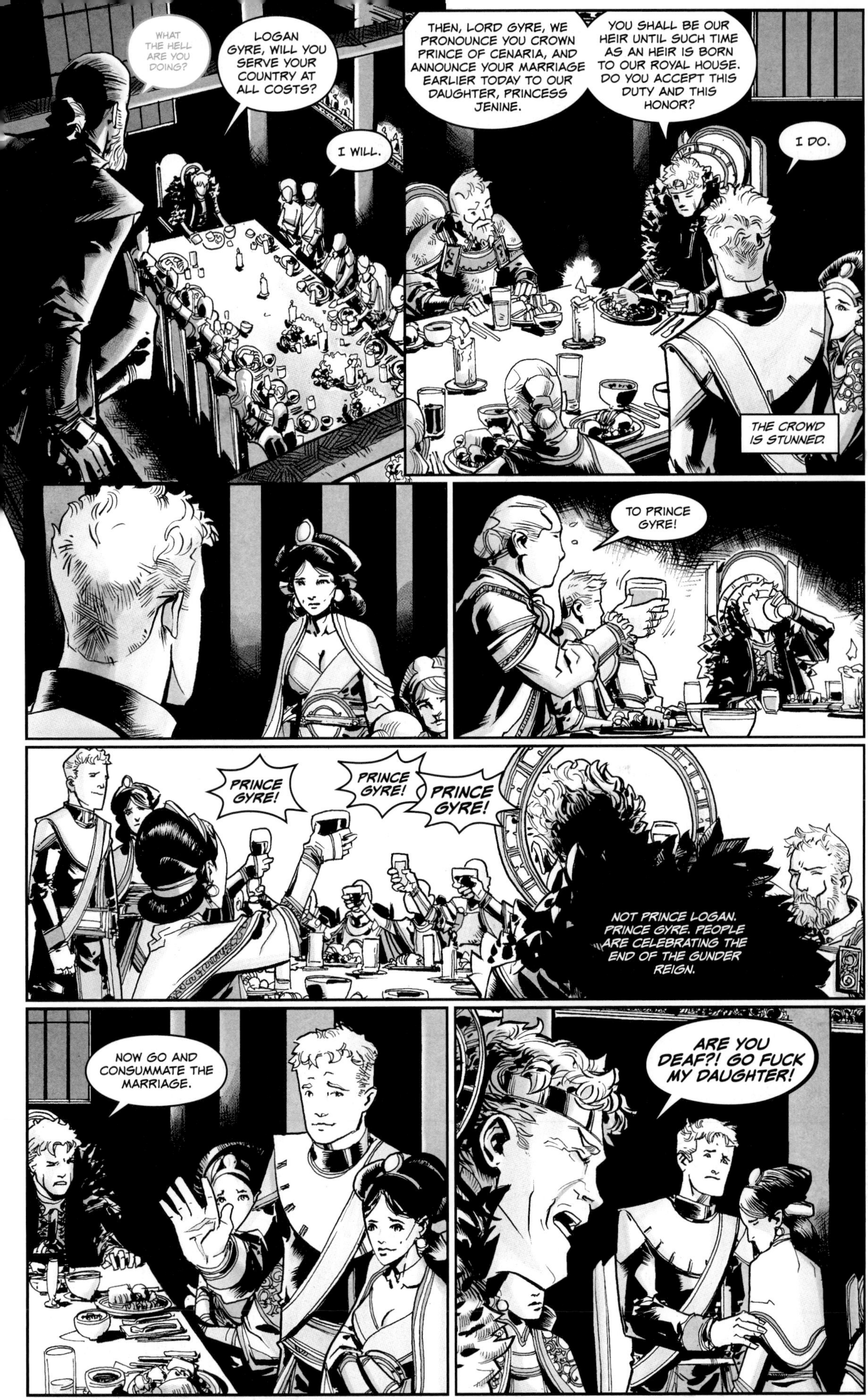
WHAT THE HELL ARE YOU DOING?
LOGAN GYRE, WILL YOU SERVE YOUR COUNTRY AT ALL COSTS?
I WILL.
THEN, LORD GYRE, WE PRONOUNCE YOU CROWN PRINCE OF CENARIA, AND ANNOUNCE YOUR MARRIAGE EARLIER TODAY TO OUR DAUGHTER, PRINCESS JENINE.
YOU SHALL BE OUR HEIR UNTIL SUCH TIME AS AN HEIR IS BORN TO OUR ROYAL HOUSE. DO YOU ACCEPT THIS DUTY AND THIS HONOR?
I DO.
THE CROWD IS STUNNED.
TO PRINCE GYRE!
PRINCE GYRE!
PRINCE GYRE!
PRINCE GYRE!
NOT PRINCE LOGAN. PRINCE GYRE. PEOPLE ARE CELEBRATING THE END OF THE GUNDER REIGN.
NOW GO AND CONSUMMATE THE MARRIAGE.
ARE YOU DEAF?! GO FUCK MY DAUGHTER!

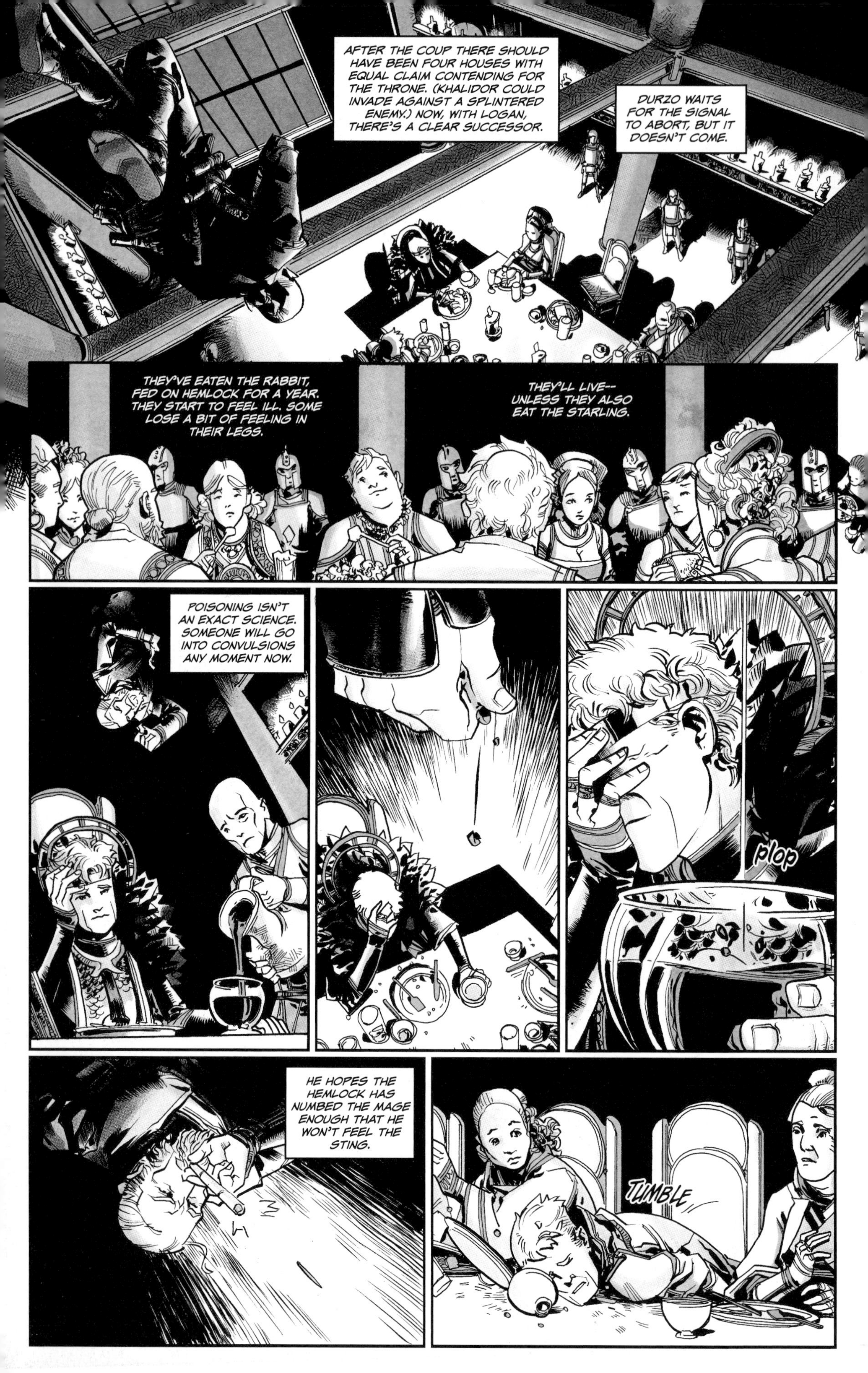
AFTER THE COUP THERE SHOULD HAVE BEEN FOUR HOUSES WITH EQUAL CLAIM CONTENDING FOR THE THRONE. (KHALIDOR COULD INVADE AGAINST A SPLINTERED ENEMY.) NOW, WITH LOGAN, THERE'S A CLEAR SUCCESSOR.
DURZO WAITS FOR THE SIGNAL TO ABORT, BUT IT DOESN'T COME.
THEY'VE EATEN THE RABBIT, FED ON HEMLOCK FOR A YEAR. THEY START TO FEEL ILL. SOME LOSE A BIT OF FEELING IN THEIR LEGS.
THEY'LL LIVE-- UNLESS THEY ALSO EAT THE STARLING.
POISONING ISN'T AN EXACT SCIENCE. SOMEONE WILL GO INTO CONVULSIONS ANY MOMENT NOW.
plop
HE HOPES THE HEMLOCK HAS NUMBED THE MAGE ENOUGH THAT HE WON'T FEEL THE STING.
TUMBLE

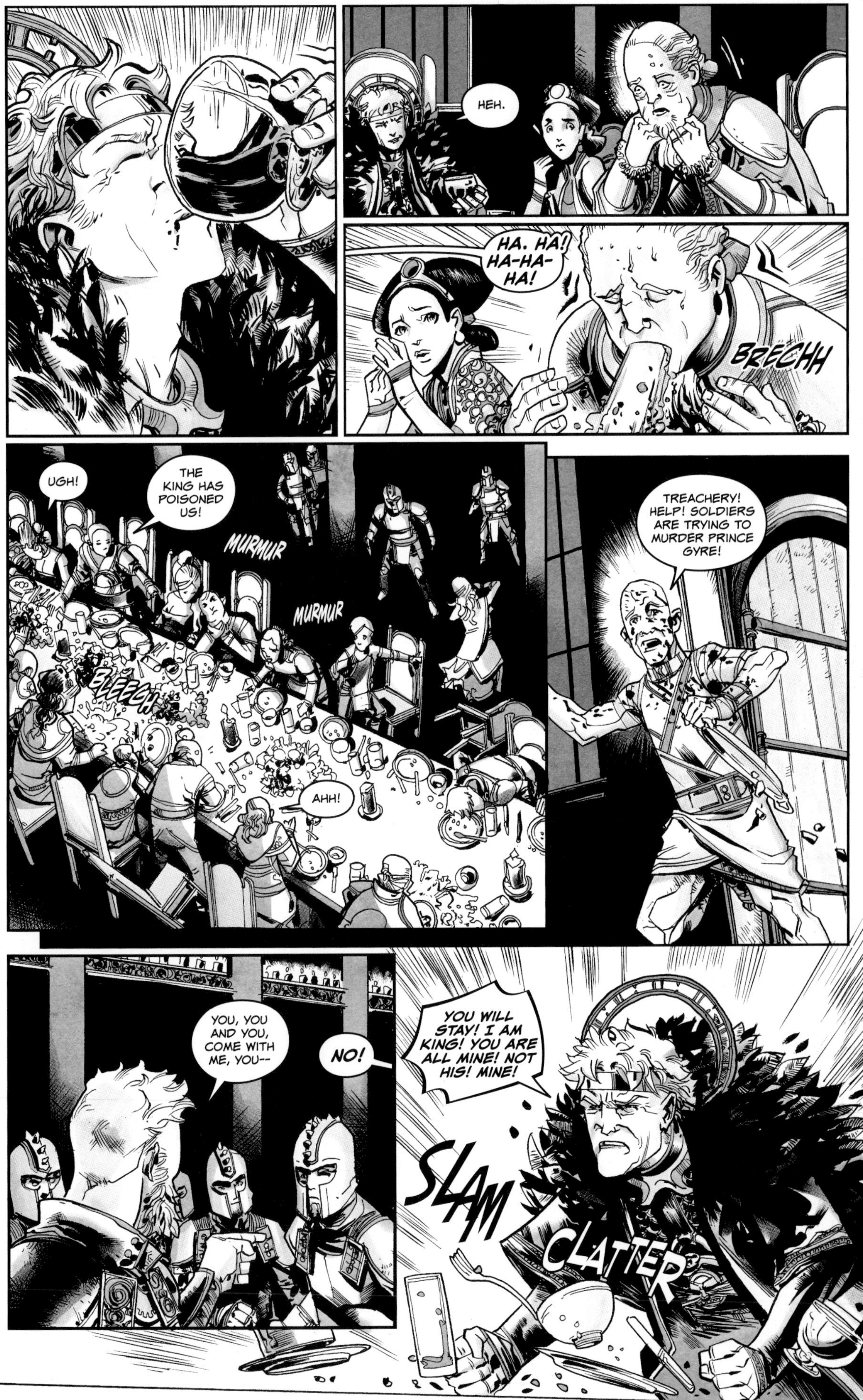
HEH.
HA. HA! HA-HA-HA!
BRECHH
UGH!
THE KING HAS POISONED US!
MURMUR
MURMUR
BLEECH
AHH!
TREACHERY! HELP! SOLDIERS ARE TRYING TO MURDER PRINCE GYRE!
YOU, YOU AND YOU, COME WITH ME, YOU--
NO!
YOU WILL STAY! I AM KING! YOU ARE ALL MINE! NOT HIS! MINE!
SLAM
CLATTER

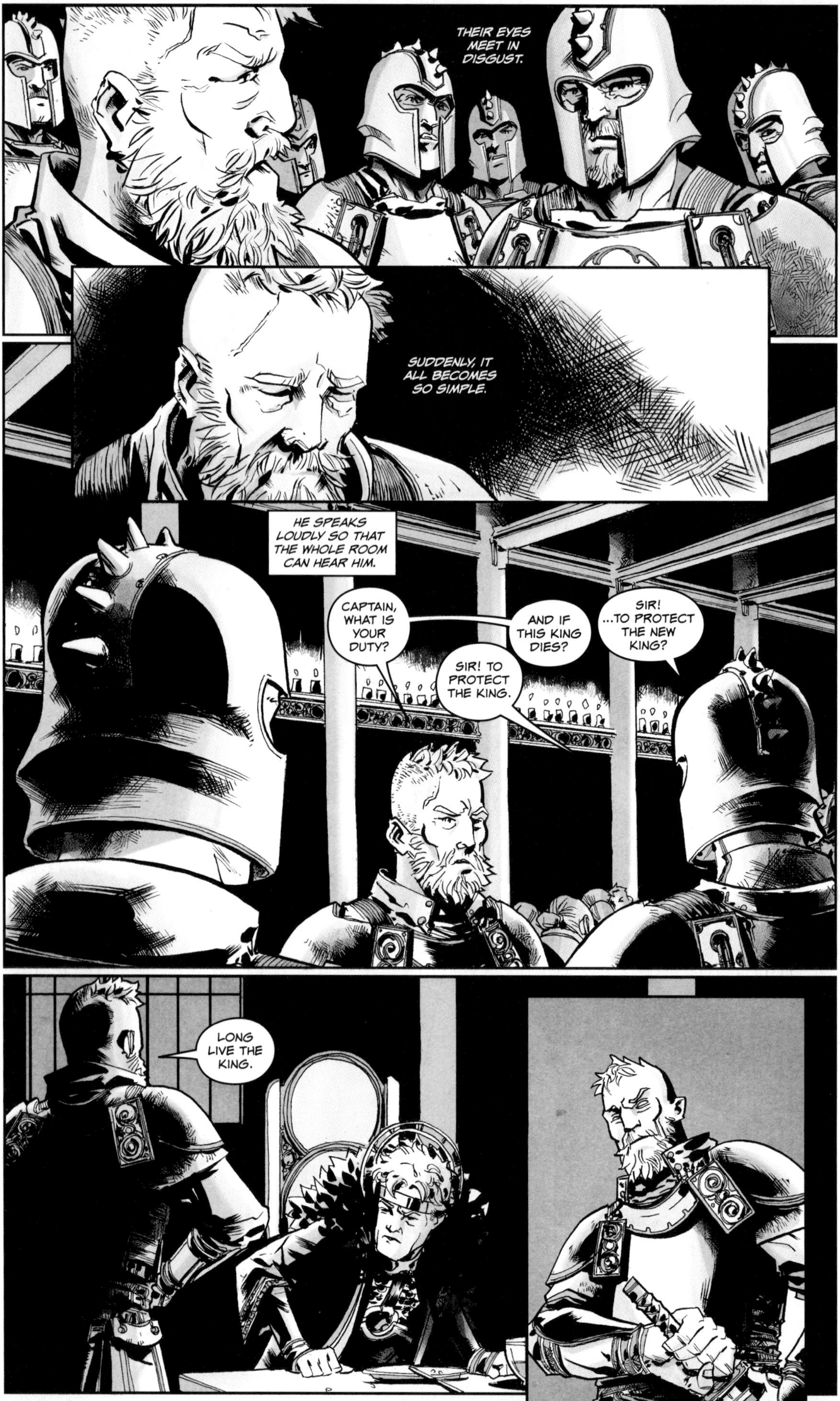
THEIR EYES MEET IN DISGUST.
SUDDENLY, IT ALL BECOMES SO SIMPLE.
HE SPEAKS LOUDLY SO THAT THE WHOLE ROOM CAN HEAR HIM.
CAPTAIN, WHAT IS YOUR DUTY?
SIR! TO PROTECT THE KING.
AND IF THIS KING DIES?
SIR! ...TO PROTECT THE NEW KING?
LONG LIVE THE KING.

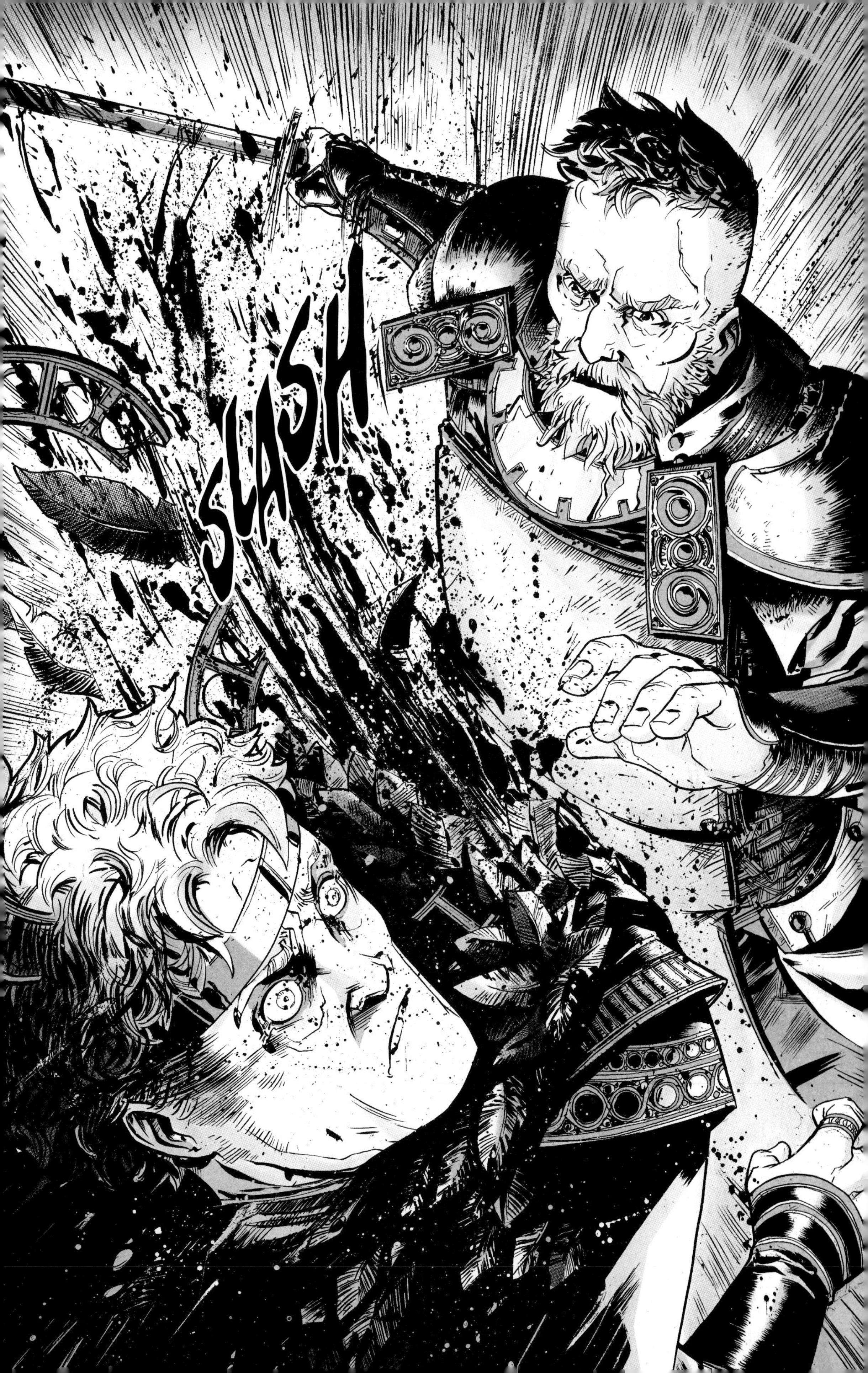
SLASH

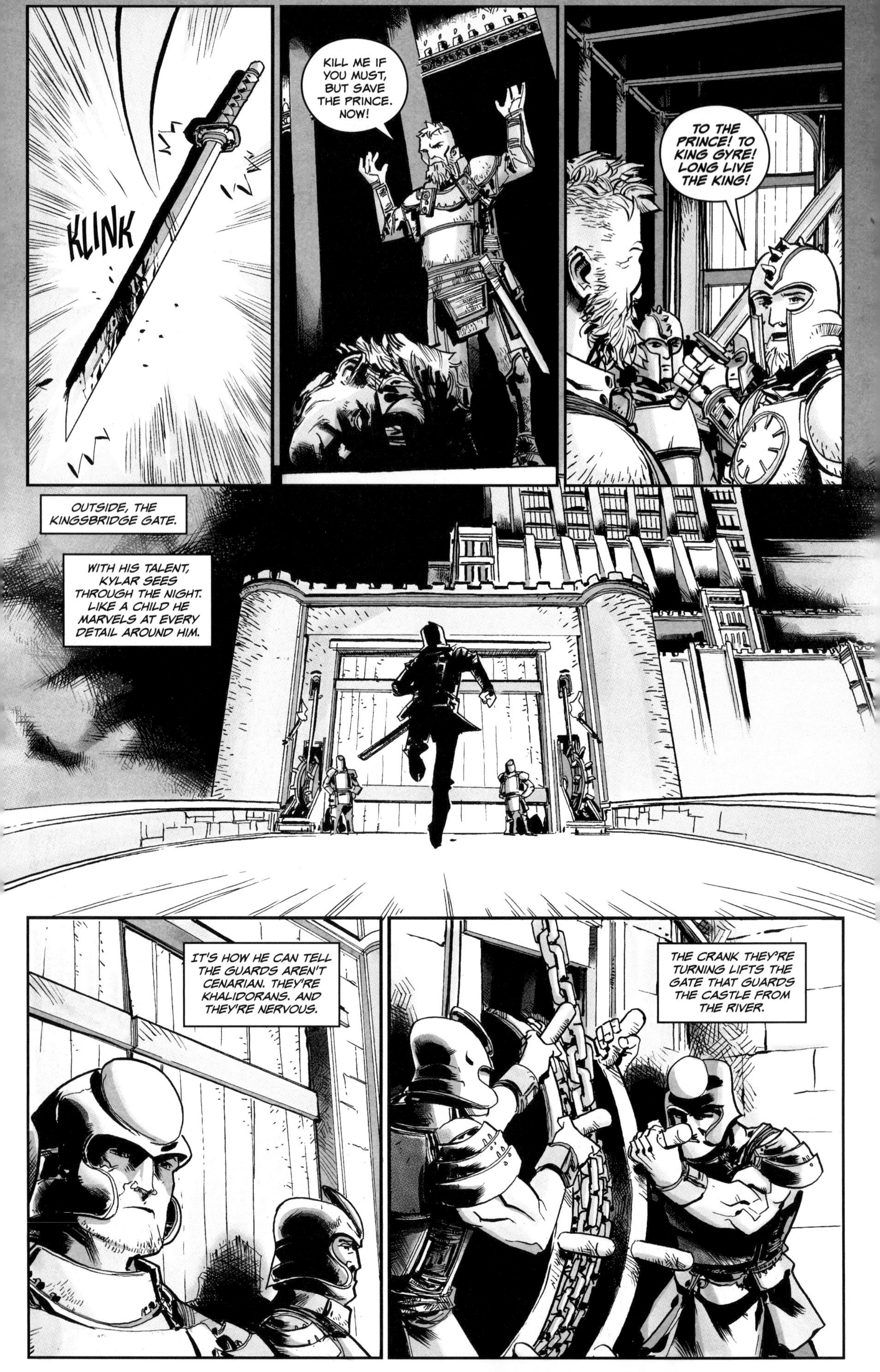
KLINK
KILL ME IF YOU MUST, BUT SAVE THE PRINCE. NOW!
TO THE PRINCE! TO KING GYRE! LONG LIVE THE KING!
OUTSIDE, THE KINGSBRIDGE GATE.
WITH HIS TALENT, KYLAR SEES THROUGH THE NIGHT. LIKE A CHILD HE MARVELS AT EVERY DETAIL AROUND HIM.
IT'S HOW HE CAN TELL THE GUARDS AREN'T CENARIAN. THEY'RE KHALIDORANS. AND THEY'RE NERVOUS.
THE CRANK THEY'RE TURNING LIFTS THE GATE THAT GUARDS THE CASTLE FROM THE RIVER.

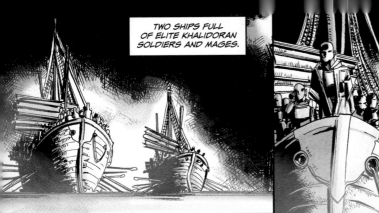

TWO SHIPS FULL OF ELITE KHALIDORAN SOLDIERS AND MAGES.

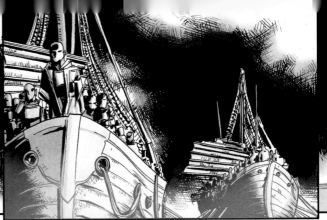

FWIP

THERE'S NO ONE MANNING THE BRIDGE DEFENSES.

FWOO

NO ONE BUT KYLAR.

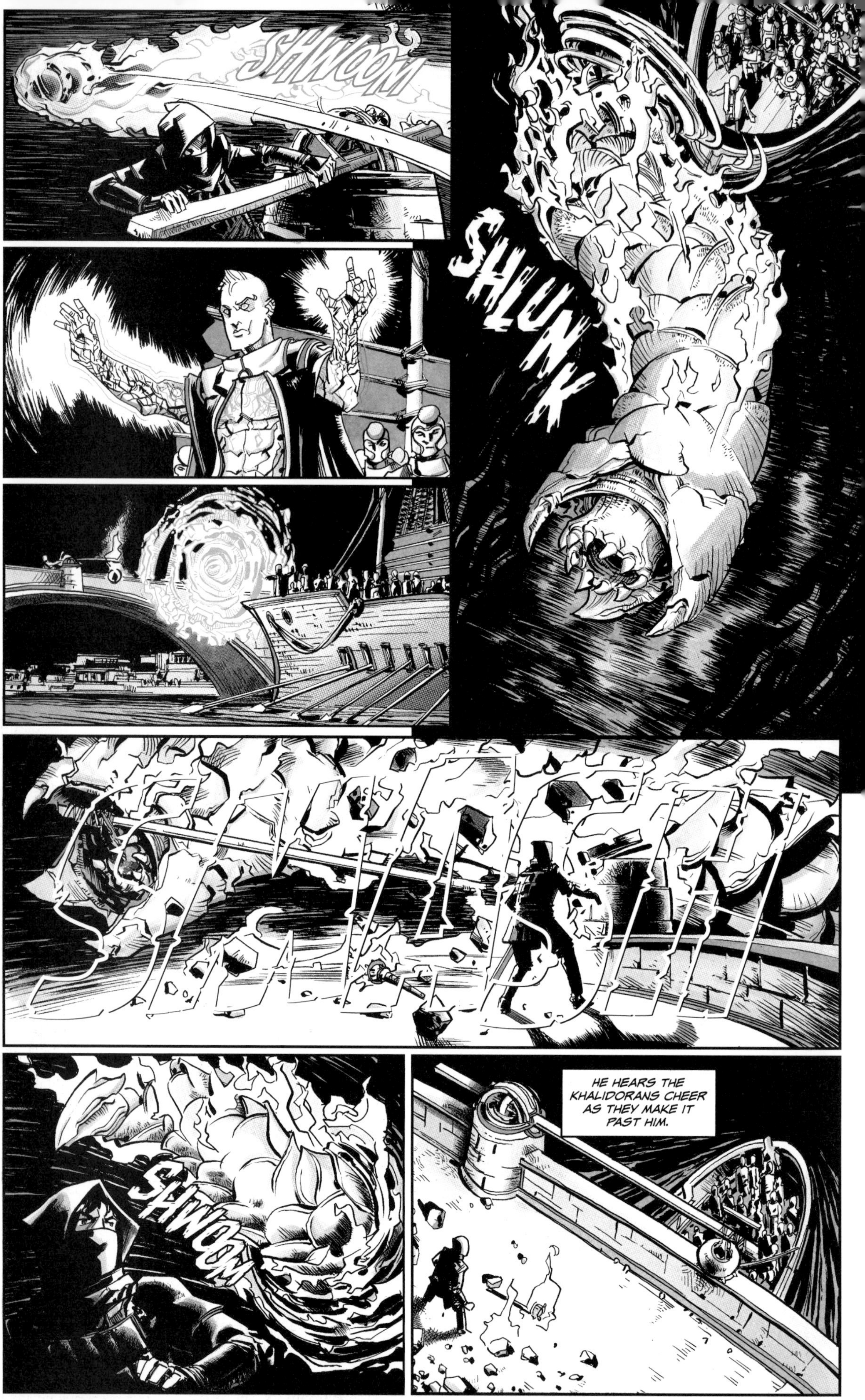
SHWOOM
SHLUNK
SHWOOM
HE HEARS THE KHALIDORANS CHEER AS THEY MAKE IT PAST HIM.

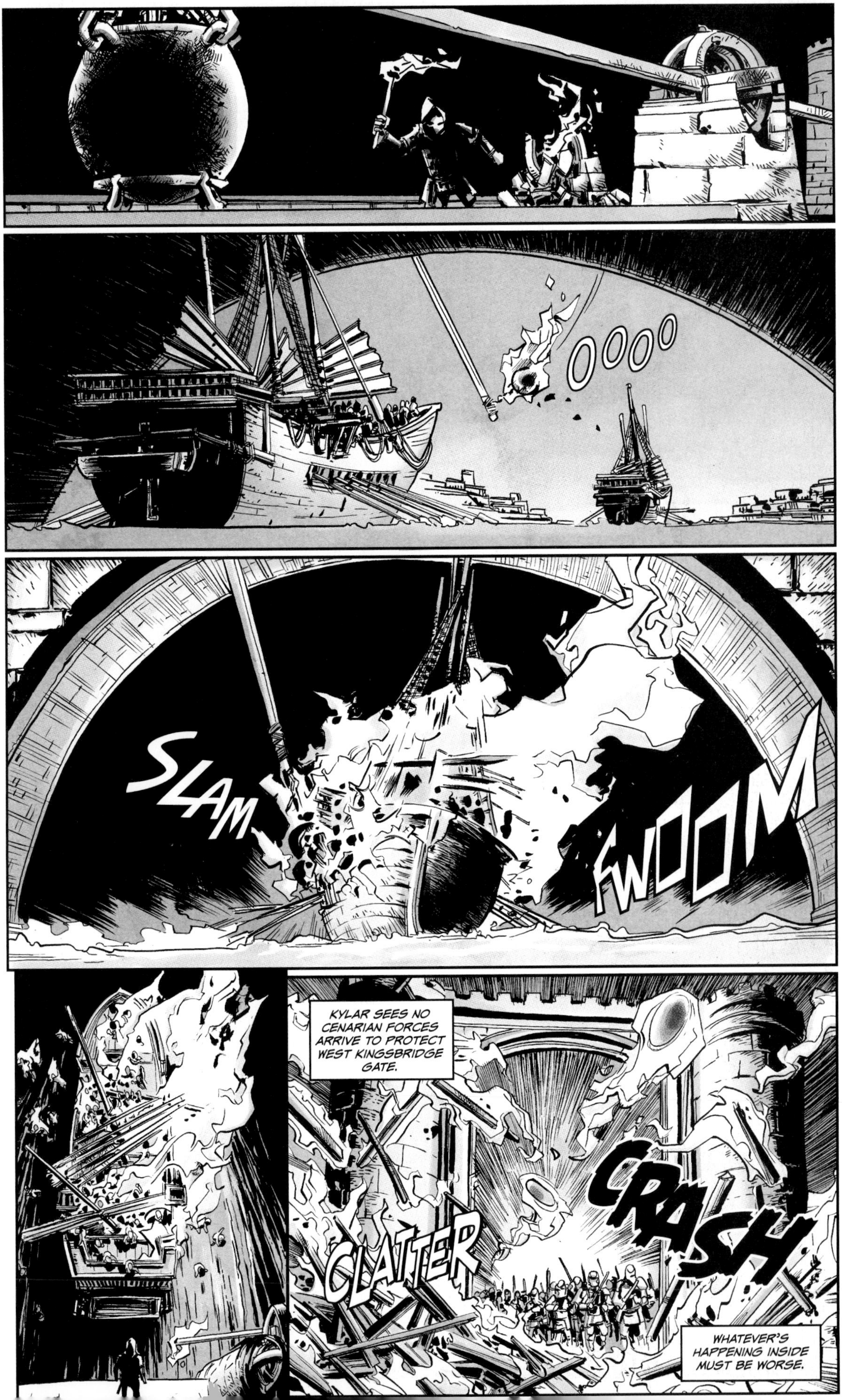
OOOO
SLAM
FWOOM
KYLAR SEES NO CENARIAN FORCES ARRIVE TO PROTECT WEST KINGSBRIDGE GATE.
CLATTER
CRASH
WHATEVER'S HAPPENING INSIDE MUST BE WORSE.

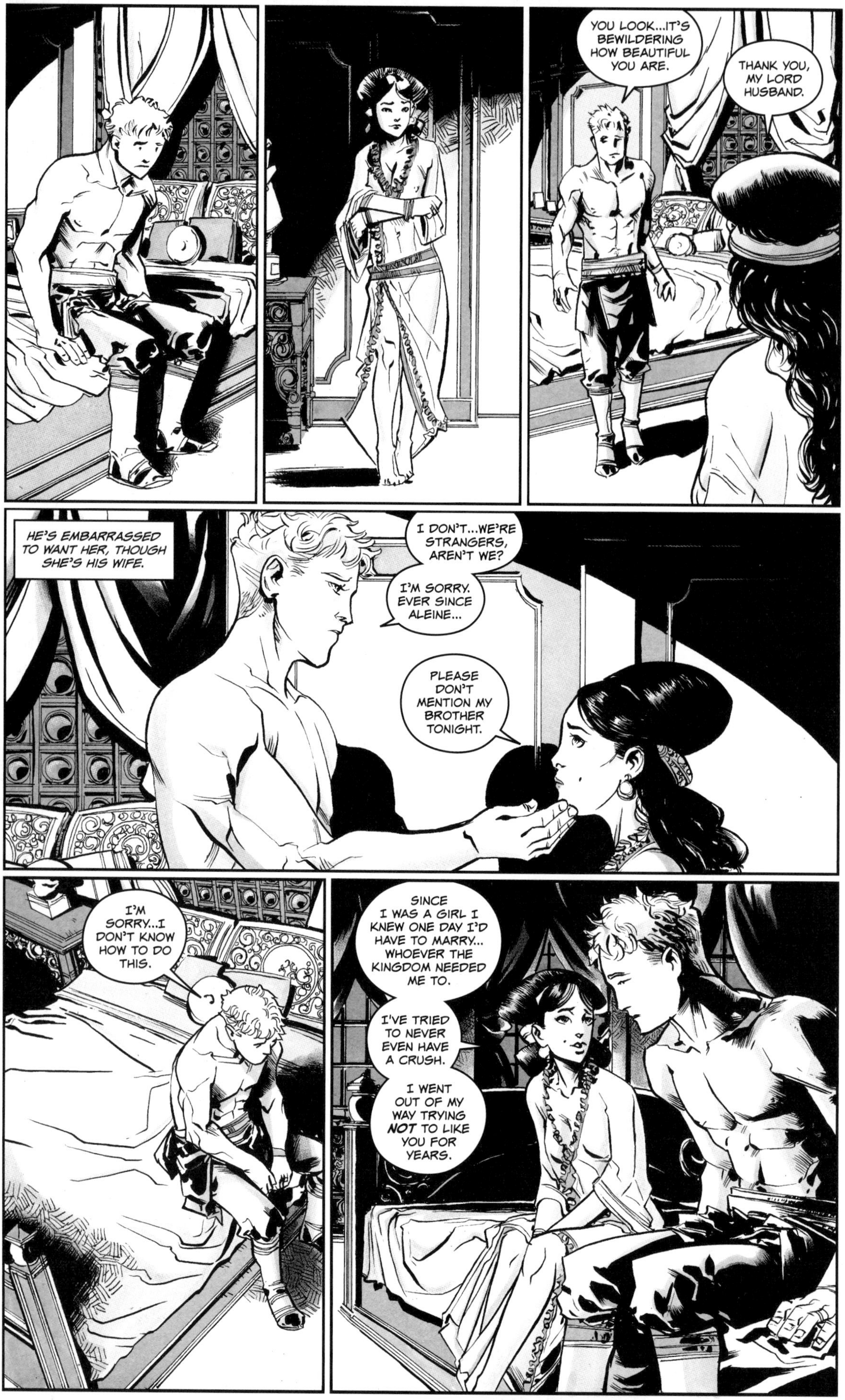
YOU LOOK...IT'S BEWILDERING HOW BEAUTIFUL YOU ARE.
THANK YOU, MY LORD HUSBAND.
HE'S EMBARRASSED TO WANT HER, THOUGH SHE'S HIS WIFE.
I DON'T...WE'RE STRANGERS, AREN'T WE?
I'M SORRY. EVER SINCE ALEINE...
PLEASE DON'T MENTION MY BROTHER TONIGHT.
I'M SORRY...I DON'T KNOW HOW TO DO THIS.
SINCE I WAS A GIRL I KNEW ONE DAY I'D HAVE TO MARRY... WHOEVER THE KINGDOM NEEDED ME TO.
I'VE TRIED TO NEVER EVEN HAVE A CRUSH.
I WENT OUT OF MY WAY TRYING NOT TO LIKE YOU FOR YEARS.

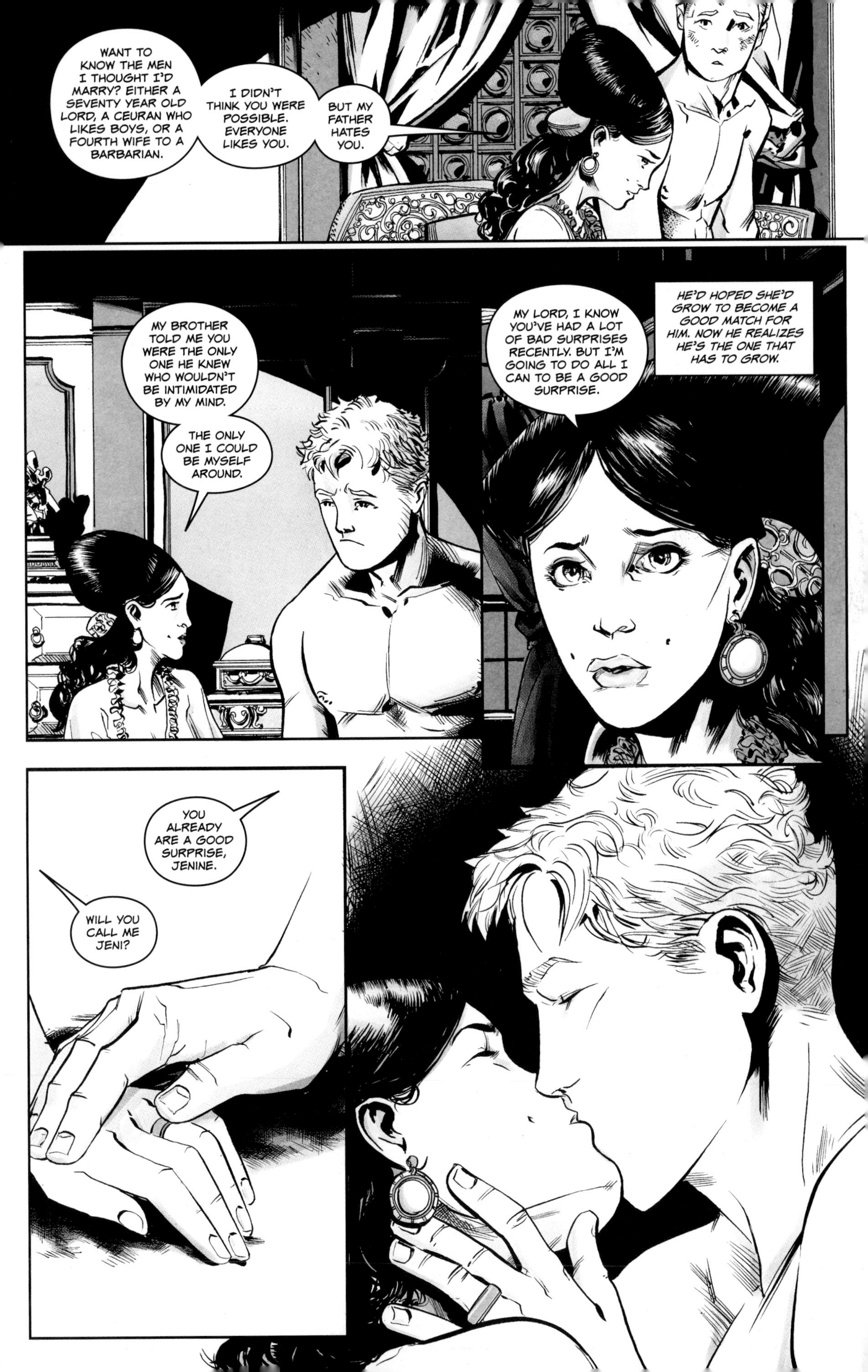

WANT TO KNOW THE MEN I THOUGHT I'D MARRY? EITHER A SEVENTY YEAR OLD LORD, A CEURAN WHO LIKES BOYS, OR A FOURTH WIFE TO A BARBARIAN.
I DIDN'T THINK YOU WERE POSSIBLE. EVERYONE LIKES YOU.
BUT MY FATHER HATES YOU.
MY BROTHER TOLD ME YOU WERE THE ONLY ONE HE KNEW WHO WOULDN'T BE INTIMIDATED BY MY MIND.
THE ONLY ONE I COULD BE MYSELF AROUND.
MY LORD, I KNOW YOU'VE HAD A LOT OF BAD SURPRISES RECENTLY. BUT I'M GOING TO DO ALL I CAN TO BE A GOOD SURPRISE.
HE'D HOPED SHE'D GROW TO BECOME A GOOD MATCH FOR HIM. NOW HE REALIZES HE'S THE ONE THAT HAS TO GROW.
YOU ALREADY ARE A GOOD SURPRISE, JENINE.
WILL YOU CALL ME JENI?

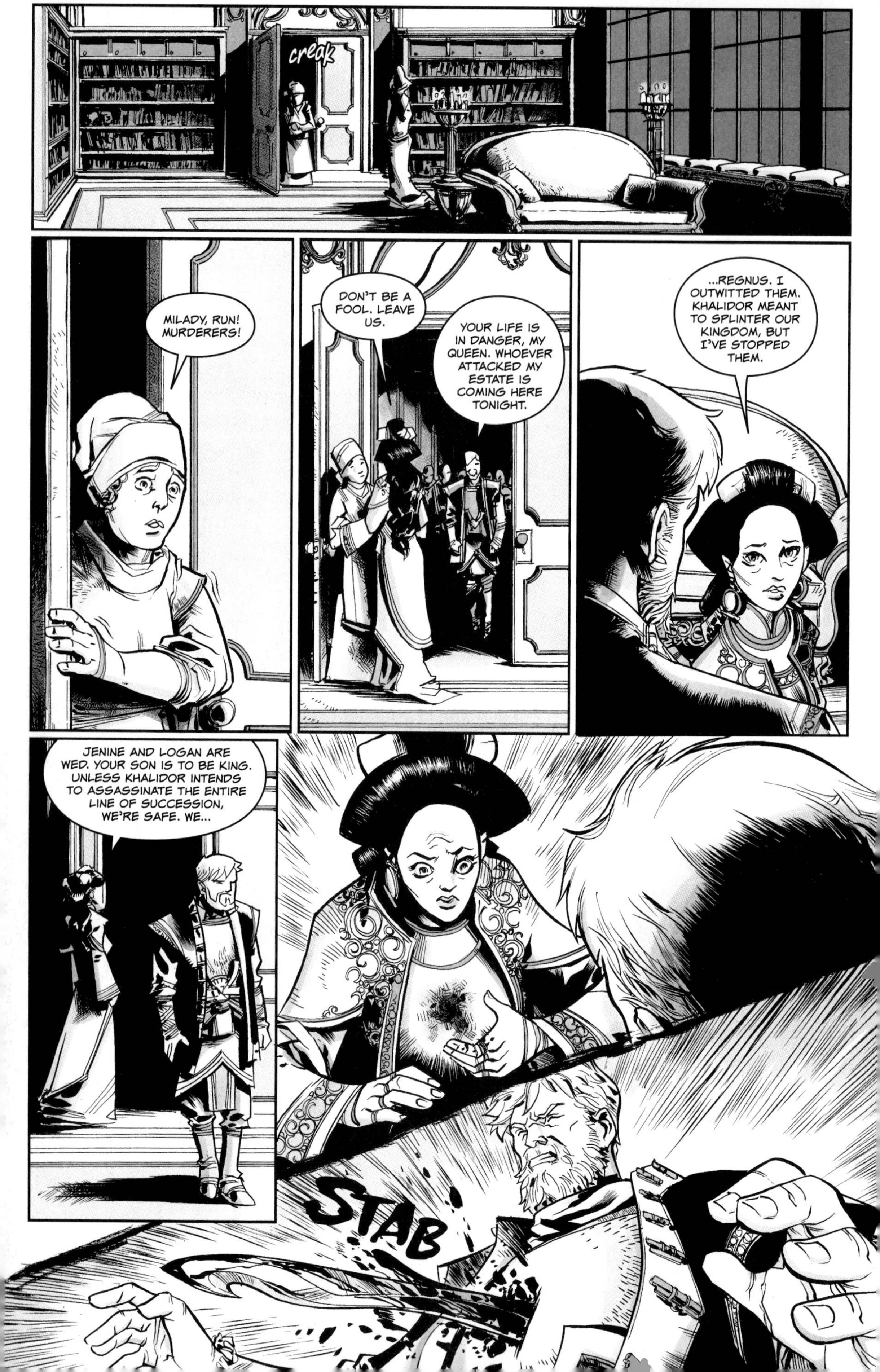
creak
MILADY, RUN! MURDERERS!
DON'T BE A FOOL. LEAVE US.
YOUR LIFE IS IN DANGER, MY QUEEN. WHOEVER ATTACKED MY ESTATE IS COMING HERE TONIGHT.
...REGNUS. I OUTWITTED THEM. KHALIDOR MEANT TO SPLINTER OUR KINGDOM, BUT I'VE STOPPED THEM.
JENINE AND LOGAN ARE WED. YOUR SON IS TO BE KING. UNLESS KHALIDOR INTENDS TO ASSASSINATE THE ENTIRE LINE OF SUCCESSION, WE'RE SAFE. WE...
STAB

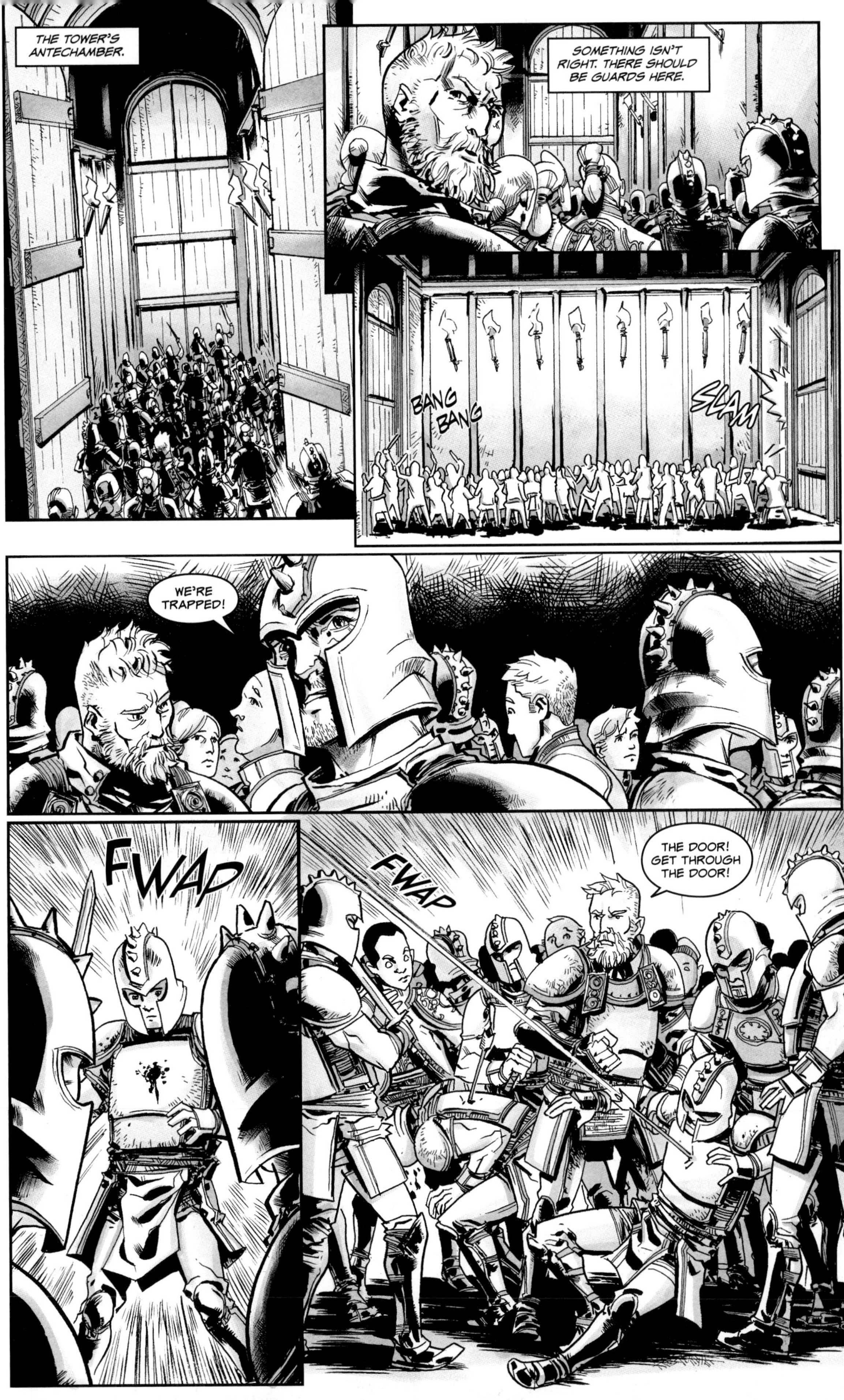
THE TOWER'S ANTECHAMBER.
SOMETHING ISN'T RIGHT. THERE SHOULD BE GUARDS HERE.
BANG BANG
SLAM
WE'RE TRAPPED!
FWAP
FWAP
THE DOOR! GET THROUGH THE DOOR!

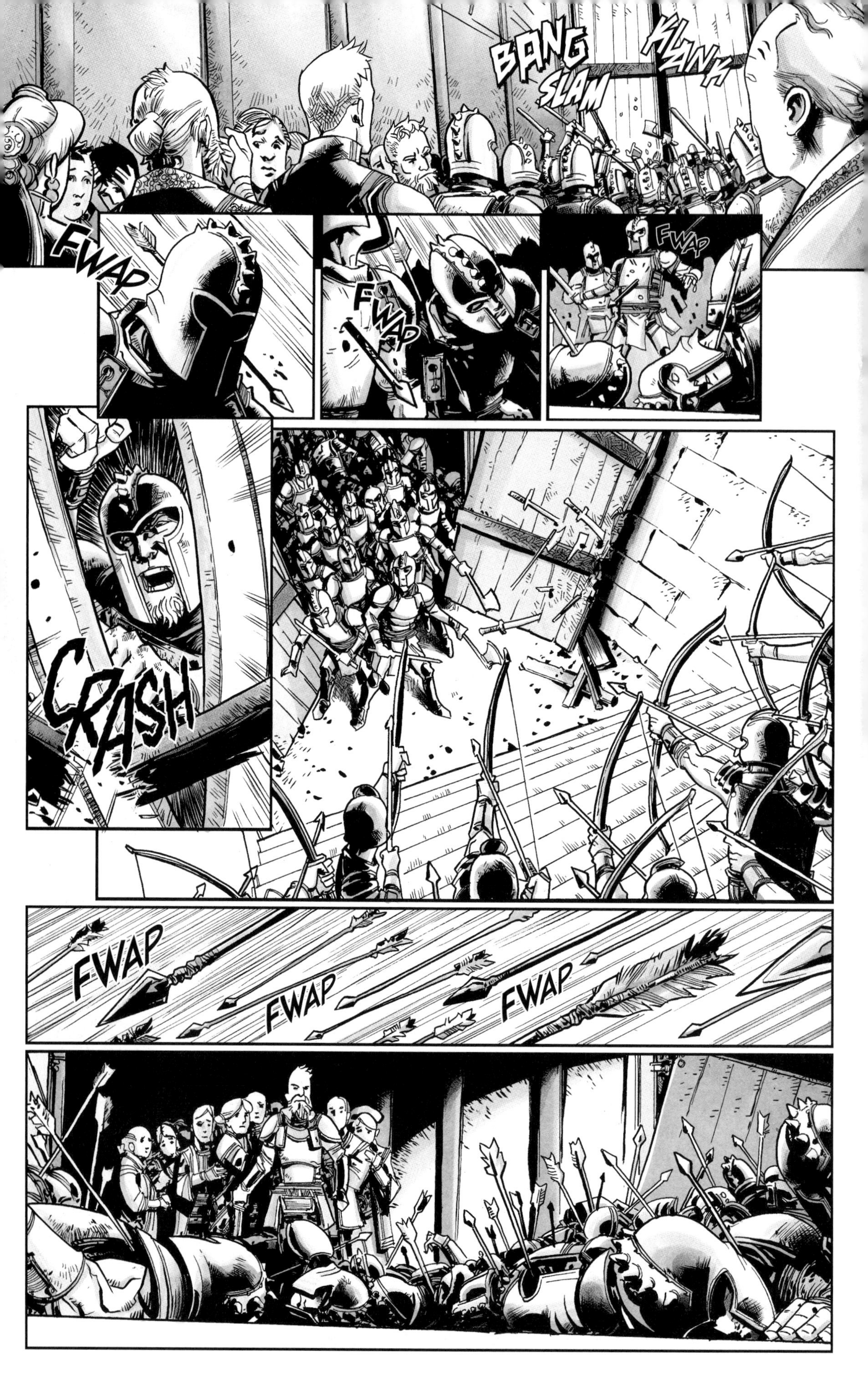
BANG
SLAM
KLANK
FWAP
FWAP
FWAP
CRASH
FWAP
FWAP
FWAP

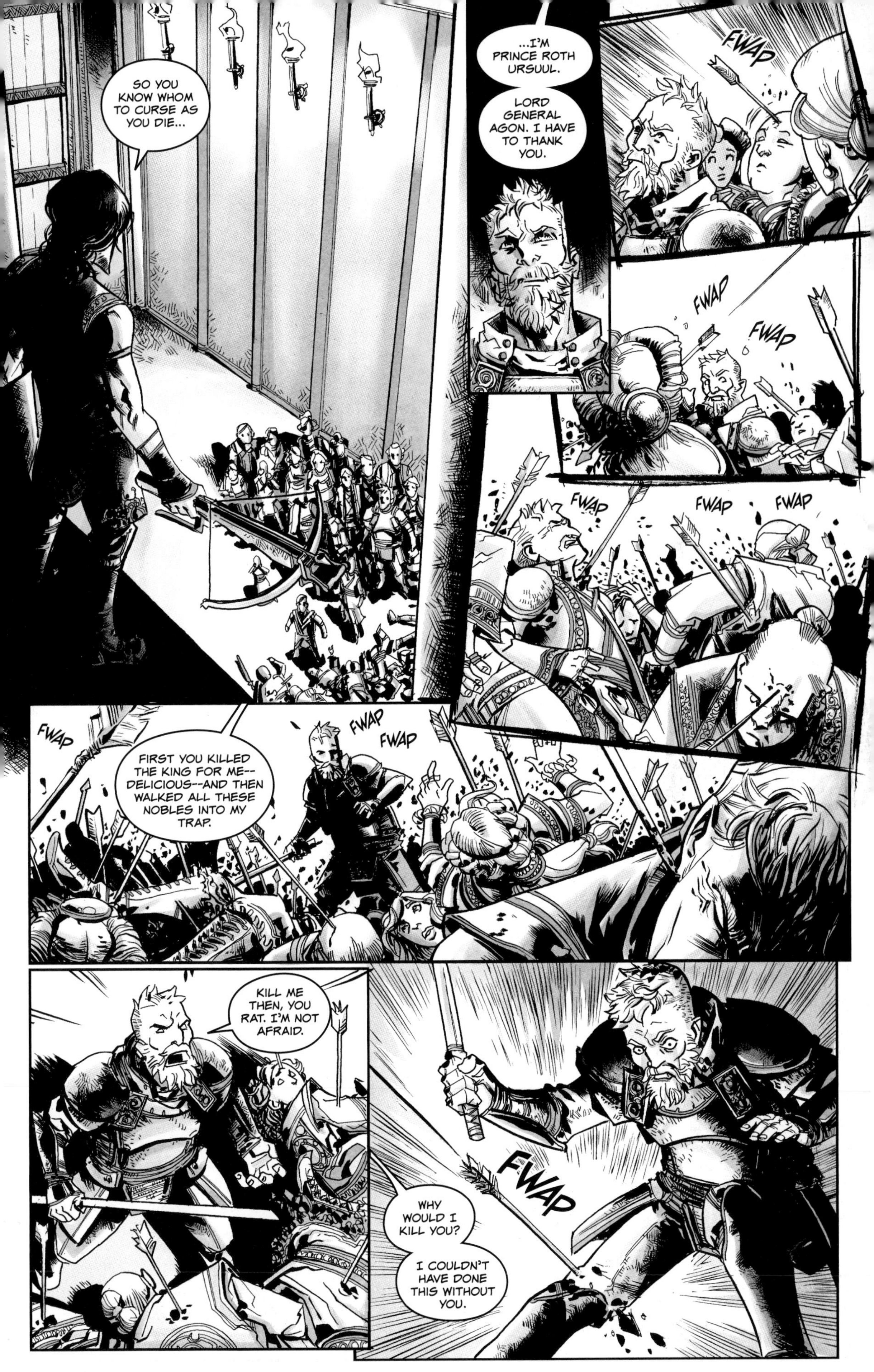
SO YOU KNOW WHOM TO CURSE AS YOU DIE...
...I'M PRINCE ROTH URSUUL.
LORD GENERAL AGON. I HAVE TO THANK YOU.
FWAP
FWAP
FWAP
FWAP
FWAP
FWAP
FWAP
FWAP
FWAP
FIRST YOU KILLED THE KING FOR ME--DELICIOUS--AND THEN WALKED ALL THESE NOBLES INTO MY TRAP.
KILL ME THEN, YOU RAT. I'M NOT AFRAID.
FWAP
WHY WOULD I KILL YOU?
I COULDN'T HAVE DONE THIS WITHOUT YOU.

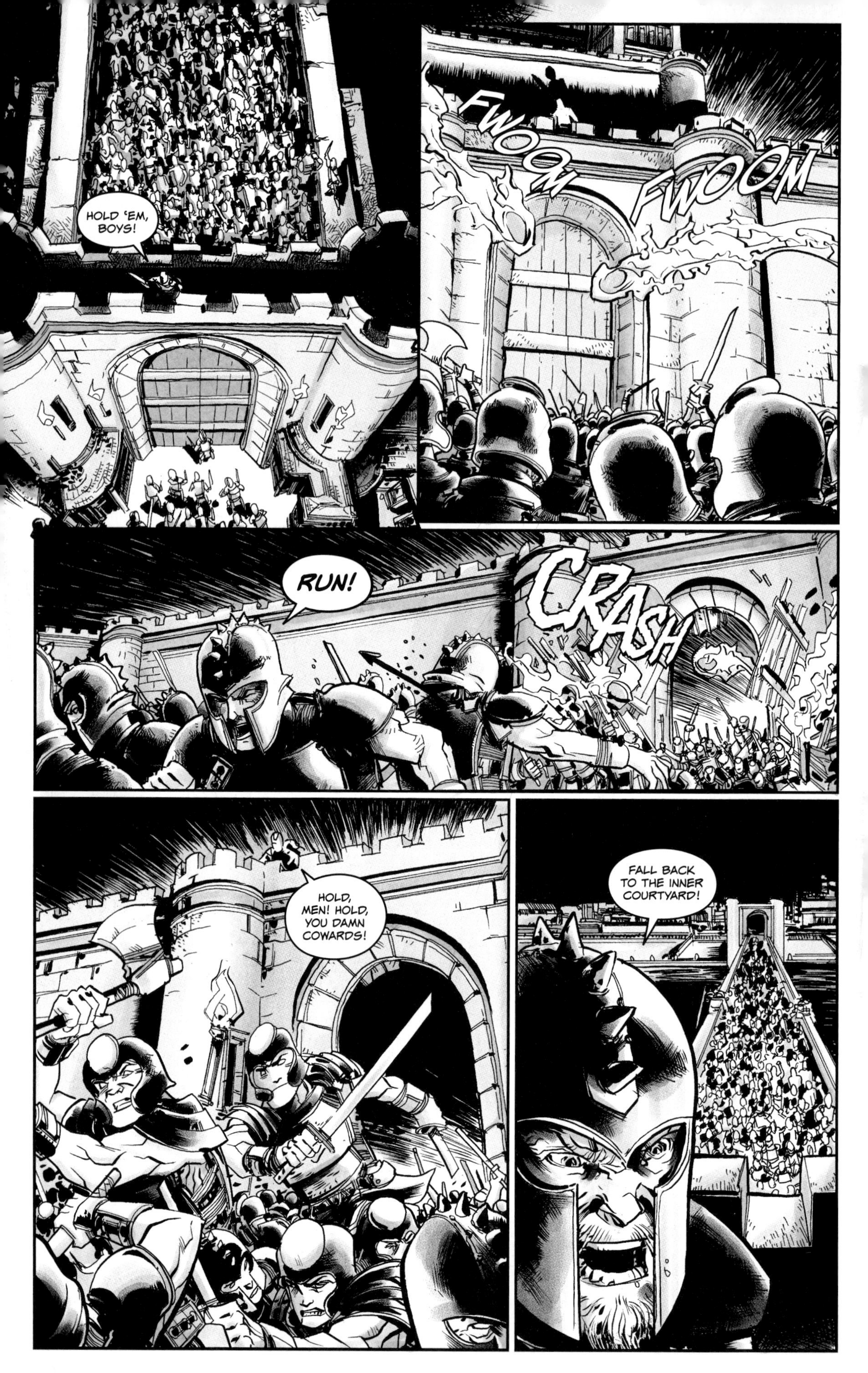
HOLD 'EM, BOYS!
FWOOM
FWOOM
RUN!
CRASH
HOLD, MEN! HOLD, YOU DAMN COWARDS!
FALL BACK TO THE INNER COURTYARD!

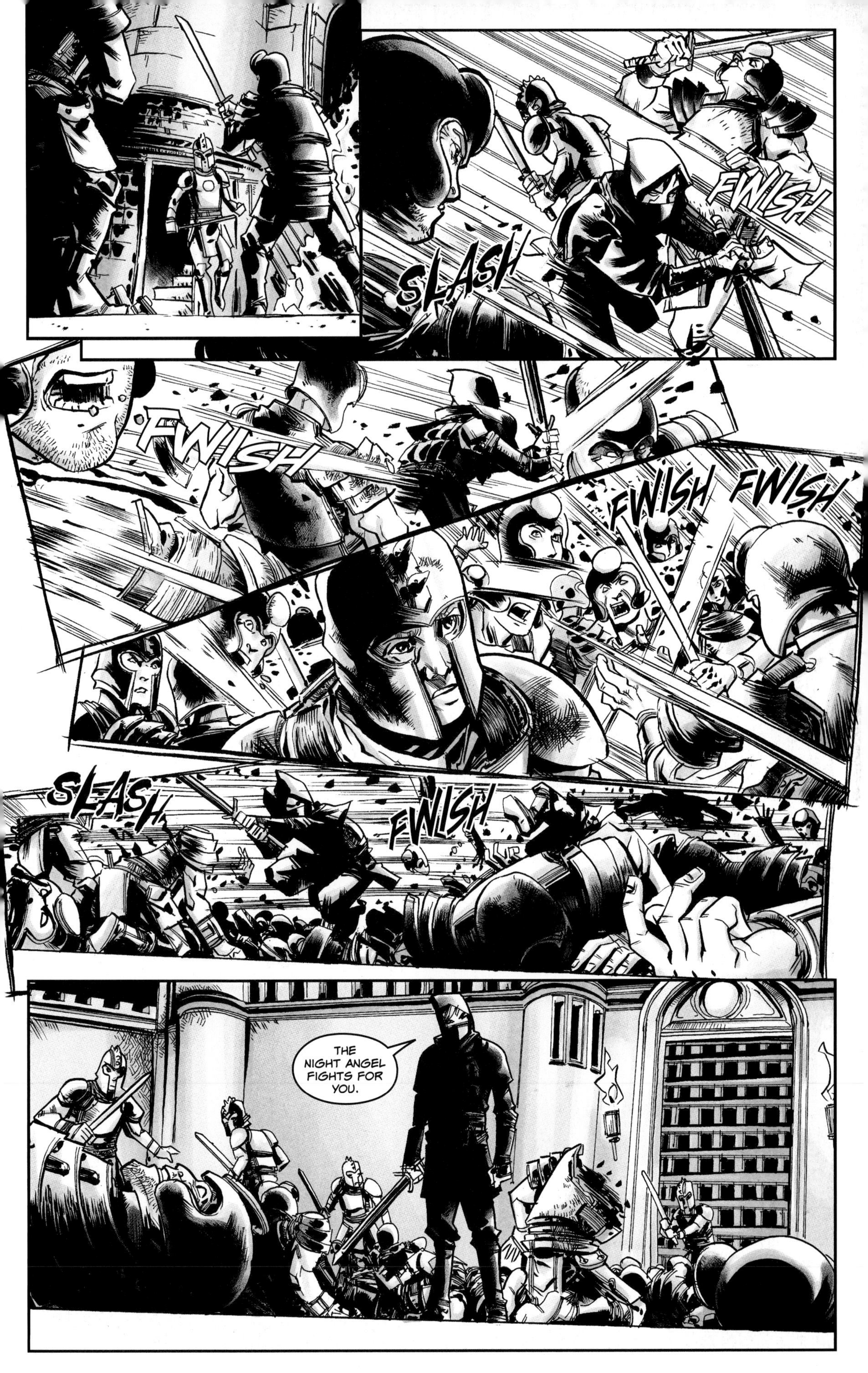
SLASH
FWISH
FWISH
FWISH FWISH
SLASH
FWISH
THE NIGHT ANGEL FIGHTS FOR YOU.

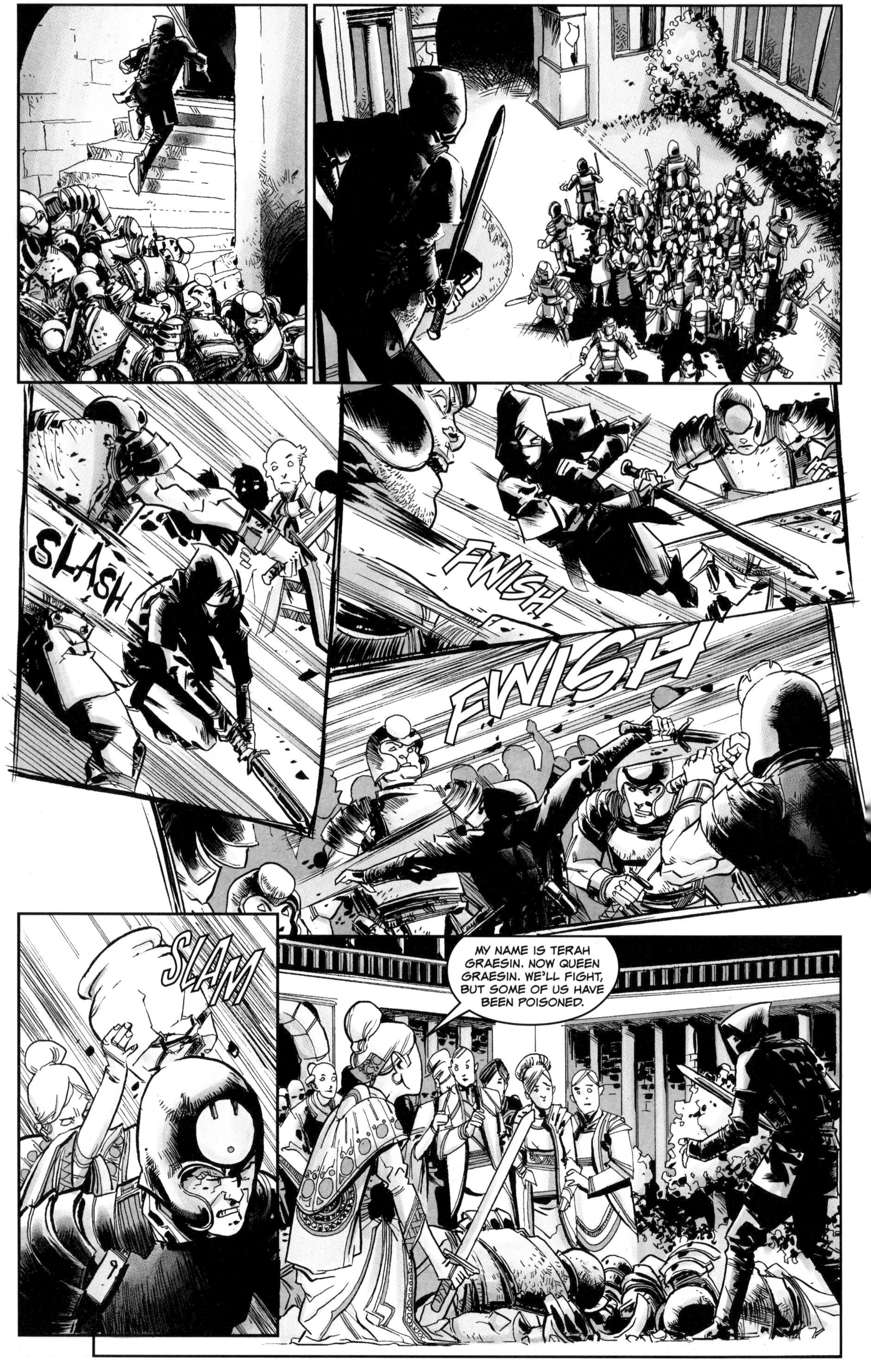
SLASH
FWISH
FWISH
SLAM
MY NAME IS TERAH GRAESIN. NOW QUEEN GRAESIN. WE'LL FIGHT, BUT SOME OF US HAVE BEEN POISONED.

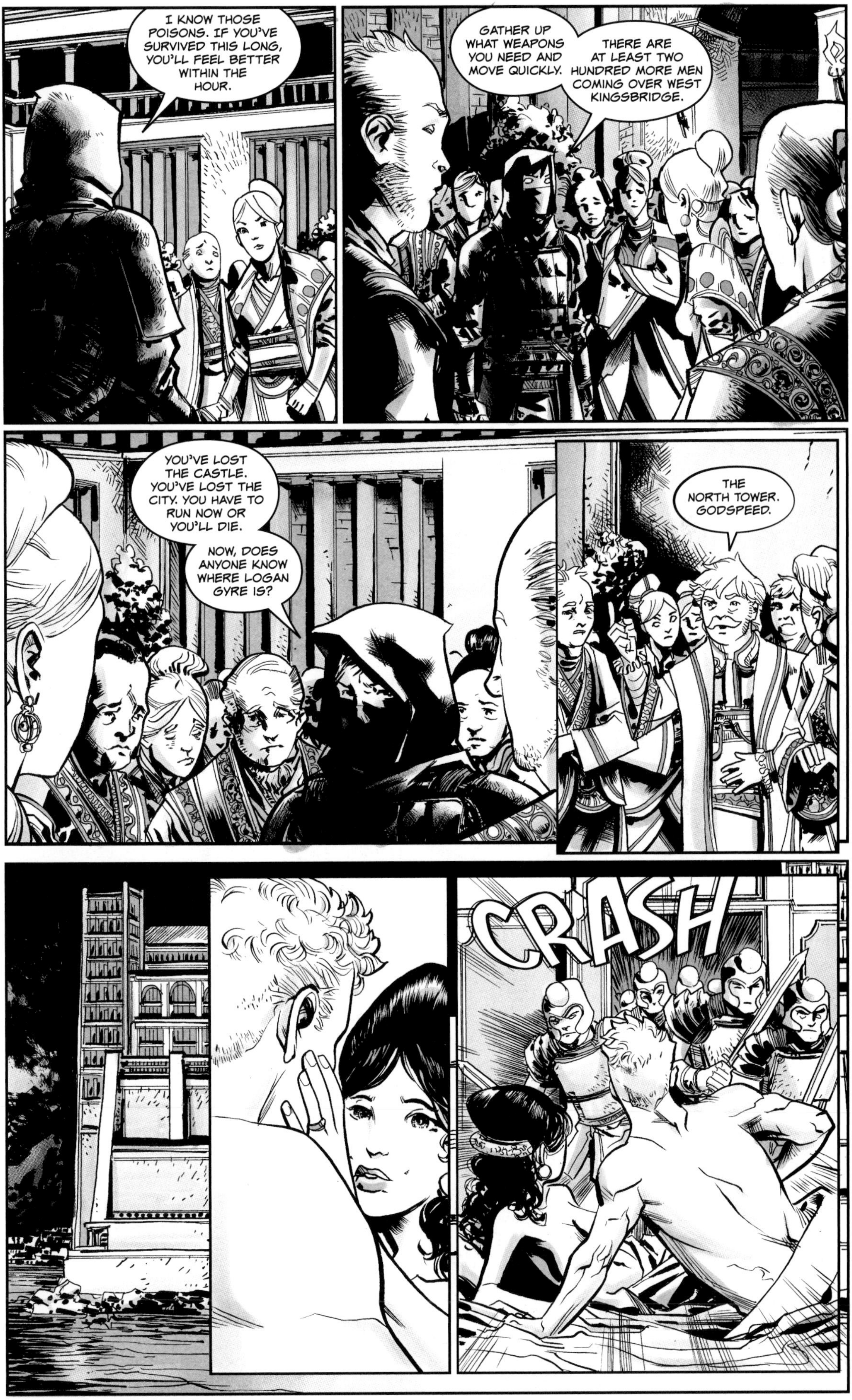
I KNOW THOSE POISONS. IF YOU'VE SURVIVED THIS LONG, YOU'LL FEEL BETTER WITHIN THE HOUR.
GATHER UP WHAT WEAPONS YOU NEED AND MOVE QUICKLY.
THERE ARE AT LEAST TWO HUNDRED MORE MEN COMING OVER WEST KINGSBRIDGE.
YOU'VE LOST THE CASTLE. YOU'VE LOST THE CITY. YOU HAVE TO RUN NOW OR YOU'LL DIE.
NOW, DOES ANYONE KNOW WHERE LOGAN GYRE IS?
THE NORTH TOWER. GODSPEED.
CRASH

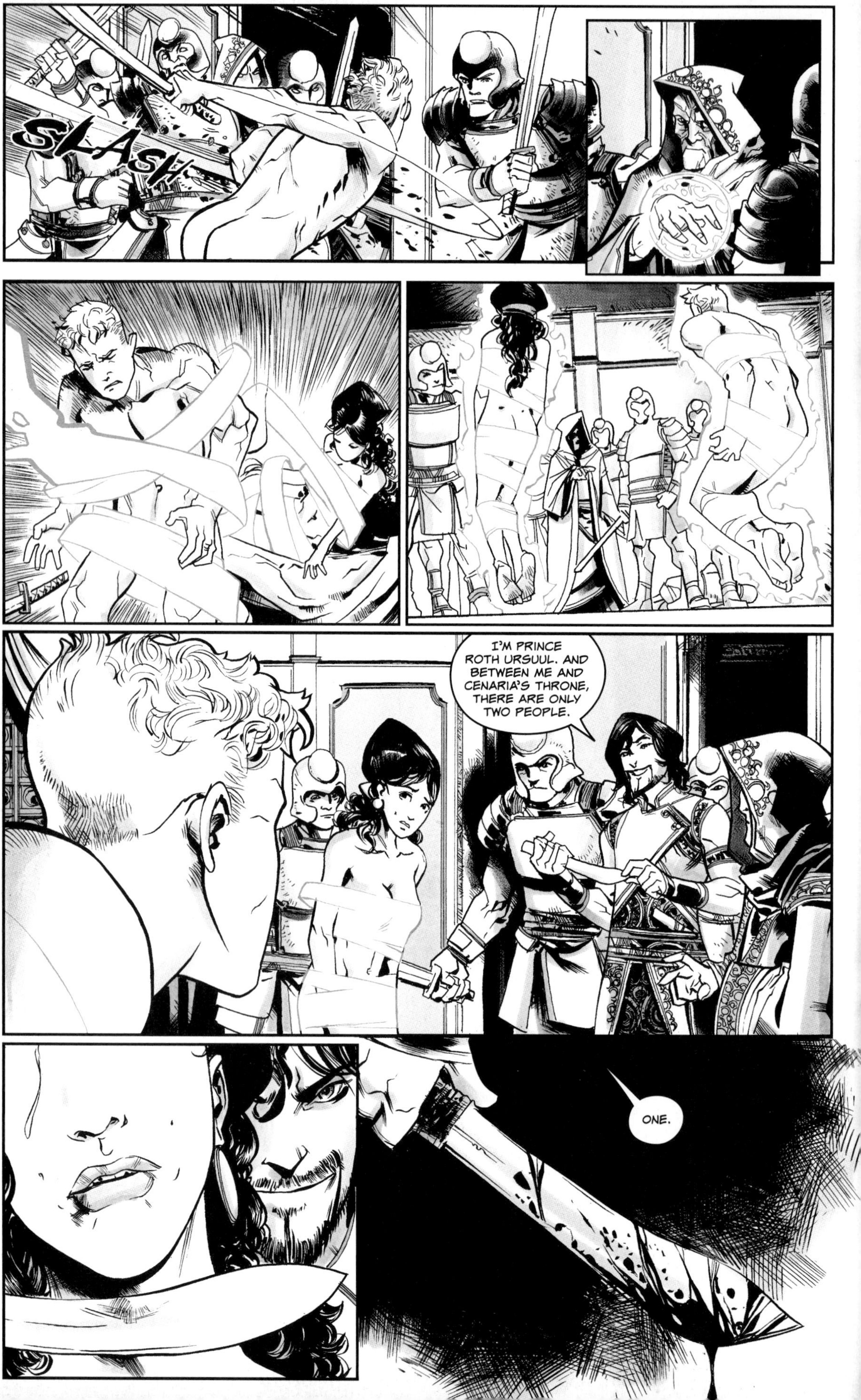
SLASH
I'M PRINCE ROTH URSUUL. AND BETWEEN ME AND CENARIA'S THRONE, THERE ARE ONLY TWO PEOPLE.
ONE.

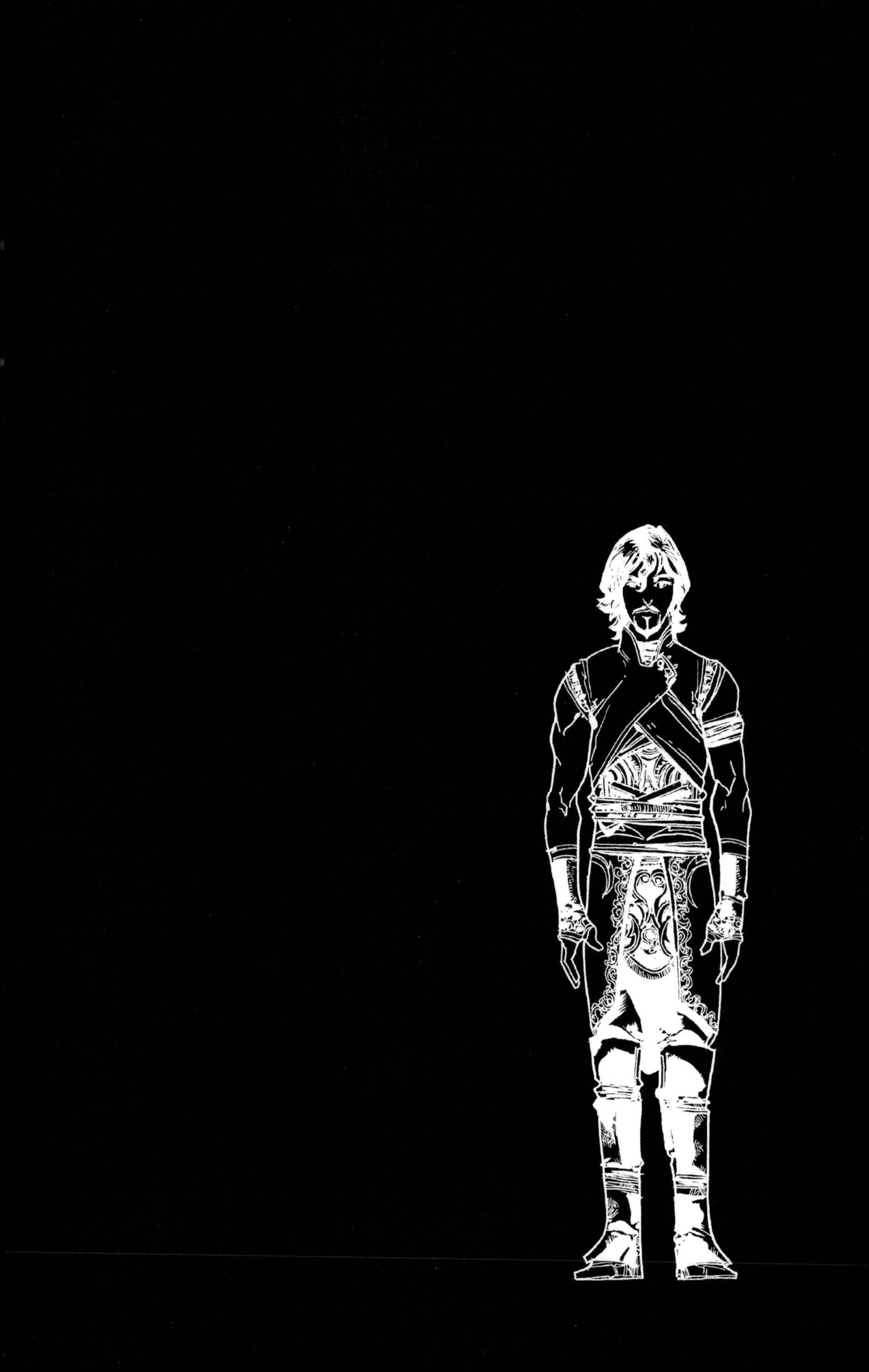

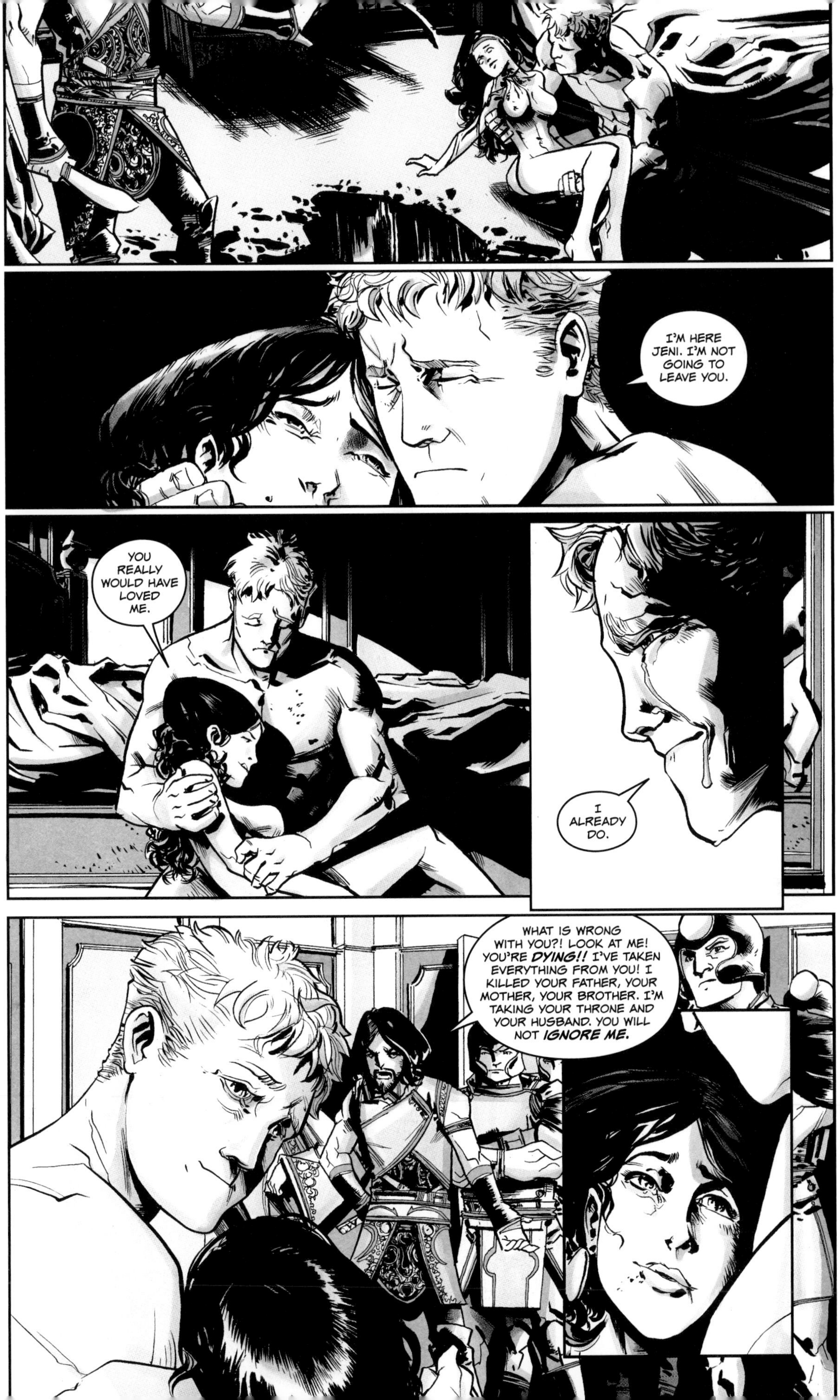
I'M HERE JENI. I'M NOT GOING TO LEAVE YOU.
YOU REALLY WOULD HAVE LOVED ME.
I ALREADY DO.
WHAT IS WRONG WITH YOU?! LOOK AT ME! YOU'RE *DYING!!* I'VE TAKEN EVERYTHING FROM YOU! I KILLED YOUR FATHER, YOUR MOTHER, YOUR BROTHER. I'M TAKING YOUR THRONE AND YOUR HUSBAND. YOU WILL NOT ***IGNORE ME.***

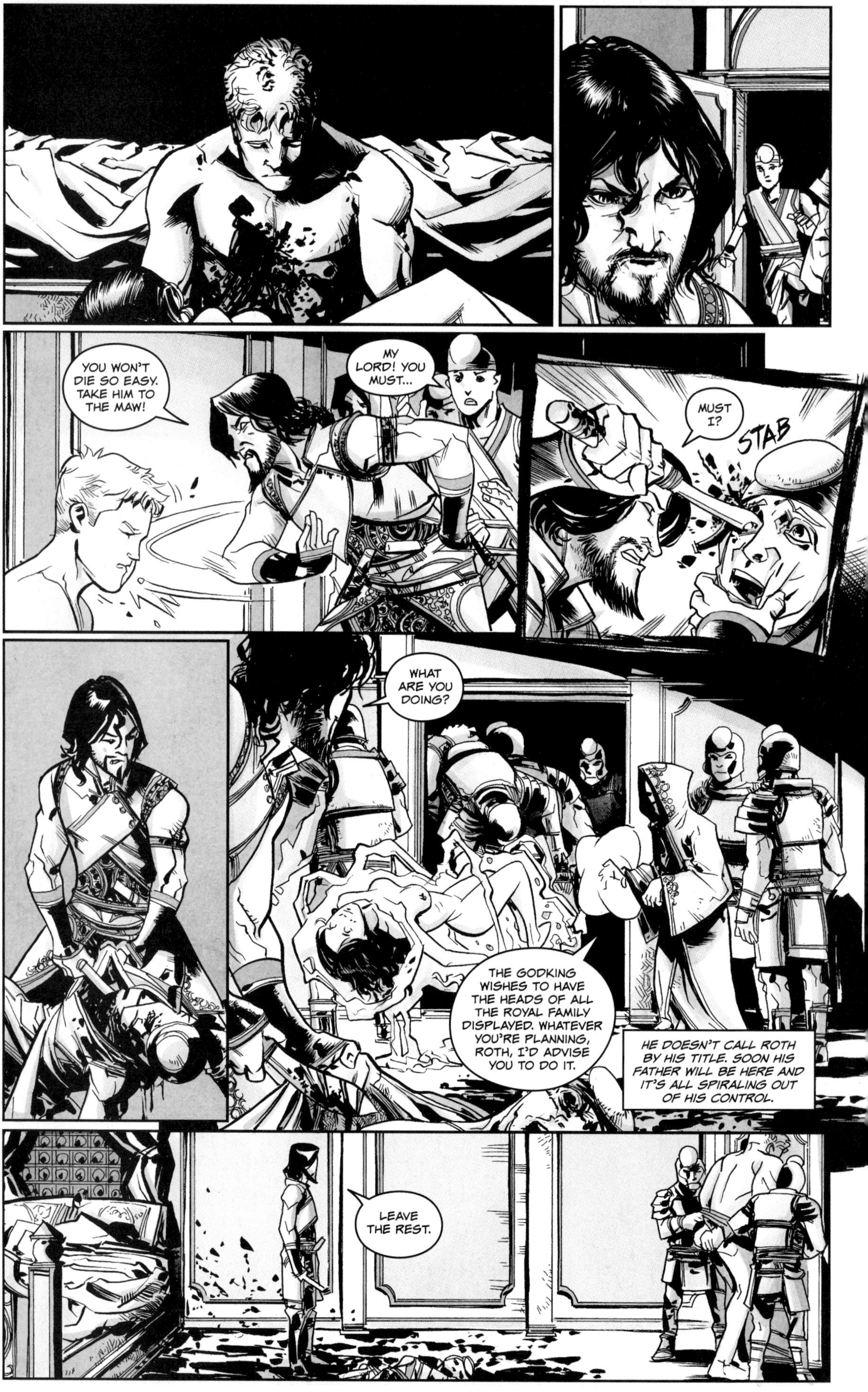
YOU WON'T DIE SO EASY. TAKE HIM TO THE MAW!
MY LORD! YOU MUST...
MUST I?
STAB
WHAT ARE YOU DOING?
THE GODKING WISHES TO HAVE THE HEADS OF ALL THE ROYAL FAMILY DISPLAYED. WHATEVER YOU'RE PLANNING, ROTH, I'D ADVISE YOU TO DO IT.
HE DOESN'T CALL ROTH BY HIS TITLE. SOON HIS FATHER WILL BE HERE AND IT'S ALL SPIRALING OUT OF HIS CONTROL.
LEAVE THE REST.

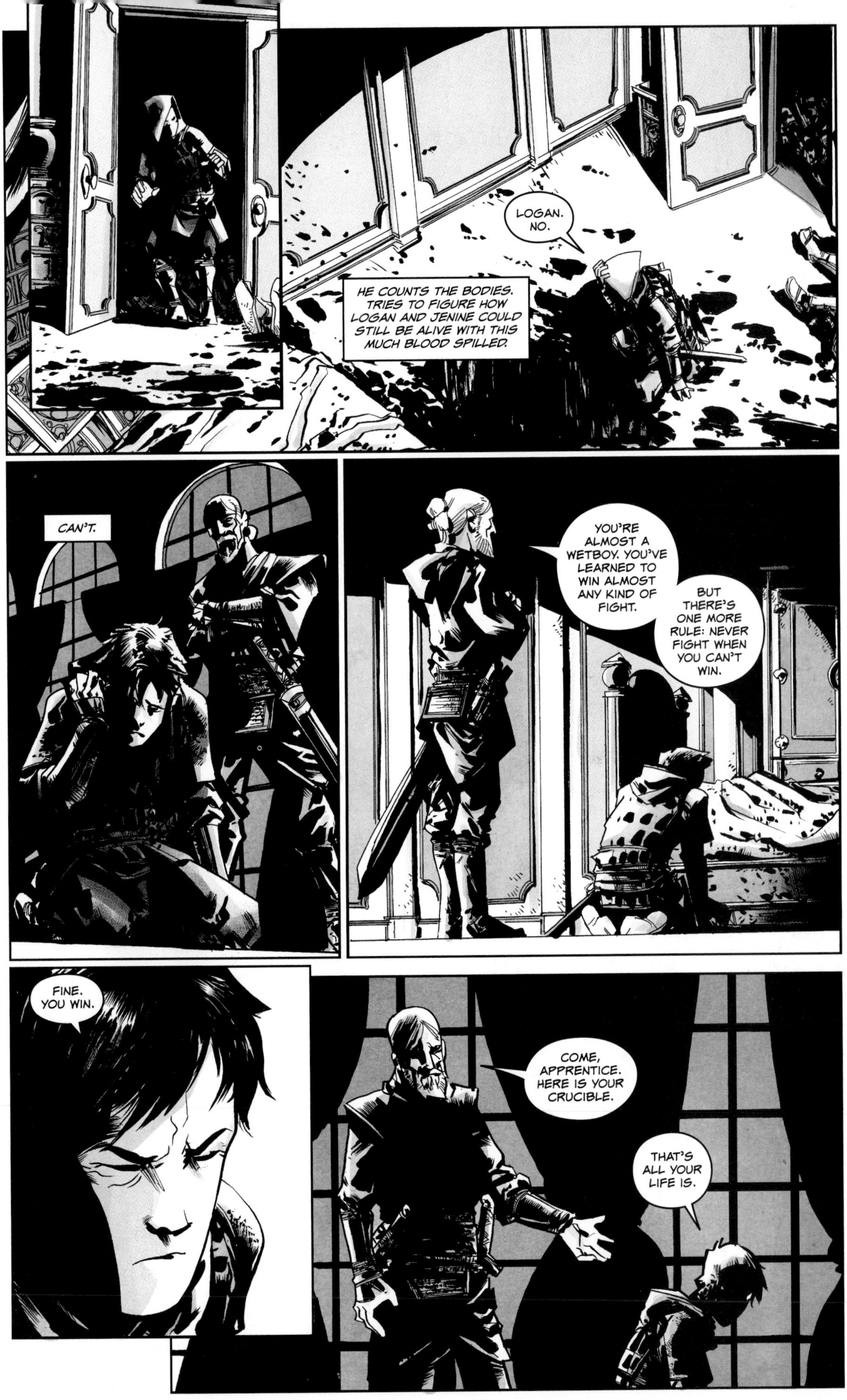
LOGAN. NO.
HE COUNTS THE BODIES. TRIES TO FIGURE HOW LOGAN AND JENINE COULD STILL BE ALIVE WITH THIS MUCH BLOOD SPILLED.
CAN'T.
YOU'RE ALMOST A WETBOY. YOU'VE LEARNED TO WIN ALMOST ANY KIND OF FIGHT.
BUT THERE'S ONE MORE RULE: NEVER FIGHT WHEN YOU CAN'T WIN.
FINE. YOU WIN.
COME, APPRENTICE. HERE IS YOUR CRUCIBLE.
THAT'S ALL YOUR LIFE IS.

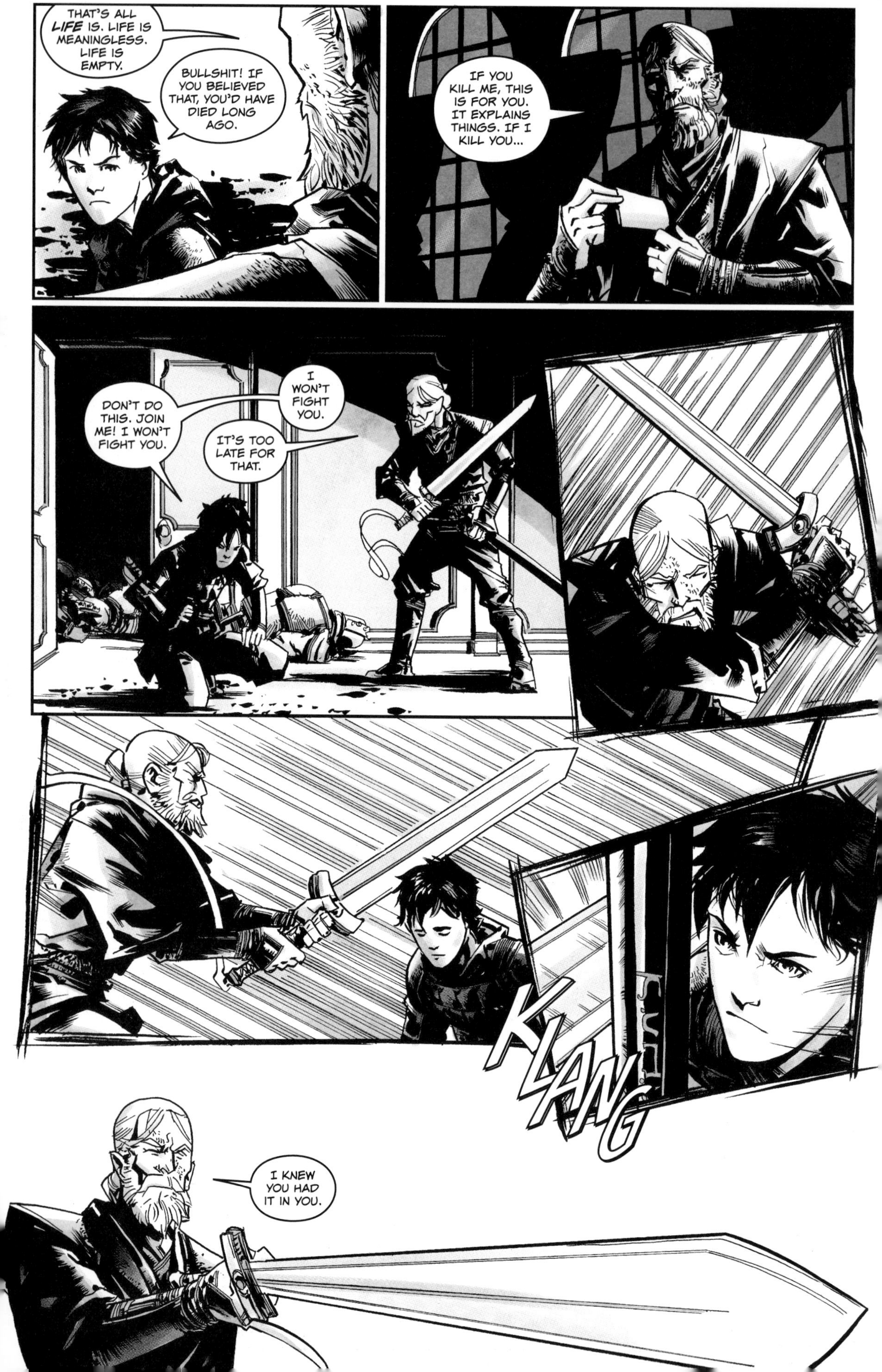
THAT'S ALL *LIFE* IS. LIFE IS MEANINGLESS. LIFE IS EMPTY.
BULLSHIT! IF YOU BELIEVED THAT, YOU'D HAVE DIED LONG AGO.
IF YOU KILL ME, THIS IS FOR YOU. IT EXPLAINS THINGS. IF I KILL YOU...
DON'T DO THIS. JOIN ME! I WON'T FIGHT YOU.
I WON'T FIGHT YOU.
IT'S TOO LATE FOR THAT.
KLANG
I KNEW YOU HAD IT IN YOU.

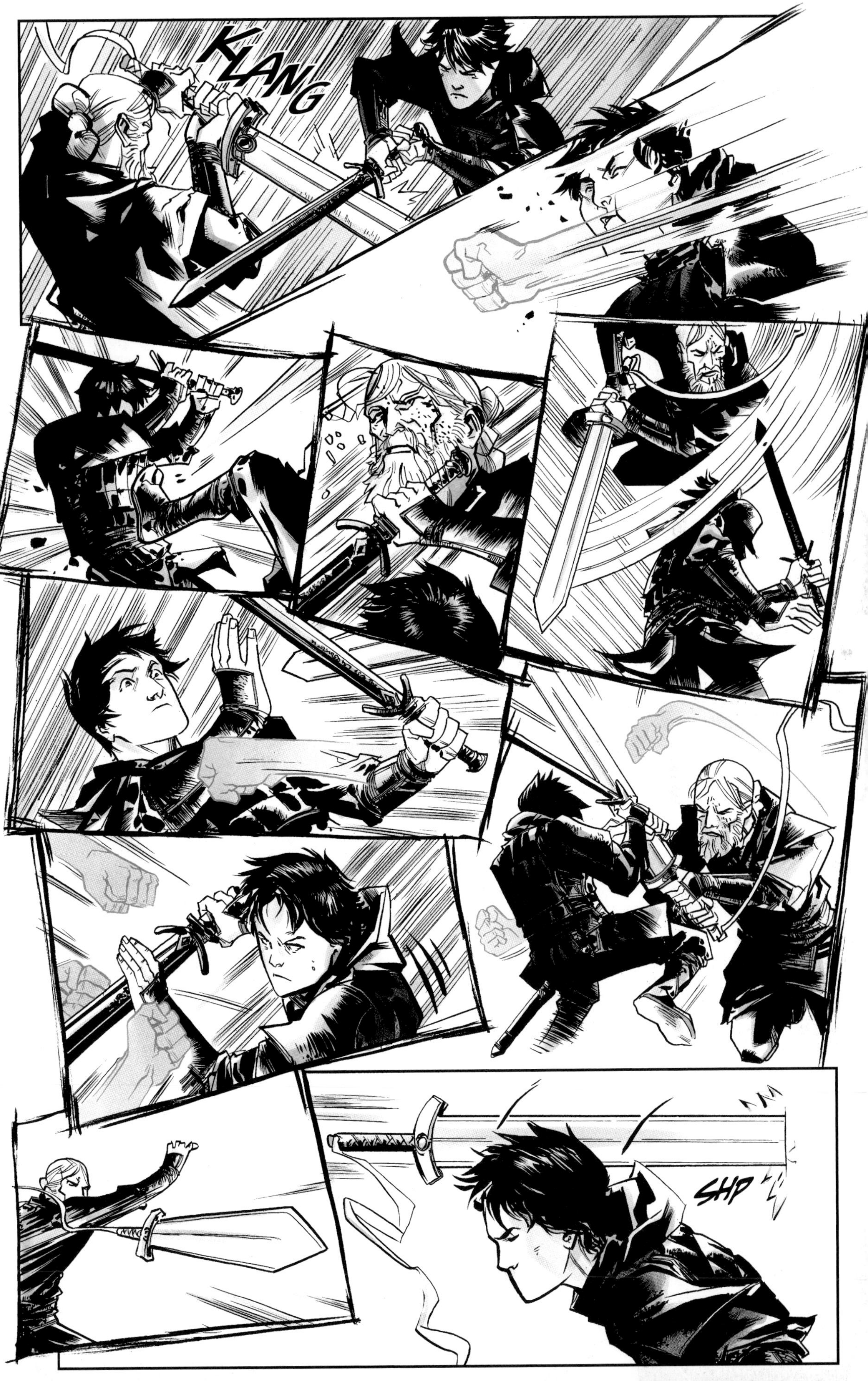
KLANG
SHP

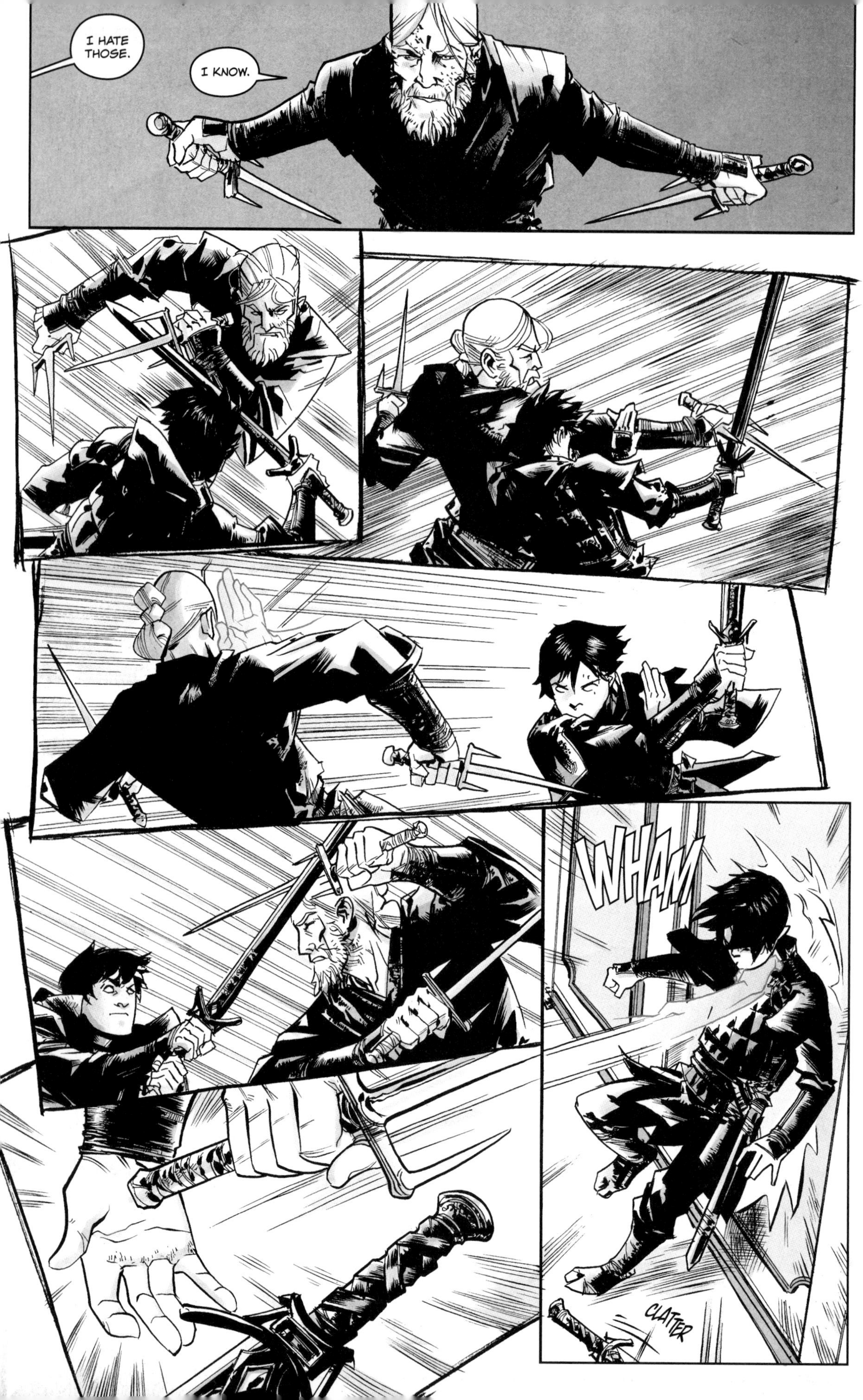
I HATE THOSE.
I KNOW.
WHAM
CLATTER

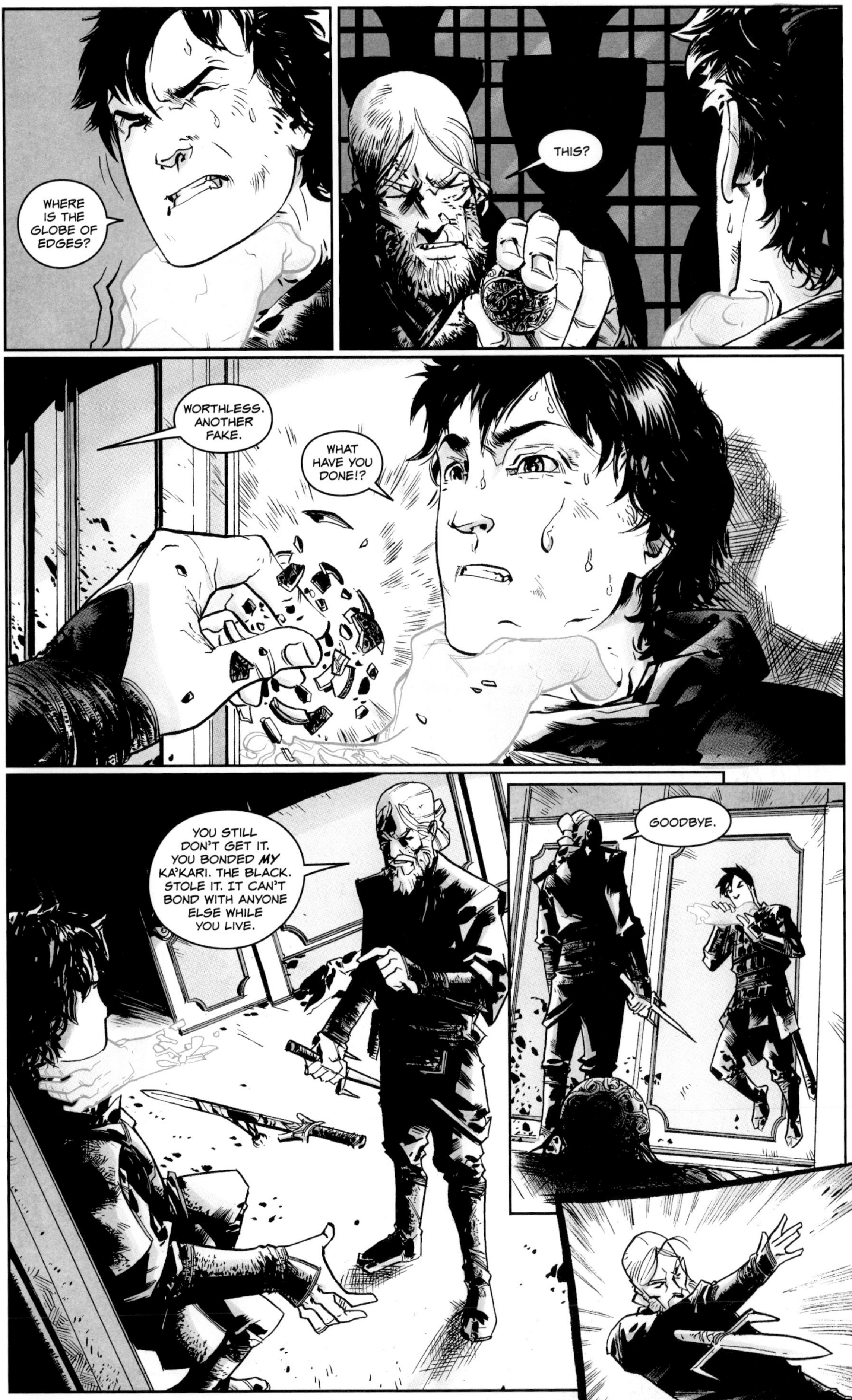
WHERE IS THE GLOBE OF EDGES?
THIS?
WORTHLESS. ANOTHER FAKE.
WHAT HAVE YOU DONE!?
YOU STILL DON'T GET IT. YOU BONDED MY KA'KARI. THE BLACK. STOLE IT. IT CAN'T BOND WITH ANYONE ELSE WHILE YOU LIVE.
GOODBYE.

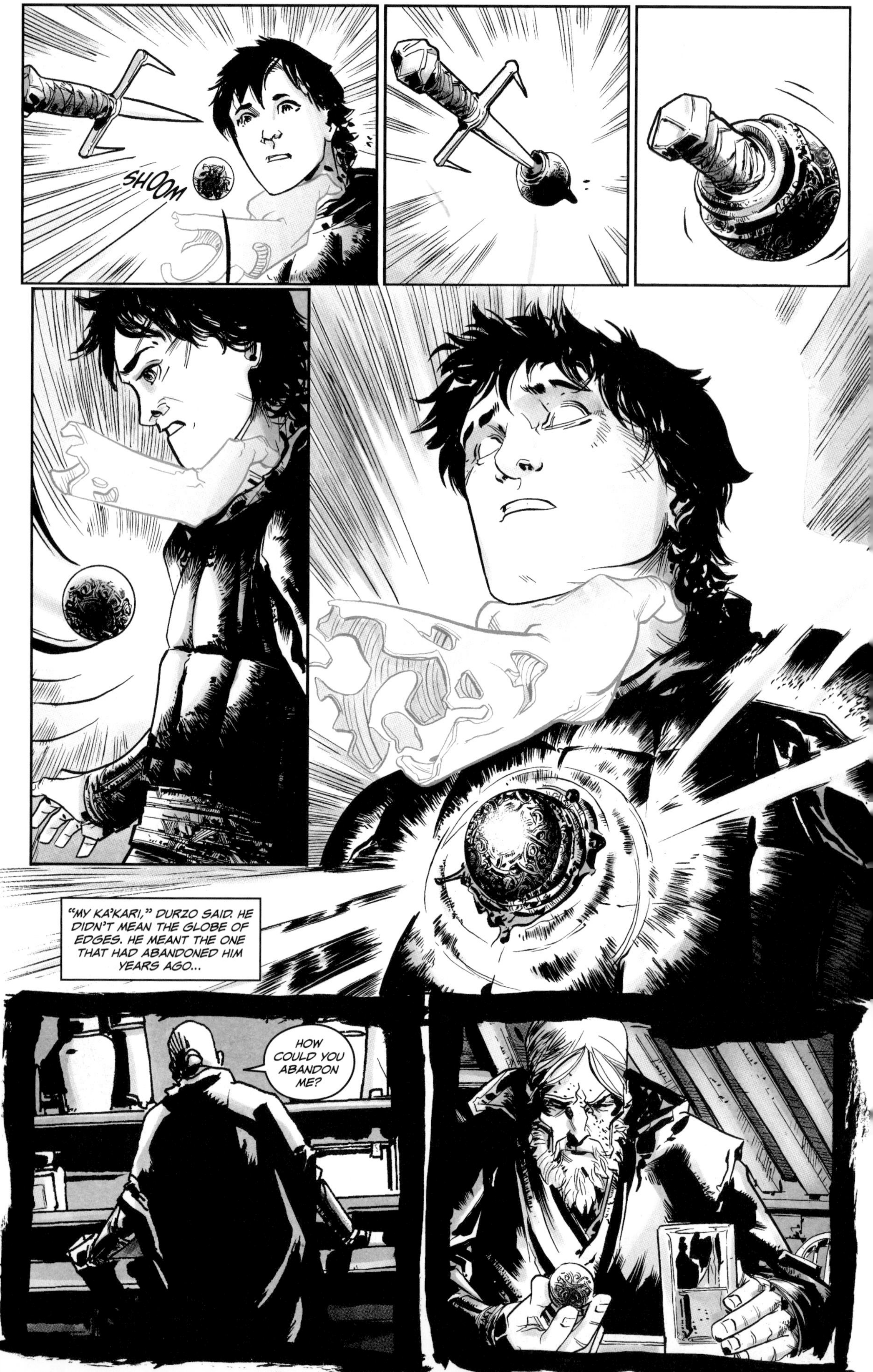
SHOOM
"MY KA'KARI," DURZO SAID. HE DIDN'T MEAN THE GLOBE OF EDGES. HE MEANT THE ONE THAT HAD ABANDONED HIM YEARS AGO...
HOW COULD YOU ABANDON ME?

...AND HAD CHOSEN KYLAR.

FWOOM

SSK

CRASH

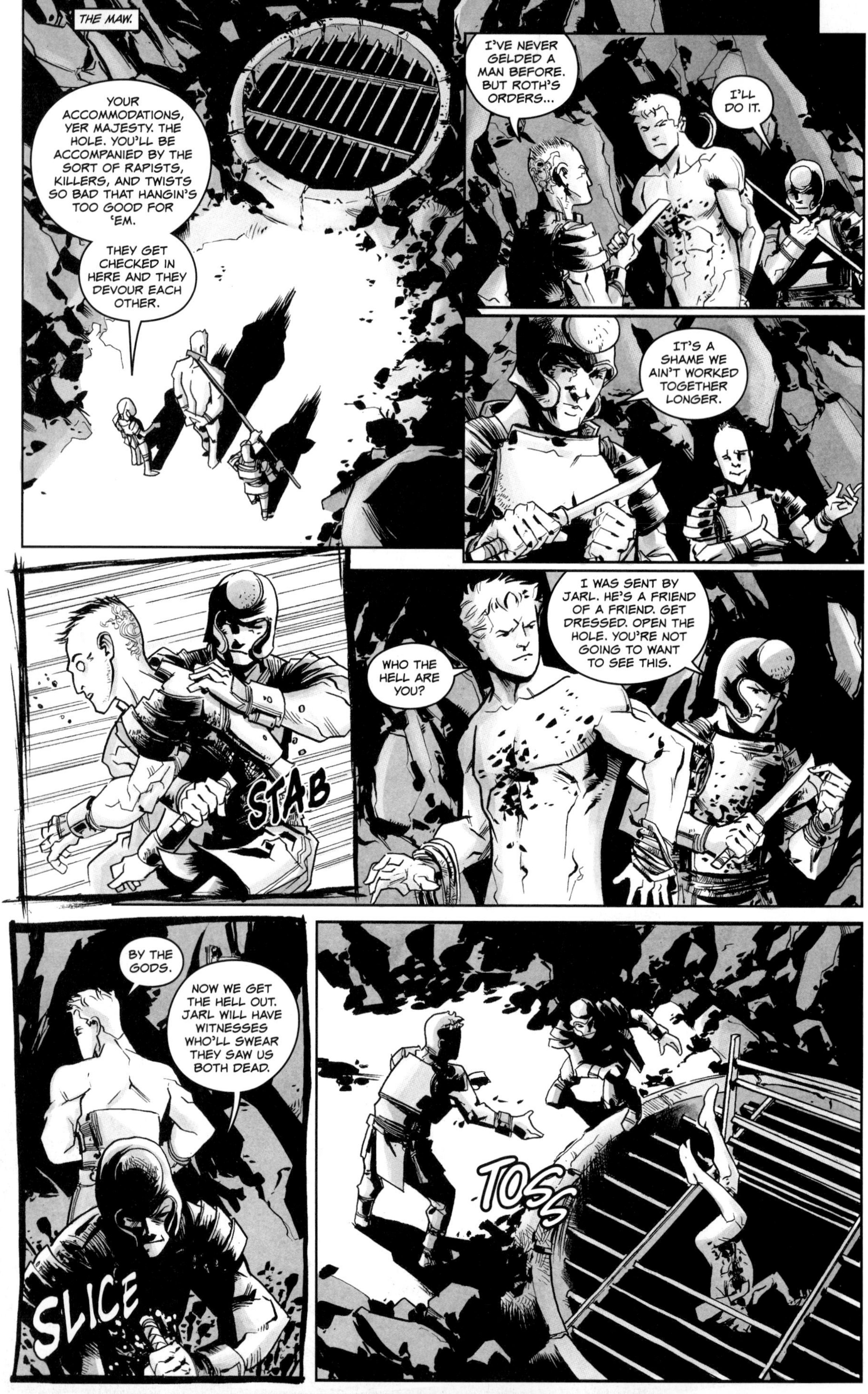
THE MAW.
YOUR ACCOMMODATIONS, YER MAJESTY. THE HOLE. YOU'LL BE ACCOMPANIED BY THE SORT OF RAPISTS, KILLERS, AND TWISTS SO BAD THAT HANGIN'S TOO GOOD FOR 'EM.
THEY GET CHECKED IN HERE AND THEY DEVOUR EACH OTHER.
I'VE NEVER GELDED A MAN BEFORE. BUT ROTH'S ORDERS...
I'LL DO IT.
IT'S A SHAME WE AIN'T WORKED TOGETHER LONGER.
STAB
WHO THE HELL ARE YOU?
I WAS SENT BY JARL. HE'S A FRIEND OF A FRIEND. GET DRESSED. OPEN THE HOLE. YOU'RE NOT GOING TO WANT TO SEE THIS.
BY THE GODS.
NOW WE GET THE HELL OUT. JARL WILL HAVE WITNESSES WHO'LL SWEAR THEY SAW US BOTH DEAD.
SLICE
TOSS

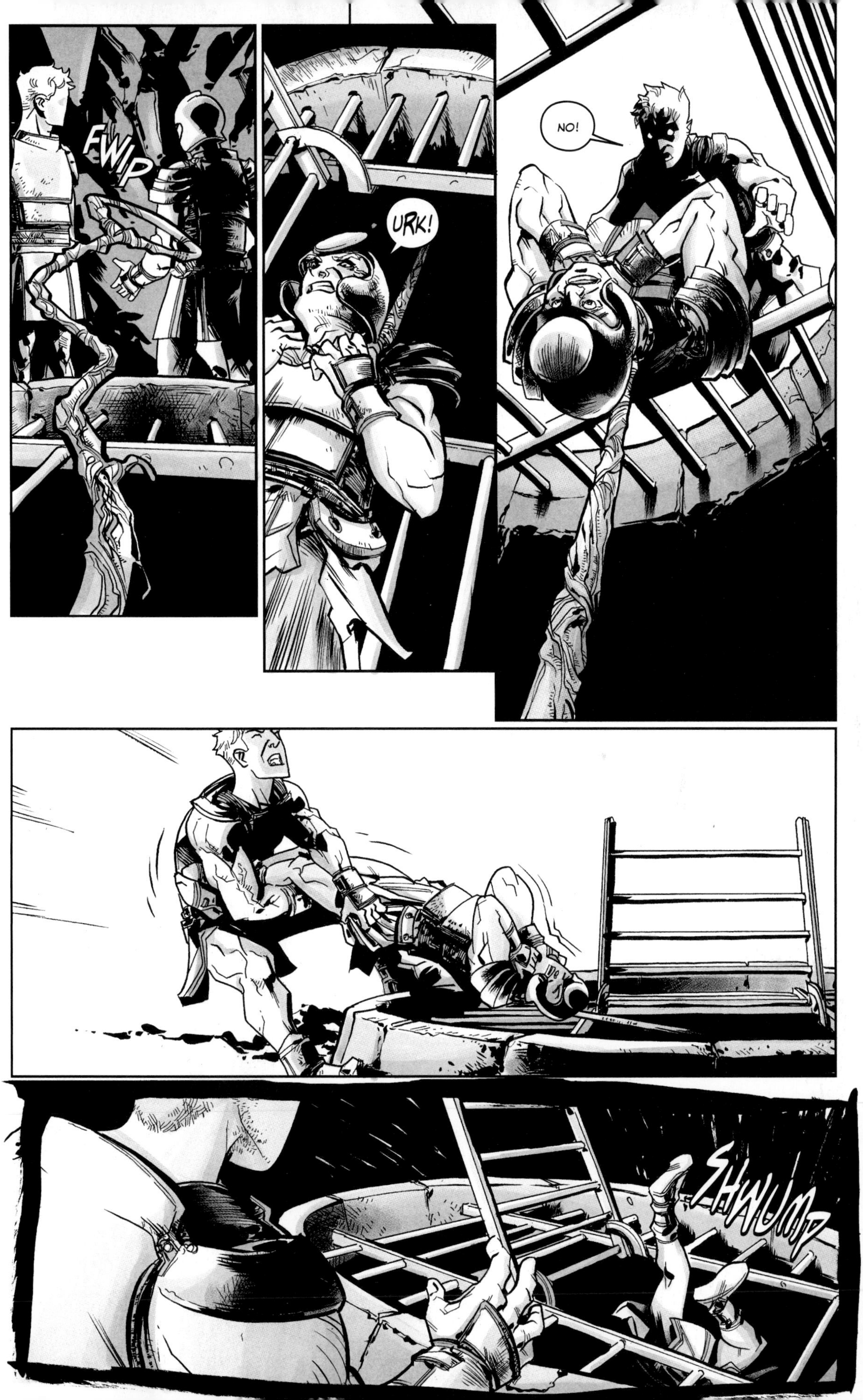
FWIP
URK!
NO!
SHWUMP

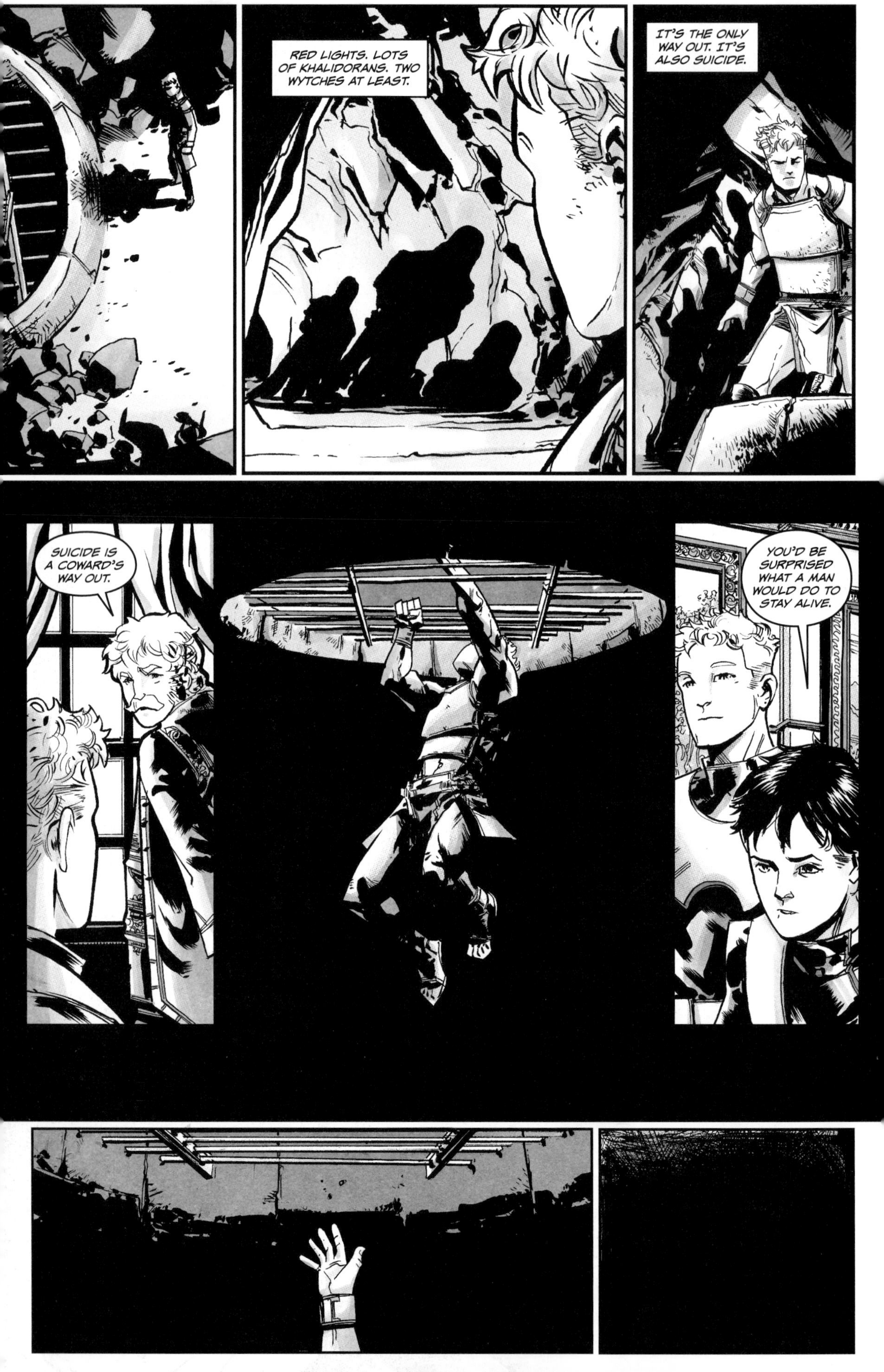
RED LIGHTS. LOTS OF KHALIDORANS. TWO WYTCHES AT LEAST.
IT'S THE ONLY WAY OUT. IT'S ALSO SUICIDE.
SUICIDE IS A COWARD'S WAY OUT.
YOU'D BE SURPRISED WHAT A MAN WOULD DO TO STAY ALIVE.

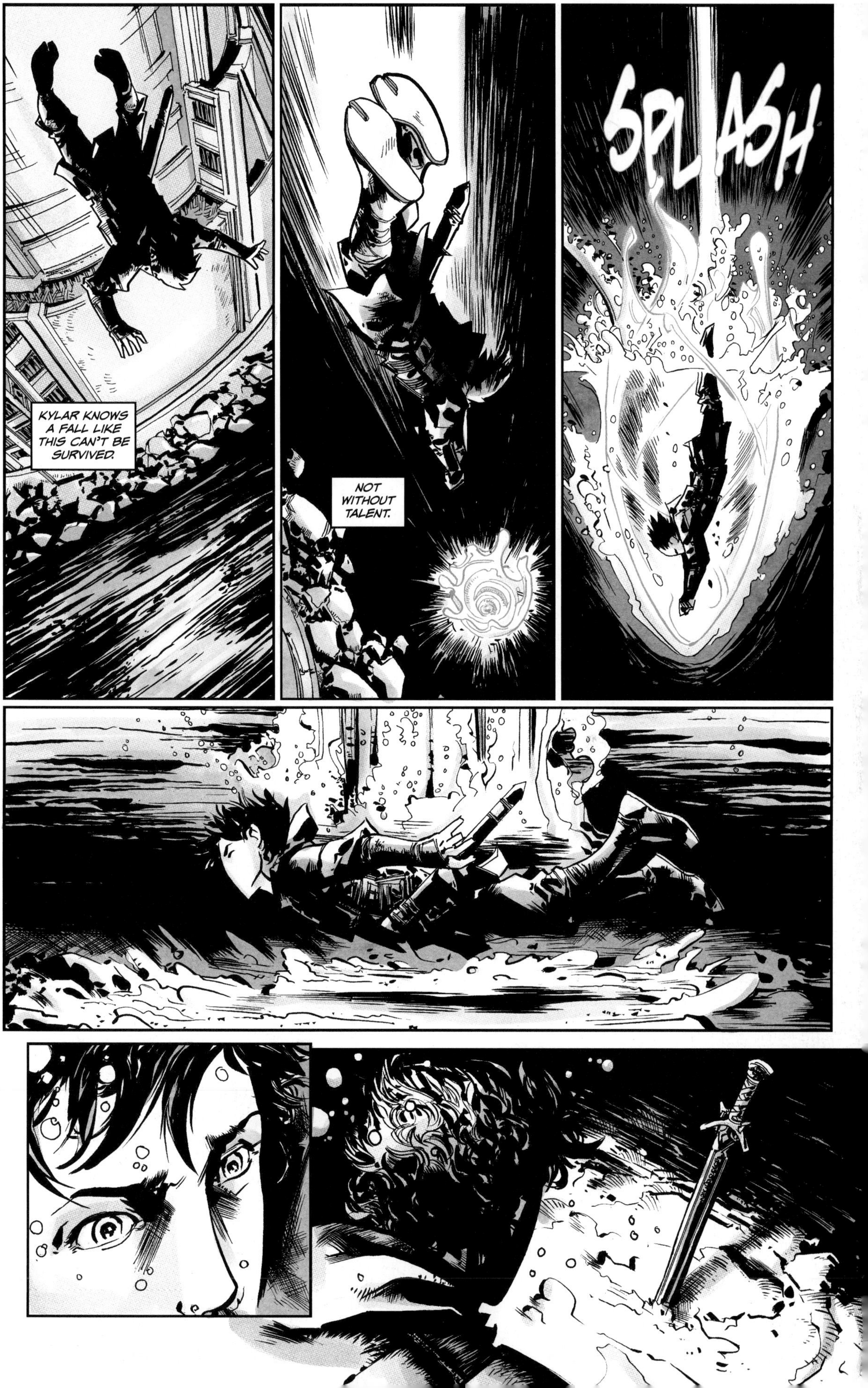
KYLAR KNOWS A FALL LIKE THIS CAN'T BE SURVIVED.
NOT WITHOUT TALENT.
SPLASH

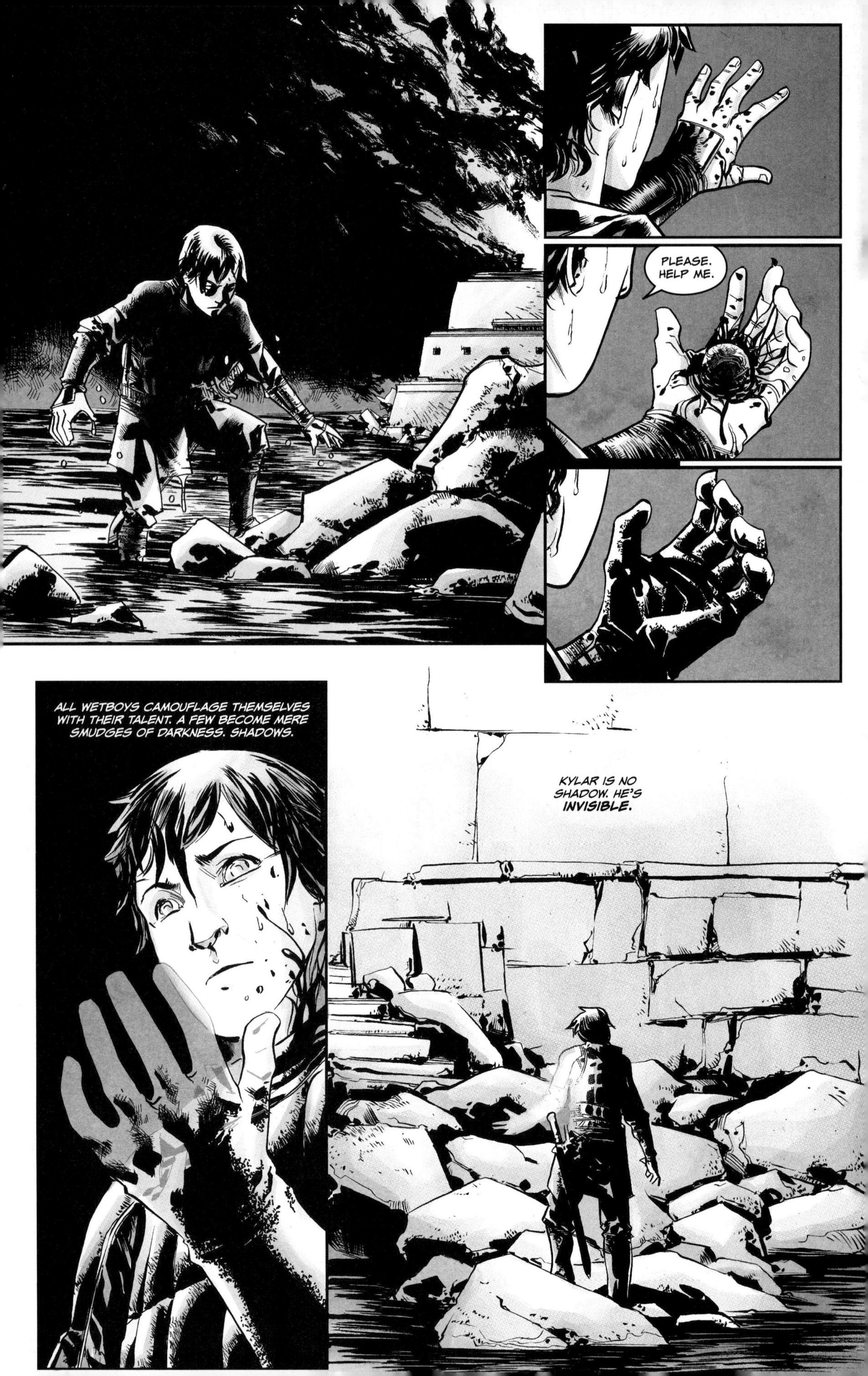
PLEASE. HELP ME.
ALL WETBOYS CAMOUFLAGE THEMSELVES WITH THEIR TALENT. A FEW BECOME MERE SMUDGES OF DARKNESS. SHADOWS.
KYLAR IS NO SHADOW. HE'S **INVISIBLE.**

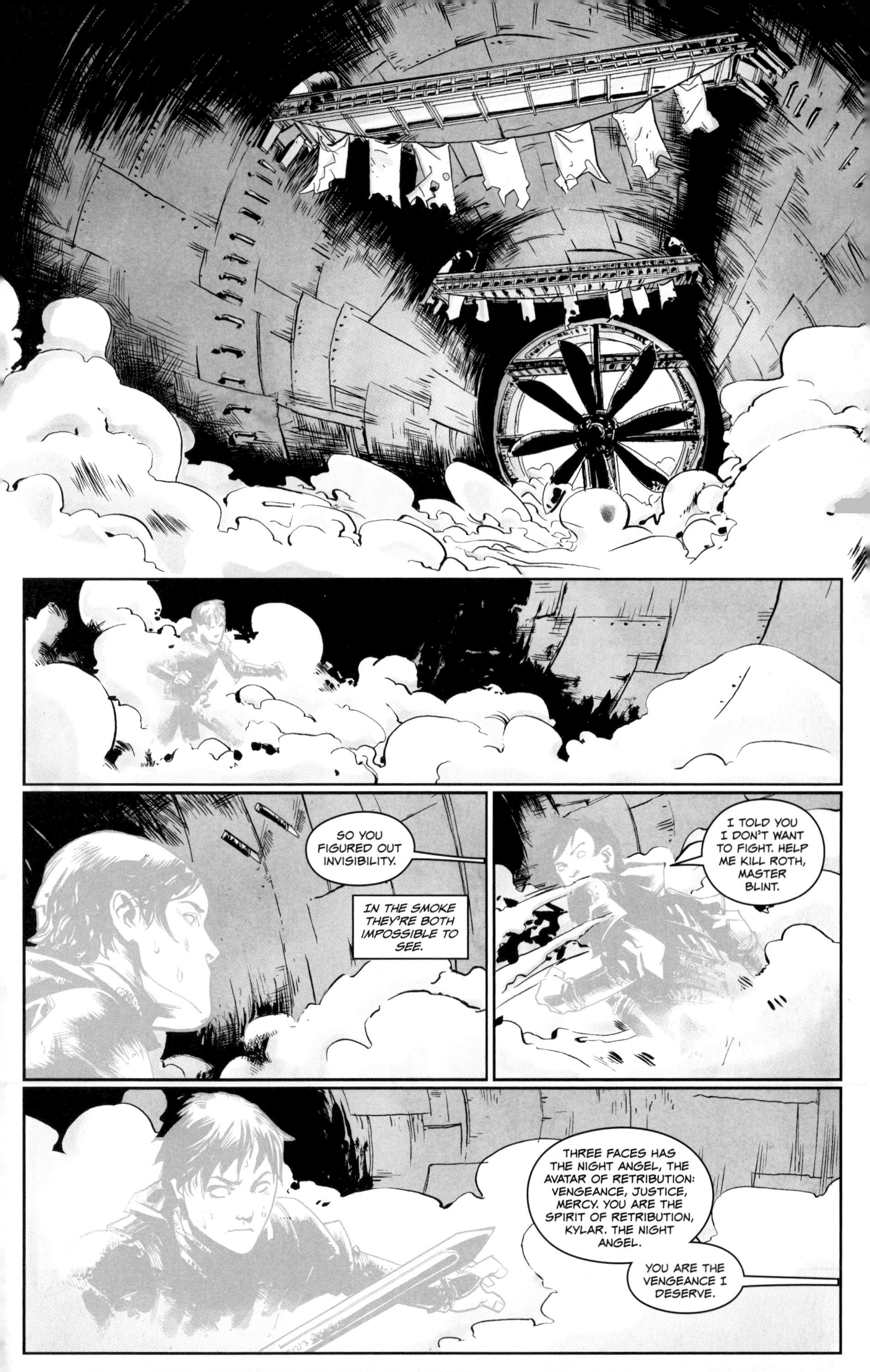
SO YOU FIGURED OUT INVISIBILITY.
IN THE SMOKE THEY'RE BOTH IMPOSSIBLE TO SEE.
I TOLD YOU I DON'T WANT TO FIGHT. HELP ME KILL ROTH, MASTER BLINT.
THREE FACES HAS THE NIGHT ANGEL, THE AVATAR OF RETRIBUTION: VENGEANCE, JUSTICE, MERCY. YOU ARE THE SPIRIT OF RETRIBUTION, KYLAR. THE NIGHT ANGEL.
YOU ARE THE VENGEANCE I DESERVE.

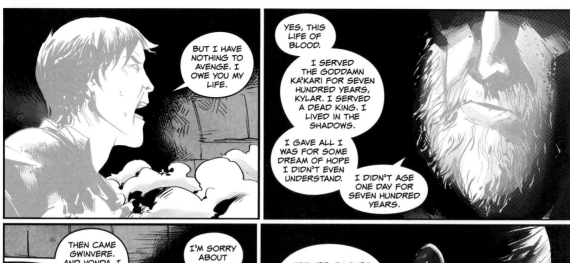

BUT I HAVE NOTHING TO AVENGE. I OWE YOU MY LIFE.

YES, THIS LIFE OF BLOOD.

I SERVED THE GODDAMN KA'KARI FOR SEVEN HUNDRED YEARS, KYLAR. I SERVED A DEAD KING. I LIVED IN THE SHADOWS.

I GAVE ALL I WAS FOR SOME DREAM OF HOPE I DIDN'T EVEN UNDERSTAND.

I DIDN'T AGE ONE DAY FOR SEVEN HUNDRED YEARS.

THEN CAME GWINVERE. AND VONDA. I LOVED HER, KYLAR.

I'M SORRY ABOUT VONDA.

NOT HER. I LOVED GWINVERE. I WANTED HER TO KNOW HOW IT FELT TO HAVE SOMEONE YOU LOVE SHARING OTHER PEOPLE'S BEDS. I PAID GWINVERE BUT IT WAS VONDA I MADE A WHORE.

THAT WAS WHY I WENT AFTER THAT SILVER KA'KARI AT FIRST. FOR GWINVERE. SO THAT SHE WOULDN'T AGE AND DIE LIKE EVERYONE I'VE EVER LOVED.

I WON'T FIGHT YOU.

BUT MY KA'KARI ABANDONED ME WHEN I LET VONDA DIE. SO THEN I NEEDED THE SILVER FOR ME. YOU WERE SUPPOSED TO CALL IT, KYLAR. INSTEAD, YOU CALLED MINE. YOU STARTED BONDING IT WHEN YOU SAVED DOLL GIRL.

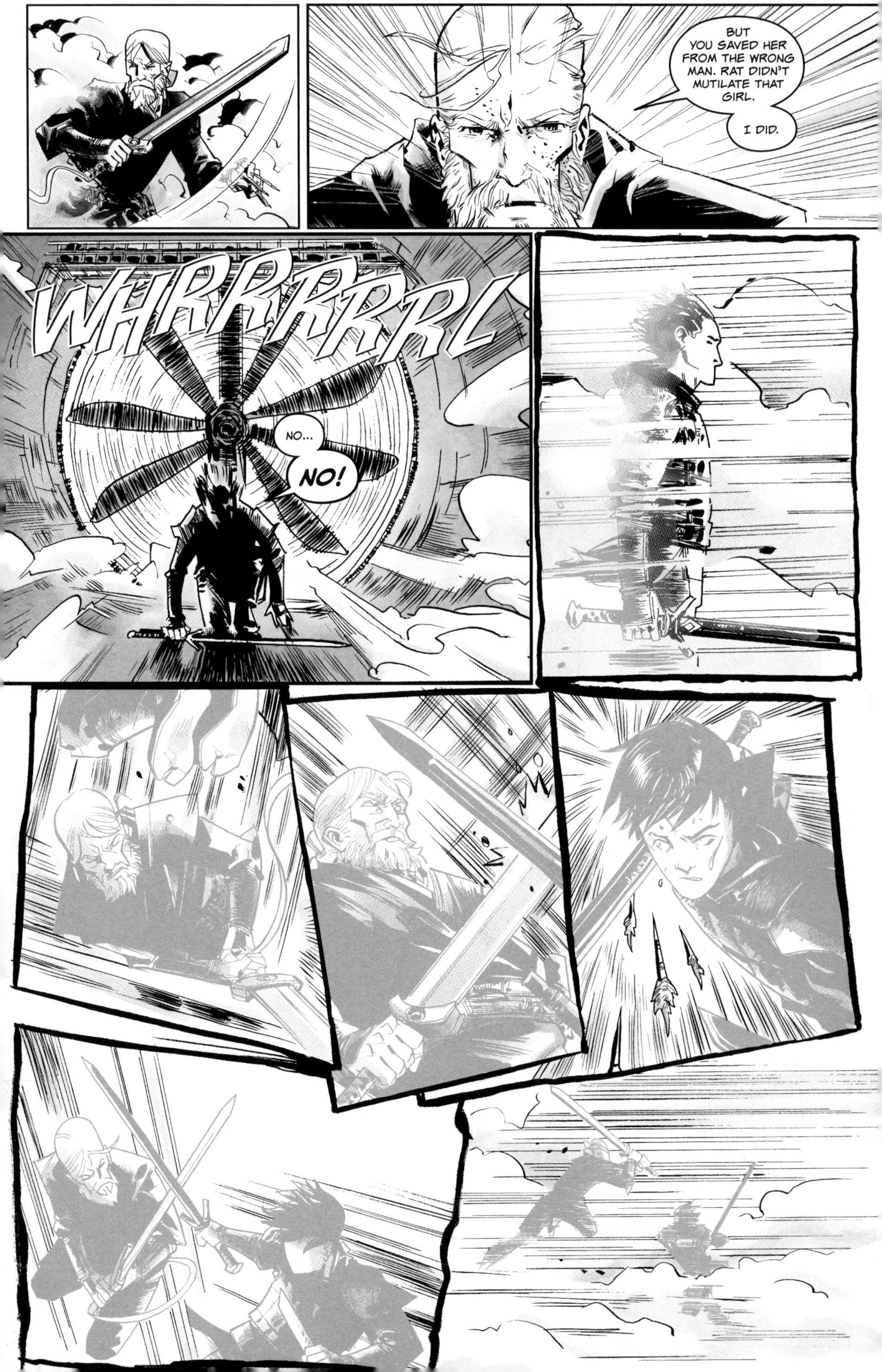
BUT YOU SAVED HER FROM THE WRONG MAN. RAT DIDN'T MUTILATE THAT GIRL.
I DID.
WHRRRRRRL
NO...
NO!

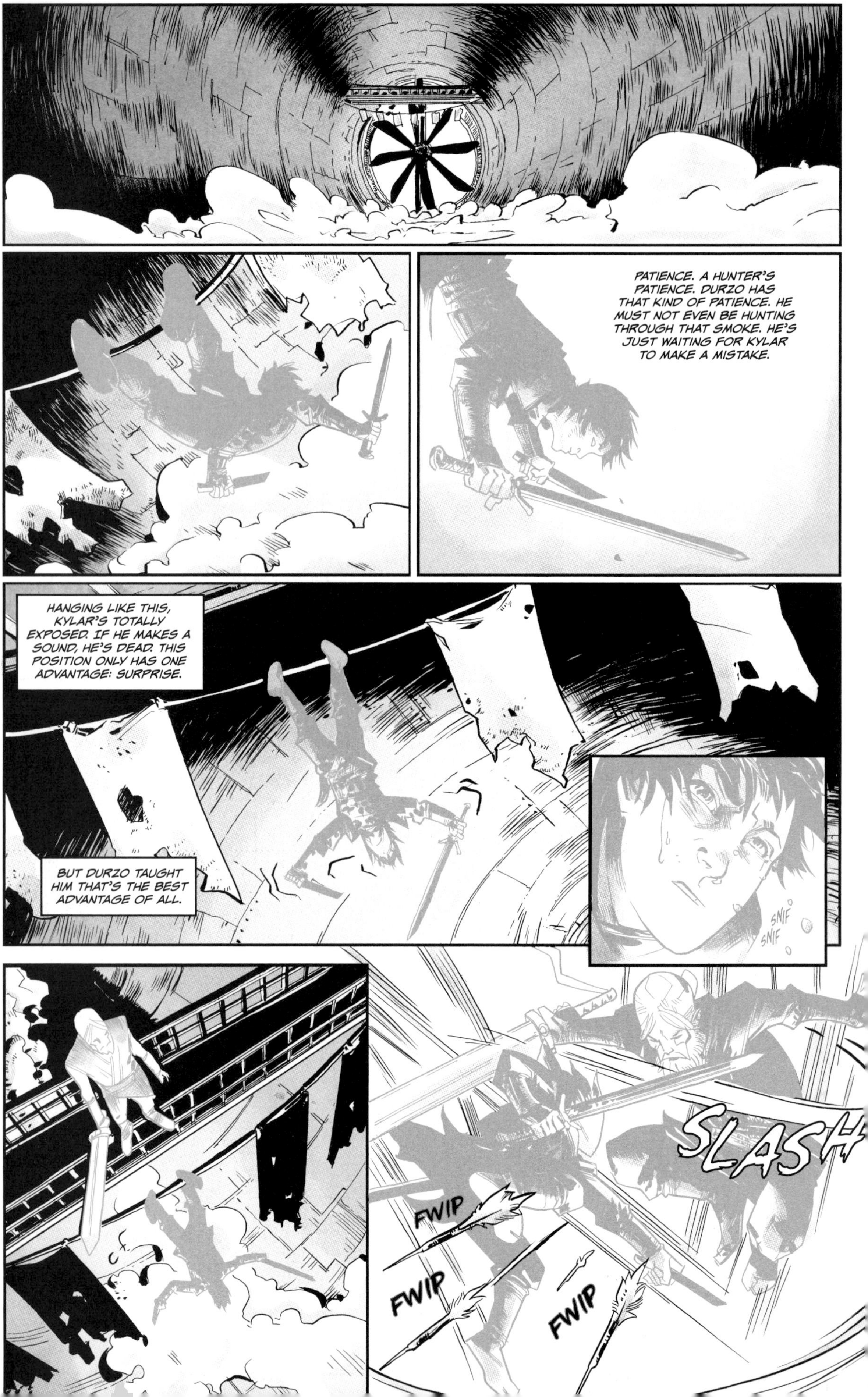
PATIENCE. A HUNTER'S PATIENCE. DURZO HAS THAT KIND OF PATIENCE. HE MUST NOT EVEN BE HUNTING THROUGH THAT SMOKE. HE'S JUST WAITING FOR KYLAR TO MAKE A MISTAKE.
HANGING LIKE THIS, KYLAR'S TOTALLY EXPOSED. IF HE MAKES A SOUND, HE'S DEAD. THIS POSITION ONLY HAS ONE ADVANTAGE: SURPRISE.
BUT DURZO TAUGHT HIM THAT'S THE BEST ADVANTAGE OF ALL.
SNIF
SNIF
SLASH
FWIP
FWIP
FWIP

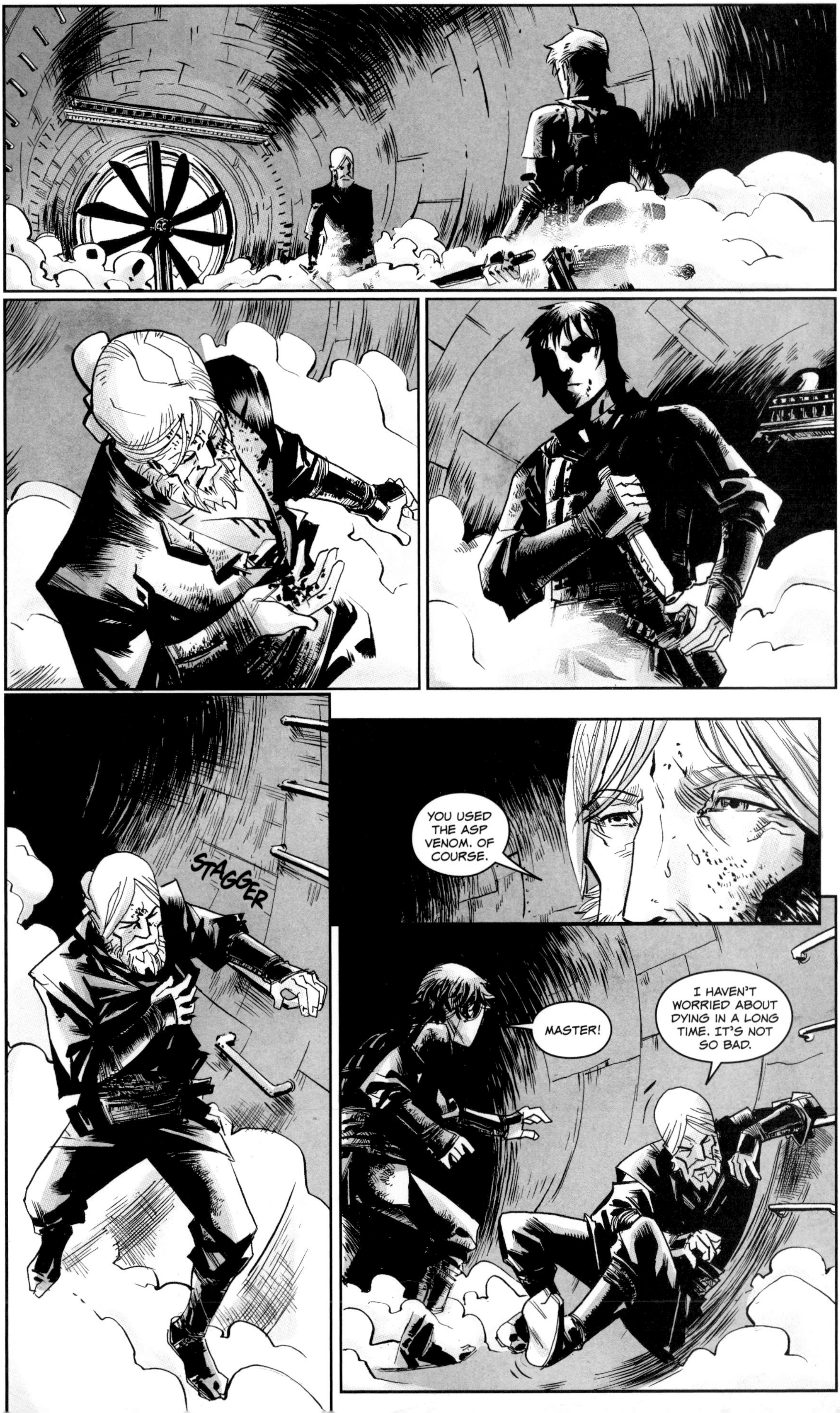
STAGGER
YOU USED THE ASP VENOM. OF COURSE.
MASTER!
I HAVEN'T WORRIED ABOUT DYING IN A LONG TIME. IT'S NOT SO BAD.

KYLAR...KILL ROTH. SAVE MY DAUGHTER.

I WOULD. I WOULD, BUT I CAN'T.

GOTCHA. BUT I DIDN'T POISON MINE. TAKE YOUR INHERITANCE, SON. IT EXPLAINS...

HA HA

rustle

KYLAR
SHOU
Y SON
NOV
FORGIVE

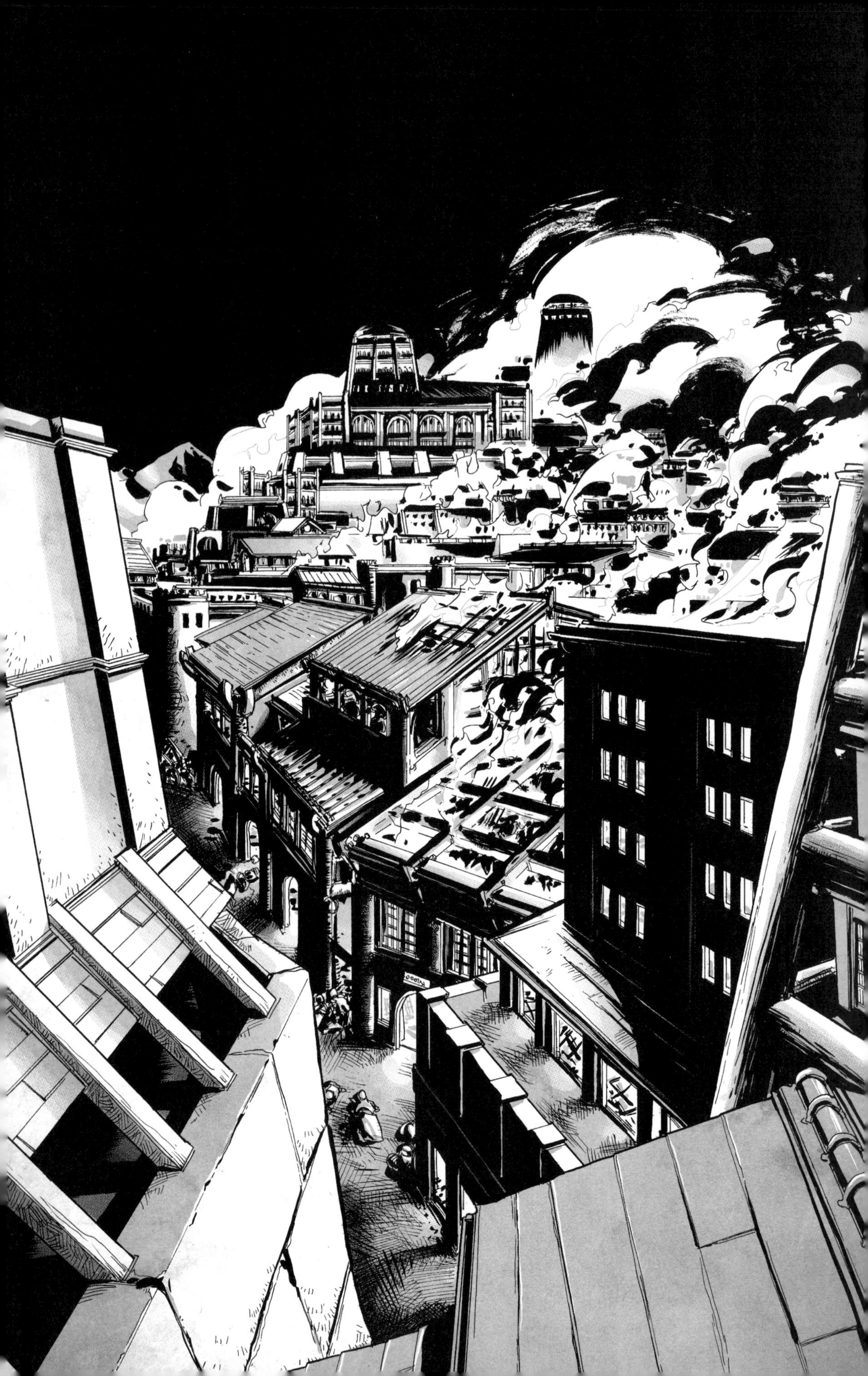

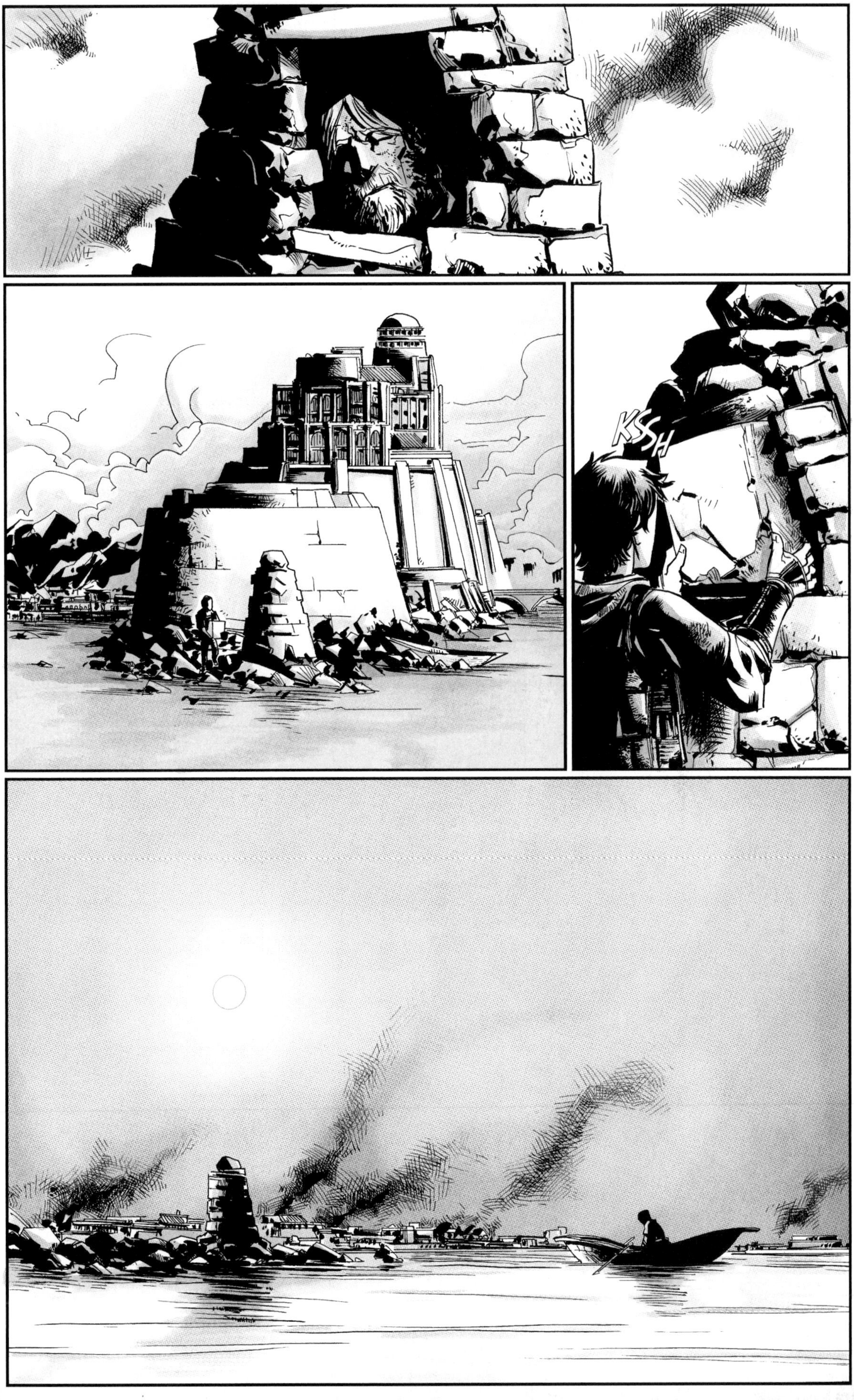
KSSH

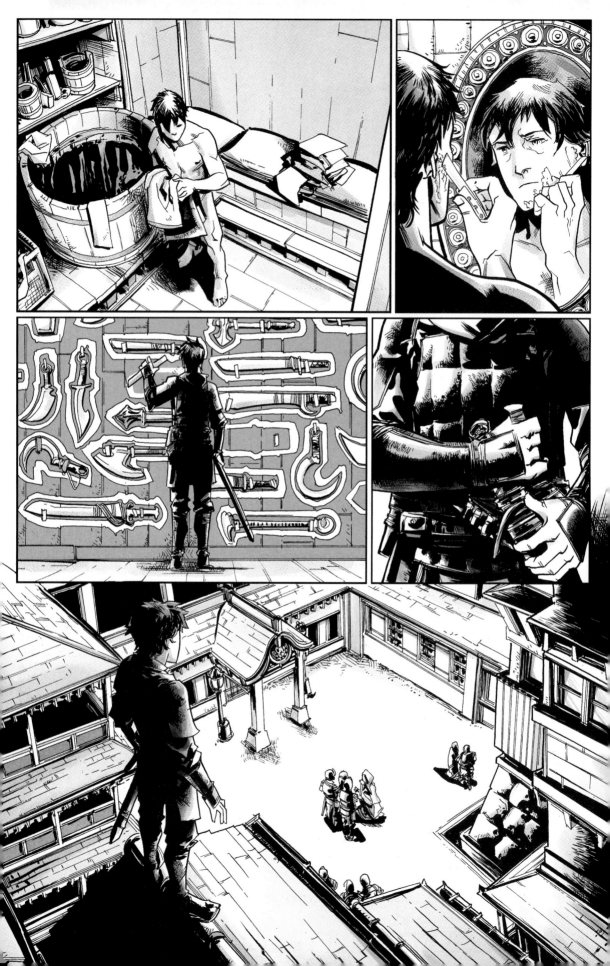

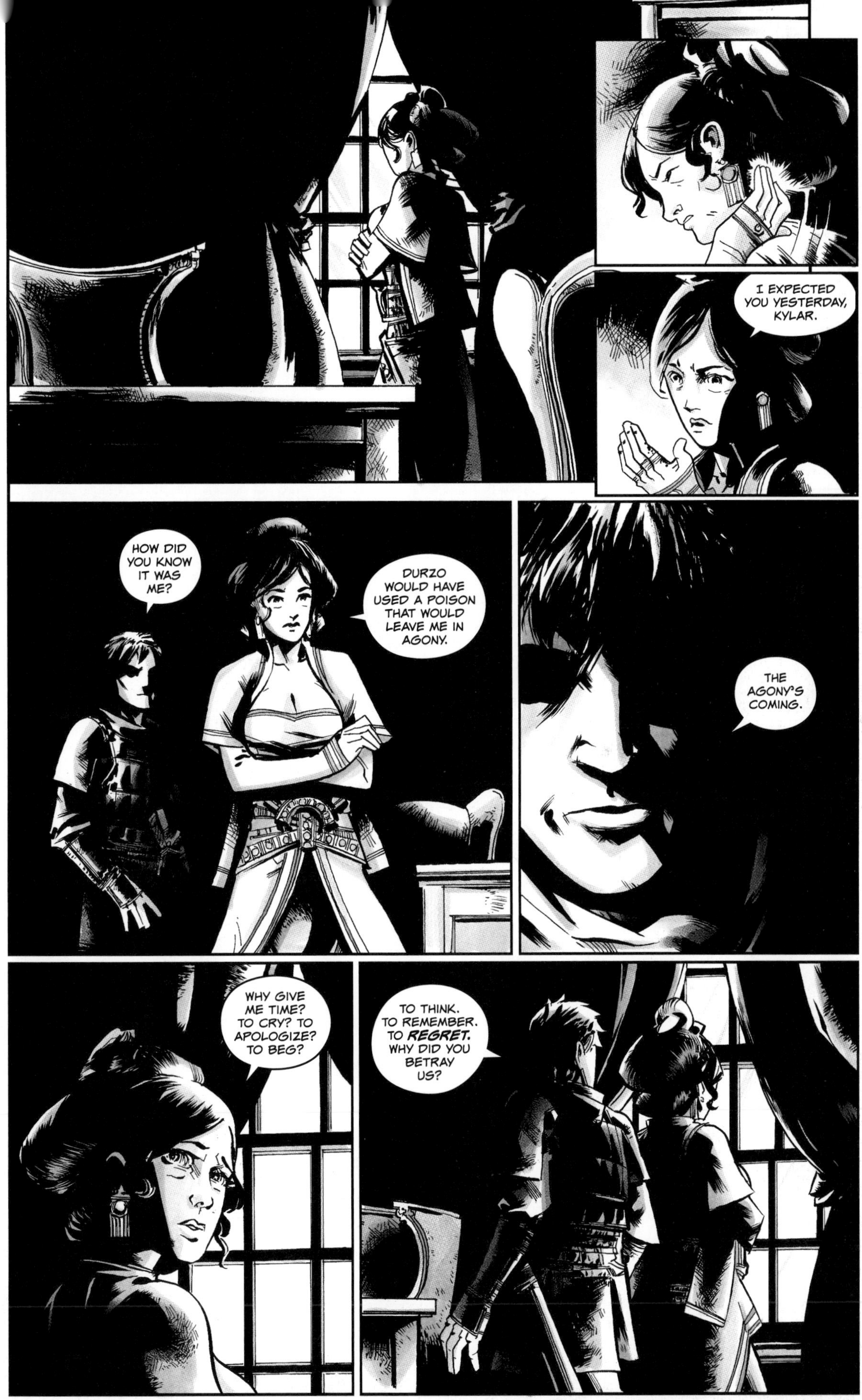
I EXPECTED YOU YESTERDAY, KYLAR.
HOW DID YOU KNOW IT WAS ME?
DURZO WOULD HAVE USED A POISON THAT WOULD LEAVE ME IN AGONY.
THE AGONY'S COMING.
WHY GIVE ME TIME? TO CRY? TO APOLOGIZE? TO BEG?
TO THINK. TO REMEMBER. TO *REGRET.* WHY DID YOU BETRAY US?

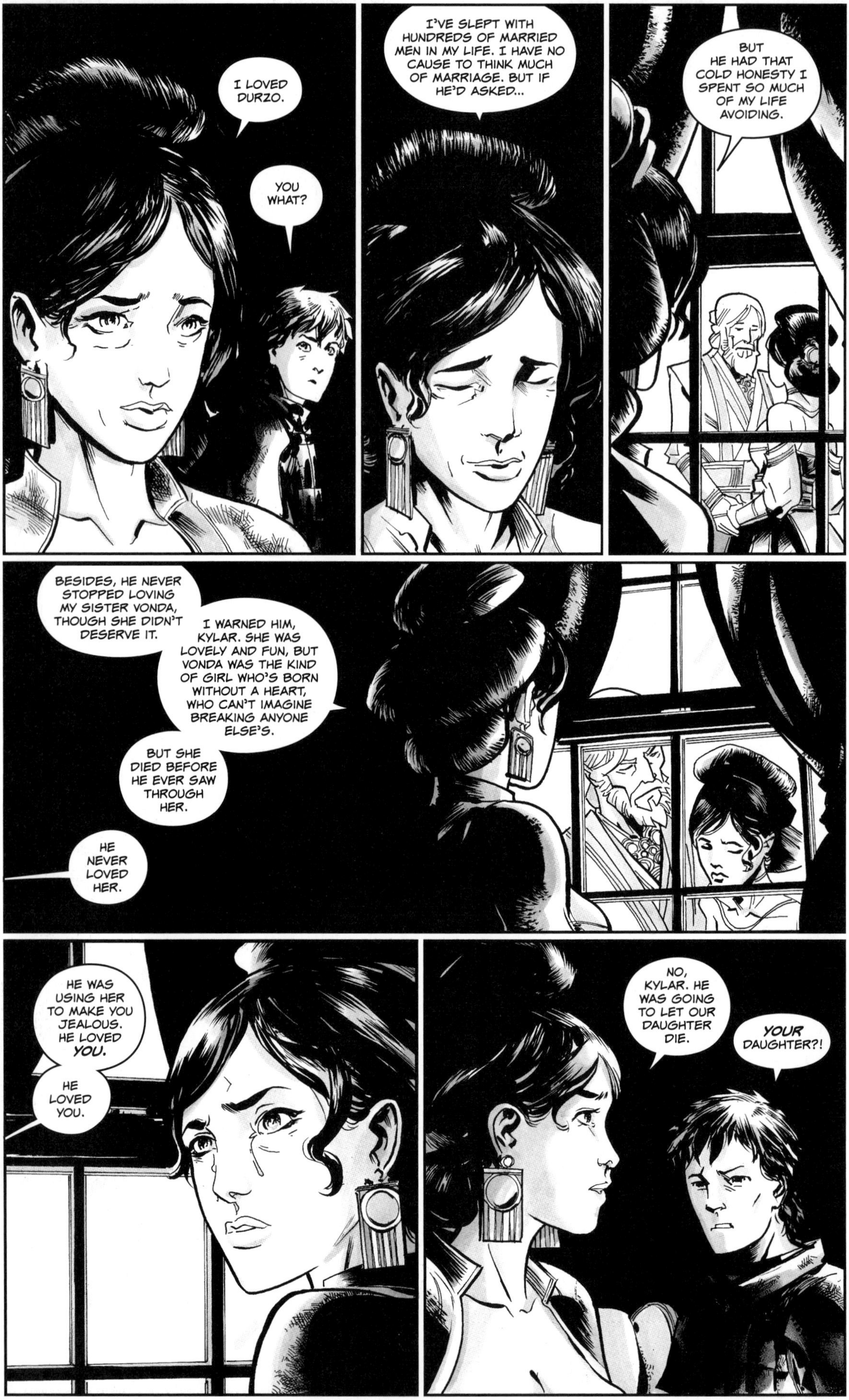
I LOVED DURZO.
YOU WHAT?
I'VE SLEPT WITH HUNDREDS OF MARRIED MEN IN MY LIFE. I HAVE NO CAUSE TO THINK MUCH OF MARRIAGE. BUT IF HE'D ASKED...
BUT HE HAD THAT COLD HONESTY I SPENT SO MUCH OF MY LIFE AVOIDING.
BESIDES, HE NEVER STOPPED LOVING MY SISTER VONDA, THOUGH SHE DIDN'T DESERVE IT.
I WARNED HIM, KYLAR. SHE WAS LOVELY AND FUN, BUT VONDA WAS THE KIND OF GIRL WHO'S BORN WITHOUT A HEART, WHO CAN'T IMAGINE BREAKING ANYONE ELSE'S.
BUT SHE DIED BEFORE HE EVER SAW THROUGH HER.
HE NEVER LOVED HER.
HE WAS USING HER TO MAKE YOU JEALOUS. HE LOVED *YOU.*
HE LOVED YOU.
NO, KYLAR. HE WAS GOING TO LET OUR DAUGHTER DIE.
YOUR DAUGHTER?!

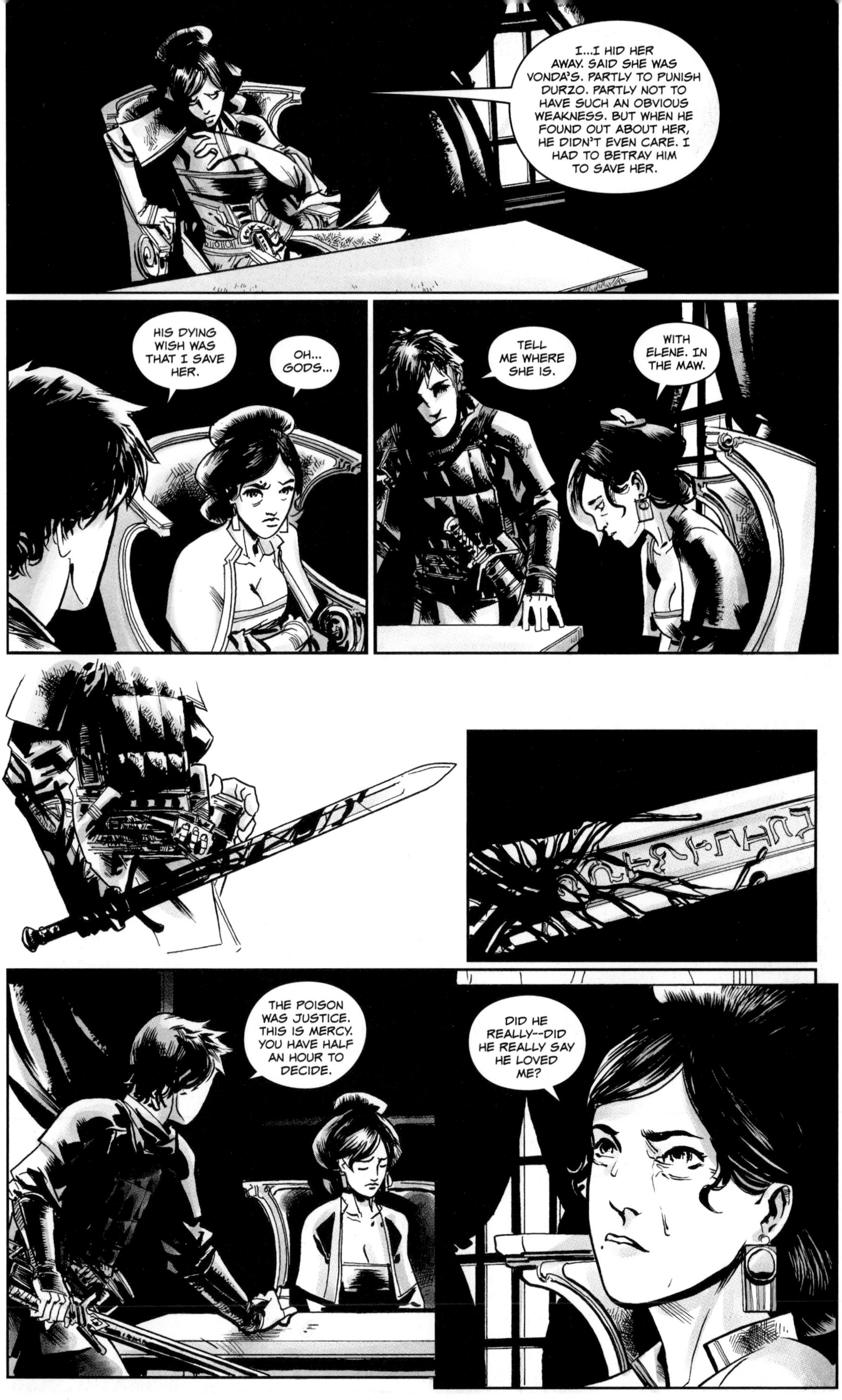
I...I HID HER AWAY. SAID SHE WAS VONDA'S. PARTLY TO PUNISH DURZO. PARTLY NOT TO HAVE SUCH AN OBVIOUS WEAKNESS. BUT WHEN HE FOUND OUT ABOUT HER, HE DIDN'T EVEN CARE. I HAD TO BETRAY HIM TO SAVE HER.
HIS DYING WISH WAS THAT I SAVE HER.
OH... GODS...
TELL ME WHERE SHE IS.
WITH ELENE. IN THE MAW.
THE POISON WAS JUSTICE. THIS IS MERCY. YOU HAVE HALF AN HOUR TO DECIDE.
DID HE REALLY--DID HE REALLY SAY HE LOVED ME?

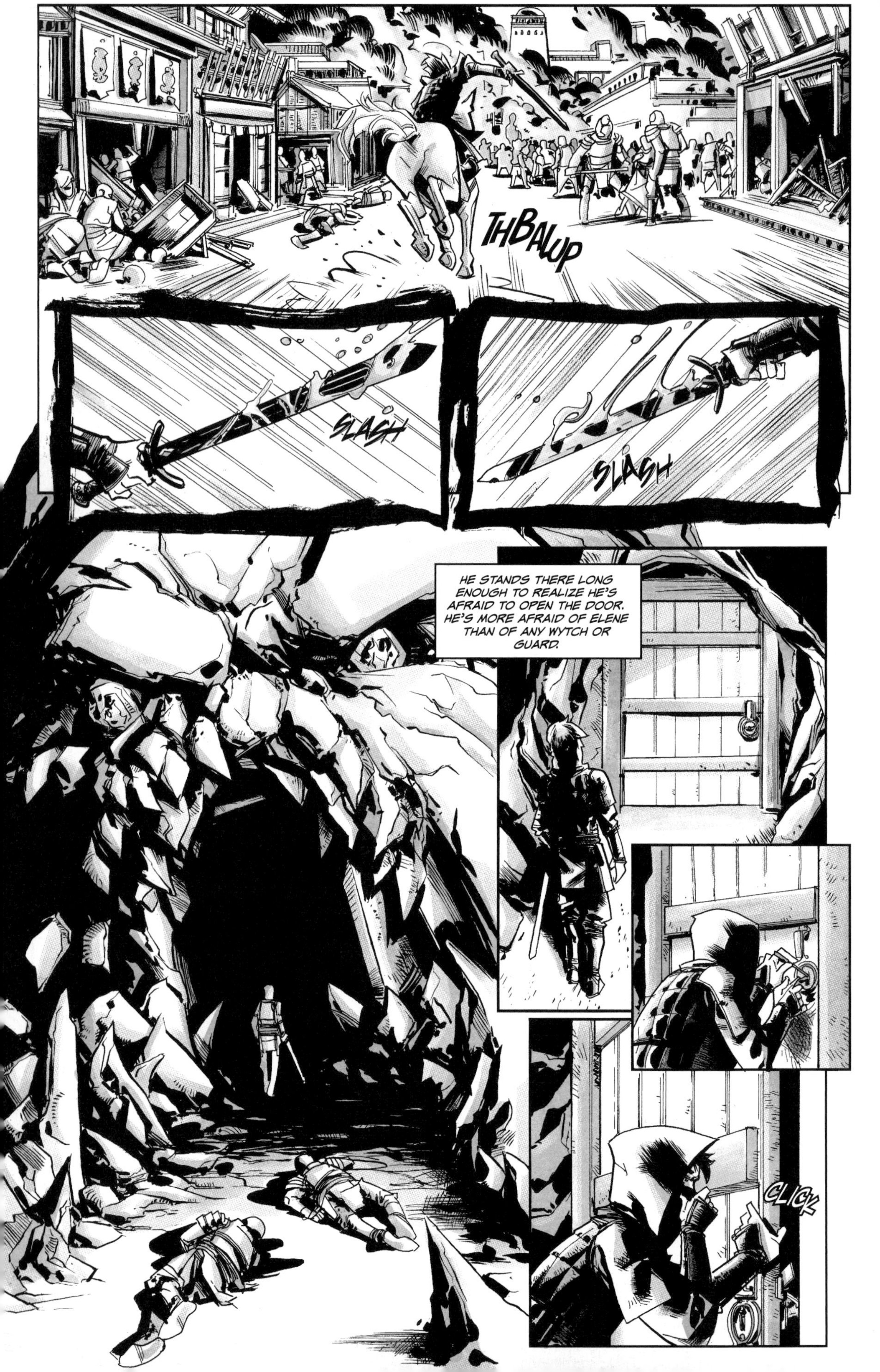
THBALUP
SLASH
SLASH
HE STANDS THERE LONG ENOUGH TO REALIZE HE'S AFRAID TO OPEN THE DOOR. HE'S MORE AFRAID OF ELENE THAN OF ANY WYTCH OR GUARD.
CLICK

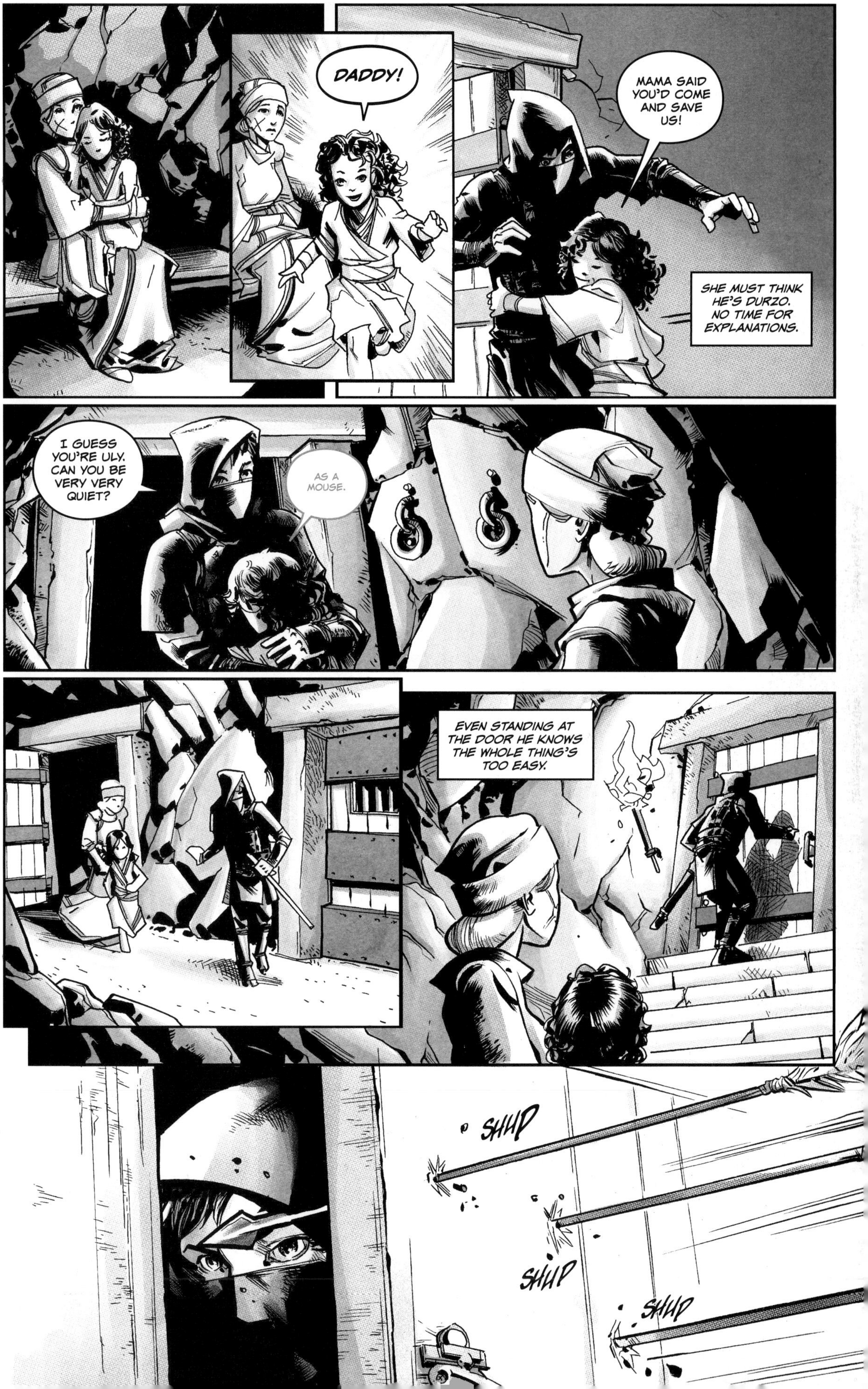
DADDY!
MAMA SAID YOU'D COME AND SAVE US!
SHE MUST THINK HE'S DURZO. NO TIME FOR EXPLANATIONS.
I GUESS YOU'RE ULY. CAN YOU BE VERY VERY QUIET?
AS A MOUSE.
EVEN STANDING AT THE DOOR HE KNOWS THE WHOLE THING'S TOO EASY.
SHUP
SHUP
SHUP

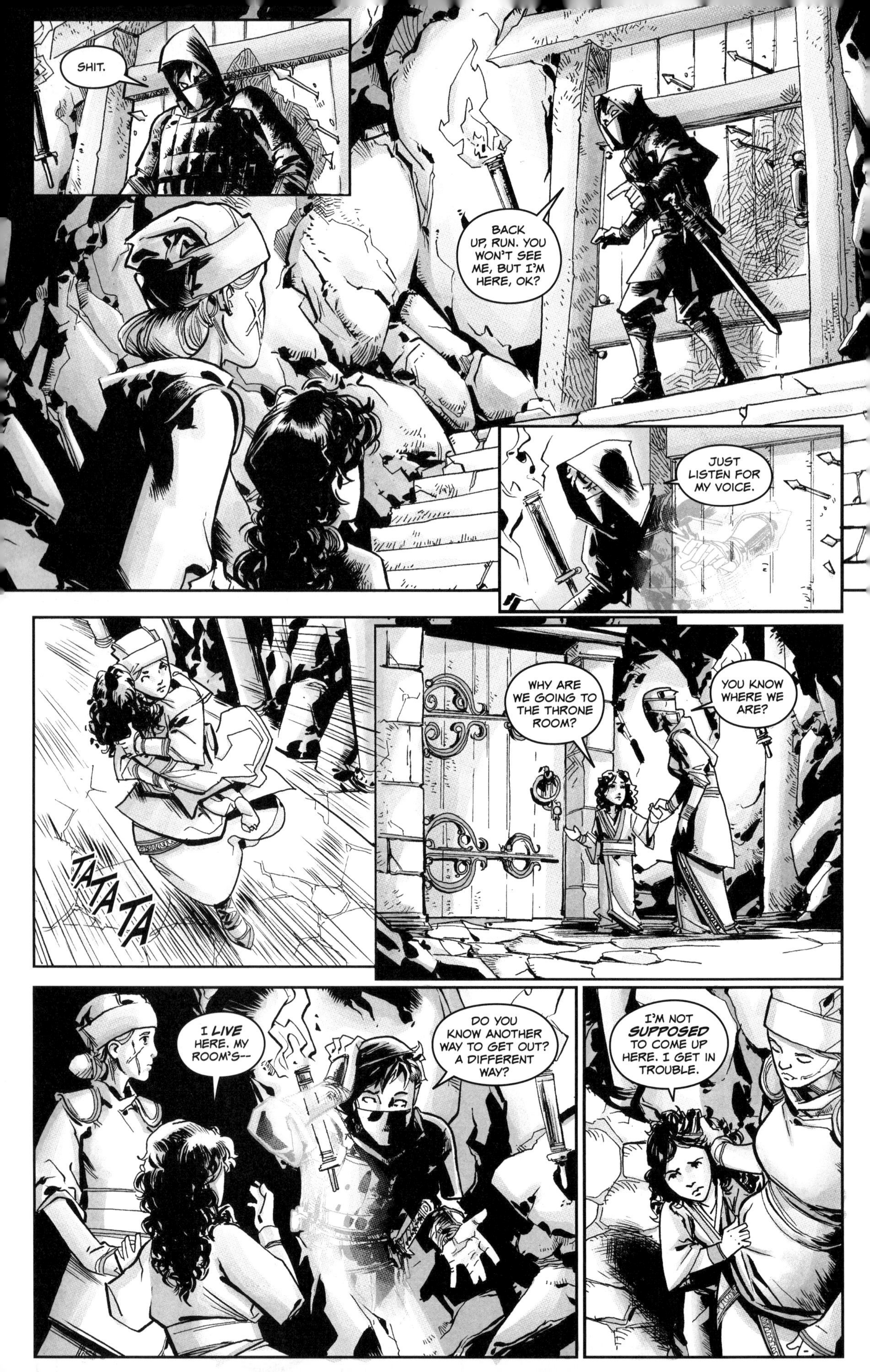
SHIT.
BACK UP, RUN. YOU WON'T SEE ME, BUT I'M HERE, OK?
JUST LISTEN FOR MY VOICE.
TATATA
WHY ARE WE GOING TO THE THRONE ROOM?
YOU KNOW WHERE WE ARE?
I *LIVE* HERE. MY ROOM'S--
DO YOU KNOW ANOTHER WAY TO GET OUT? A DIFFERENT WAY?
I'M NOT *SUPPOSED* TO COME UP HERE. I GET IN TROUBLE.

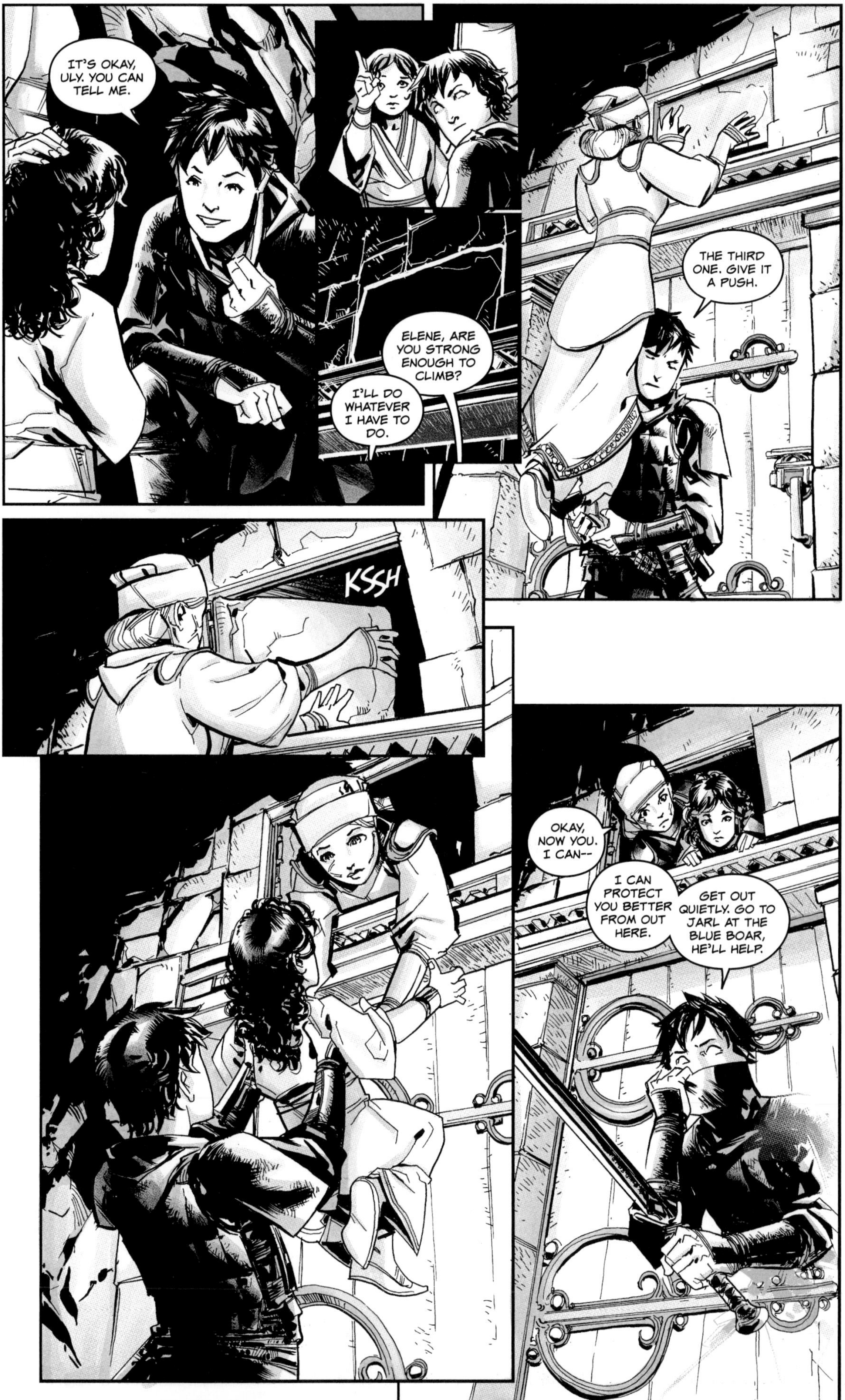
IT'S OKAY, ULY. YOU CAN TELL ME.
ELENE, ARE YOU STRONG ENOUGH TO CLIMB?
I'LL DO WHATEVER I HAVE TO DO.
THE THIRD ONE. GIVE IT A PUSH.
KSSH
OKAY, NOW YOU. I CAN--
I CAN PROTECT YOU BETTER FROM OUT HERE.
GET OUT QUIETLY. GO TO JARL AT THE BLUE BOAR, HE'LL HELP.

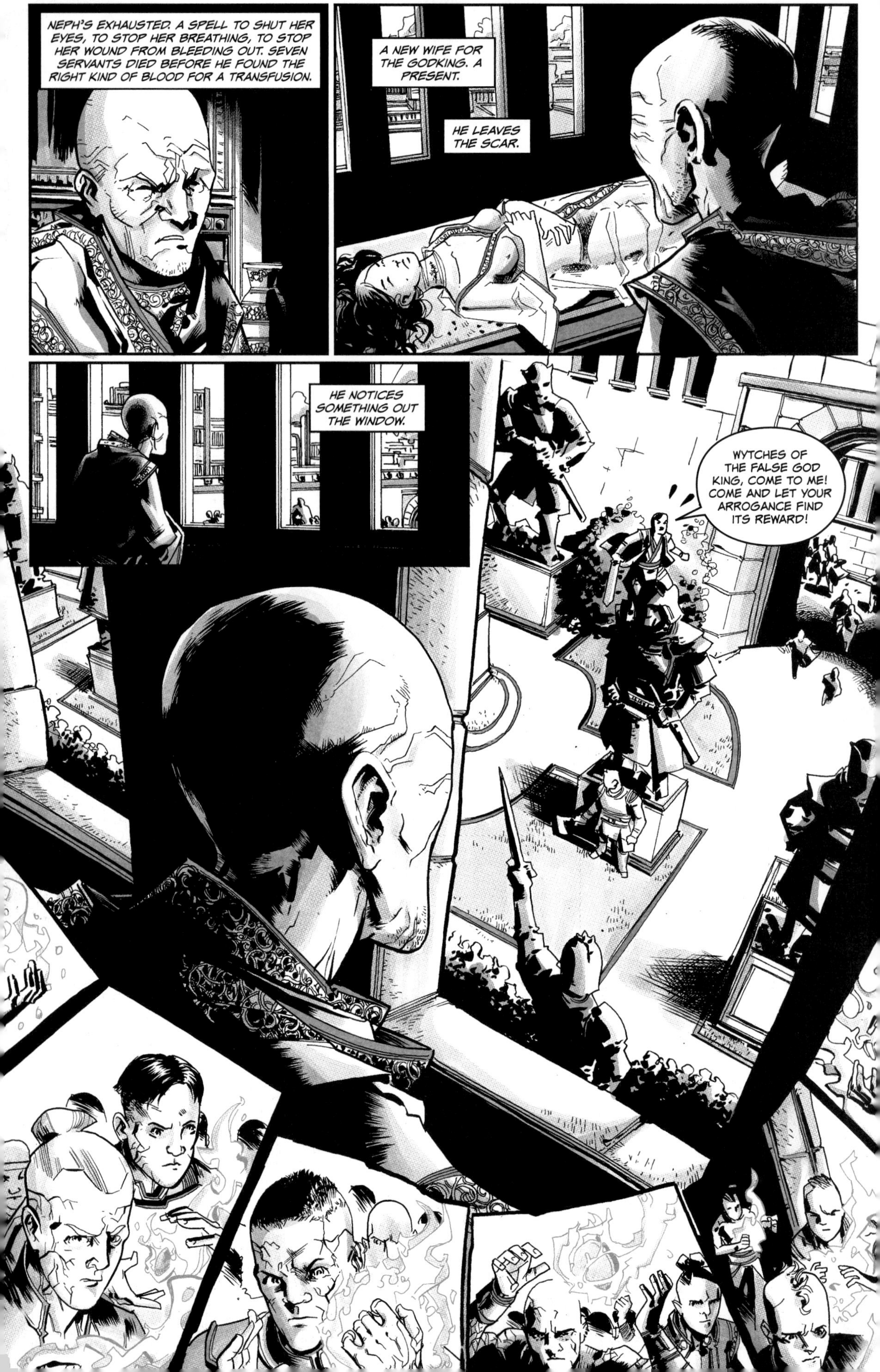
NEPH'S EXHAUSTED. A SPELL TO SHUT HER EYES, TO STOP HER BREATHING, TO STOP HER WOUND FROM BLEEDING OUT. SEVEN SERVANTS DIED BEFORE HE FOUND THE RIGHT KIND OF BLOOD FOR A TRANSFUSION.
A NEW WIFE FOR THE GODKING. A PRESENT.
HE LEAVES THE SCAR.
HE NOTICES SOMETHING OUT THE WINDOW.
WYTCHES OF THE FALSE GOD KING, COME TO ME! COME AND LET YOUR ARROGANCE FIND ITS REWARD!

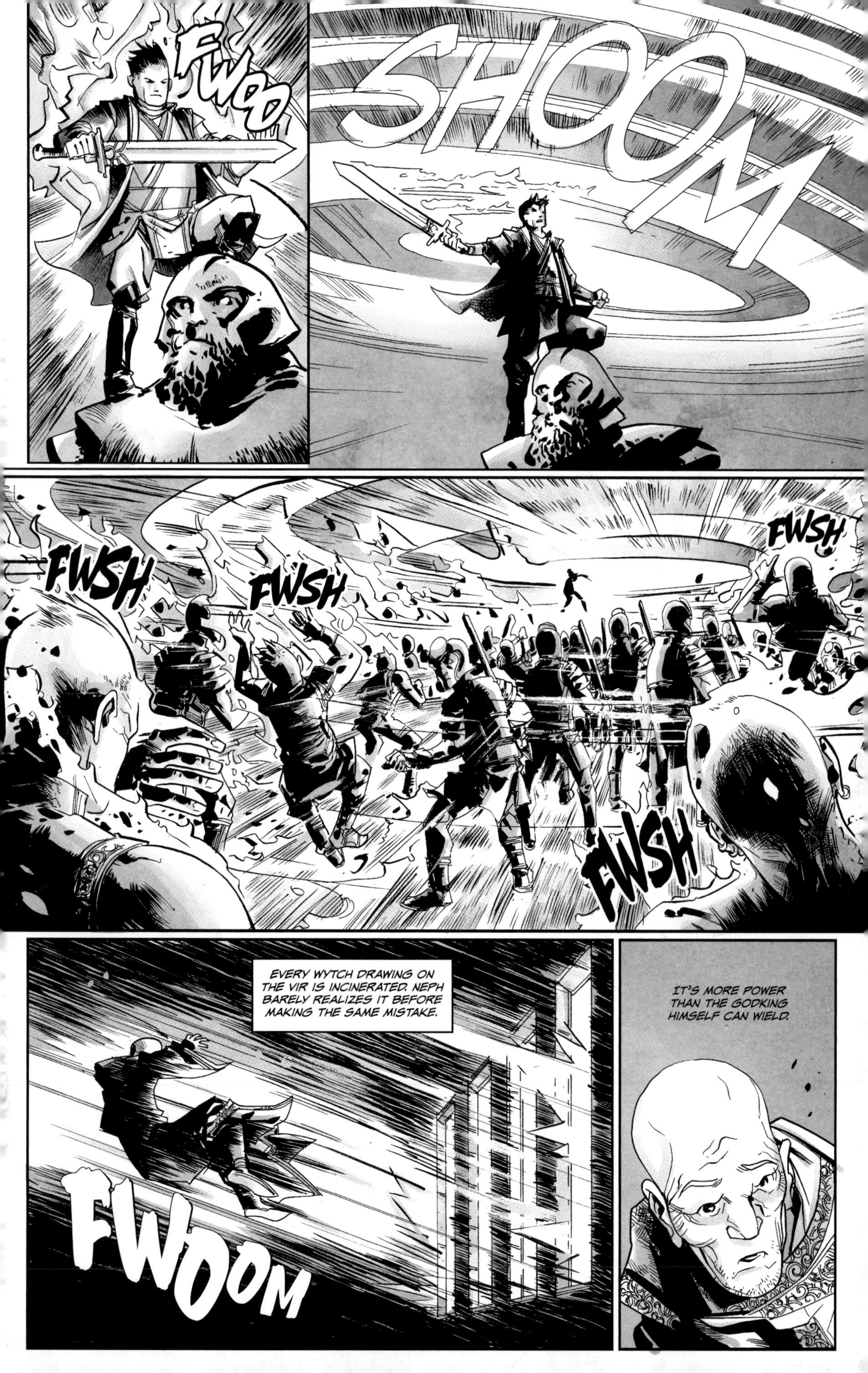
FWOO
SHOOM
FWSH
FWSH
FWSH
FWSH
EVERY WYTCH DRAWING ON THE VIR IS INCINERATED. NEPH BARELY REALIZES IT BEFORE MAKING THE SAME MISTAKE.
FWOOM
IT'S MORE POWER THAN THE GODKING HIMSELF CAN WIELD.

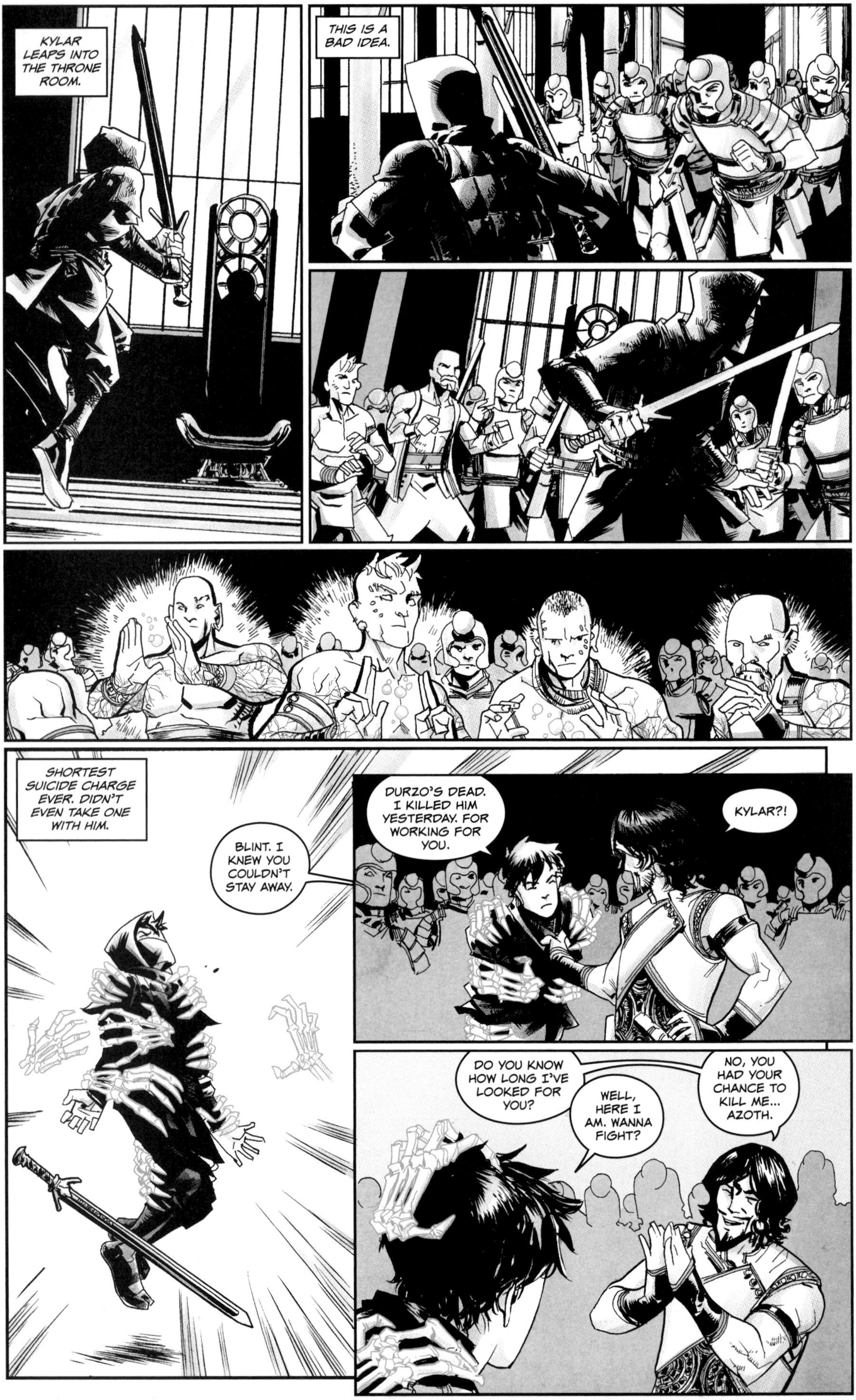
KYLAR LEAPS INTO THE THRONE ROOM.
THIS IS A BAD IDEA.
SHORTEST SUICIDE CHARGE EVER. DIDN'T EVEN TAKE ONE WITH HIM.
BLINT. I KNEW YOU COULDN'T STAY AWAY.
DURZO'S DEAD. I KILLED HIM YESTERDAY. FOR WORKING FOR YOU.
KYLAR?!
DO YOU KNOW HOW LONG I'VE LOOKED FOR YOU?
WELL, HERE I AM. WANNA FIGHT?
NO, YOU HAD YOUR CHANCE TO KILL ME... AZOTH.

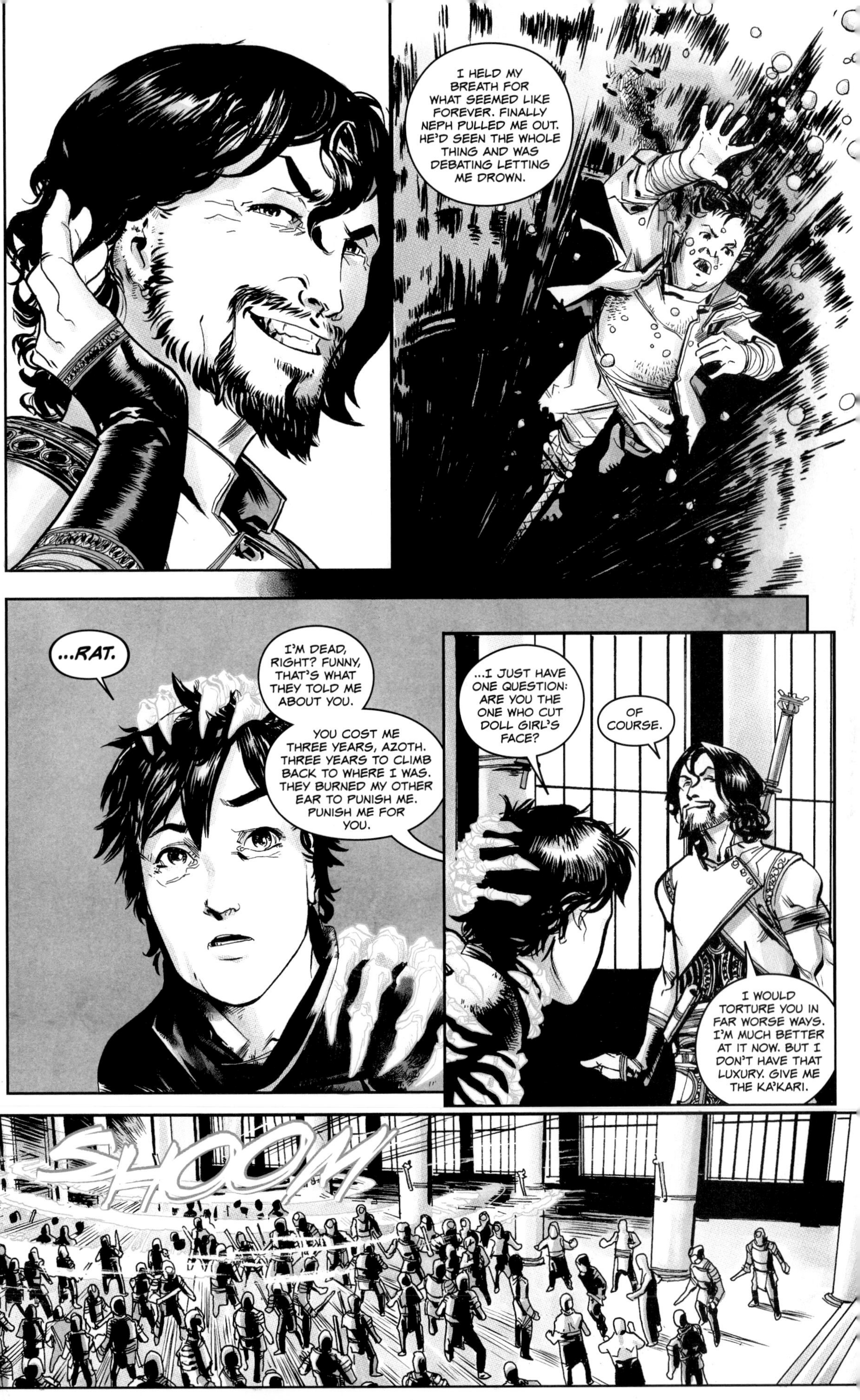
I HELD MY BREATH FOR WHAT SEEMED LIKE FOREVER. FINALLY NEPH PULLED ME OUT. HE'D SEEN THE WHOLE THING AND WAS DEBATING LETTING ME DROWN.
...RAT.
I'M DEAD, RIGHT? FUNNY, THAT'S WHAT THEY TOLD ME ABOUT YOU.
YOU COST ME THREE YEARS, AZOTH. THREE YEARS TO CLIMB BACK TO WHERE I WAS. THEY BURNED MY OTHER EAR TO PUNISH ME. PUNISH ME FOR YOU.
...I JUST HAVE ONE QUESTION: ARE YOU THE ONE WHO CUT DOLL GIRL'S FACE?
OF COURSE.
I WOULD TORTURE YOU IN FAR WORSE WAYS. I'M MUCH BETTER AT IT NOW. BUT I DON'T HAVE THAT LUXURY. GIVE ME THE KA'KARI.
SHOOM

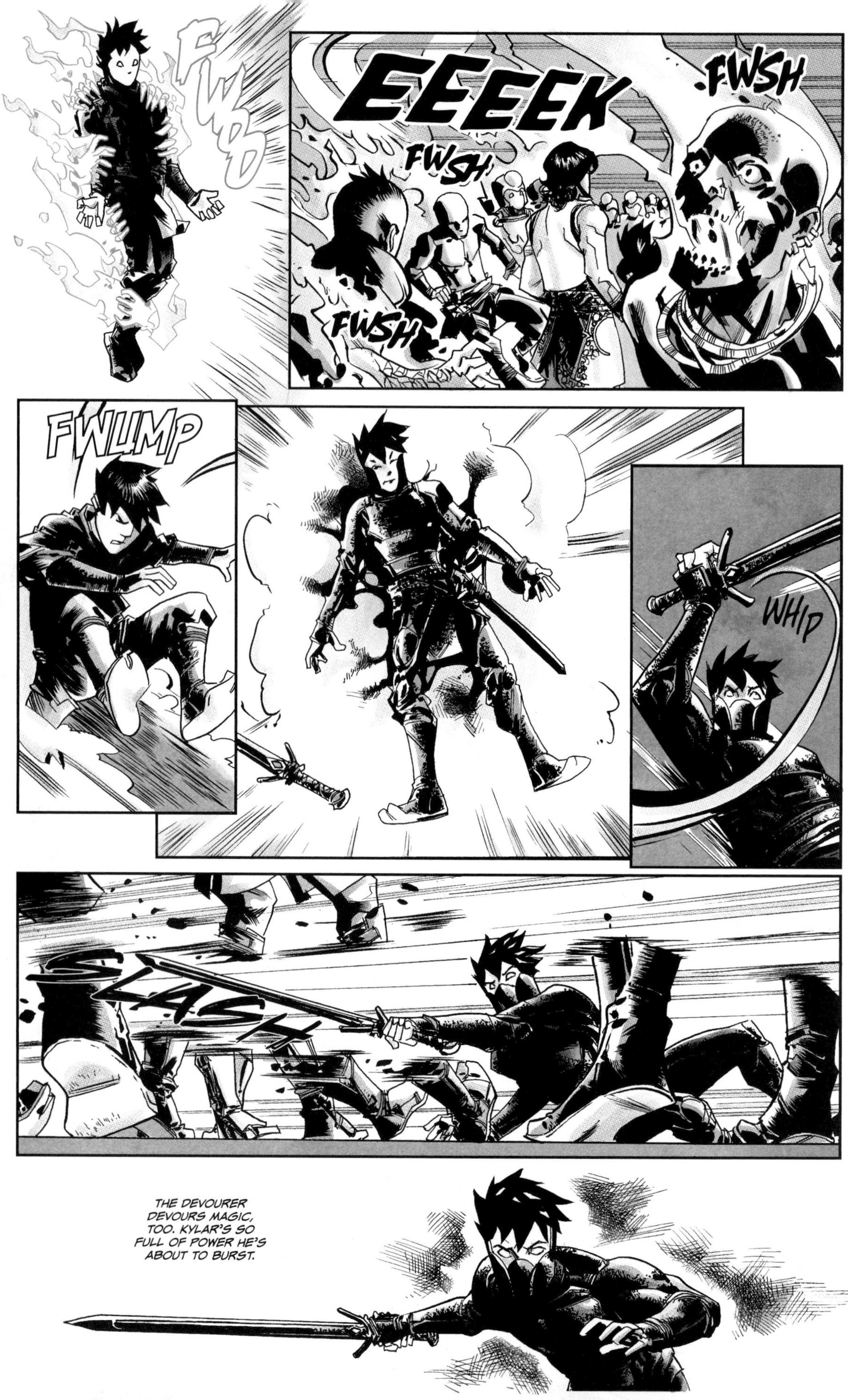
FWBD
EEEEK
FWSH
FWSH
FWSH
FWUMP
WHIP
SLASH
THE DEVOURER DEVOURS MAGIC, TOO. KYLAR'S SO FULL OF POWER HE'S ABOUT TO BURST.

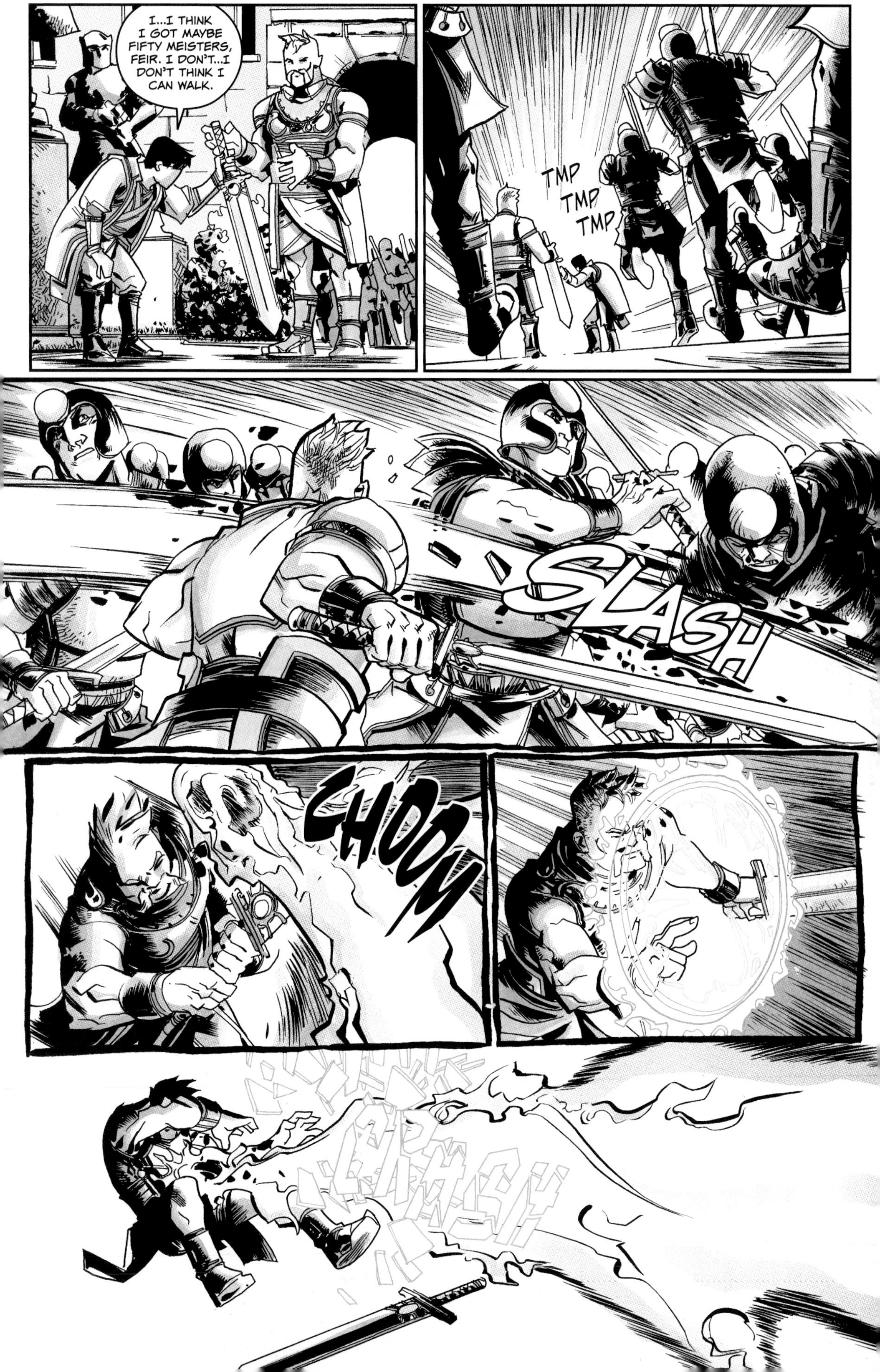
I...I THINK I GOT MAYBE FIFTY MEISTERS, FEIR. I DON'T...I DON'T THINK I CAN WALK.
TMP TMP TMP
SLASH
CHOOM
CRASH

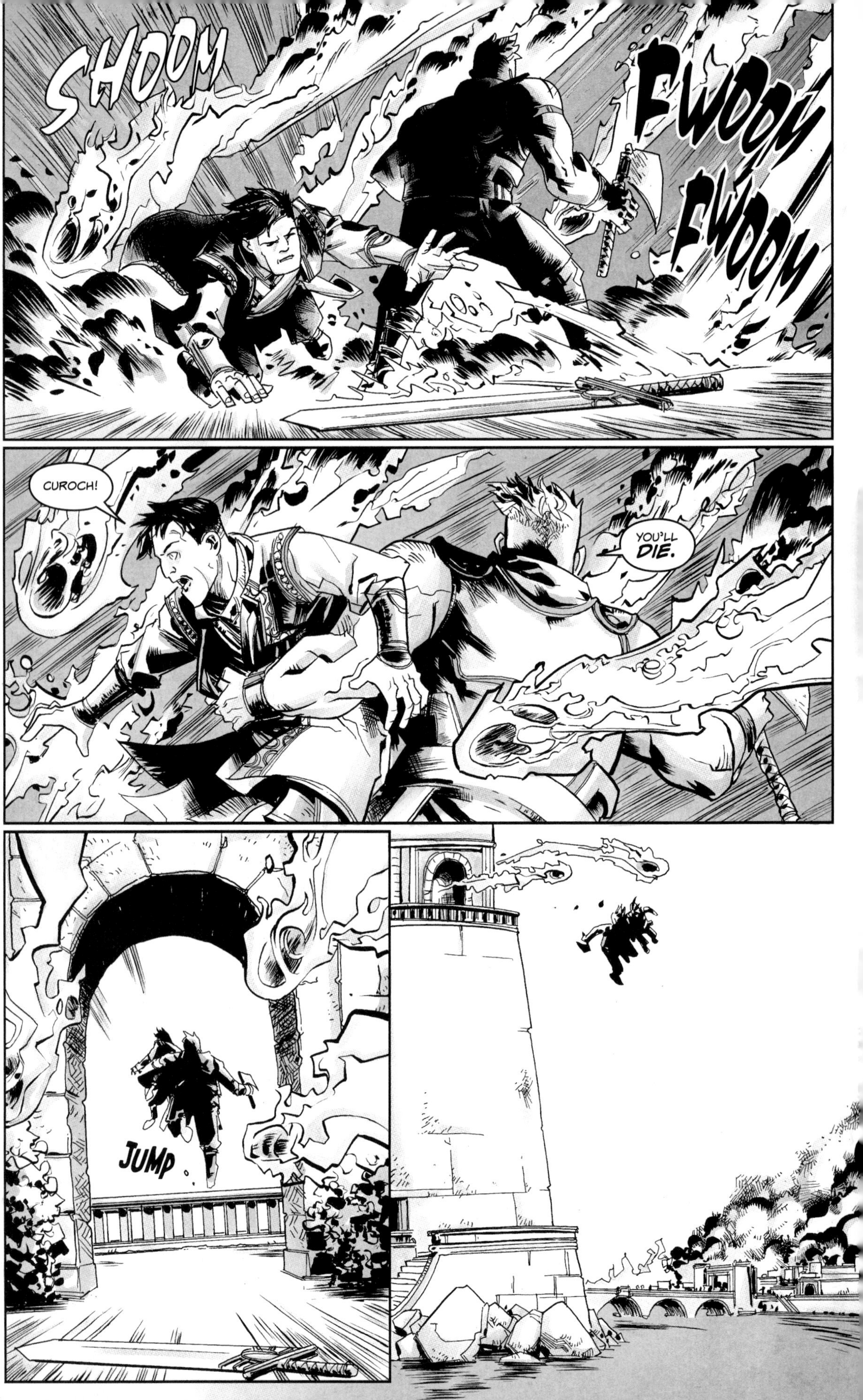
SHOOM
FWOOM
FWOOM
CUROCH!
YOU'LL DIE.
JUMP

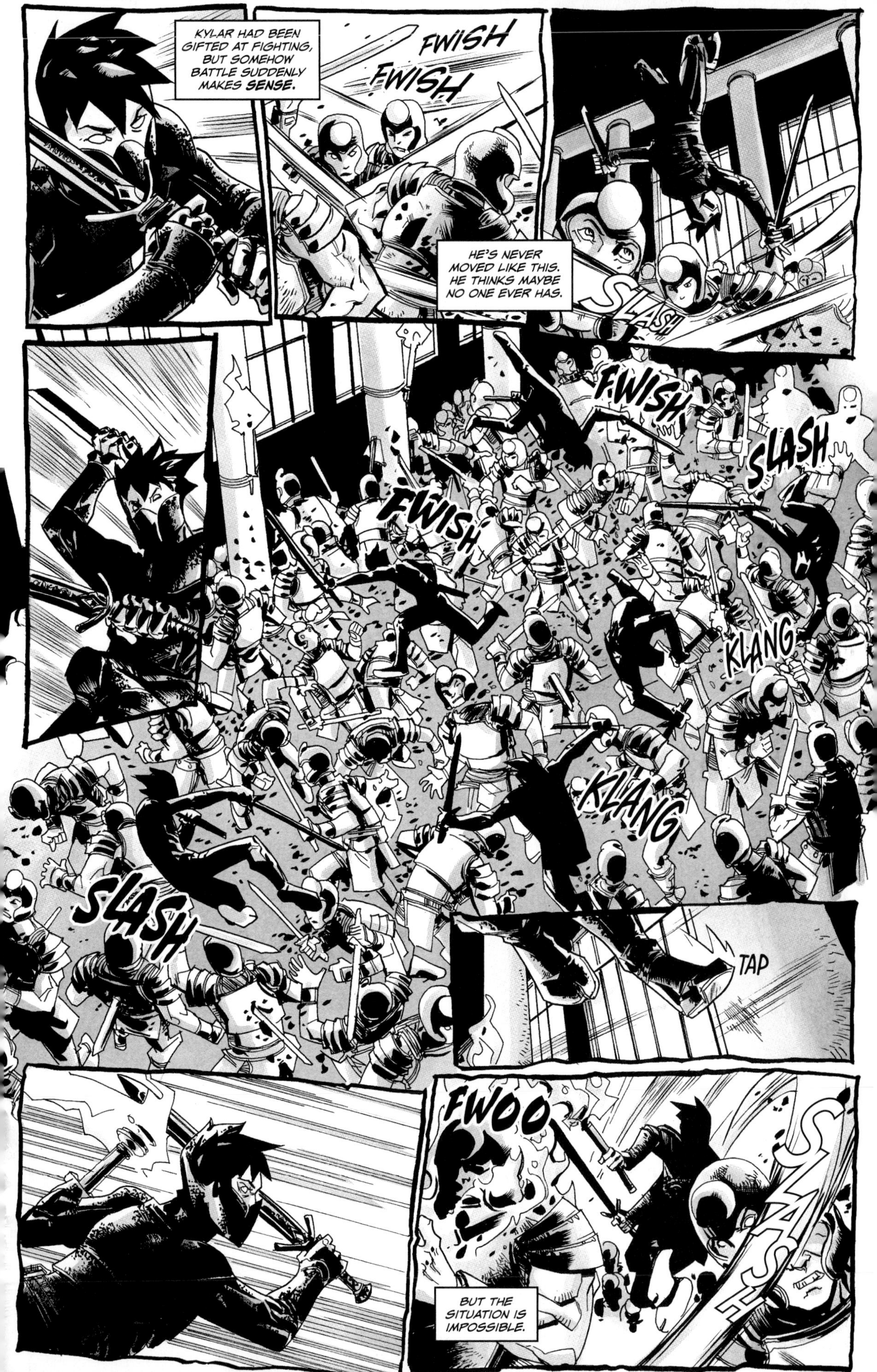
KYLAR HAD BEEN GIFTED AT FIGHTING, BUT SOMEHOW BATTLE SUDDENLY MAKES SENSE.
FWISH
FWISH
HE'S NEVER MOVED LIKE THIS. HE THINKS MAYBE NO ONE EVER HAS.
SLASH
FWISH
SLASH
FWISH
KLANG
KLANG
SLASH
TAP
FWOO
SMASH
BUT THE SITUATION IS IMPOSSIBLE.

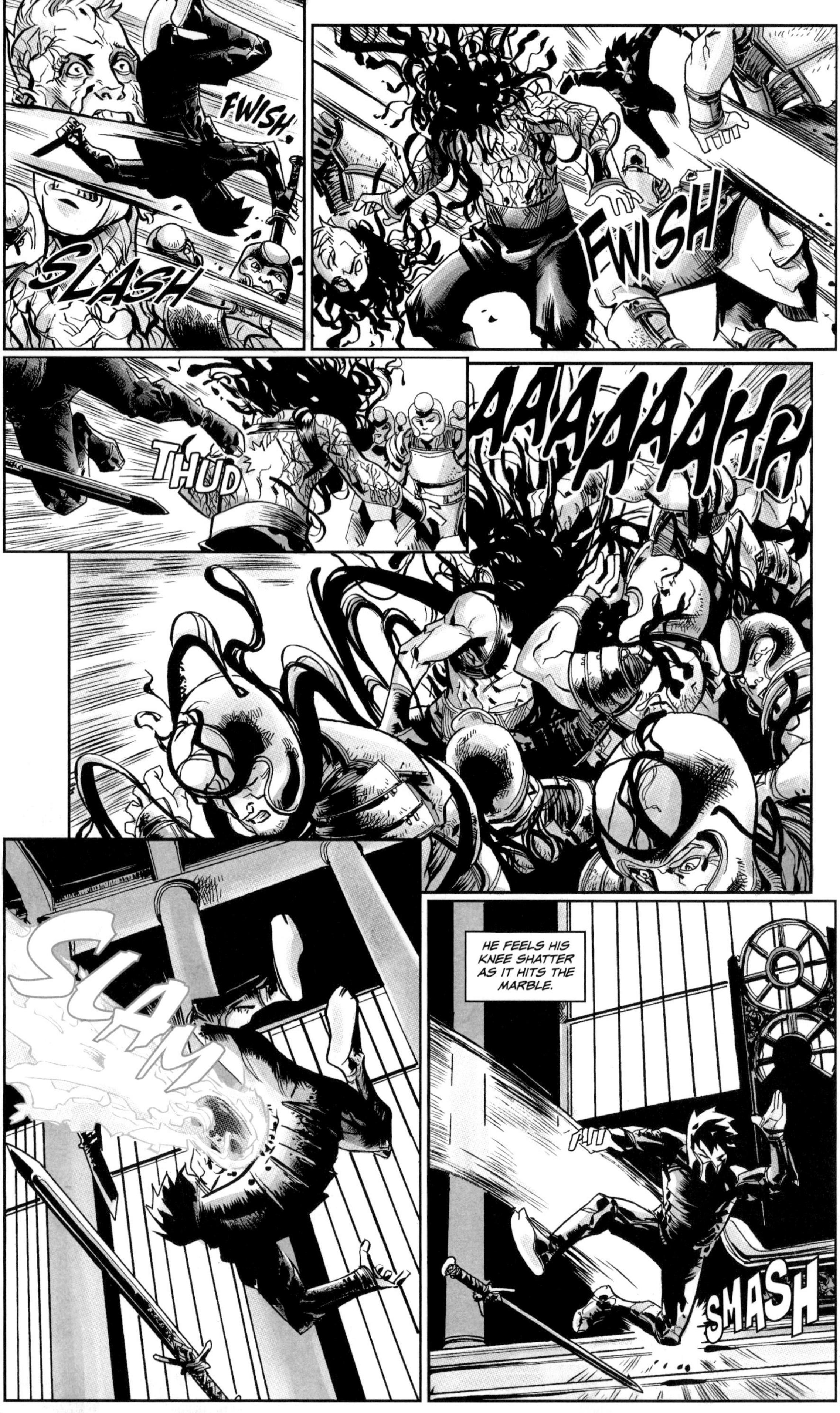
FWISH
SLASH
FWISH
THUD
AAAAAAAHH
SLAM
HE FEELS HIS KNEE SHATTER AS IT HITS THE MARBLE.
SMASH

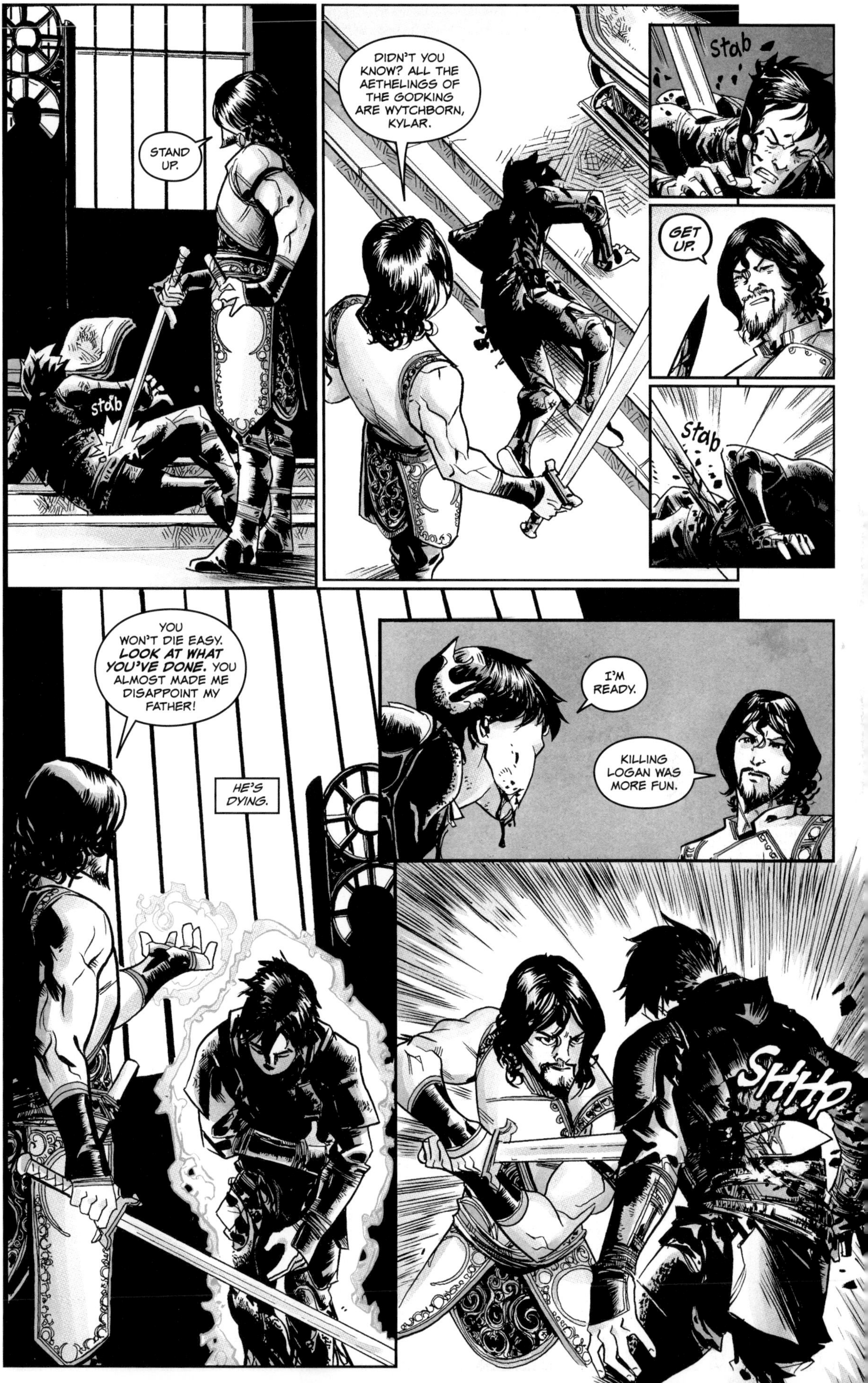
STAND UP.
stab
DIDN'T YOU KNOW? ALL THE AETHELINGS OF THE GODKING ARE WYTCHBORN, KYLAR.
Stab
GET UP.
Stab
YOU WON'T DIE EASY. **LOOK AT WHAT YOU'VE DONE.** YOU ALMOST MADE ME DISAPPOINT MY FATHER!
HE'S DYING.
I'M READY.
KILLING LOGAN WAS MORE FUN.
SHHP

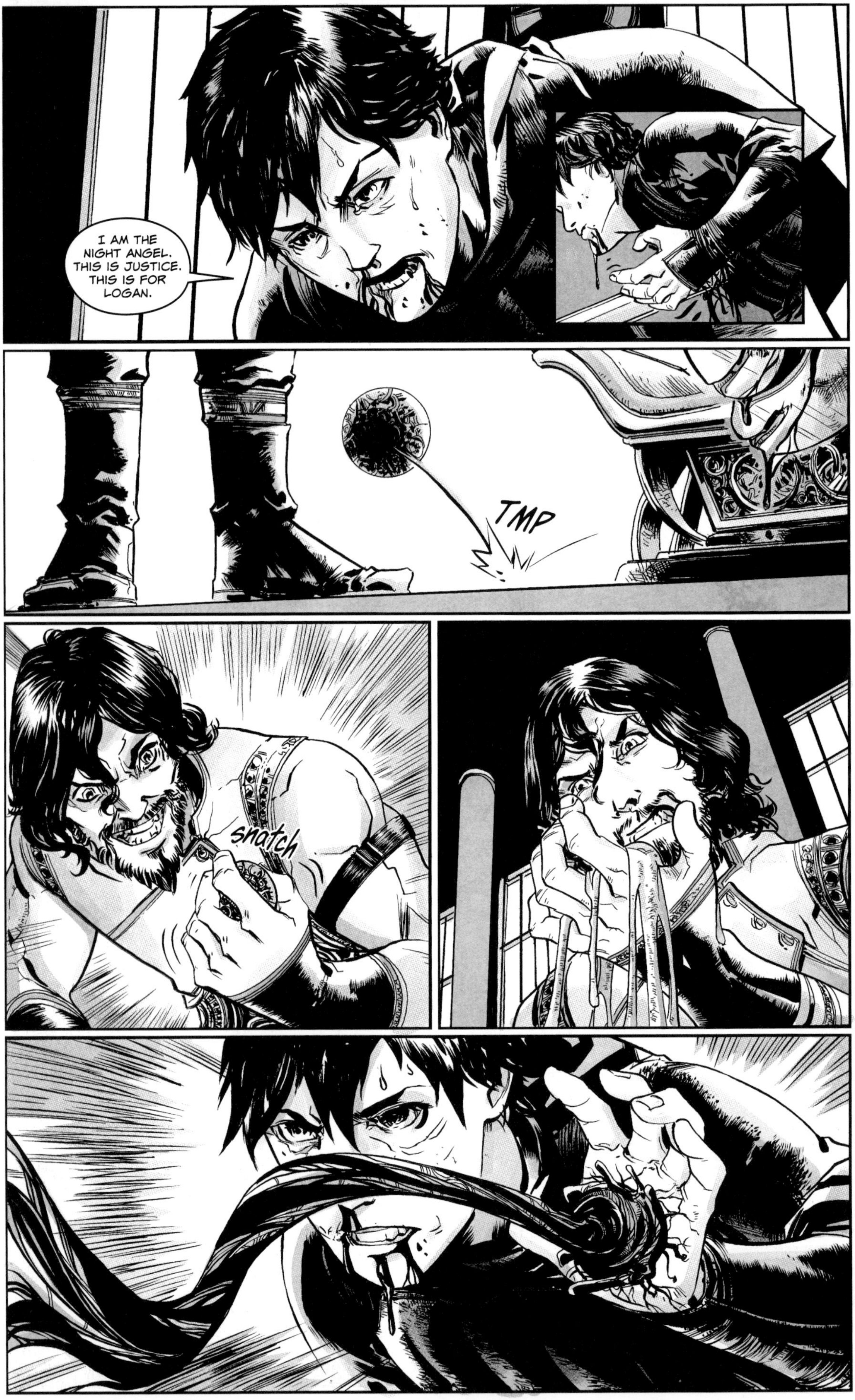
I AM THE NIGHT ANGEL. THIS IS JUSTICE. THIS IS FOR LOGAN.
TMP
snatch

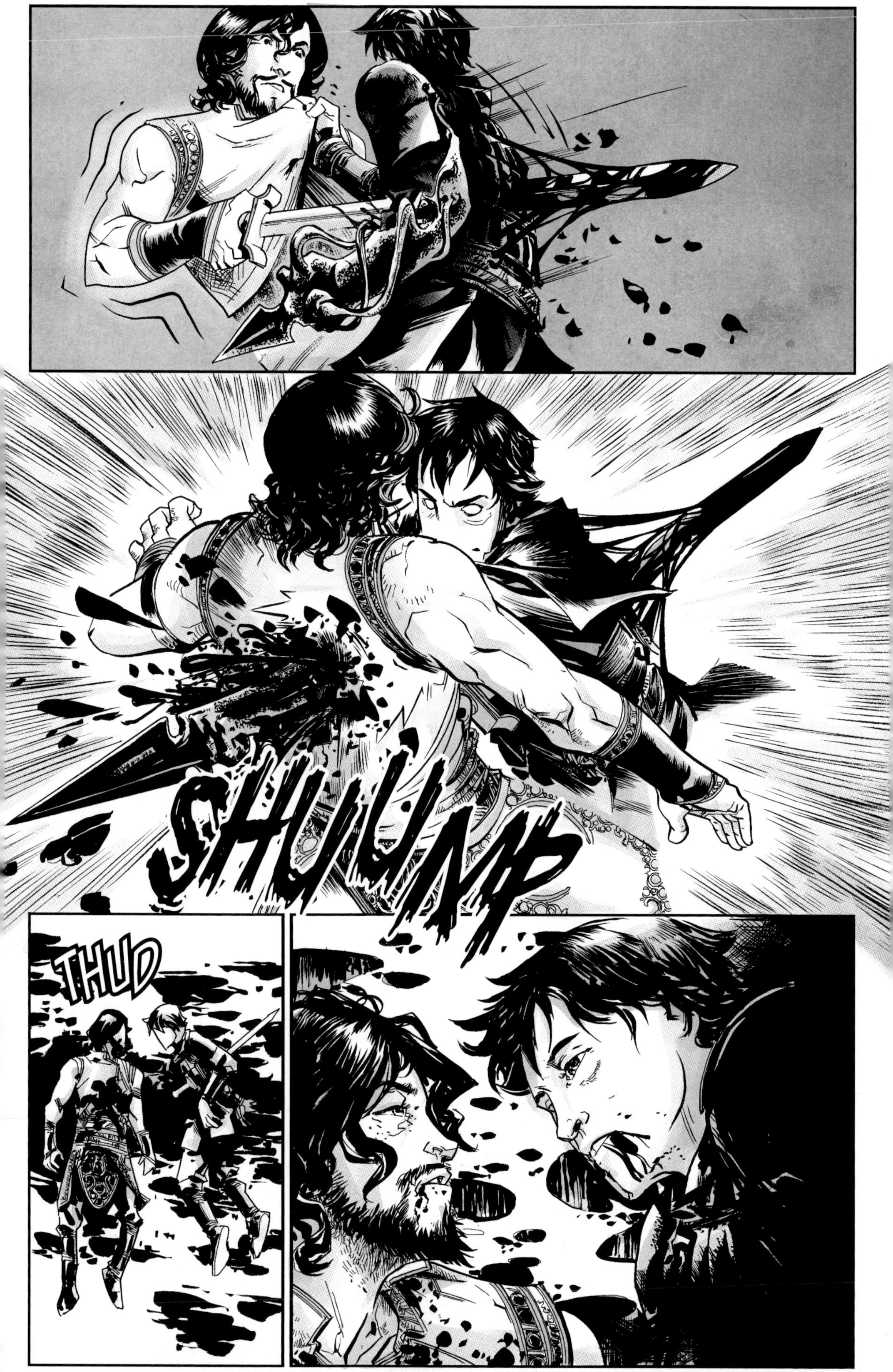
SHUUMP
THUD

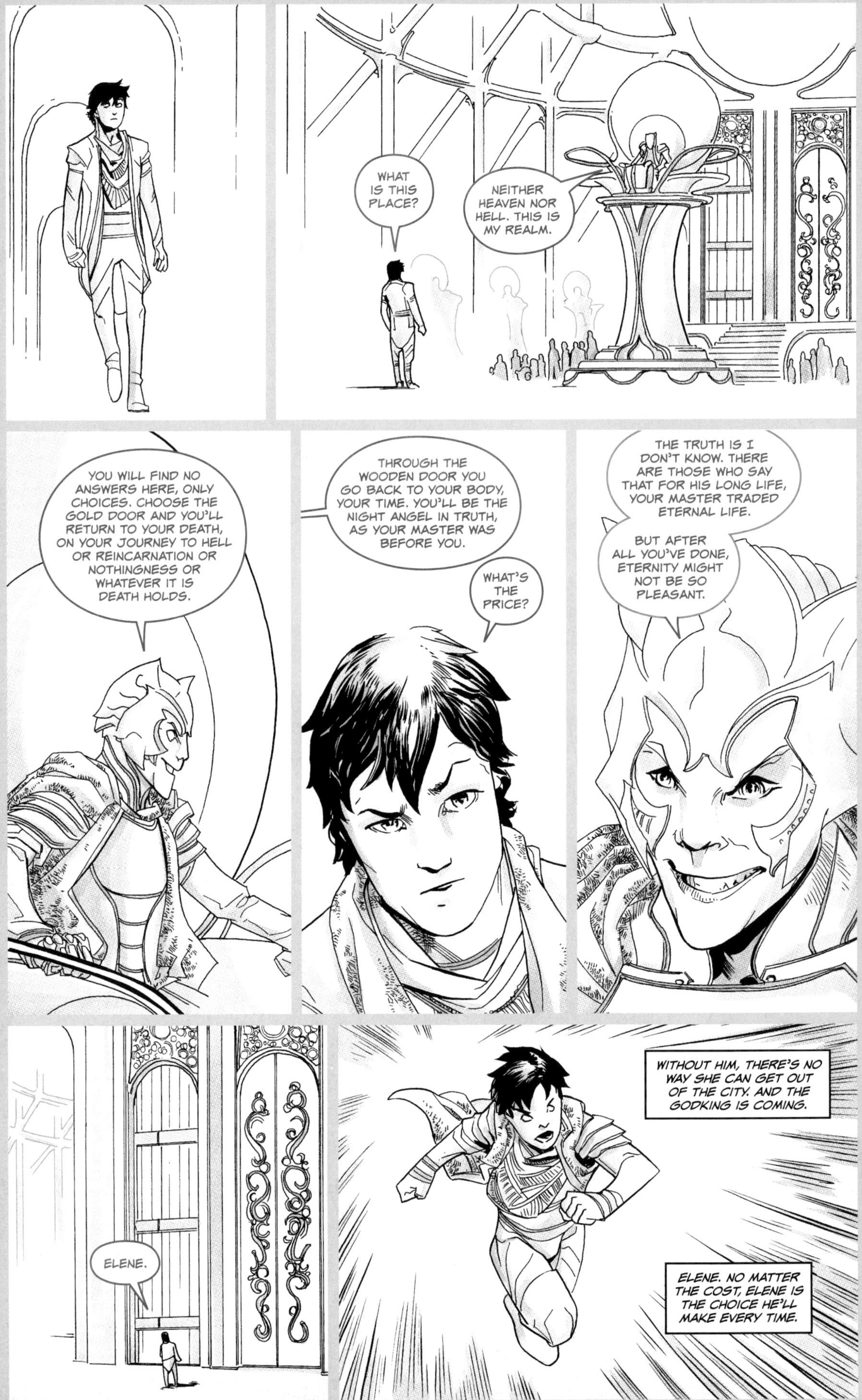
WHAT IS THIS PLACE?
NEITHER HEAVEN NOR HELL. THIS IS MY REALM.
YOU WILL FIND NO ANSWERS HERE, ONLY CHOICES. CHOOSE THE GOLD DOOR AND YOU'LL RETURN TO YOUR DEATH, ON YOUR JOURNEY TO HELL OR REINCARNATION OR NOTHINGNESS OR WHATEVER IT IS DEATH HOLDS.
THROUGH THE WOODEN DOOR YOU GO BACK TO YOUR BODY, YOUR TIME. YOU'LL BE THE NIGHT ANGEL IN TRUTH, AS YOUR MASTER WAS BEFORE YOU.
WHAT'S THE PRICE?
THE TRUTH IS I DON'T KNOW. THERE ARE THOSE WHO SAY THAT FOR HIS LONG LIFE, YOUR MASTER TRADED ETERNAL LIFE.
BUT AFTER ALL YOU'VE DONE, ETERNITY MIGHT NOT BE SO PLEASANT.
ELENE.
WITHOUT HIM, THERE'S NO WAY SHE CAN GET OUT OF THE CITY. AND THE GODKING IS COMING.
ELENE. NO MATTER THE COST, ELENE IS THE CHOICE HE'LL MAKE EVERY TIME.

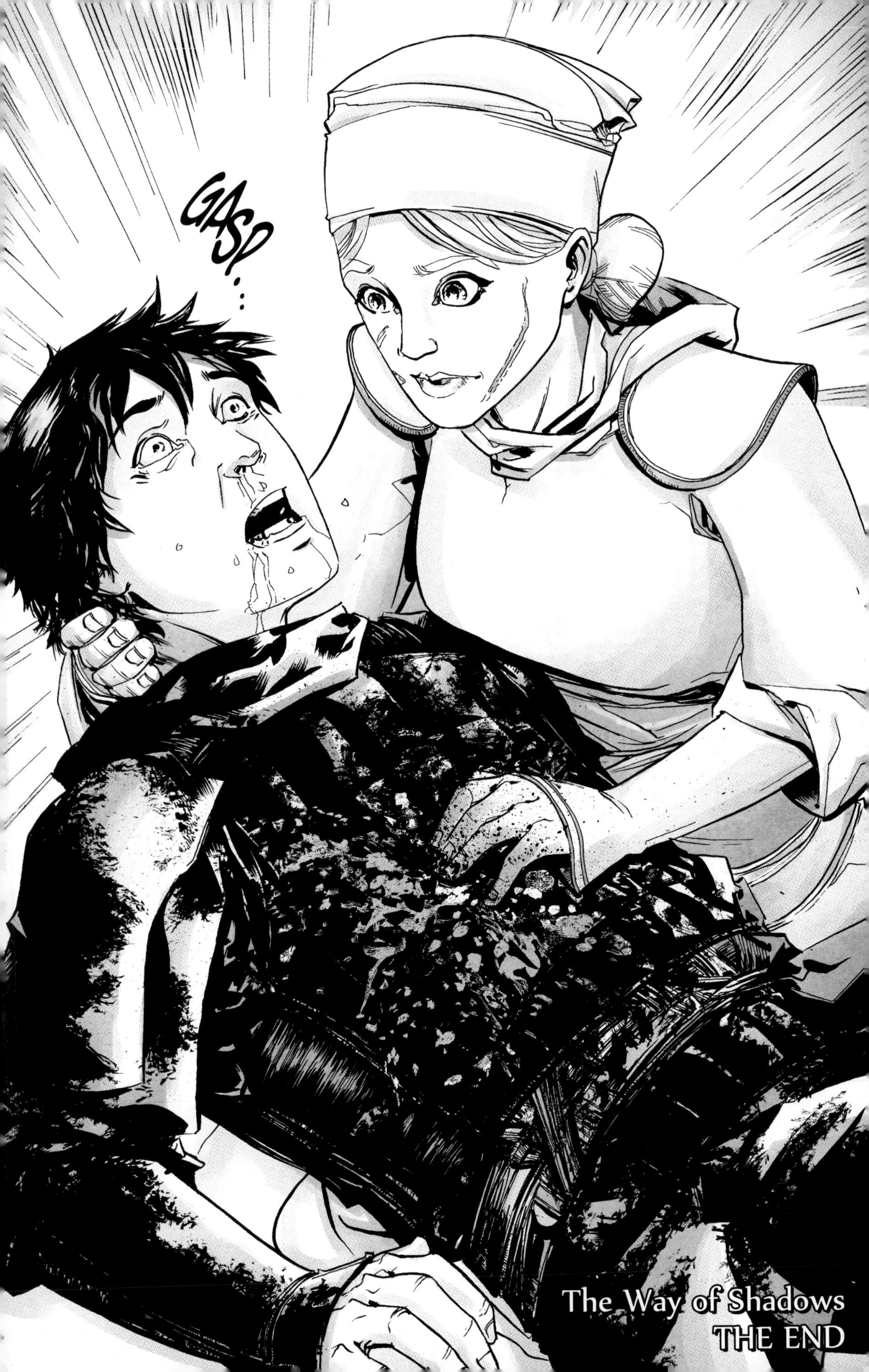
GASP...
The Way of Shadows
THE END

THE WAY OF SHADOWS: THE GRAPHIC NOVEL

ART: ANDY MACDONALD
ADAPTATION: IVAN BRANDON

LETTERING: ANDWORLD DESIGN

YEN PRESS
HACHETTE BOOK GROUP
1290 AVENUE OF THE AMERICAS
NEW YORK, NY 10104

WWW.HACHETTEBOOKGROUP.COM
WWW.YENPRESS.COM

YEN PRESS IS AN IMPRINT OF HACHETTE BOOK GROUP, INC.
THE YEN PRESS NAME AND LOGO ARE TRADEMARKS OF
HACHETTE BOOK GROUP, INC

FIRST EDITION: OCTOBER 2014

ISBN: 978-0-316-21298-4

10 9 8 7 6 5 4 3 2

WOI

PRINTED IN TH
UNITED STATES OF AMERIC